Functional Syntax

Susumu Kuno

Functional Syntax

Anaphora, Discourse
and Empathy

The University of Chicago Press
Chicago and London

Susumu Kuno is professor of linguistics at Harvard University and the author of *The Structure of the Japanese Language.*

The University of Chicago Press, Chicago 60637
The University of Chicago Press, Ltd., London

© 1987 by The University of Chicago
All rights reserved. Published 1987
Printed in the United States of America

95 94 93 92 91 90 89 88 87   5432

Library of Congress Cataloging-in-Publication Data

Kuno, Susumu, 1933–
    Functional syntax.

    Bibliography: p.
    Includes index.
    1. Grammar, Comparative and general—Syntax.
2. Functionalism (Linguistics) 3. Discourse
analysis.   I. Title.
P295.K86   1987   415   86-3149
ISBN 0-226-46200-5
ISBN 0-226-46201-3 (pbk.)

Contents

Preface

This book originated from my attempt, begun in 1977–78, to collect in one volume some of the papers on functional syntax which I have published in various journals and edited volumes. I soon realized that I was involved in a much more difficult task than simply selecting the papers for the volume and writing an introduction and epilogue. For one thing, I had to eliminate overlaps between some of the papers and incorporate new findings on the same topics. For another, there were inconsistencies among the papers, mainly due to the differing grammatical frameworks in which they had been written. Furthermore, as the book was being prepared, my understanding of the phenomena that these papers dealt with grew and my grammatical perspective evolved. I eventually abandoned the idea of putting the papers together in favor of writing a new book, based on these papers but including reviews of research results of other scholars and my own new research. What I have here includes only about half of the areas in functional syntax that I had originally intended the book to cover. But believing that this is already more than enough for a book, I am presenting this first attempt to synthesize my past research results in functional syntax. A separate book or books will follow to cover any aspects that this book has not addressed.

This book presents many of the results of research that I have been carrying out at Harvard University for the past ten years or so. During these years, my research has been supported in part, but continuously, by the National Science Foundation (the current grant no. BNS-82-14193). I want to thank the NSF for their continuing support, without which my research would not have made as much progress as I believe it has. I also want to thank the Guggenheim Foundation for the fellowship I received from them in 1977–78. This fellowship freed me from teaching and administrative obligations to start working on the ideas in the book.

I had the first draft of the manuscript of this book ready around the fall of 1981. Since then, I have gone through five or six major revisions of the manuscript on the basis of numerous comments that I have received from colleagues and students. My deepest gratitude goes to John Whitman and Akio Kamio, both of whom read an earlier version of the book and gave me many invaluable comments. The reader will find the contributions of these two scholars in every chapter of this book.

The manuscript has also been read in one version or another by others, to whom I would also like to express my appreciation. I am particularly indebted to Victoria Bergvall, Eileen Nam, and Margaret Thomas for their valuable comments on both content and exposition. Peter Bosch, Heather Cavanaugh, John Goldsmith, Elanah Kutik, James D. McCawley, Kiyoko Masunaga, and Shelley Waksler all provided insights on the contents that are found throughout the book. I am beholden to Kyle Johnson, Young-Se Kang, Jaklin Kornfilt, Mamoru Saito, and Larry Solan for particular comments on my treatment of the anaphora problems in the framework of the government and binding theory (found in Chapter 2). Kevin Knight deserves my thanks for the computer plotting of the sentence structure diagrams throughout the book. Finally, I want to express my gratitude to Lindsey Eck for his editorial and proofreading work.

I reiterate my indebtedness to all of these people who aided me in the preparation of this book. Naturally, the final decisions have all been mine, and I also absolve them of responsibility for any faults that may be found.

On a purely personal level, the preparation of a book of this size is bound to take its toll. It has clearly affected the fulfillment of my responsibilities as husband and father. I want to thank my wife Yoko and daughters Alisa and Erika for having been sympathetic to my work, and for having given up vacation trips for many summers and winters.

Susumu Kuno

April 22, 1985
Cambridge, Massachusetts

1 Introduction

This book presents an account of pronouns, reflexives, and many other linguistic phenomena in the framework of functional syntax. I will examine these phenomena from a multitude of angles, and present not only the syntactic conditionings that control their usage, but also the semantic and discourse-based principles bearing on them. We will see that such principles interact with each other as well as with syntactic conditionings. This approach pays full attention to the communicative functions that a given linguistic phenomenon performs, and seeks to explain the usage of the phenomenon on the basis of these functions. Examples are mainly drawn from English, but there are occasional references to corresponding phenomena in other languages. This book attempts to offer natural explanations for what superficially look like chaotic linguistic data—explanations which are easy to follow and which do not require the whole apparatus of a formal theory of grammar.

Functional syntax is, in principle, independent of various past and current models of grammar such as case grammar, Montague grammar, relational grammar, generalized phrase structure grammar, lexical functional grammar, and various versions of Chomskian generative theory such as standard theory, extended standard theory, revised extended standard theory, and government and binding theory.[1] Each theory of grammar must have a place or places where various functional constraints on the well-formedness of sentences or sequences of sentences can be stated, and each can benefit from utilizing a functional perspective in the analysis of concrete syntactic phenomena. Therefore, in theory there is no conflict between functional syntax and, say, the government and binding theory of generative grammar. Given a linguistic process that is governed purely by syntactic factors, this process will be described in the syntactic component of grammar both by pure syntacticians and by functional syntacticians. On the other hand, given a linguistic process that is governed by both syntactic and, say, discourse factors, the syntactic aspect will be formulated in the syntactic component, while discourse factors that interact with this syntactic characterization will be described in the discourse component of grammar. Pure syntacticians would concentrate on the former characterization and functional syntacticians on the latter. There need not be any disagreement between the two.

In practice, however, there are numerous conflicts between the outlooks of pure and functional syntacticians with respect to how to analyze a given linguistic phenomenon. Pure syntacticians tend to give syntactic characterizations to linguistic phenomena which are in fact controlled by nonsyntactic factors. Or they label them as nonsyntactic phenomena and brush them aside, without attempting to find out what kind of nonsyntactic factors are in control. In the rest of this chapter, I will illustrate the kind of mistaken generalizations that pure syntactic approaches often make by using three linguistic phenomena: (i) interpretation of coordinate structure in a sentence, (ii) extraction from picture nouns with possessive noun phrases (NPs), and (iii) extraction from picture nouns without possessive NPs. In the course of arguing against the particular syntactic generalizations that have been proposed for these phenomena, I will show how functional syntacticians would analyze the same phenomena. This analysis arrives at generalizations that both are free from the problems of the original syntactic generalizations and are capable of accounting for new sets of facts that pure syntacticians have failed to take into consideration.

1.1 Lexical and Contextual Meaning[2]

Observe the following sentence:

(1.1)   Beavers build dams.

Each element in the sentence carries with it two types of meaning. For example, *beavers* in the sentence represents the following semantics:

(1.2)   (A)   *beaver:* an amphibious rodent of the genus *Castor,* valued for its fur and formerly for castor, and noted for its ingenuity in damming streams with trees, branches, stones, mud, etc. (*American College Dictionary*)
         (B)   a.   Generic
                b.   Agent

The meaning (A) comes directly from the lexicon. I will call it the lexical meaning of *beavers* (ignoring the problem of singular and plural nouns). On the other hand, the fact that *beavers* in (1.1) refers to the whole class of beavers—that is, the fact that it is a generic noun—and the fact that it is an agent of the action *build dams* cannot be retrieved from the lexicon. These are meanings that *beavers* acquires as it is used in sentences. I will call (B) the "contextual meaning" of *beavers* in (1.1).[3]

Similarly, observe the following sentences:

(1.3)   a.   The lady wanted to talk to *a bachelor* in linguistics, but she could not find anyone who was willing to talk to her.
         b.   The lady wanted to talk to *a bachelor* in the British Order of the Garter, but he refused to talk to her.

The lexical meaning of *a bachelor* in (1.3a) is 'a holder of a B.A. degree.' Its contextual meanings are [−specific] in that there was no particular individual that the lady wanted to talk to, and [goal] in that it is in the goal case. In contrast, the lexical meaning of *a bachelor* in (1.3b) is 'a young knight serving under the standard of another knight.' Its contextual meanings are [+specific] in that there was a particular individual that the lady wanted to talk to, and [goal] in that it is in the goal case.

The syntactic process called *one*-substitution cannot ignore differences in lexical meaning of two commonly shared lexical items. For example, observe *one ~ sub* the following sentences:

(1.4) a. Jane wanted to talk to a bachelor in linguistics, and Mary wanted to talk to a bachelor in mathematics.

   b. Jane wanted to talk to a bachelor in linguistics, and Mary wanted to talk to *one* in mathematics.

(1.5) a. Jane wanted to talk to a bachelor in linguistics, and Mary wanted to talk to a bachelor in the British Order of the Garter.

   b. *Jane wanted to talk to a bachelor in linguistics, and Mary wanted to talk to *one* in the British Order of the Garter.

The two tokens of *a bachelor* in (1.4a) share the same lexical meaning, that is, that of 'a holder of a B.A. degree.' The second can be replaced with *one,* as shown in (1.4b). In contrast, the two tokens of *a bachelor* in (1.5a) represent two different lexical meanings: 'a holder of a B.A. degree' for the first, and 'a young knight serving under the standard of another knight' for the latter. This difference in lexical meaning cannot be ignored in *one*-substitution. Note that (1.5b) is totally unacceptable if *one in the British Order of the Garter* is to be interpreted as 'a young knight serving under the standard of another knight in the British Order of the Garter.' (*i.e. not a linguist in the BOG*)

Now let us examine to see if *one*-substitution can or cannot ignore differences in contextual meaning. Observe, first, the following sentences:

(1.6) a. Beavers [+generic, agent] build dams. John caught a beaver [+specific, object] in the trap yesterday.

   b. Beavers build dams. John caught *one* in the trap yesterday.

(1.7) a. Our competitor hired a bachelor in linguistics [+specific, object]. We want to hire a bachelor in linguistics [−specific, object], too, but can we find any?

   b. Our competitor hired a bachelor in linguistics. We want to hire *one,* too, but can we find any?

In (1.6a), the first *beavers* is [+generic], and it is in the agent case, while the second *a beaver* is [+specific], and it is in the object case. *One*-substitution can ignore these differences in contextual meaning and replace the latter with *one*. Similarly, in (1.7), the first *a bachelor in linguistics* is [+specific] while the second is [−specific]. *One*-substitution can ignore this difference, and replace the latter with *one*.

The above contrast between differences in lexical meaning and differences in contextual meaning is not limited to *one*-substitution. It extends to all processes that involve reduction and deletion. For example, observe the following sentences:

(1.8)   a.   The curry was hot.
         b.   The coffee was hot.

The word *hot* is ambiguous between (i) peppery and (ii) hot in temperature. Example (1.8a) is ambiguous between these two interpretations. On the other hand, since in our culture coffee is not peppery, (1.8b) is unambiguous and means only that the coffee was hot in temperature.

Now observe the following sentences:

(1.9)   a.   The curry and the coffee were both hot.
         b.   The curry was hot, and so was the coffee.
         c.   The curry was hotter than the coffee.
         d.   The curry was hot, but the coffee was not.

In these sentences, there is only one surface realization of the word *hot*. Note that these sentences all mean 'the curry was hot in temperature.' This interpretation is forced on the sentences because in order for the *hot* for the coffee to be collapsed with the *hot* for the curry as in (a), or in order for it to be reduced to *so* as in (b), or deleted as in (c, d), it has to represent the same lexical meaning as the *hot* for the curry. The interpretation of *hot* that is shared by both is that of 'hot in temperature,' and hence arises the unambiguity of these sentences.[4]

Let us now compare the above situation with reduction processes involving different *contextual* meanings. Observe the following sentences:

(1.10)   a.   John [experiencer] loves everyone [object] and he [object] is loved by everyone [experiencer].
         b.   John loves, and is loved by, everyone.
(1.11)   a.   John wanted to marry a blonde [−specific], and Bill married a blonde [+specific].
         b.   John wanted to marry, and Bill did marry, a blonde.

In (1.10b), *John [experiencer]* and *he (= John) [object]* are collapsed into one token *John,* and *everyone [object]* and *everyone [experiencer]* are collapsed into one token *everyone*. Similarly, in (1.11b), *a blonde [−specific]* and *a blonde [+specific]* are collapsed by Right-Node Raising into one token *a blonde*.[5]

Let us use the term "reduction processes" to refer to the processes in which two identical constituents are reduced into one by collapsing, by replacement with a pronominal form (such as *so* as in (1.9b)), or by deletion. The above observations lead to the following generalization:

(1.12)   *Semantic Constraint on Reduction Processes:* Reduction processes, when they apply to commonly shared lexical items, can ignore differences in "contextual meaning" but not differences in "lexical meaning."

It is important to emphasize here that in using the term "reduction" in the above formulation, I am not implying that the "reduced" sentences are necessarily derived transformationally (by replacement with pro-forms or by deletion) from the structures underlying the unreduced full-fledged sentences. The generalization represented in this formulation holds regardless of the particular syntactic derivations of the sentences involved. Therefore, in the framework in which (1.4b), for example, is generated from the underlying structure which already has *one* in the second clause, the semantic component of grammar would have to reconstruct the semantics of this pro-form on the basis of the first clause: *Jane wanted to talk to a bachelor in linguistics.* In this framework, the Semantic Constraint on Reduction Processes given in (1.12) can be considered to be a constraint that would limit the semantics of *bachelor* that would replace *one* in the reconstructed semantic representation to the semantics of *bachelor* in the first clause (i.e., 'a holder of a B.A. degree'). Expressions such as "reduction," "deletion," "one-substitution," "collapsing" and so on that are used in this book should be interpreted as being neutral with respect to whether the sentences under discussion are to be derived transformationally, or whether they are present in reduced form in the underlying structures and the semantic component would reconstruct the full semantics of the "reduced" sentences.

[handwritten margin note: warning:]

Let us now examine the following sentence:

(1.13)   *John and a hammer broke the window.

Fillmore (1968) observed the following as an illustration of the explanatory power of his case grammar:

(1.14)   Only noun phrases representing the same case may be conjoined.

According to this constraint, (1.13) is ungrammatical because two noun phrases in different cases, one in the agent case and the other in the instrument case, are conjoined in the sentence. However, in view of the fact that reduction processes can ignore differences in contextual meaning, we must ask whether it is really true that noun phrase coordination is blocked by differences in semantic case.

A careful examination of the facts of coordination in English shows that Fillmore's constraint cannot be maintained. For example, observe the following sentences:

(1.15) a. The boys attacked a policeman [object], and the girls were attacked by a fireman [agent].
         b. The boys attacked, and the girls were attacked by, a policeman [object] and a fireman [agent], respectively.

(1.16) a. The children [experiencer] liked the teachers [object], and the parents [object] were liked by the teachers [experiencer].
         b. The children [experiencer] and the parents [object] respectively liked and were liked by the teachers.[6]

The situations that (1.15b) and (1.16b) describe are artificial, and the sentences are a little strained. However, they seem to be far better than (1.13), and I believe that they can be called acceptable sentences. This fact disproves the existence of a constraint such as (1.14).

If Fillmore's hypothesis is invalid, the explanation for the unacceptability of (1.13) must be sought elsewhere. I attribute it primarily to the fact that, while the coordination of *John* and *a hammer* as subject of *broke the window* suggests that the two played equally important roles in the act of breaking the window, there is nothing in the sentence to justify this equation. Sentences of the pattern of (1.13) become acceptable if they offer enough information that would justify the above equation. For example, observe the following sentence:

(1.17)   John and his hundred-pound hammer must have broken this steel door.

In the above sentence, *John* is [agent] and *his hundred-pound hammer* is [instrument], but the coordination of the two NPs is possible because *his hundred-pound hammer* is considered to have been as instrumental as John himself to the breaking of the steel door. Likewise, observe the following sentence:

(1.18)   John and his five-dollar screwdriver opened the safe in sixty seconds.

In (1.17) and (1.18), I have shown instances of [agent] and [instrument] NPs conjoined with *and*. In the following example, it is not clear what case each of the two NPs is in. The sentence is meant to describe the situation in which John was running around carrying a hundred-pound hammer and ran into a big glass door without knowing it. As a consequence, the glass door broke under the impact of both John and the hammer.

(1.19)   John and the hammer together broke the window.

? It is clear that *John* is not [instrument], but it is not clear whether it is an [agent] NP or not on the reading that is assumed here. On the other hand, it seems that *the hammer* is not [instrument] because John did not use it as an instrument. In any case, examples such as (1.17) and (1.18), as well as (1.15b) and (1.16b), firmly establish that it is possible to conjoin NPs of different semantic cases.

I have shown above that the claim that noun phrases of different semantic cases cannot be conjoined is hard to maintain. A similar questionable claim was made some time ago about the coordination of noun phrases of different markings with respect to specificity. Observe the following sentences:

(1.20)   a.   John wanted to see a lawyer. [±specific]
         b.   John wanted to see a psychotherapist. [±specific]
         c.   John wanted to see a lawyer and a psychotherapist.

Example (1.20a) is ambiguous with respect to whether or not John had a specific lawyer that he wanted to see. The following continuations disambiguate the sentence:

(1.21)   a.   . . . , but he was out of town. [+specific]
         b.   . . . , but he couldn't find one who was available. [−specific]

Example (1.20b) is ambiguous in the same way. One might expect that when these two sentences, each two ways ambiguous, are conjoined, with a reduction process applied to the resulting sentence, four different interpretations would emerge. Contrary to this expectation, (1.20c) has only two interpretations, one with *a lawyer* and *a psychotherapist* both interpreted as [+specific], and the other with these two noun phrases both interpreted as [−specific]. It is not possible to interpret *a lawyer* as [+specific] and *a psychotherapist* as [−specific], or vice versa. On the basis of this fact, it was proposed that noun phrases with different markings with respect to specificity could not be conjoined. However, this constraint is not consistent with the claim of the Semantic Constraint on Reduction Processes given in (1.12) and with the coordination facts that we observed in (1.15)–(1.18).

A further examination of the coordination facts involving noun phrases of different specificity marking leads us to sentences of the following kind:

(1.22)   Mary decided to see a lawyer, and an old friend of hers from Iowa who had once been in the same situation.

It is possible to interpret *a lawyer* as [−specific] and *an old friend of hers from Iowa who had once been in the same situation* as [+specific], vindicating the proposed hypothesis that noun phrases of different specificity markings can be conjoined.

We have to ask, then, why (1.22) allows a mixed interpretation, while (1.20c) does not. We can attribute this contrast to the following constraint:

(1.23)   *Parallel Interpretation Tendency:* Parallel structures tend to be interpreted in a parallel fashion unless there is external pressure for non-parallel interpretations.

In (1.22), assume that *a lawyer* is interpreted as [−specific]. Now one comes to the next indefinite noun phrase. A parallel interpretation of this noun phrase would mean 'any of her old friends from Iowa who had once been in the same situation.' However, such an interpretation would be pragmatically implausible: it is not likely that Mary had more than one such friend. Thus, pragmatics forces a nonparallel interpretation of the second noun phrase as 'a certain old friend of hers from Iowa . . . .' In contrast, there is nothing in (1.20c) that would force a nonparallel interpretation of *a lawyer* and *a psychotherapist*. Therefore, we obtain only parallel interpretations.

The same parallel interpretation tendency is in operation in our interpretation of

(1.24)   The curry was hot and the coffee was hot.

The primary and predominant interpretation of the sentence is that of 'both the curry and the coffee were hot in temperature.' However, because the association of curry with pepperiness is also very strong in this universe, it is possible to obtain a secondary and weak interpretation which says that the curry was peppery and the coffee was hot in temperature. With a little more external reinforcement, a mixed interpretation becomes stronger:

(1.25)   The curry was so hot that the guests had to drink a lot of water with it, and the coffee served after dinner was so hot that some of the guests burned their tongues.

The fact that we tend to interpret parallel structures in a parallel fashion unless otherwise required is not peculiar to our linguistic performance, but seems to be common to our cognitive process in general. For example, observe the following Necker cube:

(1.26)

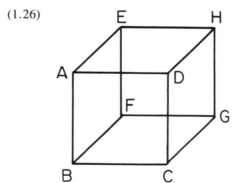

As is well known, this cube is ambiguous with respect to whether the surface ABCD or surface EFGH is interpreted as the one facing you. Everyone has his own first interpretation, but a switch to the other interpretation usually takes place after a short interval.[7] From that time on, there is a constant switch back and forth between these two interpretations.

Now, assume that we have two such Necker cubes next to each other.

(1.27)

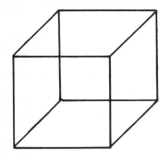 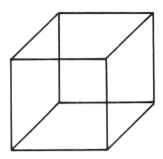

As observed in Kuno (1972a, p. II-17), if one looks at these two Necker cubes from some distance so that they are in one's view at the same time, they are interpreted in a parallel fashion. A switch in interpretation of one Necker cube is accompanied by a switch in interpretation of the other. This illustrates a parallel interpretation tendency in visual process.

Is it possible to force a mixed interpretation to the parallel Necker cubes? The answer is yes. For example, observe the following:

(1.28)

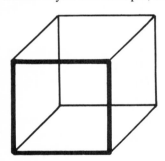 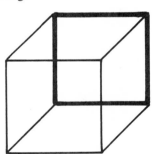

If bold lines are used to outline the surfaces that are supposed to be facing you, it becomes much easier to interpret the two cubes in two different ways. Similarly, observe the following:

(1.29)

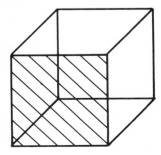 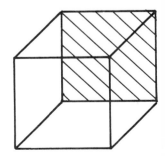

The shading of the surfaces intended to be facing the viewer accomplishes a similar effect. Examples (1.28) and (1.29) are the visual counterpart of the linguistic phenomenon (1.22) and (1.25).

The parallel interpretation tendency in language extends to embedded structures as well. For example, observe the following sentence:

(1.30)   While the curry was extremely hot, the coffee was not that hot.

The predominant interpretation of this sentence is that of 'hot in temperature' for both occurrences of *hot*. A visual counterpart of this phenomenon can be seen in the following figure:

(1.31)

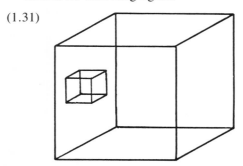

In the above, a small Necker cube is embedded in a large one. Here again, the two cubes are interpreted in a parallel fashion.

In the embedded structure also, it is possible to force a nonparallel interpretation:

(1.32)   In addition to the fact that the curry was so hot that the guests had to drink a lot of water with it, the coffee was so hot that some of the guests burned their tongues drinking it.

Similarly, a mixed interpretation can be forced on the embedded Necker cubes:

(1.33)

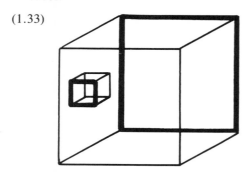

I am not claiming above that the linguistic facts that I have discussed here and the visual interpretation facts concerning Necker cubes and their variations are exactly identical. For example, the ambiguity of sentences such as *the curry was hot* or *John wanted to talk to a lawyer,* once learned, seems to be recognizable instantaneously—it is basically a matter of whether one knows it or one doesn't. There does not seem to be any significant time lag in switching from one interpretation to another. In contrast, regardless of how familiar a viewer is with the ambiguity of a Necker cube, there is always a significant time lag in switching from his favorite interpretation to another. Furthermore, the likelihood that a switch in interpretation will take place increases as time t increases. This phenomenon does not have any linguistic counterpart.[8] Similarly, for a Necker cube, after the first and second interpretations have been made, one switches back and forth between the two. But again there is no linguistic counterpart.[9] Thus, there are significant differences in the meaning of "ambiguity" between linguistic and visual data. In spite of this, there does not seem to be any doubt that a parallel interpretation tendency observable in language is attributable to a parallel interpretation tendency in cognitive processes in general (including visual processes). If this is true, it might be that the constraint given in (1.23) need not be stated in grammar but can be stated as a general constraint that applies to many cognitive processes.

[margin handwriting: cognitive & lingtc]

The discussion in this section suggests the kind of difficulty that a linguist must face in his analysis of a given linguistic phenomenon. The direct counterexample to Fillmore's generalization can be found only in sentences such as (1.15)–(1.18), which are difficult to come by, especially if the linguist is working on a language of which he does not have a native or native-like command. The indirect counterevidence can be found in a more general problem of whether reduction process can ignore differences in "contextual meaning." Therefore, the linguist must always be examining his target phenomenon in a larger perspective than is immediately called for by the phenomenon itself. Furthermore, that larger perspective might involve nonlinguistic cognitive processes as well. The linguist must look at his object of analysis from a multitude of angles.

1.2 **Specified Subject Condition**[10]

Compare the following two pairs of sentences:

(2.1) a. Did you buy a portrait of Marilyn Monroe?
　　　 b. Who did you buy a portrait of?

(2.2) a. Did you buy Mary's portrait of Marilyn Monroe?
　　　 b. *Who did you buy Mary's portrait of?

[margin handwriting: ? the portrait... because, pragmatically, if portrait is definite, then you'd most likely know, as well, wt. or who it was a portrait of...]

Why is (2.1b) acceptable and (2.2b) unacceptable? Pure syntacticians' immediate reaction to such data would be to assume that (2.2b) is unacceptable due to a violation of some syntactic constraint. They assume that there is a constraint that says nothing can be moved out of a picture noun construction that has a possessive NP in the determiner position, that is, a structure that can be represented as [NP's N Prep X]$_{NP}$. Some syntacticians relate it to an independently motivated, though dubious, constraint that says that no rule can apply, with a trigger upstairs, to a constituent within an NP or S that has a specified subject. More formally stated, this constraint reads as follows (Chomsky 1973):

picture noun constructions

(2.3)   *Specified Subject Condition:* No rule can involve X, Y in the structure
$$\ldots X \ldots [_\alpha \ldots Z \ldots -W\,Y\,V \ldots] \ldots$$
where Z is the specified subject of WYV in α, and α is either NP or S.[11]

Let us compare the structures of (2.1b) and (2.2b) at the time of application of a movement transformation that places *who(m)* in sentence-initial position:

(2.4)   a.   [$_{\bar{s}}$ Q [$_{s}$ you did buy [$_{NP}$ a portrait of who]]
         b.   [$_{\bar{s}}$ Q [$_{s}$ you did buy [$_{NP}$ *Mary's* portrait of who]]

The transformation that moves *who* into the sentence-initial Q, call it *Wh*-Q Movement, involves X = Q, and Y = *who,* with α = NP. *Wh*-Q Movement legitimately applies to (2.4a) because the embedded NP does not have a specified subject, but it cannot apply to (2.4b) because *Mary's* is the specified subject of *portrait of who.*[12]

The same constraint is invoked for explaining the ungrammaticality of the following (b) sentences:

(2.5)   a.   It is Marilyn Monroe who I want to buy a portrait of.
         b.   *It is Marilyn Monroe who I want to buy Mary's portrait of.
(2.6)   a.   Marilyn Monroe, I don't want to buy a portrait of.
         b.   *Marilyn Monroe, I don't want to buy Mary's portrait of.
(2.7)   a.   Yesterday, I met the actress who I had bought a portrait of.
         b.   *Yesterday, I met the actress who I had bought Mary's portrait of.

?/✗ ———→ (as well as ✗the portrait)

Some syntacticians believe that the Specified Subject Condition is not a condition that needs to be stated in grammars of individual languages but is a condition on the construction of grammatical rules, namely, a part of the theory of grammar with which humans are born.

UG

Before adopting a syntactic explanation for the unacceptability of (2.2b), (2.5b), (2.6b), and (2.7b) such as the one represented by the Specified Subject Condition, functional syntacticians examine more data involving extraction from picture nouns, suspecting that there might be semantic or discourse-based explanations for the unacceptability of these sentences. Sooner or later

functionalist method

they will come across sentences such as those given below, which have the same sentence pattern as (2.7b) but which are perfectly acceptable:

(2.8) a. This is the story that I haven't been able to get Mary's version of.[13]

b. This is the event that I liked CBS's reporting of best of all.

Mary's in (2.8a) and *CBS's* in (2.8b) are the specified subjects of their respective picture nouns. In spite of this fact, I have not come across any native speakers of English who find anything wrong with these sentences. There is nothing artificial or strained in these sentences. Therefore, they show that the Specified Subject Condition is not even a plausible constraint in English, to say nothing of its status as a language universal condition that humans are born with.

Having dispensed with the Specified Subject Condition as an explanation for the unacceptability of (2.2b), (2.5b), (2.6b), and (2.7b), functional syntacticians must offer a new explanation for the unacceptability of these sentences vis-à-vis the acceptability of (2.8a) and (2.8b). There must be something in the semantic or discourse-based nature of the picture nouns in the latter two sentences that is not shared by those in the first four sentences. Functional syntacticians soon arrive at the following two observations. First, the expression *Mary's version of the story,* even without any prior context, immediately suggests that there are other people's versions of the same story. In other words, the lexical item *version* makes it possible, or rather forces one, to interpret *Mary's* contrastively. In contrast, the expression *Mary's picture of Marilyn Monroe,* out of context, does not imply that there are other people's portraits of Marilyn Monroe. In other words, it is difficult to interpret *Mary's* contrastively in (2.2). This semantic contrast must be responsible for the difference in acceptability of (2.2b) and its likes and (2.8a). Second, for (2.8b), functional syntacticians note that in the United States there are three major television networks that report on national and international events. The expression *CBS's reporting of the event* immediately suggests that there are ABC's and NBC's reportings of the same event. Therefore, in this sentence, too, it is easy to interpret the possessive NP (i.e., Chomsky's specified subject) of the picture noun in a contrastive sense. From the above two observations, functional syntacticians can form an initial hypothesis that extraction from picture nouns with possessive NPs yields acceptability if the possessive NPs are readily interpretable contrastively. In fact, (2.8a) and (2.8b) require that *Mary's* and *CBS's* be pronounced with a focus intonation.

Observe, further, the following sentence:

(2.9) ??This is the story that I haven't been able to get Mary's latest version of.[14]

The expression *Mary's latest version of the story,* out of context, is usually interpreted with *latest* as the focus, and not with *Mary's* as the focus. For many speakers, this sentence is unacceptable. There are speakers who regard it as acceptable, but they say that they get only the interpretation in which there are several people's latest versions of the same story and the speaker has not received Mary's yet. In this interpretation, *Mary's*, and not *latest*, is the focus. This fact supports the hypothesis that extraction from picture nouns with possessive NPs does not result in unacceptability when the possessive NPs are readily interpretable as the focus of picture nouns.

Likewise, observe the following sentences:

(2.10) a. A politician of this kind, I wouldn't dream of buying even Avedon's portrait of.

  b. (?)This morning, I bumped into a man who I had just bought a local artist's portrait of.

  c. (?)A politician of this kind, I wouldn't dream of buying anybody's portrait of.

In (2.10a), the use of *even* makes clear that the possessive NP *Avedon's* is used here contrastively. In (2.10b, c) the fact that the possessive NPs are indefinite indicates that they represent new, unpredictable information. The common denominator of "contrastive" possessive NPs and "new, unpredictable" possessive NPs is that they represent *focus* information, that is, information with a high degree of newness and unpredictability.[15] Therefore, it can be hypothesized that extraction from picture nouns with possessive NPs is allowed when the possessive NPs represent focus information.

It still needs to be explained why extraction from picture nouns results in acceptability when possessive NPs are the foci of the picture nouns, and that it results in unacceptability when they are not. Grosu (1978) attributes the unacceptability of the latter type of extraction to the fact that it involves a conflict in topic-comment organization. Let us backtrack a little here and go back to my observation (Kuno 1973, chaps. 20 and 21; 1976a) that only a constituent that qualifies as the topic of a relative clause can be relativized. For example, observe the following Japanese sentences:

(2.11) a. [Sono hito ga sinda noni]   dare mo kanasimanakatta.
        the man died although nobody was-saddened
        'Although the man died, nobody was saddened.'

  b. Sono hito wa, [∅ sinda noni]   dare mo kanasimanakatta.
      the man   died although nobody was-saddened
      'That man, although (he) died, nobody was saddened.'

  c. [[∅ sinda noni]   dare mo kanasimanakatta] hito . . .
      died although nobody was-saddened   person
      'the man who (lit.) although (he) died, nobody was saddened'

(2.12) a. [Sono hito ga dekinakereba] watakusi ga yaru.
        the man if-cannot   I   do
        'If that man cannot do it, I will do it.'

    b. *Sono hito wa, [Ø dekinakereba] watakusi ga yaru.
        '*That man, if (he) cannot do it, I will do it.'
    c. *[[Ø dekinakereba] watakusi ga yaru] hito . . .
            if-cannot   I   do   person
        '*the person who if (he) cannot do it, I will do it . . .'

In (2.11a), *sono hito* 'the/that man' is a constituent in an adverbial clause. The acceptability of (2.11b) shows that this element can serve as the topic of the entire sentence. Note in (2.11c) that this constituent can be relativized.[16] In (2.12a), too, *sono hito* 'the/that man' is a constituent in an adverbial clause. However, the unacceptability of (2.12b) shows that in the given sentence this constituent cannot serve as topic. This is undoubtedly due to the fact that while 'although he died, no one was saddened' in (2.11b) qualifies as an attribute (i.e., as a comment) of *sono hito*, 'the/that man,' 'if he cannot do it, I will do it' of (2.12b) does not qualify as an attribute of the man under discussion. Observe that the relativization of *sono hito* 'the/that man' results in unacceptability, as shown in (2.12c). On the basis of the pervasive parallelism between topicalization and relativization, I proposed that in Japanese what is relativized is the theme of the relative clause. For example, the underlying structure of (2.11c) is something like

(2.13)   [*sono hito wa* [*sono hito ga* sinda noni] dare mo kanasimanakatta] hito
          |the man   ↓ the man died although nobody was saddened   man
          ↓   *topic-copy deletion*
     relativization by topic deletion

As is shown above, what is relativized in Japanese is not *sono hito (ga)* as the subject of the adverbial clause in (2.13), but *sono hito (wa)* as the topic of the entire relative clause.

The claim that only the constituents in a sentence that qualify as the topic of the sentence can be relativized applies to English, also. For example, observe the following sentences:

(2.14)   a. This person alone passed the test.
          b. *The person who alone passed the test was a sixty-year-old self-taught engineer.

In (2.14a), *this person* represents the new, unpredictable, focus information. The sentence is not a statement about the person, but about 'Who passed the test?' The sentence is synonymous with

(2.15)   The only person who passed the test was THIS PERSON.

Observe in (2.14b) that this constituent cannot be relativized. This example, as well as some others, shows that both in Japanese and English it is the case that only those constituents that qualify as topics of relative clauses can be relativized to yield acceptable relative clause constructions.[17] In Kuno (1976a),

I extended this observation to *wh*-question and *it*-clefting constructions and hypothesized that only those constituents that qualify as topics can undergo unbounded movement transformations.

preferred/
natural
topic-comment
structures

Grosu (1978) points out that it has also been shown that certain constructions (both sentences and noun phrases) have "natural" or "preferred" topic-comment structures, that is, structures that they tend to assume in out-of-the-blue situations (Keenan 1974). In particular, in a sentence, the subject tends to be selected as topic, and in a noun phrase of the [NP's N Prep X] pattern, the possessive NP, and not X, tends to be perceived as a topic.

Thus, given

(2.16)   The man bought the woman's portrait of the actress.

It is easiest to interpret the sentence as a statement about *the man*. It is next easiest to interpret it as a statement about *the woman's portrait of the actress* or about *the woman's*. However, it is extremely difficult to interpret the sentence as a statement about *the actress*. This is reflected in the relativizability of the four NPs:

(2.17)   a.   This is the man who bought the woman's portrait of the actress yesterday.
          b.   This is the woman's portrait of the actress which the man bought yesterday.
          c.   This is the woman whose portrait of the actress the man bought yesterday.
          d.   *This is the actress who the man bought the woman's portrait of yesterday.

What this fact shows is that the subject priority for the status of topic is not strong vis-à-vis other constituents in the sentence, but the possessive NP priority in picture nouns vis-à-vis the object of the preposition is extremely strong.

The above observations make it possible to explain why some sentences involving extraction of X out of [NP's N Prep X] are acceptable and why others are unacceptable. For example, observe the following sentences:

(2.18)   a.   [Q you bought [a portrait of Marilyn Monroe]]
          b.   Who did you buy a portrait of? (= 2.1b)
(2.19)   a.   [Q you bought [Mary's portrait of Marilyn Monroe]]
          b.   *Who did you buy Mary's portrait of? (= 2.2b)
(2.20)   a.   [I haven't been able to get [Mary's version of this story]]
          b.   This is the story that I haven't been able to get Mary's version of. (= 2.8a)

In (2.18a), the noun phrase in square brackets does not involve a genitive noun phrase, and therefore *Marilyn Monroe* (or a noun phrase that fills that slot) can readily qualify as the topic of the sentence. Hence, the noun phrase in this position can undergo *Wh*-Q Movement (as well as *Wh*-Relative Movement, Topicalization, and *It*-Clefting). Hence the acceptability of the sentence. In (2.19a), on the other hand, in the out-of-the-blue situation, *Mary* qualifies more readily than *Marilyn Monroe* for the status of topic, and hence the unacceptability of (2.19b) because a constituent that is least likely to qualify as the topic of the relative clause has been relativized in this sentence. In (2.20a), on the other hand, *Mary* does not qualify as topic because, due to the semantic nature of *version, Mary's* has to be interpreted as contrastive focus information. Hence, *this story,* which is otherwise much lower than the possessive NP in the pecking order, becomes eligible as the topic of this relative clause and can undergo relativization.

The above explanation suggests that extraction of X out of the [NP's N Prep X] pattern might be possible even when the genitive NP is not the focus of the phrase just in case X qualifies as a prominent topic, whereas the possessive NP serves as a latent topic (say, a paragraph topic). Such a situation would arise when the possessive NP is semantically transparent, and represents information that is so presupposed (i.e., taken for granted) that one would not characterize the rest of the sentence as a statement about that possessive NP. For example, observe the following discourse, which is based on Grosu's observation:

(2.21)   I have been collecting a separate picture of each Hollywood actress, and I can show them to you if you like. But I need to tell you in advance, I cannot show you my picture of Marilyn Monroe.

In a sense, the entire discourse can be said to be a statement about the speaker. But the information content that *I* or *my* represents is so low (that is, it is so presupposed) that it qualifies only as a hyper-topic (i.e., a latent topic, e.g., a paragraph topic or a conversation topic), and it makes more sense to say that in the last sentence, *Marilyn Monroe,* and not *I/my,* is the prominent topic. Note that the following sentence, which is due to Grosu, can replace the last sentence of (2.21):

(2.22)   But there is one particular actress who I will NEVER show you my picture of Ø.

It is interesting, in this respect, to note that all the counterexamples to the Specified Subject Condition given in Grosu's paper that do not have the possessive NP as focus have either *my* or *your* in the possessive NP position—the two possessive pronouns that are most presupposed, and most transparent from discourse points of view.[18]

This, of course, does not mean that only the first- and second-person possessive pronouns allow extraction of the pattern of (2.22). For example, observe the following sentence:

(2.23)   This is the term that I don't like Chomsky's definition of.

This sentence, which is acceptable for all speakers with whom I have checked it, is amenable to two interpretations:

(2.24) a. (with *Chomsky's* stressed)
Among various terms under discussion, there is one such that I like all the various definitions of it given by various scholars, except for the one given by Chomsky.

  b. (with *Chomsky's* destressed)
Among the definitions of various terms given by Chomsky, there is one that I don't like—and it is the definition of this term.

In (2.24a), *Chomsky's* is a focus, while in (2.24b), it is a hyper-topic. Example (2.23) is acceptable in interpretation (2.24a) because *Chomsky's* does not qualify as the topic, and hence control for the topic of the whole clause can be transferred to *the term,* a noun phrase that is to be relativized. The same sentence is also acceptable in interpretation (2.24b) because in this interpretation, *Chomsky's* is a transparent paragraph topic, and therefore it can yield control for the topic of the entire relative clause to *the term.*

If the above explanation of the acceptability of (2.23) in interpretation (2.24b) is correct, then why is it that the sentence that we started out with, namely, (2.2b), and the relative clause version of it are unacceptable?

(2.25) a. *Who did you buy Mary's portrait of? (= 2.2b)
  b. *Yesterday, I met the actress who I had bought Mary's portrait of. (= 2.7b)

coming up
w/contexts

↑

acceptability
depends
on this...

It seems that the difference between (2.23) and (2.25) lies in how easy it is to come up with a context that would justify the presuppositions that are involved in these sentences. Sentence (2.23) presupposes that there are definitions by Chomsky of various linguistic terms. Such a presupposition does not require any special context. Furthermore, (2.23), in interpretation (2.24b), presupposes that the preceding context has been Chomsky's definition of various linguistic terms. It is not difficult at all for the hearer to come up with such a context. On the other hand, (2.25b), for example, in the interpretation in which *Mary's* does not receive a focus stress, presupposes that there is a portrait by *Mary* of the man under discussion, as well as of many other persons/objects. Such a presupposition is difficult to justify under the out-of-the-blue situation. The sentence also presupposes that the preceding discourse has been about the fact that the speaker is accustomed to buying Mary's portraits. This presupposition is necessary in order to interpret *Mary's* not as a prominent topic, but as a hyper-topic. These two presuppositions are unusual, and require much more special context than is required for (2.23). It seems that ordinary speakers of English reject (2.25) because they cannot easily come up with the context of this kind. This explanation is supported by the fact that (2.26) is considerably better than (2.25b) if the hearer knows that Avedon is a well-known photographer:

(2.26)   Yesterday, I met the model who I just bought Avedon's portrait of.

I have shown above that the unacceptability of (2.2b) cannot be attributed to a syntactic constraint such as the Specified Subject Condition and must be explained as semantic and discourse-based. But this realization cannot be obtained as long as one keeps looking at ordinary sentences such as (2.2b). One has to dig deep into the phenomenon under discussion before one discovers sentences such as (2.8a, b), (2.10a, b, c), and (2.22, 23).

1.3   NP Constraint, Subjacency, and Restructuring of Picture Nouns

In the preceding section, we examined semantic and discourse-based conditions for extraction from picture nouns with possessive NPs, but we proceeded as if there were no problem for extraction from picture nouns without possessive NPs. We did not discuss in any depth the acceptability of sentences such as

(3.1)   Who did you buy a portrait of?

However, the fact that sentences such as (3.1) are acceptable requires explanation because it is not the case that all sentences of this pattern are acceptable. Below, I give examples of acceptable and unacceptable sentences, all involving extraction from picture nouns without possessive NPs:

(3.2)   a.   What did you buy a book on?
         b.   Who did you see a picture of?
         c.   What have you bought a book about?
         d.   Which book did you read a review of?
(3.3)   a.   *What did you lose a book on?
         b.   *Who did they destroy pictures of?[19]
         c.   *Who did you see a book about?
         d.   *What did John burn a large green book about?

The fact that there are well-formed sentences such as those given in (3.1) and (3.2), and that there are unacceptable sentences such as those given in (3.3), has long been known. How do linguists go about accounting for this fact? Bach and Horn (1976) have hypothesized that (3.3) represented the normal state of affairs and have attributed the unacceptability of these sentences to the following constraint:

(3.4)   *The NP Constraint:* No constituent that is dominated by NP can be moved or deleted from that NP by a transformational rule.

In order to account for the acceptability of (3.1) and (3.2), they have hypothesized that extraposition has applied to the prepositional phrase within each picture noun before extraction applied. That is, they have hypothesized that this extraposition rule has turned the structure of (3.5a), for example, to that of (3.5b):

(3.5)   a. $[_{\bar{S}}$ Q $[_S$ you did buy $[_{NP}$ a portrait $[_{PP}$ of who]]]]
          b. $[_{\bar{S}}$ Q $[_S$ you did buy $[_{NP}$ a portrait] $[_{PP}$ of who]]]

Since *of who* of (3.5b) is not dominated by NP, they claim that *Wh*-Q Movement applies freely to this structure and produces (3.1).

Chomsky (1977) also assumes that (3.3) represents the normal state of affairs and attributes the unacceptability of these sentences to the following constraint:

(3.6)   *Subjacency:* No rule can involve X, Y, X superior to Y, if there is more than one cyclical node boundary between X and Y.

Chomsky assumes that $S/\bar{S}$ and NP are cyclical nodes for English. According to this condition, extraction of the *wh*-word out of the picture noun in (3.5a) is blocked because this extraction involves two cyclical node boundaries, S and NP, but extraction of the same *wh*-word out of the prepositional phrase of (3.5b) is allowable because this process involves only one cyclical node boundary, namely, S. Thus, Chomsky, too, assumes that extraposition of prepositional phrases has taken place in (3.1) and (3.2), but not in (3.3).[20]

Let us see what the restructuring analysis has actually accomplished. In Bach and Horn's case, this analysis has removed a set of sentences which are counterexamples to the NP Constraint. In Chomsky's case, it has removed a set of sentences which are counterexamples to Subjacency, which Chomsky assumes to be independently motivated. However, neither Bach and Horn nor Chomsky provides us with any conditions as to when restructuring fails to take place, as is the case with the sentences of (3.3). Thus, the problem of how to reconcile the acceptability of (3.1) and (3.2) with the NP Constraint, and Subjacency has simply been replaced by the problem of how to reconcile the unacceptability of (3.3) with the restructuring rule involving extraposition of prepositional phrases. We do not know any more about the phenomenon under discussion than we used to know before the restructuring analysis was introduced.

Bach and Horn observe parallelism between the extractability of NPs and that of PPs out of picture nouns. For example, consider the following sentences:

(3.7)   a.   Who did John write a book about?
          b.   About whom did John write a book?[21]
(3.8)   a.   *Who did they destroy a book about?
          b.   *About whom did they destroy a book?

They claim that a PP within a picture noun can be fronted in its entirety only when it has been extraposed out of the picture noun by the restructuring rule under discussion. According to them, (3.8a) and (3.8b) are both unacceptable because *about* wh-*someone,* for reasons that they have left unexplained, cannot undergo extraposition out of the picture noun *a book about* wh-*someone.*

The above parallelism, however, quickly dissolves as we examine further data:

(3.9)   a.   Who did you buy a book about?
        b.   *About whom did you buy a book?
(3.10) a.   What did you borrow a book about from the library?
        b.   *About what did you borrow a book from the library?
(3.11) a.   Who did you like stories about best of all?
        b.   *About whom did you like stories best of all?[22]

In the above examples, extraposition of a smaller NP out of the picture noun is possible, but fronting of the prepositional phrase in its entirety results in unacceptability.[23]

Bach and Horn also observe parallelism between the extractability of a smaller NP and the passivizability of the head NP. For example, observe the following sentences, which are taken from Bach and Horn (1976):

(3.12) a.   Who did they write a book about?
        b.   A book was written about Nixon by John.
(3.13) a.   *Who did they destroy a book about?
        b.   *A book was destroyed about Nixon by John.

According to their restructuring analysis, *a book* has become the sole object of *write* after *about NP* has been extraposed out of the picture noun. They claim that passivization of the head NP of picture nouns is possible only under this condition. They claim that (3.13b) is unacceptable because, as witnessed by the unacceptability of (3.13a), the prepositional phrase *about Nixon* is still part of the object NP of *destroy.*

Here, too, the above parallelism does not extend far beyond the sentences that they have discussed in the paper. For example,

(3.14) a.   What did John buy a book about?
        b.   *A book was bought about Nixon by John.
(3.15) a.   What did you borrow a book about from the library?
        b.   *A book was borrowed from the library about Nixon. ⟵ oK

In spite of the fact that extraction of the object of *about* is possible, as shown by the acceptability of (3.14a) and (3.15a), the passivization of *a book* results in unacceptability.

Furthermore, Bach and Horn's restructuring analysis, which is based on the extraposability of PPs out of picture nouns, makes wrong predictions because extraction is sometimes banned from the extraposed PPs:

(3.16) a.   Einstein attacked a theory about the predictability of the movements of atoms with vengeance.

b.   Einstein attacked a theory, with vengeance, about the predictability of the movements of atoms.
c.   *What did Einstein attack a theory about? (Bach and Horn)
d.   *About what did Einstein attack a theory? (Bach and Horn)

Example (3.16b) shows that the expression *a theory about NP* allows extraposition of *about NP*. In spite of this fact, neither the fronting of the smaller NP, nor the PP is allowable, as shown by the unacceptability of (3.16c, d).

Bach and Horn observe parallelism between extractability out of picture nouns and the pronominalizability of the head picture noun:

(3.17)   a.   Bill wrote it about Nixon.
         b.   Einstein formulated it about relativity.
(3.18)   a.   *John destroyed it about Nixon.
         b.   *Einstein attacked it about relativity.

However, in this case, too, the parallelism does not extend too far:

(3.19)   a.   *Bill bought it about Nixon. cf. (3.2a)
         b.   *Bill borrowed it about Nixon from the library. cf. (3.10a)

The above observations show that, although Bach and Horn are correct in assuming that certain picture noun sentences have prepositional phrases outside picture nouns, this fact explains only a subset of cases where extraction is possible out of picture nouns. That is, the subset that they have dealt with consists of sentences in which the semantics of the prepositional phrases matches that of the verbs involved. For example, observe the following two sentences.

(3.20)   a.   John wrote a book about Nixon.
         b.   John bought a book about Nixon.

The concept *write about something* exists. Thus, *about Nixon* in (3.20a) can be interpreted adverbially, as a prepositional phrase modifying *bought* and outside the picture noun. Hence the acceptability of (3.7b), (3.12b), and (3.17a). On the other hand, the concept *buy about something* does not exist. Thus, *about Nixon* in (3.20b) cannot be interpreted adverbially, as a prepositional phrase modifying *bought* and outside the picture noun.

The above claim that (3.20a), at least in one of its derivations, has *about Nixon* as an adverbial prepositional phrase can be supported by the fact that the following sentence seems to be acceptable:

(3.21)   John wrote a book on political chicanery about Nixon.

It seems that in the above sentence, *on political chicanery* is part of the picture noun while *about Nixon* is a verb modifier. This analysis is confirmed by the very tests that Bach and Harms used:

(3.22)   a.   A book on political chicanery was written about Nixon.
           b.   *A book was written on political chicanery about Nixon.
           c.   *A book on political chicanery about Nixon was written.

Example (3.22a) shows that *a book on political chicanery* is the object of *wrote* in (3.21), while (3.22b) shows that *on political chicanery* cannot be an element outside the picture noun. Similarly, (3.22c) shows that *a book on political chicanery about Nixon* cannot form a single constituent.

Now observe the following sentence:

(3.23)   What aspects of political activities did you write a book on about Nixon?

I believe that this sentence is acceptable in spite of the fact that the sentences in (3.22) have shown that *a book on political chicanery* is an NP and that extraposition of PP (i.e., *on political chicanery*) has not taken place. This diametrically contradicts Bach and Horn's claim that no constitutent that is dominated by NP can be moved from that NP by a transformational rule.[24]

Clearly, Bach and Horn's and Chomsky's restructuring analysis cannot account for the phenomenon under discussion. What, then, is the real explanation for the contrast between (3.1, 2) and (3.3)? In order to find out if there is any syntactic, semantic, or discourse-based difference between these two sets of sentences, let us examine the corresponding sentences without extraction. For example, compare the following two sentences:

(3.24)   a.   Yesterday, on my way home, I bought a book on John Irving.
           b.   Yesterday, on my way home, I lost a book on John Irving.

In a highly intuitive sense, we feel that the fact that the book under discussion was on John Irving is much more *relevant* in (3.24a) than in (3.24b).[25] This is undoubtedly due to the fact that one buys books, but one does not lose them, because of their content.[26] Thus, (3.25) would be a natural continuation of (3.24a) but not of (3.24b):

(3.25)   He is one of the contemporary authors that I like, and I have read all the novels that he has published.[27]

We can say that John Irving readily qualifies as the theme of the sentence in (3.24a) but not in (3.24b). This distinction seems to be responsible for the difference in acceptability between (3.2a) and (3.3a). We see here that the discourse condition that we discussed in the preceding section is in operation here, too:

(3.26)   *Topichood Condition for Extraction:* Only those constituents in a sentence that qualify as the topic of the sentence can undergo extraction processes (i.e., *Wh*-Q Movement, *Wh*-Relative Movement, Topicalization, and *It*-Clefting).

Koster (1978) seems to assume that extractability is due to lexical idiosyncrasies of verbs, but this is not correct. He compares the following sentences:

(3.27) a. Who did you see a picture of?
        b. *Who did you destroy a picture of?

objects,

verb semantics

vs.

relevance

and states that the difference in acceptability is due to the different verbs *see* and *destroy*. This observation is true only to the extent that the lexical meanings of verbs clearly have something to do with assigning relevance values to the smaller NP of picture nouns. But it stops far short of capturing the real conditioning factor involving extraction out of picture nouns.

It is clearly illustrated that extractability depends heavily upon how relevant the content of the smaller NP is to what the rest of the sentence says, or, to put it differently, how well the smaller NP qualifies as the topic of the entire sentence. Compare (3.27b) with the following:

(3.28) Speaker A: Right after Chairman Mao died, they started taking pictures of the Central Committee members off the wall.
        Speaker B: Who did they destroy more pictures of, Chairman Mao or Jiang Qing?

Speaker B knows that the destroying of pictures was carried out on the basis of who they portrayed. Therefore, the content of the pictures is relevant to the rest of the sentence. In other words,

(3.29) They destroyed pictures of Chairman Mao.

can be interpreted as a statement about Chairman Mao in this kind of context. Hence the acceptability of (3.28B). Example (3.27b) is acceptable for those who can imagine contexts such as (3.28A) and unacceptable for those who cannot. In any case, the acceptability of (3.28B) shows that, contrary to Koster's assumption, the extractability problem can be decided upon only when one looks at the entire sentence and cannot be solved simply on the basis of the verbs used.

Another illustration of the pragmatic nature of the phenomenon under discussion is the contrast that is observable between the following two sentences:

(3.30) a. What did you see pictures of?
        b. *Who did you see a book about?

Bach and Horn consider (3.30a) fully acceptable and (3.30b) unacceptable. I believe that there is total agreement among speakers of English with respect to the acceptability of (3.30a). Although I suspect that there are wide differences of judgment in the acceptability of (3.30b), it is, in any case, important to recognize the fact that there are speakers who consider (3.30a) acceptable and (3.30b) unacceptable when these two sentences are given in isolation. Since the two sentences have the same verb *see* used in the same meaning, it is clear that we cannot resort to the lexical meanings of the verbs involved in order to account for extractability out of picture nouns. The difference between (3.30a) and (3.30b) clearly lies in the fact that when one sees a picture, one has seen its content, while when one sees a book, one usually does not see *what* the book is about, to say nothing of *who* it is about.

The above observations make Bach and Horn's and Chomsky's restructuring analysis rather futile—they would have to claim that restructuring has taken place in (3.27a), (3.28B), and (3.30a), but not in (3.27b) and (3.30b). There is no basis to assume that (3.27b) and (3.28B) have two different structures, nor that (3.30a) and (3.30b) do. Even if their claim about restructuring is justified within their own theories, it is a rather trivial claim because it is a claim that is necessitated by the theory, and it has very little to do with actual facts.

Erteschik-Shir (1981), who deals with the same kind of examples I have dealt with in this section, proposes an interesting hypothesis. First, let us observe her examples, which she attributes to Cattell (1979):

(3.31)   a.   John wrote a book about Nixon.
         b.   Who did John write a book about?
(3.32)   a.   John destroyed a book about Nixon.
         b.   *Who did John destroy a book about?
(3.33)   a.   I like the gears in that car.
         b.   Which car do you like the gears in?
(3.34)   a.   I like the girl in that car.
         b.   *Which car do you like the girl in?

She hypothesizes that the crucial concept that determines extractability from picture nouns is that of "dominance," which she defines as follows:

(3.35)   *Dominance:* A constituent c of a sentence S is dominant in S if and only if the speaker intends to direct the hearer's attention to the intension (semantic content) of c, by uttering S.
(3.36)   *Dominance Principle:* A constituent that undergoes extraction must be dominant in the S.

She gives the following as one of the operational tests for identifying which constituents of particular sentences can be dominant.

(3.37)   Sam said: John wrote a book about Nixon.
         Which is a lie—it was about a rhinoceros.
(3.38)   Sam said: John destroyed a book about Nixon.
         *Which is a lie—it was about a rhinoceros.

The test applied to (3.31a) (in (3.37)) indicates that *about Nixon* can be dominant. Erteschik-Shir says that this is because the hearer's attention is drawn to the fact that the book is about Nixon. Therefore it is possible to refute just this part of the sentence. The unacceptable response in (3.38), which signals that the prepositional phrase *about Nixon* is not dominant here, can be explained in terms of the semantic force of the verb *destroy*. The speaker intends to focus the hearer's attention on the act of destruction rather than on the content of the book. Erteschik-Shir observes that if we know that John characteristically destroys books, then the semantic force of the verb is neutralized and in this context the discourse (3.38) would be acceptable, suggesting that in the same context (3.32b) would also be acceptable.

The lie test applied to (3.33) and (3.34) gives the following results:

(3.39)   Sam said: John likes the gears in that car.
    a.   Which is a lie—he never saw the car.
    b.   Which is a lie—he never tried the gears.
(3.40)   Sam said: John likes the girl in that car.
    a.   *Which is a lie—he never saw the car.
    b.   Which is a lie—he never saw the girl.

According to her lie test, *that car* can be dominant in (3.39) but not in (3.40). The extractability of *which car* in (3.33) and the unextractability of *which car* in (3.34) follows from this.

Concerning the reason why *that car* can be interpreted as being dominant in (3.39), but not in (3.40), Erteschik-Shir refers to Cattell's earlier observation: ". . . *the gears* have a relationship to *that car* which does not hold between *the girl* and *that car:* that of a functional part to a whole" (Cattell 1979, p. 170). As the test (3.39) shows, it is possible to use the sentence (3.33a) in a context where *the gears* is intended to be dominant. She assumes that the reading where *the gears* is dominant would be the prevalent one. The alternative reading, where *that car* is dominant, is possible because the speaker, by uttering (3.33a), is not necessarily drawing the hearer's attention to the existence of gears in cars, but to the fact that *that car* is being liked because of its gears. In other words, where the main point is the specific car, the sentence could be paraphrased as:

(3.41)   I like that car for its gears.

She observes that (3.34b) is unacceptable because (3.34a) cannot be paraphrased as:

(3.42)   *I like that car for its girl.

She adds that (3.34b) is much improved if we imagine a society in which every car came with a girl and buyers chose cars partly on the basis of the girls in them. She observes that the same context similarly improves the response (3.40a), attesting to the correlation between the lie test and the extraction facts.

Erteschik-Shir's Dominance Principle attempts to capture the same generalization that the topichood condition does from a different angle—from the point of view of the speaker's intention. It nicely succeeds in solving the problem that both topicalization processes (Topicalization and Relativization) and focusing processes (*Wh*-Q Movement and *It*-Clefting) are subject to the same constraint. However, it leaves unresolved the problem of why, for example, a speaker *cannot intend* to direct the hearer's attention to the intension of *that car* in (3.40). The same problem exists for the Topichood Condition: Why is it that *that car* cannot serve as the topic of the sentence? Why is a part-whole relationship relevant for dominance and topichood?

There is some likelihood that another factor, which is related to a whole-part relationship, is interacting with extraction phenomena. First, observe the following two discourses:

(3.43)   I met a man with a telescope. It was a gigantic telescope, more than six feet long and about six inches in diameter. It had an expensive-looking camera attached to it . . .

(3.44)   The witness said that he met a man with a telescope in the park.—Which is a lie—it was a double-barreled shotgun.

In (3.43), *a telescope* becomes the topic of the whole discourse. In (3.44), Erteschik-Shir's lie test shows that *a telescope* can be dominant in the first sentence. In spite of these facts, the following sentence is awkward, marginal, or unacceptable for many speakers:

(3.45)   ✓/?/??/*What did you meet a man with?

Therefore, something more than dominance or topichood is involved in extraction. We note that in those cases in which extraction is possible, the head noun is an attribute of the extracted NP (a list head). For example, observe the following sentences:

(3.46)   a.   I have forgotten the name of that person.
          b.   Who have you forgotten the name of?
(3.47)   a.   I have read a book about Nixon.
          b.   Who have you read a book about?

The name of a person (a list head) is his/her attribute. The fact that there is a book about a person is his/her attribute. On the other hand, the fact that there is a man carrying a telescope is not an attribute of that telescope. This difference seems to be at least partly responsible for the acceptability of (3.46b) and (3.47b) and the marginality or unacceptability of (3.45).

Similarly, observe the following:

(3.48)   a.   I fully recognize the problem with this solution.
          b.   This is the kind of solution which I fully recognize the problem with.
(3.49)   a.   I don't like solutions with this kind of problem.
                (= 'I don't like solutions that have this kind of problem.')
          b.   *This is the kind of problem that I don't like any solution with.

Solutions may have problems (= difficulties). A particular difficulty may be an attribute of a particular solution (a list head). But a particular solution is not an attribute of a particular difficulty (= problem). In (3.48b), the relativized NP is a list head, and the remaining NP (plus a preposition) is its attribute. In contrast, in (3.49b), the relativized NP is not a list head, and the remaining NP not an attribute of the relativized NP. This difference must be responsible, at least in part, for the acceptability of (3.48b) and the unacceptability of (3.49b).

Observe, further, the following sentences:

(3.50)   a.   I know the people in that workshop best.
          b.   Which workshop do you know the people in best?
(3.51)   a.   I know the people in that workshop room best.
          b. ??Which workshop room do you know the people in best?

Workshops (list heads) can have their respective lists, psychologically permanent, of participants as their attribute values. On the other hand, workshop rooms usually cannot. The people who happen to be in a given workshop room at a given time do not constitute the workshop room's attribute. This difference seems to account for the difference in acceptability between (3.50b) and (3.51b).

Returning to the contrast between (3.33b) and (3.34b), we observe that while gears are a legitimate attribute of a car, a girl who happens to be in a car does not constitute a legitimate attribute of that car. The above observations suggest that the following condition exists for extraction:

(3.52)   *List-Head Attribute Relationship Requirement:* Extraction of X from [NP Prep X] is possible only when X is a list head, and NP is an attribute of X.

It is not surprising that such a constraint should exist. A list head is, so to speak, the topic of the list, and its attributes are the comments about the topic. Therefore, the above condition is consistent with the Topichood Condition for Extraction and is perhaps derivable from it.

In this section, we have looked into extraction from picture nouns without possessive NPs. I believe that I have shown convincingly that Bach and Horn's NP Constraint, Chomsky's Subjacency, and their PP extraposition analysis fail to account for the phenomenon. In their place, I have presented a nonsyntactic account of the phenomenon, on the basis of the Topichood Condition, Erteschik-Shir's Dominance Principle, and the List-Head Attribute Requirement. These nonsyntactic formulations are still in their developing stage, and they are not without difficulties. The most serious problem is how to determine what constituents in a given sentence can qualify as the topic of the whole sentence, and what constituents are dominant. We need many more tests than Erteschik-Shir's lie test or a topic continuation test. Crude though these formulations may still be, they are nevertheless the only hope for accounting for the phenomenon under discussion in the face of the failure of the syntactic approaches. Since there does not seem to be any syntactic clue for the solution, the most profitable research avenue seems to be that of continuing to refine and objectivize our functional approach.

1.4 About This Book

There are four areas, among others, in which functional approaches have been particularly fruitful in accounting for what used to be regarded as "syntactic" phenomena or for what used to be put aside as "nonsyntactic" (and therefore, implicitly, "unworthy of serious research"). They are:

(4.1)   *Perceptual Strategies*
This area offers explanation for "syntactic phenomena" on the basis of perceptual strategies or other performance factors.

(4.2)   *Flow of Information in Sentences in Discourse*
This area examines arrangements of elements in a sentence or/and a sequence of sentences from points of view such as
(i)   topic and comment: what is the topic of the sentence or sentences
(ii)   presupposition: what part of the sentence is taken for granted as true
(iii)   old and new information: how much new information a given element in the sentence adds to the development of a story
(iv)   activated and inactivated: what part of the sentence the speaker assumes to be in the awareness of the hearer at the time of the utterance.

(4.3)   *Direct Discourse Perspective*
This area examines subordinate clauses that represent the utterance, thought, or internal feeling of the referent of a main clause element and contrasts them with those that do not. It observes that certain syntactic patterns occur only in the former type of subordinate clauses and attributes them to the fact that they relate to the "speaker/experiencer/thinker/feeler/knower/hearer" of what the subordinate clauses represent.

(4.4)   *Empathy Perspective*
The speaker, in describing an event or state, can choose various "camera angles": He can place himself at a distance from the participants of the event/state and give an objective, detached description. Alternatively, he can position himself closer to one participant than to the others, or, in some special cases, he can completely identify himself with one participant and describe the event/state from this participant's camera angle. The empathy perspective examines syntactic manifesta-

tions of the speaker's camera angles in sentences and in a sequence of sentences.

The first section of this chapter, which dealt with the coordination phenomena of English, is in the area of "perceptual strategies." The second and third sections, which dealt with extraction from picture nouns, belong to the area of "flow of information in sentences in discourse." There is a considerable amount of research results, including my own, in these two areas, part of which is summarized in Kuno (1975a, 1978b). Space limitation prevents my including much further discussion on these areas in this book.

This book deals primarily with the "direct discourse perspective" and the "empathy perspective." My approach is to demonstrate how these two perspectives can account for various phenomena involving pronouns and reflexives in English which have not been adequately accounted for, which have been "accounted for" by erroneous syntactic conditions, or which have been completely ignored by past researchers. The direct discourse perspective was first proposed in Kuno (1972b), and the empathy perspective, in its preliminary form by Kuno (1972b) and in a much more expanded and formalized form in Kuno and Kaburaki (1975). A large portion of this book is based on these two papers and on other papers that I have published in the same perspectives. However, this book represents my first major attempt to synthesize my past research in these two fields, and it also introduces many new findings that have not been published before.

At the beginning of this chapter, I observed that functional syntax is independent of various current models of grammar. The generalizations that are presented in this book are of the kind that need to be incorporated into any theory of grammar. I assume, in this book, a model of grammar that is close to the theory represented in Chomsky's *Aspects of the Theory of Syntax*. However, in order to make my generalizations palatable to broader audiences, I will attempt to present them alternatively in more recent theories of grammar, including government and binding theory. Also, since I start out with a discussion of the pronominalization and reflexivization phenomena dating back to the early 1960s, I will have to use the then-current model of generative grammar as a basis for discussing early works. I have to repeat here that the generalizations I present in this book are independent of the particular grammatical framework that one may be working in—therefore, I ask the reader not to be distracted by disagreement between theoretical frameworks and lose sight of the true objectives of the book.

2 Pronouns and Reflexives (1)

2.1 Ross's and Langacker's Formulations

It has long been recognized that pronouns can sometimes precede their "ante-cedents" in sentences, but in pre-generative traditional grammars, no attempt was made to examine the syntactic relationship that must hold between pro-nouns and their antecedents in such cases. For example, consider the follow-ing four sentences, in which the index *i* attached to *John* and *he* is meant to show that they are coreferential:

(1.1) a. If John$_i$ is around, he$_i$ will do it.
     b. If he$_i$ is around, John$_i$ will do it.
     c. John$_i$ will do it if he$_i$ is around.
     d. *He$_i$ will do it if John$_i$ is around.

The question here is how to state conditions for the use of pronouns in such a way as to account for the fact that (1.1a, b, c) are acceptable, while (1.1d) is unacceptable if *John* and *he* are interpreted as coreferential. Statements of the sort often found in traditional grammars such as, "Pronouns can sometimes precede their antecedents in sentences," would be unable to distinguish be-tween (1.1b), which is acceptable, and (1.1d), which is unacceptable.

Serious attempts to examine conditions for use of pronouns began with Ross's (1967a) and Langacker's (1969) now classic works. Both hypothesized that pronouns appear in the deep structure as unpronominalized full-fledged noun phrases and that they are turned into pronouns transformationally by a rule called "pronominalization."

The theory of generative grammar has undergone numerous important revi-sions. It is now generally assumed that pronouns are realized as pronouns in underlying structure and that semantic interpretive rules establish their corefer-ence (or lack thereof) with other noun phrases in the same sentence. Those whose theoretical framework is drastically different from the one that Ross and Langacker used might object that a discussion of their formulations of pronominalization rules is anachronistic. This objection is unwarranted be-cause, in spite of all the developments in generative theory of grammar since their time, little progress has been made in the empirical issues of this area of research. Most of the difficulties subsequently discovered in the Ross-

Langacker formulation still remain unresolved. In this sense, this chapter presents not only a historical account of research on the syntax of pronouns but also a synchronic account of the difficulties in the analysis of pronouns that still need to be resolved. I will begin with an examination of what is right and what is wrong with the Ross-Langacker analysis.

Let us first examine Ross's formulation. He hypothesized that the following two conditions hold.

(1.2) a. Forward pronominalization is unconditional.
  b. Backward pronominalization is allowable only if the first of the two coreferential NPs is in a subordinate clause that does not dominate the second.

If pronominalization applies to the structures shown below, it is clear that the above generalizations are consistent with the data in (1.1):

(1.3) a. [[If John$_i$ is around], John$_i$ will do it]
  b. [John$_i$ will do it [if John$_i$ is around]]

Forward pronominalization, which is unconditional according to (1.2a), applies to (1.3a) and (1.3b) and produces (1.1a) and (1.1c). Backward pronominalization can apply to (1.3a) because the first *John* is in a subordinate clause that does not dominate the second *John,* but it cannot apply to (1.3b) because the first *John* is not in a subordinate clause at all. This explains the unacceptability of (1.1d).

It is necessary to show here that Ross's explanation is independent from the problem of whether (1.3a) or (1.3b) should be regarded as representing the underlying word order. If (1.3a) is taken to be the underlying word order, a postposing transformation, call it "adverb postposing," will be needed. On the other hand, if (1.3b) is taken to be the underlying word order, then a preposing transformation, call it "adverb preposing," will be needed. Either way, the above explanation depends on the assumption that pronominalization is applied to the output of adverb postposing or preposing, namely, to the structures shown in (1.3).[1] It is easy to demonstrate that the reverse order of application would be inconsistent with the generalizations of (1.2). Assume, for a moment, that (1.3a) represents the underlying word order and that pronominalization applied before adverb postposing. Then we have the following derivations, in which ^{P*} and ^{PV} are used to indicate the acceptability judgments predicted by Ross's generalizations.

(1.4) a. Underlying structure
      [[If John$_i$ is around], John$_i$ will do it]
  b. Pronominalizations
      (i)   Forward: ^{PV}If John$_i$ is around, he$_i$ will do it.
      (ii) Backward: ^{PV}If he$_i$ is around, John$_i$ will do it.

c. Adverb preposing (optional)
   (iii)   (applied to (i)): ^{PV}He$_i$ will do it if John$_i$ is around.
   (iv)   (applied to (ii)): ^{PV}John$_i$ will do it if he$_i$ is around.

The above derivations predict that all four sentences would be acceptable. But we have already observed that (iii) is unacceptable in the intended interpretation. Hence, the assumption that (1.4a) represents the underlying word order, and that pronominalization applies before adverb postposing, makes the wrong prediction.

Next, let us assume that (1.3b) represents the underlying word order and that pronominalization applies before adverb preposing:

(1.5)   a. Underlying structure
           [John$_i$ will do it [if John$_i$ is around]]
       b. Pronominalization
           (i)   Forward: ^{PV}John$_i$ will do it if he$_i$ is around.
           (ii)   Backward: ^{P*}He$_i$ will do it if John$_i$ is around.
       c. Adverb preposing
           (iii)   (applied to (i)): ^{PV}If he$_i$ is around, John$_i$ will do it.
           (iv)   (applied to (ii)): ^{P*}If John$_i$ is around, he$_i$ will do it.

The above derivations predict that (iv), which is derived from the ungrammatical intermediate structure (ii), is ungrammatical. However, as we have already seen, (iv) is a perfectly acceptable sentence. This shows that the assumption that (1.5a) represents the underlying word order and that pronominalization applies before adverb preposing makes the wrong prediction about the acceptability of the sentences involved. Since (1.4) and (1.5) exhaust the possibilities for the relative order of the if-clause and the main clause in a sentence, the incorrect predictions made by (1.4) and (1.5) must be due to their common assumption that pronominalization applies before adverb postposing/preposing. On the other hand, if we apply pronominalization to the output of adverb postposing/preposing, Ross's formulation makes the correct prediction about the acceptability of (1.1a, b, c) and the unacceptability of (1.1d). Therefore, only the assumption that pronominalization follows adverb postposing/preposing is consistent with Ross's formulation of forward and backward pronominalization.

Now let us examine Langacker's formulation of pronominalization:

(1.6)   NP^a may be used to pronominalize NP^P unless
       (i)   NP^P precedes NP^a; and
       (ii)   either (a) NP^P commands NP^a,
              or (b) NP^a and NP^P are elements of separate conjoined structures.

This formulation is often referred to as the "precede-command" constraint on pronominalization. Let us recall that the command relationship is defined in the following way:

(1.7)   A commands B if and only if the first S(entence) node that dominates A also dominates B.

Now, let us apply Langacker's formulation to see whether it is consistent with the facts of (1.1). Since the *unless*-condition of (1.6) does not refer to the forward pronominalization cases, forward pronominalization is unconditional in Langacker's formulation as well. Thus, the acceptability of (1.1a) and (1.1c) is automatically explained. Example (1.1b) is acceptable because the target of pronominalization, the first *John,* does not command the second *John:*

(1.8)

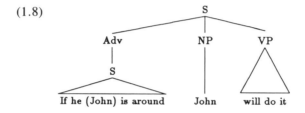

On the other hand, in (1.1d), the target NP both precedes and commands the second NP:

(1.9)

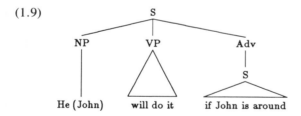

Structure (1.9) shows that the first S-node that dominates the left-hand *John* also dominates the second *John.* Therefore, the left-hand *John* both precedes and commands the right-hand *John.* Langacker's formulation predicts that (1.1d) is unacceptable because backward pronominalization has applied in violation of the precedence-command constraint.

Ross's and Langacker's formulations of the conditions on pronominalization are very similar and make identical predictions in most cases. For example, both can explain the acceptability status of the following sentences:

(1.10)   a.   All who know John$_i$ admire him$_i$.
          b.   All who know him$_i$ admire John$_i$.
(1.11)   a.   John$_i$ is admired by all who know him$_i$.
          b.   *He$_i$ is admired by all who know John$_i$.

If it is assumed that passivization applies before pronominalization, the structures to which pronominalization would apply would be:

(1.12)   a.   [$_S$ All [$_S$ who know John$_i$] admire John$_i$]
          b.   [$_S$ John$_i$ is admired by all [$_S$ who know John$_i$]]

In both Ross's and Langacker's formulations, there is no constraint on forward pronominalization, and therefore this rule, when applied to (1.12a, b), yields (1.10a) and (1.11a). Now, in (1.12a), the left-hand *John* is in a subordinate clause that does not dominate the second *John*, and therefore Ross's formulation allows backward pronominalization to apply to this structure to yield (1.10b). Similarly, although the first *John* in (1.12a) precedes the second, it does not command it, and therefore Langacker's formulation, too, would allow the rule to apply, yielding (1.10b). On the other hand, in (1.12b), the left-hand *John* is not in a subordinate clause, and therefore, Ross's formulation blocks backward pronominalization from applying to this structure. This explains why (1.11b) is unacceptable. Similarly, in (1.12b), the left-hand *John* both precedes and commands the second, and therefore Langacker's formulation, too, blocks backward pronominalization from applying. Hence the unacceptability of (1.11b).

Ross's and Langacker's formulations also agree in predicting that the following sentences are both acceptable:

(1.13)   a.   That John$_i$ is absent today means that he$_i$ is seriously sick.
          b.   That he$_i$ is absent today means that John$_i$ is seriously sick.

As shown below, the first underlying *John* in (1.13) is in a subordinate clause that does not dominate the second. Therefore, Ross's condition for backward pronominalization is met. Similarly, the first *John*, although it precedes the second, does not command it, and therefore pronominalization of the first *John* is also allowed by Langacker's precede-command constraint.

(1.14)

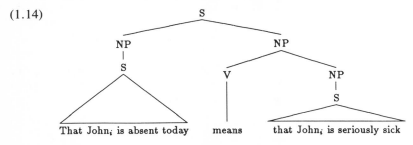

However, Ross's and Langacker's formulations cannot explain the acceptability of (1.15b) below:

(1.15)   a.   John$_i$'s father dislikes him$_i$.
          b.   His$_i$ father dislikes John$_i$.

This is because in

(1.16)

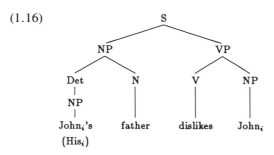

John$_i$'s   father   dislikes   John$_i$
(His$_i$)

the first *John* is not in a subordinate clause, and it both precedes and commands the second *John*. Therefore, it fails to meet Ross's condition on backward pronominalization and satisfies Langacker's *unless*-condition against pronominalization. The sentence should be unacceptable, but it is not.

It seems that the best way to accommodate cases such as (1.15b), as well as those that are adequately handled by the precede-command condition, is to redefine, as later proposed by Lasnik (1976), the concept of "command" as follows:

(1.17)   *A* kommands *B* if and only if the first S(entence) or NP node that dominates *A* also dominates *B*.

Lasnik distinguished the above concept of "command" from the one given in (1.7) by spelling it as "kommand." I will refer to it as "k-command" in this book. Our crucial example (1.15b) does not involve violation of the precede-command condition if the above definition of "command" is used. This is because, as shown in (1.16), the first S or NP node that dominates [his]$_{NP}$ is the NP node corresponding to *his father,* and this NP node does not dominate *John.* Similarly, (1.13b) is acceptable because the first S or NP node that dominates [he]$_{NP}$ is the S node corresponding to *he is absent today,* and this S node does not dominate [John]$_{NP}$. Likewise, (1.1b) is acceptable because the first S or NP node that dominates [he]$_{NP}$ is the S node for the subordinate clause, which does not dominate [John]$_{NP}$ in the main clause. In contrast, (1.1d) is unacceptable because the first S or NP node that dominates [he]$_{NP}$ is the S for the entire sentence, and this S dominates [John]$_{NP}$ in the subordinate clause. Similarly, observe the following sentences:

(1.18)   a.   I saw his$_i$ sister's portrait of John$_i$.
         b.   *I saw his$_i$ portrait of John$_i$'s sister.

According to Langacker's definition of "command," [his]$_{NP}$ commands [John]$_{NP}$ both in (1.18a) and (1.18b) because the first S node that dominates [his]$_{NP}$ also dominates [John]$_{NP}$. Therefore, both sentences should be unacceptable. However, it is only (1.18b) that is unacceptable. This can be ac-

counted for automatically by the new concept of "k-command" given in
(1.17). That is, in (1.18a), the first S or NP node that dominates [his]$_{NP}$ is the
NP node corresponding to *his sister,* which does not dominate [John]$_{NP}$.
Hence, the sentence does not involve violation of the precede-command condition using the new concept of k-command. On the other hand, in (1.18b),
the first S or NP node that dominates [his]$_{NP}$ is the NP node for the entire
object (*his portrait of John's sister*), and this NP dominates *John.* Hence the
unacceptability of (1.18b).

K-command also accounts for the acceptability of the following:

(1.19)   a.   A picture of John$_i$ with a prostitute ruined his$_i$ reputation.
         b.   A picture of him$_i$ with a prostitute ruined John$_i$'s reputation.
(1.20)   a.   An oil painting by John$_i$ of Madam Hollander established his$_i$
              reputation.
         b.   An oil painting by him$_i$ of Madam Hollander established John$_i$'s
              reputation.

Backward pronominalization is not blocked in (1.19) and (1.20) because the
NPs corresponding to *a picture of him* and *an oil painting by him,* which are
the first S or NP nodes dominating [him]$_{NP}$ in these sentences, do not dominate [John('s)]$_{NP}$.

In the above account of how the precede-command condition using the
"k-command" concept works, I have used expressions such as "the first S or
NP node that dominates [he]$_{NP}$ does not dominate [John]$_{NP}$," rather than expressions such as "the first S or NP node that dominates *he* does not dominate
John." This is because the conditions for pronominalization apply not to lexical items *he* and *John,* but to the NP nodes that immediately dominate them.
Observe the following structure:

(1.21)   *He$_i$ dislikes John$_i$'s father.

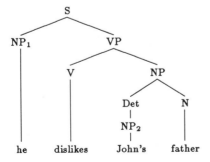

In the above structure, *he* does not k-command *John's* because the first S or
NP node that dominates *he* is not S but NP$_1$, which does not dominate *John's.*
It is the [he]$_{NP}$ that k-commands *John's,* and therefore the precede-command

condition against backward pronominalization should apply to NP_1 and not to *he*. In the rest of the book, expressions such as "*he* commands *John*" will sometimes be used, but they should always be understood as abbreviations for more cumbersome expressions such as "the NP that dominates *he* commands the NP that dominates *John*" or "[he]$_{NP}$ commands [John]$_{NP}$."

2.2 Lakoff's Rule Ordering Paradox

Ross's and Langacker's formulations, as we have seen above, initially appeared to have captured the essential facts of pronominalization, and became showcase examples of the power of generative grammar to account for linguistic phenomena that would otherwise have been unexplainable. However, closer examination of data involving pronominalization uncovered numerous counterexamples to their formulations. The first such class of data are suggested by Lakoff (1968). Observe the following sentences; the recorded acceptability judgments are Lakoff's:[2]

(2.1) a. John$_i$ found a snake near him$_i$.
     b. *He$_i$ found a snake near John$_i$.
     c. *Near John$_i$, he$_i$ found a snake.
     d. Near him$_i$, John$_i$ found a snake.

Lakoff argues that the above set of data can be explained if it is assumed that the locative expression appears sentence-finally, as in (2.1a), in underlying structure and that pronominalization precedes adverb preposing. Let us follow the line of argument for this rule ordering step by step. We start with the structure shown in (2.2):

(2.2) [John$_i$ found a snake near John$_i$]

Let us see what problems arise if we assume that pronominalization follows adverb preposing. Since adverb preposing is an optional rule, we obtain both (2.2) and (2.3) as input to pronominalization:

(2.3) [Near John$_i$, John$_i$ found a snake]

Since forward pronominalization is unconditional, it should apply both to (2.2) and (2.3). Also, since the first *John* in (2.2) and (2.3) is not in a subordinate clause (or since the first *John* both precedes and commands the second *John*), backward pronominalization should not apply. Thus, this assumption predicts the following judgments (indicated by [P]). The actual acceptability status of each sentence is shown to the right of the slash.

(2.4) a. [P]√/√John$_i$ found a snake near him$_i$.
     b. [P]*/*He$_i$ found a snake near John$_i$.
     c. [P]√/*Near John$_i$, he$_i$ found a snake.
     d. [P]*/√Near him$_i$, John$_i$ found a snake.

Thus, the assumption that pronominalization follows adverb preposing makes wrong predictions about the acceptability status of (2.4c) and (2.4d).

Now let us explore the contrary assumption that pronominalization precedes adverb preposing. Assuming that pronominalization is obligatory, we obtain the following results:

(2.5)   Underlying structure
        [John$_i$ found a snake near John$_i$]
        a.   Forward pronominalization
             $^{PV}/^V$John$_i$ found a snake near him$_i$.
        b.   Backward pronominalization
             $^{P*}/^*$He$_i$ found a snake near John$_i$.
        c.   Adverb preposing applied to (b)
             $^{P*}/^*$Near John$_i$, he$_i$ found a snake.
        d.   Adverb preposing applied to (a)
             $^{PV}/^V$Near him$_i$, John$_i$ found a snake.

According to the assumption that pronominalization precedes adverb preposing, (c) is correctly predicted to be unacceptable because its source sentence (b) is unacceptable (due to violation of the condition on backward pronominalization), and (d) is also currently predicted to be acceptable because its source sentence (a) is acceptable. Thus, this assumption makes the correct prediction about the acceptability status of each of the sentences in (2.4) and must be regarded as correct. This leads us to:

(2.6)   *Conclusion I:* Pronominalization precedes adverb preposing.

Let us keep in mind that this conclusion is contrary to the one that we arrived at in Section 2.1, that is, that pronominalization must apply after *if*-clauses are moved around.

Let us now examine the following set of data, which pattern after Lakoff's original examples:

(2.7)   a.   John$_i$ found a snake behind the girl he$_i$ was talking with.
        b.   *He$_i$ found a snake behind the girl John$_i$ was talking with.
        c.   Behind the girl John$_i$ was talking with, he$_i$ found a snake.
        d.   Behind the girl he$_i$ was talking with, John$_i$ found a snake.

We see below what predictions each of the two possible orderings of pronominalization and adverb preposing makes about the acceptability status of each sentence in (2.7):

(2.8)   Assumption: Pronominalization follows adverb preposing
        Underlying structure: (i)   [John$_i$ found a snake behind the girl
                                       [$_S$ John$_i$ was talking with]]
        Adverb preposing: (ii)   [Behind the girl [$_S$ John$_i$ was talking with]
                                       John$_i$ found a snake]

    a.   Forward pronominalization applicable in (i)
            ^{PV}/^{V}John$_i$ found a snake behind the girl he$_i$ was talking with.

    b.   Backward pronominalization inapplicable in (i)
            ^{P*}/*He$_i$ found a snake behind the girl John$_i$ was talking with.

    c.   Forward pronominalization applicable in (ii)
            ^{PV}/^{V}Behind the girl John$_i$ was talking with, he$_i$ found a snake.

    d.   Backward pronominalization inapplicable in (ii)
            ^{PV}/^{V}Behind the girl he$_i$ was talking with, John$_i$ found a snake.

Therefore, the assumption that pronominalization follows adverb preposing correctly predicts the acceptability status of the sentences involved.

Now let us examine the contrary assumption that pronominalization precedes adverb preposing:

(2.9)   Assumption: Pronominalization precedes adverb preposing
        Underlying structure: [John$_i$ found a snake behind the girl [$_s$ John$_i$ was talking with]]

    a.   Forward pronominalization applicable
            ^{PV}/^{V}John$_i$ found a snake behind the girl he$_i$ was talking with.

    b.   Backward pronominalization inapplicable
            ^{P*}/*He$_i$ found a snake behind the girl John$_i$ was talking with.

    c.   Adverb preposing applied to (a)
            ^{PV}/^{V}Behind the girl he$_i$ was talking with, John$_i$ found a snake.

    d. ^{P*}/^{V}Behind the girl John$_i$ was talking with, he$_i$ found a snake.

The above order of application of the two rules involved predicts that (d) would be unacceptable because its source structure (b) is unacceptable. But (d) is an acceptable sentence. Since (2.8) makes all the right predictions, while (2.9) makes the wrong prediction for (2.9d), we must conclude the following:

(2.10)   *Conclusion II:* Pronominalization follows adverb preposing.

But Conclusion I and Conclusion II are contradictory. Since the preposing rule that is responsible for moving *near NP* in (2.5) and the one that is responsible for moving *behind NP + relative clause* must be one and the same rule, the above contradiction is irreconcilable. Thus, Conclusion I and Conclusion II produce a rule ordering paradox in which pronominalization must both precede and follow adverb preposing.

As I will show in the subsequent sections, Lakoff's rule ordering paradox remains a paradox in *all* the later hypotheses (including Chomsky's [1981, 1982] binding theory) except for the one that will be proposed later on in this chapter.

2.3 **Postal's Analysis**

Postal (1970) produced an argument that the rule of pronominalization must apply either last-cyclically after *Wh*-Q Movement, or postcyclically. This argument was based on assumptions that are no longer widely held. However, the sentences which led Postal to hypothesize that pronominalization could not be made to apply cyclically are still highly relevant to the present state of the art for determining the exact conditions for pronominal reference. This is because, as will be shown in subsequent sections in this chapter, few of the later hypotheses about pronominal reference can handle Postal's sentences adequately. Therefore, I will summarize his argument in this section.

Postal observed that the following sentences are both acceptable:

(3.1)   a.   Which of the men who visited her$_i$ do you think Betty$_i$ hated?

      b.   Which of the men who visited Betty$_i$ do you think she$_i$ hated?

Let us examine the derivation of these sentences in Ross and Langacker's framework:

(3.2)

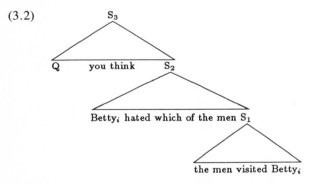

If pronominalization applies cyclically and obligatorily, then it should apply in the S_2 cycle and pronominalize the second *Betty*.[3] Since the first *Betty* is not in a subordinate clause with respect to S_2, and since it both precedes and commands the second *Betty*, it is impossible to pronominalize the first *Betty*:

(3.3)   a. ^{PV}[$_{S_2}$ Betty$_i$ hated which of the men [$_{S_1}$ who visited her$_i$]]

      b. ^{P*}[$_{S_2}$ she$_i$ hated which of the men [$_{S_1}$ who visited Betty$_i$]]

In the S_3 cycle, *Wh*-Q Movement applies, and preposes *which of the men who . . .* to sentence-initial position. Example (3.1a) is derived from applying this rule to the structure containing the grammatical (3.3a), and therefore it should be, and is, grammatical. On the other hand, (3.1b), which is derived by applying the rule to the structure containing the ungrammatical (3.3b), should be ungrammatical, but it is a perfectly acceptable sentence. Therefore, the assumption that pronominalization is cyclical makes the wrong prediction. However, if we assume that pronominalization applies last-cyclically after *Wh*-Q Movement, or postcyclically, there is no problem in accounting for the acceptability of (3.1a) and (3.1b). Under this assumption, pronominalization cannot and does not apply in the S_2 cycle. In the S_3 cycle, *Wh*-Q Movement applies and produces the following structure:

(3.4)   [$_{S_3}$ Which of the men [$_{S_1}$ who visited Betty$_i$] do you think [$_{S_2}$ Betty$_i$ hated]]

Pronominalization applies to the above structure. Since forward pronominalization is unconditional, it applies to (3.4) and produces (3.1b). Alternatively, since the first *Betty* is in a subordinate clause that does not dominate the second *Betty*, it can apply backward, yielding (3.1a). This explains the acceptability of (3.1a) and (3.1b).

It would not be amiss to consider here what alternative conclusion Postal could have drawn from the acceptability of (3.1b). His conclusion that pronominalization is last- or postcyclical crucially depended upon the assumption that pronominalization is obligatory at the first opportunity that it becomes applicable. This obligatory application marks (3.3b) ungrammatical and blocks derivation of (3.1b). Postal could have proposed, however, that pronominalization apply optionally. According to this hypothetical proposal, the following two structures would be obtained at the end of the second cycle of derivation from (3.2):

(3.5)   a.   Optional application of pronominalization
              [$_{S_2}$ Betty$_i$ hated which of the men [$_{S_1}$ who visited her$_i$]]
         b.   Optional nonapplication of pronominalization
              [$_{S_2}$ Betty$_i$ hated which of the men [$_{S_1}$ who visited Betty$_i$]]

In the third cycle, application of *Wh*-Q Movement to (a) would produce (3.1a). On the other hand, application of *Wh*-Q Movement to (b) would produce

(3.6)   [$_{S_3}$ Which of the men [$_{S_1}$ who visited Betty$_i$] do you think [$_{S_2}$ Betty$_i$ hated]]

Pronominalization would apply again to this entire structure. If it applies forward, it would yield (3.1b). If it applies backward, it would yield (3.1a), thus producing a dual derivation of (3.1a). Let us assume that this kind of false ambiguity is not a serious problem.

Optional pronominalization does raise problems with other sentences, however. For example, it does not have to apply to (3.6), which might not be a serious problem for our particular example because (3.6) is only slightly awkward. But there are sentence patterns that require obligatory application of pronominalization, as in:

(3.7)   a.   John$_i$ adores his$_i$ mother.
         b.   *John$_i$ adores John$_i$'s mother.

Therefore, the above optional pronominalization approach would need a surface filter of the following kind:

(3.8)   *Filtering Rule:* A sentence that contains two unpronominalized NPs that are coreferential such that one k-commands the other is ungrammatical.[4]

Then, (3.1a) and (3.1b), which led Postal to hypothesize that pronominalization is last- or postcyclical, could have been dealt with using optional cyclical application of pronominalization and a surface filtering rule which would weed out derivations in which pronominalization has not applied between two coreferential NPs. Jackendoff's analysis of pronouns, which we will look into in the next section, is similar to this "optional pronominalization and surface filter" approach.

2.4   Jackendoff's Interpretive Rules

Jackendoff (1972) assumed that pronouns are realized in underlying structure as pronouns and that a set of interpretive rules would assign a coreferential interpretation to pronouns and their antecedents in the sentence. He proposed the following two rules:

(4.1)   Rule 1:   Optionally mark an NP as coreferential with a pronoun unless the pronoun both precedes and commands the NP. (Cyclical)
         Rule 2:   If for any NP$_1$ and NP$_2$ pair in a sentence, the coreference linkage has not been established, mark them as noncoreferential. (Last-cyclical)

Let us see how these two rules apply. First, observe the following sentence:

(4.2)   [John will come if I ask him]

If Rule 1 does not apply, there is no change in (4.2). Rule 2 then would mark *John* as [−coref] with respect to *him*. This is the interpretation that holds when *him* refers not to *John,* but someone else who has been talked about in the preceding discourse. Alternatively, if Rule 1 does apply to (4.2), *John* gets marked as [+coref] with respect to *him*. If this takes place, Rule 2 is inapplicable.

Assume next that the following underlying structure is given for the backward pronominalization situation.

(4.3)   He will come if I ask John.

Since *he* both precedes and commands *John,* Rule 1 cannot mark the two NPs as coreferential. We proceed to Rule 2, which marks *John* as [−coref] with respect to *he*.

Let us now see how Jackendoff's interpretive rules would apply *cyclically* to Postal's examples, which, as we have seen, seem to indicate that pronominalization should apply last-cyclically or postcyclically if *wh*-expressions are to be fronted by a Q-triggered *Wh*-Q Movement rule. In Jackendoff's framework, Postal's examples are derived from the following underlying structures:

(4.4)   a.   [$_{S_3}$ You think [$_{S_2}$ Betty hated which of the men [$_{S_1}$ the men visited her]]]

　　　　b.   [$_{S_3}$ You think [$_{S_2}$ she hated which of the men [$_{S_1}$ the men visited Betty]]]

We start with the derivation of the surface sentence corresponding to (4.4a). Jackendoff's Rule 1 is optional, and therefore, it may or may not apply in the S_2 cycle. Assume first that the rule has applied. Then, *Betty* and *her* are marked as [+coref]. In the S_3 cycle, *Wh*-Q Movement applies and preposes the *wh*-expression, yielding:

(4.5)   Which of the men who visited her do you think Betty hated?

　　　　　　　　　　　　　　　　　　　　[+coref]

On the other hand, if Rule 1 has not applied in the S_2 cycle, we obtain the following structure after application of *Wh*-Q Movement:

(4.6)   Which of the men who visited her do you think Betty hated?

　　　　　　　　　　　　　　　(coreference unspecified)

Now, Rule 1, which is cyclical, can apply to establish coreference between *her* and *Betty*. If it does apply, we get the same reading as the one represented in (4.5). If it does not apply, the last-cyclical Rule 2 would apply and yield:

(4.7)   Which of the men who visited her do you think Betty hated?

　　　　　　　　　　　　　　　　　　[−coref]

Next, we examine the derivation which (4.4b) represents. In the S_2 cycle, Rule 1 cannot apply to establish coreference between *she* and *Betty* because *she* both precedes and commands *Betty*. Thus, their coreference is left unspecified. That Rule 1 does not mark *she* and *Betty* as [−coref] at this stage is the most important feature of Jackendoff's system. In the S_3 cycle, *Wh*-Q Movement applies and yields the following structure:[5]

(4.8)   Which of the men who visited Betty do you think she hated most?

　　　　　　　　　　　　　　　(coreference unspecified)

The application of Rule 1 in this cycle establishes the coreference linkage between *Betty* and *she*. On the other hand, if Rule 1 is not applied, Rule 2 will mark the two as noncoreferential. This accounts for the fact that *she* of (4.8) can be interpreted either as being coreferential or noncoreferential with *Betty*.

Although Jackendoff's system can explain Postal's "last- or postcyclical" data in a "cyclical" fashion, it, too, is incapable of explaining Lakoff's rule ordering paradox. Observe the following derivation:

(4.9)   Underlying structure   a.   [John found a snake near him]
                                 b.   [He found a snake near John]
         Adverb preposing   a′. [Near him, John found a snake]
                                 b′. [Near John, he found a snake]
         Rule 1   a″. [Near him, John found a snake]
                                       |____|
                                      (unspecified) = [−coref] (Rule 2)
                                 b″. [Near John, he found a snake]
                                       |____|
                                      (i)   [+coref]
                                      (ii)   (unspecified) = [−coref] (Rule 2)

If we assume that adverb preposing applies before Rule 1, as shown above, Rule 1 would fail to establish coreference between *him* and *John* in (4.9a″) because *him* both precedes and commands *John*. The same assumption would also incorrectly establish coreference between *John* and *he* in (4.9b″). On the other hand, if we apply Rule 1 before adverb preposing, as shown below, the correct coreference relations can be established:

(4.10)   Underlying structure   a.   [John found a snake near him]
                                 b.   [He found a snake near John]
         Rule 1   a′. [John found a snake near him]
                                       |_____|
                                      (i)   [+coref]
                                      (ii)   (unspecified)
                                 b′. [He found a snake near John]
                                       |_____|
                                      (unspecified)
         Adverb preposing   a″. [Near him, John found a snake]
                                       |____|
                                      (i)   [+coref]
                                      (ii)   (unspecified) = [−coref] (Rule 2)
                                 b″. [Near John, he found a snake]
                                       |____|
                                      (unspecified) = [−coref] (Rule 2)

Therefore, Rule 1 must apply before adverb preposing. Furthermore, Rule 1 must be prevented from applying after adverb preposing because if it were allowed to apply again, it would incorrectly establish coreference between

John and *he* in (4.10b″). This means that Rule 1 and adverb preposing must be extrinsically ordered.

Let us next consider the following underlying structures:

(4.11)   a.   [John found a snake behind the girl [he was talking with]]
          b.   [He found a snake behind the girl [John was talking with]]

Rule 1 applies first, as dictated by the preceding conclusion, and establishes the following coreference linkages:

(4.12)   a.   [John found a snake behind the girl [he was talking with]]
                |_____|

                (i)   [+coref]
                (ii)   (unspecified)
          b.   [He found a snake behind the girl [John was talking with]]
                |_____|

                           (unspecified)

Adverb preposing applies next, yielding the following structures:

(4.13)   a.   [Behind the girl [he was talking with], John found a snake]
                           |_____|

                    (i)   [+coref]
                    (ii)   (unspecified) = [−coref] (Rule 2)
          b.   [Behind the girl [John was talking with], he found a snake]
                           |_____|

                       (unspecified) = [−coref] (Rule 2)

Since (4.10) showed specifically that Rule 1 cannot be applied again after adverb preposing, it is not possible to apply the rule to (4.13b) to establish coreference between *John* and *he*. Therefore, the rule application ordering that has been established for (4.10) cannot account for the coreferential interpretation of *John* and *he* of (4.13b).

It is easy to see that Jackendoff's interpretive rules would establish correct coreference and noncoreference linkages for (4.11a) and (4.11b) if it could be assumed either that (i) Rule 1 applies after adverb preposing or that (ii) Rule 1 and adverb preposing are not extrinsically ordered and they apply whenever they are applicable. But this conclusion contradicts the conclusion we drew from (4.9) and (4.10). Thus we find here the same kind of rule ordering paradox that we saw in Ross's and Langacker's formulation of pronominalization.

2.5 Lasnik's Surface Interpretive Rule

Lasnik (1976), like Jackendoff, assumed that pronouns are realized in underlying structure as pronouns, and that a set of interpretive rules would establish coreference linkage between pronouns and their antecedents in the sentence.

Unlike Jackendoff, however, Lasnik assumed that (i) coreference or lack thereof between two NPs can be determined on the basis of surface structure alone, without recourse to cyclical stages of derivation, and that (ii) it is easier to arrive at conditions for lack of coreference (disjoint reference) than to arrive at conditions for coreference.

Lasnik proposed the following condition:

(5.1)   *Lasnik's Formulation:* If NP_1 precedes and kommands NP_2, and NP_2 is not a pronoun, then NP_1 and NP_2 are noncoreferential (and otherwise, they can be coreferential).
Definition: A kommands B if and only if the minimal cyclic node (S or NP) dominating A also dominates B.

I will henceforth refer to Lasnik's "kommand" concept as *k-command* and Ross and Langacker's "command" concept as *S-command* (because it crucially depends upon the minimal S node) to avoid confusion.

Let us examine some sentences to see how Lasnik's k-command analysis works. First, observe the following sentences:

(5.2)   a. $John_i$ found a snake near him_i.

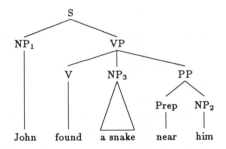

b.   *He_i found a snake near $John_i$.

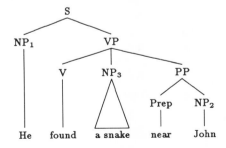

Lasnik's constraint allows for the possibility of coreferential interpretation whenever the right-hand NP (i.e., NP_2) is a pronoun. Therefore it can correctly assign coreference linkage between $[John]_{NP_1}$ and $[him]_{NP_2}$ in (5.2a). On the other hand, in (5.2b), [he]$_{NP_1}$ k-commands [John]$_{NP_2}$ because the minimal cyclic node that dominates NP$_1$ is the S dominating the whole sentence, which dominates NP$_2$, a nonpronominal NP. Thus, all of the three conditions in Lasnik's constraint (i.e., k-command, precede, and nonpronominal NP$_2$) are met, and therefore the rule determines that *he* and *John* cannot be coreferential.

In contrast, observe the following sentences:

(5.3) a. All who know him admire John. (him = John)
       b. If he can, John will do it. (him = John)

The minimal cyclic node that dominates [him/he]$_{NP_1}$ in each of the two sentences above is the S node dominating the subordinate clause. Therefore, the k-command condition is not met, and hence the possibility for coreference interpretation between *him/he* and *John* is not ruled out.

Lasnik's formulation accounts for backward pronominalization into possessive NPs without any difficulty. For example, observe the following sentences:

(5.4) a. *He$_i$ loves John$_i$'s mother.
       b. His$_i$ mother loves John$_i$.
(5.5) a. *John$_i$ loves John$_i$'s mother.
       b. John$_i$'s mother loves John$_i$.

Example (5.4a) is unacceptable in the coreferential interpretation because [he]$_{NP_1}$ precedes and k-commands [John('s)]$_{NP_2}$, and the latter is nonpronominal. In contrast, (5.4b) is acceptable because [his]$_{NP_1}$ does not k-command [John]$_{NP_2}$: the minimal cyclic node dominating NP$_1$ is the NP node for *his mother*, which does not dominate NP$_2$. This formulation can also handle the contrast between (5.5a) and (5.5b) in an elegant way. Note that the "precede and k-command" constraint does not say anything about the nature of NP$_1$: therefore, the constraint applies regardless of whether NP$_1$ is a pronoun or not. In (5.5a), the left-hand [John]$_{NP_1}$ k-commands the right-hand [John]$_{NP_2}$, which is not a pronoun, because the minimal cyclic node dominating NP$_1$ is the S for the entire sentence. Hence, these two occurrences of *John* cannot be coreferential. On the other hand, in (5.5b), [John('s)]$_{NP_1}$ does not k-command [John]$_{NP_2}$ because the minimal cyclic node dominating NP$_1$ is the NP for *John's mother*, which does not dominate NP$_2$. Hence the possibility of an interpretation of coreference between these two occurrences of *John*.

Now observe the following two sentences:

(5.6) a. John$_i$, his$_i$ mother loves dearly.
       b. *Him$_i$, John$_i$'s mother loves dearly.

For these two sentences, too, Lasnik's formulation makes the correct predictions. Example (5.6a) is acceptable because NP$_2$ is pronominal. On the other hand, (5.6b) is unacceptable in the coreferential interpretation because [him]$_{NP_1}$ both precedes and k-commands [John]$_{NP_2}$, a nonpronominal NP.

Likewise, observe the following sentences:

(5.7)   a.   I saw his$_i$ sister's portrait of John$_i$.
         b.   *I saw his$_i$ portrait of John$_i$'s sister.

The picture noun of (5.7a) has the structure shown in (5.8a), and that of (5.7b) has the structure shown in (5.8b):

(5.8)   a.

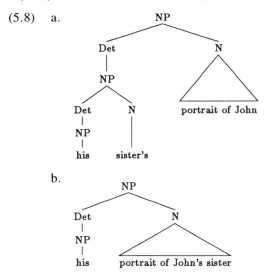

         b.

In (5.8a), [his]$_{NP}$ k-commands only *sister's,* and it does not k-command *John.* In contrast, in (5.8b), [his]$_{NP}$ k-commands *portrait of John's sister.* Thus, the "precede and k-command" analysis can account for the fact that (5.7a) is acceptable and (5.7b) unacceptable.

Lasnik's k-command analysis has some nice features and seems to work rather well when simple sentences which have not undergone word order change are involved. However, it too cannot account for the acceptability status of the following two crucial sentences:

(5.9)   a.   *Near John$_i$, he$_i$ found a snake.
         b.   Near him$_i$, John$_i$ found a snake.

Since Lasnik's formulation assumes that coreference or lack thereof between two NPs can be determined on the basis of surface structure alone, and since it allows for a coreferential interpretation whenever the right-hand NP is a pronoun, it predicts that (5.9a) would be acceptable. Likewise, since *him* of (5.9b) k-commands *John,* which is not a pronoun, Lasnik's formulation predicts that the sentence would be unacceptable. These predictions are both incorrect.[6] There must be something wrong with Lasnik's assumption that coreferentiality, or lack thereof, between two NPs can be determined in a simple fashion by applying interpretive rules to surface structure alone.

2.6 Reinhart's C-Command Analysis

Reinhart (1976, 1981, 1983) assumes that what determines coreference or lack thereof between two NPs in a sentence is neither the concept of Ross's and Langacker's S(entence)-command, nor that of Lasnik's k-command (namely, S- or NP-command), but rather that of c(onstituent)-command. She defines c-command as follows:

(6.1)   *C-Command:* Node A c(onstituent)-commands node B if and only if the first branching node α_1 dominating A
    (i)   either dominates B, or
    (ii)   is immediately dominated by a node α_2 which dominates B, and α_2 is of the same category type as α_1.[7]

For example, observe the following structures:

(6.2)   a.

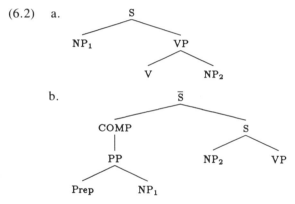

b.

In (6.2a), NP_1 c-commands NP_2 because S, which is the first branching node that dominates NP_1, dominates NP_2. On the other hand, NP_2 does not c-command NP_1 because the VP node, which is the first branching node that dominates NP_2, does not dominate NP_1. In (6.2b), NP_1 does not c-command NP_2 because the PP node, which is the first branching node that dominates NP_1, does not dominate NP_2. In contrast, NP_2 c-commands NP_1 because S, the first branching node that dominates NP_2, is immediately dominated by $\overline{S}$, which dominates NP_1, and $\overline{S}$ is of the same category type as S.

Like Lasnik, Reinhart assumes that coreference or lack thereof between two NPs in a sentence can be determined effectively on the basis of surface structure configurations alone. She also assumes that the use of her c-command concept makes it possible to eliminate the "precede" concept. She formulates her constraint as follows:

(6.3)   *Reinhart's Formulation:* If NP_1 c-commands NP_2, and NP_2 is not a pronoun, NP_1 and NP_2 cannot be coreferential.

Let us now examine some of our crucial sentences to see how Reinhart's c-command formulation works. First, observe the following sentences and their corresponding surface structures:

(6.4)   a. John$_i$ adores his$_i$ mother.
         b. *John$_i$ adores John$_i$'s mother.
         c. *He$_i$ adores John$_i$'s mother.

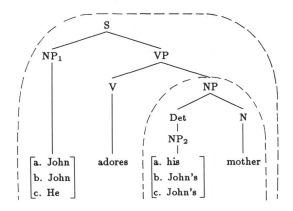

In (6.4), NP$_1$ c-commands NP$_2$ because its most immediate branching node is the S node, which dominates NP$_2$. Thus, this rules out a coreferential interpretation between *John* and *John('s)* of (b) and between *he* and *John('s)* of (c). In the same structure, NP$_2$ does not c-command NP$_1$ because its most immediate branching node is the NP for *his/John's mother,* which does not dominate NP$_1$. Therefore, Reinhart's formulation does not rule out the possibility of a coreferential interpretation between [John]$_{NP_1}$ and [his]$_{NP_2}$.

Next observe the following:

(6.5)   a. John$_i$'s mother adores him$_i$.
         b. John$_i$'s mother adores John$_i$.
         c. His$_i$ mother adores John$_i$.

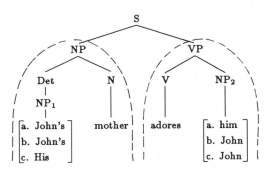

In (6.5), NP$_1$ does not c-command NP$_2$ because its immediate branching node NP does not dominate NP$_2$. Neither does NP$_2$ c-command NP$_1$ because NP$_2$'s immediate branching node is VP, which does not dominate NP$_1$. Therefore there is no constraint on coreferential interpretation between NP$_1$ and NP$_2$, and hence all three versions are allowed.

Let us now observe how Reinhart's formulation performs with respect to sentences that involve adverb preposing. First observe the following sentences (Reinhart assumes that constituents that are extracted from VP and fronted to sentence-initial position are placed in the COMP position):

(6.6)   a.   Near him$_i$, John$_i$ found a snake.
         b.   *Near John$_i$, he$_i$ found a snake.

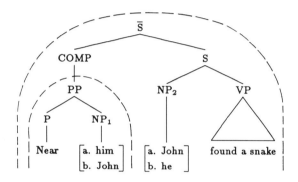

In the left-to-right application of Reinhart's formulation to (6.6a), [him]$_{NP_1}$ does not c-command [John]$_{NP_2}$ because NP$_1$'s first branching node PP does not dominate NP$_2$. On the other hand, in the right-to-left application of her rule, [John]$_{NP_2}$ does c-command [him]$_{NP_1}$ because NP$_2$'s first branching node S is immediately dominated by $\overline{S}$, which is of the same category type as S. Let us refer to this c-command situation by stating that NP$_2$ c-commands NP$_1$ via an S to $\overline{S}$ projection. In (6.6a), [John]$_{NP_2}$ thus c-commands [him]$_{NP_1}$ via an S to $\overline{S}$ projection, but since the latter is a pronoun, Reinhart's formulation does not apply. Since (6.6a) does not violate Reinhart's condition regardless of whether it is applied left to right or right to left, *him* and *John* can be considered to be coreferential. Note that this is where Lasnik's formulation failed: NP$_1$ k-commands NP$_2$ because NP$_1$'s minimal cyclic node in (6.6) is $\overline{S}$, which dominates NP$_2$, a nonpronominal NP.[8]

As already mentioned, in the surface structure of (6.6), NP$_2$ c-commands NP$_1$ via an S to $\overline{S}$ projection. Thus, in (6.6b) Reinhart's formulation successfully rules out the coreference possibility between [he]$_{NP_2}$ and [John]$_{NP_1}$.[9] Recall that Lasnik's formulation failed here: his k-command analysis allows for coreferential interpretation between NP$_1$ and NP$_2$ as long as the right-hand NP is a pronoun. Thus it erroneously predicts that (6.6b) should be acceptable.

Similarly, observe the following sentences:

(6.7)   a.   *John$_i$'s mother, he$_i$ adores dearly.[10]
        b.   *John$_i$'s mother, John$_i$ adores dearly.

We saw in the preceding section that Lasnik's k-command analysis erroneously allows for coreferential interpretation between [John('s)]$_{NP_1}$ and [he/John]$_{NP_2}$ because NP$_1$ does not k-command NP$_2$. Reinhart's c-command analysis correctly marks these sentences unacceptable because NP$_2$ c-commands the nonpronominal NP$_1$. Here, too, Reinhart's analysis is superior to Lasnik's.

Reinhart's c-command analysis, however, leaves many pronominalization facts unaccounted for. First, as pointed out by Carden (1980, 1981), it erroneously predicts that (6.8b) should be acceptable:

(6.8)   a.   Near him$_i$, the investigator believed that John$_i$ found a snake.
        b.   *Near John$_i$, the investigator believed that he$_i$ found a snake.

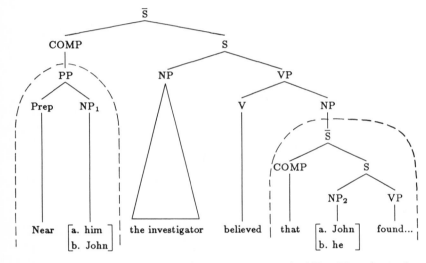

In the above structure, NP$_2$ no longer c-commands NP$_1$. Therefore, the c-command analysis incorrectly predicts that (6.8b) should be acceptable.

Similarly, observe the following sentences:

(6.9)   a.   Near the girl he$_i$ was talking with, John$_i$ found a snake.
        b.   Near the girl John$_i$ was talking with, he$_i$ found a snake.

These sentences have the same structure as (6.6) except that NP$_1$ is further embedded in the relative clause. In (6.9b), the main clause subject [he]$_{NP_2}$ c-commands the nonpronominal [John]$_{NP_1}$ via an S to $\overline{S}$ projection. Therefore, Reinhart's formulation erroneously predicts that the sentence should be unacceptable. Recall that (6.6) and (6.9) are the sentences which Lakoff used to demonstrate that the Ross-Langacker constraint would fall into a rule ordering paradox. The above observation shows that Reinhart's analysis has not resolved this paradox.

In attempting to account for these sentences, Reinhart speculates that her disjoint reference rule obeys Chomsky's Subjacency Condition. This is contrary to the generally held view that only movement rules obey the Subjacency Condition. Y is subjacent to X if and only if there is at most one cyclical node (S or NP) boundary between Y and X. The Subjacency Condition dictates that no rule involve X, Y, where X is superior to Y, if Y is not subjacent to X. In (6.9b), the antecedent of *he* is not subjacent to the pronoun because there are at least two cyclical node boundaries between the two:

(6.10)   Near [the girl [*John* was talking with]$_S$]$_{NP}$, *he* found a snake.

Reinhart speculates that her disjoint reference rule does not disallow coreference in (6.10) because *John* and *he* are not subjacent: she assumes that this is why a coreferential interpretation between *John* and *he* is not ruled out.

To assume that the disjoint reference rule obeys the Subjacency Condition, however, opens a Pandora's box. As Reinhart herself is aware, it would predict incorrectly that the following sentences would all be acceptable:

(6.11)   a.   *He$_i$ disliked [$_{NP}$ most of [$_{NP}$ John$_i$'s office mates]]
          b.   *He$_i$ read [$_{NP}$ the book [$_S$ John$_i$ bought at the bookstore]]
          c.   *After days of search, he$_i$ was finally found in [$_{NP}$ a sleazy hotel room [$_S$ that Dr. Levin$_i$ had rented under a false name]]. (Reinhart)

This forces Reinhart to state that the disjoint reference rule obeys the Subjacency Condition in general except when NP$_1$ is the subject and NP$_2$ is in the VP, but she does not explain why the Subjacency Condition applies selectively. Therefore, it must be assumed that there is no account in her analysis of the acceptability of (6.9b).

A problem that is as troublesome to Reinhart's analysis as the acceptability of (6.9b) is the fact, noted by Solan (1983), that both the following sentences are marginal or unacceptable:

(6.12)   a.   ??In John$_i$'s bed, he$_i$ put Sam.
          b.   ??In John$_i$'s bed, Sam put him$_i$.

Reinhart's disjoint reference rule predicts that (a) would be unacceptable because *he* c-commands *John('s)* via an S to $\bar{S}$ projection, but that (b) would be acceptable because the c-command domain of *him* is cut off by the VP node that dominates it. This prediction turns out to be incorrect. The kind of asymmetry that her analysis predicts does not seem to exist between (a) and (b).

There are many other serious problems with Reinhart's disjoint reference rule, which include (i) its order-free formulation and (ii) its dependence on the concept of c-command. I will discuss these problems in Sections 2.8 and 2.11, where I give a critical review of Chomsky's binding conditions.

2.7 The First Phase of Trace Theory

Postal (1971) observed that *who* and *him* in (7.1a) can be coreferential but that *who* and *he* in (7.1b) cannot be:

(7.1) a. Who said Mary kissed him?
       b. Who did he say Mary kissed?

He attributed the impossibility of obtaining coreferential interpretation for (7.1b) to the fact that if *who* and *he* in this sentence were coreferential, they would have crossed each other in the derivation of the sentence, and that this would have violated a general ban on cross-over of coreferential noun phrases that are clause mates.[11] He motivated the constraint on the basis of sentences such as the following:

(7.2) a. John killed himself.
       b. *John was killed by himself.
(7.3) a. John talked to Mary about herself.
       b. *John talked about Mary to herself.

Observe that the rendition of the cross-over constraint in the framework of an interpretive theory of pronouns would require that interpretive rules for pronominal reference refer to the phrase structures before and after application of movement transformations.

Wasow (1972, 1979) and Chomsky (1975) claimed that interpretive rules for coreference linkage can still be made to apply only to surface structure in the cases under discussion if it is assumed that application of a movement transformation leaves a trace, call it *t*, in the original position of the moved constituent. Thus, the surface structures of (7.1a) and (7.1b), according to this "trace theory," can be informally represented as follows:

(7.4) a. Who [$_s$ t said Mary kissed him]
       b. Who [$_s$ he said Mary kissed t]

Wasow and Chomsky argued that it is easy to convert surface structures with *wh*-phrases and traces to their *logical forms*, to which semantic rules for coreference linkage would apply. A relatively trivial interpretive rule would map (7.4) directly to (7.5):

(7.5) a. for which person x, x said Mary kissed him?
       b. for which person x, he said Mary kissed x?

It is assumed here that the predication part of the logical form retains all the phrase structure configuration that the surface structure contains. Wasow and Chomsky assumed that the bound variable x functions roughly as a name (e.g., *John*), and that (7.5a) and (7.5b), therefore, would have interpretations analogous to (7.6a) and (7.6b), respectively:

(7.6) a.   John said Mary kissed him.
       b.   He said Mary kissed John.

In other words, the interpretive rule for pronominal reference can establish coreference between the variable x and the pronoun *him* in (7.5a), but not between *he* and x in (7.5b). For the rest of this section, I will assume that this interpretive rule is identical with Reinhart's disjoint reference rule, but in order to avoid confusion that might arise from the fact that Reinhart's c-command formulation, as it was proposed by her, is a rule that applies to *surface structure,* while the c-command rule under discussion here is a semantic rule that applies to *logical forms,* I will refer to the latter simply as "trace theory."

It is easy to see that trace theory does a slightly better job than Reinhart's disjoint reference rule in accounting for various facts about pronominal reference. For example, observe the following sentences:

(7.7) a.   Who did he say Mary kissed? (= 7.1b)
       b.   Who do you think he said Mary kissed?

Neither (a) nor (b) has an interpretation in which *who* and *he* are coreferential. Reinhart's disjoint reference rule can rule out coreferential interpretation from (a) because *he* c-commands *who* in the surface structure via an S to $\bar{\text{S}}$ projection:

(7.8)

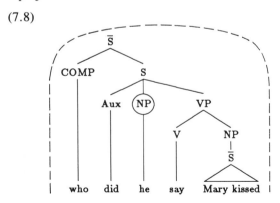

On the other hand, Reinhart's analysis erroneously fails to rule out coreference linkage between *who* and *he* for (7.7b) because *he* does not c-command *who* in the surface structure of the sentence.

(7.9)

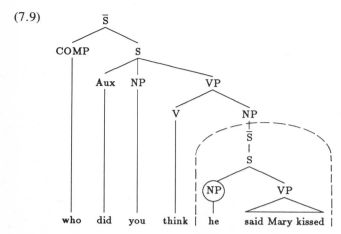

who   did   you   think | he   said Mary kissed |

In contrast, trace theory is able to block coreference interpretation of
(7.7b), as well as of (7.7a), because the surface structure of the sentence has a
trace in the object position of *kissed:*

(7.10)   a.   who [$_S$ you think he said Mary kissed t]
         b.   Logical Form: for which person x, you think he said Mary kissed x.

The interpretive rule for pronominal reference, applied to (7.10b), would correctly fail to establish coreference between *he* and *x.*

Nevertheless, although it works better than Reinhart's disjoint reference rule
here, trace theory does not seem to go much further in correctly predicting
unacceptable coreference interpretations. For example, observe the following
sentences:

(7.11)   a.   Whose father does he adore most?
              cf. Who adores his father most?
         b.   Whose father do you think he adores most?
              cf. Who do you think adores his father most?

What is at issue here is the impossibility of obtaining a coreferential interpretation between *whose* and *he* in (a) and (b).[12] Note that the surface structures of these sentences in the framework of trace theory propounded in
Wasow (1972) and Chomsky (1975) are as follows:

(7.12)   a.   Whose father [$_S$ he adores t most]
         b.   Whose father [$_S$ you think he adores t most]

Crucially, the trace *t* in (7.12) is a trace of the moved constituent *whose father,* and not a trace of *whose.* Therefore, the logical forms that would be
needed to establish disjoint reference *whose* and *he* and to block coreference
between the two, that is,

(7.13)   a.   for which person x, he adores x's father most?
         b.   for which person x, you think he adores x's father most?

are not directly derivable from (7.12).[13]

Trace theory cannot handle our crucial sentences with preposed prepositional phrases, either. Observe the following sentences:

(7.14)   a.   Next to John, the investigators believe that he put a basket of roses.
         b.   Next to the woman John was courting, the investigators believe that he put a basket of roses. (Carden)

John and *he* of (7.14a) cannot be coreferential, while *John* and *he* of (7.14b) can be. Trace theory cannot block the coreferential interpretation of *John* and *he* in (7.14a) because even if application of adverb preposing left a trace, it would be a trace of the whole prepositional phrase and not that of *John*. Therefore, the information that the *he* c-commands *John* in the corresponding logical form is not available to the pronominal rule. Moreover, even if it were made available, the trace theory would not be able to handle the phenomenon under discussion because then it would also block coreferential interpretation from (7.14b), which allows for such an interpretation. Thus, trace theory also fails to solve the paradox that has confronted all the past analyses of pronominal reference.

2.8   Government and Binding (GB) Theory

In this section, I will examine how Chomsky's government and binding (GB) theory fares with respect to our crucial sentences involving coreference and disjoint reference. The GB theory has the following three binding conditions that are relevant to the present discussion.

(8.1)   Condition A: An anaphor is bound in its governing category.
        Condition B: A pronominal is free in its governing category.
        Condition C: An R-expression is free.

This is not a place for discussing the technical details of these conditions or the background that led Chomsky to hypothesize them. I will give here only nontechnical paraphrases in order to give the reader who is not initiated into GB theory a vague idea of what it can or cannot do for pronominal analysis.

For the present discussion, we can interpret the expression 'an anaphor' of Condition A as 'a reflexive pronoun,' and 'its governing category' as referring to 'its closest parent NP or S.' Binding in Condition A, as well as in the other two conditions, operates under the condition of c-command. What Condition A states, then, is that a reflexive must be coindexed with an NP that c-commands it within the reflexive's closest parent NP or S category. Thus, given

(8.2) a. [$_S$ John criticized himself]
       b. Mary looked at [$_{NP}$ John's portrait of himself]

himself of (8.2a) must be coindexed with its clause mate (more accurately, its S-mate) *John,* and *himself* of (8.2b) is obligatorily coindexed with its NP-mate *John('s).*

Condition B states that a pronominal cannot be coreferential with an NP- or S-mate that c-commands it. For example, observe the following sentences:

(8.3) a. John criticized him.
       b. Mary asked John about him.
       c. Mary looked at John's portrait of him.

John and *him* of (8.3a) and (8.3b) are clause mates (i.e., S-mates), and the former c-commands the latter. Therefore, *him* cannot be coindexed with *John.* Similarly, *John('s)* and *him* of (8.3c) are NP-mates and the former c-commands the latter. Therefore, *him* cannot be coindexed with *John('s).* Observe, further, the following sentences:

(8.4) a. John's brother criticized him.
       b. John criticized his brother.

In (8.4a), *him* cannot be coindexed with *John's brother,* which c-commands it within the former's minimal S, but it can be coindexed with *John('s)* because the latter does not c-command it. In (8.4b), *his* can be coindexed with *John* because what Condition B dictates is that *his* be free (i.e., not coindexed with any other NP) only within its governing category NP (dominating *his brother*).[14]

Condition C states that R(eferring)-expressions (i.e., nonpronominal NPs such as *John, Mary, the visitor,* etc.) are free. What the condition means is that 'An R-expression NP_2 is free from NP_1 (i.e., is not to be coindexed with NP_1) if NP_1 c-commands NP_2.' Thus, observe the following sentences:

(8.8) a. John/He criticized John.
       b. John/He criticized John's brother.

In both (8.8a) and (8.8b), NP_1 = *John/He* c-commands NP_2 = *John('s).* Therefore, the latter cannot be coindexed with the former. On the other hand, see the following examples:

(8.9) a. John's mother adores John.
       b. His mother adores John.

In (8.9a), NP_1 = *John's* does not c-command NP_2 = *John.* Neither does NP_2 c-command NP_1. Therefore, these two NPs are coindexable. Similarly, in (8.9b), NP_1 = *his* does not c-command NP_2 = *John.* Therefore, the latter is not prevented from being coindexed with the former. Condition B, as it is applied to NP_1, does not disallow the coindexing of *his* with *John*, either, be-cause the latter does not c-command the former. Hence the possibility of co-indexing the two NPs.

I have illustrated what Conditions A, B, and C mean as if they applied to surface structure, but in the first part of Chomsky (1981) these conditions are intended to apply to logical forms, now referred to as LF-representation.[15] Let us now examine some diagnostic sentences to see how these conditions (especially Conditions B and C) work. First observe the following sentences, which involve movement:

(8.10)   a.   Who did he criticize severely?
         b.   Who did he say Mary kissed?

As in the earlier form of trace theory, it is also assumed in GB theory that the movement of a category leaves behind a coindexed empty category (trace):

(8.11)   a.   Who$_i$ [$_S$ he criticized [$_{NP_i}$ e] severely]
         b.   Who$_i$ [$_S$ he said Mary kissed [$_{NP_i}$ e]]

The corresponding LF-representation is

(8.12)   a.   for which person x, he criticized x severely?
         b.   for which person x, he said Mary kissed x?

Variables are R-expressions. Therefore, Condition C applies to the x in the open-sentence part of (8.12a, b), that is, to the x of *he criticized x severely* and *he said Mary kissed x*. It determines that x cannot be coindexed with *he* because *he* c-commands x. Hence there is no possibility of interpreting (8.10a, b) with *he* as coreferential with *who*.

The pronominal analysis in GB theory is fraught with problems. First of all, it erroneously disallows a coreferential interpretation of *John* and *him* in sentences such as:

(8.13)   a.   John found a snake near him.
              LF-representation: for x = John, x found a snake near him.
         b.   John put the blanket under him.
              LF-representation: for x = John, x put the blanket under him.

In the LF-representation of (8.13a) and (8.13b), x and *him* are S-mates, and *him* is c-commanded by x. Therefore, Condition B erroneously dictates that *him* be marked for disjoint reference with *John*.[16]

Let us now proceed to discuss sentences which involve movement. Observe, first, the following example:

(8.14)   Whose brother did he see?

If the movement of *whose brother* leaves only an empty category behind as its trace, the surface structure, now referred to in GB theory as S-structure, of the above sentence is

(8.15)   Whose brother$_i$ [$_S$ he saw [$_{NP_i}$ e]]

Chomsky (1981, pp. 89–90) observes that in order to block a coreferential interpretation of *whose* and *he,* which does not exist in (8.14), it is necessary to obtain the LF-representation for the sentence that is shown below:

(8.16)   for which person x, he saw x's brother.

If the above LF-representation were available, Condition C would block co-indexing of *he* and x because *he* c-commands x. Chomsky observes that the above logical form is not directly derivable from (8.15) and that its reconstruction would require a trace theory that would leave a structured trace behind, with a doom marker (D) indicating that it does not have a surface realization:

(8.17)   Whose brother$_i$ [$_S$ he saw [$_{NP_i}$, $_D$ whose brother]]

He further notes that the following sentence allows for coreferential interpretation between *John* and *he:*

(8.18)   Which book that John likes did he read?

The coreferential interpretation would be blocked if Condition C applied to the LF-representation that derived from structured trace:

(8.19)   . . . y = John . . . he read the book that y likes

In this LF-representation, *he* c-commands y, and thus the coindexing of the two would be blocked by Condition C. Therefore, it is presumably the case that Condition C applies to the LF-representation without structured trace in the case of (8.18) so that *he* should not c-command y (= *John*):

(8.20)   for which x, x a book that John likes, he read x.

Chomsky admits that there are many problems that arise in this connection but says that it is beyond the scope of his book. He dismisses trace theory with structured trace of the type shown in (8.17) and continues to adopt trace theory with empty category, as shown in (8.15). He thus leaves unexplained the fact that *he* cannot be coreferential with *whose* in (8.14).

Since Chomsky entertains the possibility, albeit briefly, of resorting to trace theory with structured trace rather than trace theory with empty category, I will examine here what would happen in the framework of trace theory with structured trace. For this purpose, let us observe the following sentence:

(8.21)   Near John, he found a snake.

This is a sentence that does not allow for coreferential interpretation between *John* and *he.*[17] In order to block such an interpretation, it is necessary to be able to obtain the following LF-representation corresponding to the sentence:

(8.22)   for x = John, he found a snake near x.

This LF-representation requires a trace with inner structures. Assume that trace theory with structured trace is adopted. Then coindexing of *he* and *x* would be correctly blocked.

Now observe the following sentence:

(8.23)   Near the girl that John was talking with, he found a snake.

This is a sentence that allows for coreferential interpretation between *John* and *he*. However, the LF-representation that is derived from the surface structure of the sentence with structured trace would be:

(8.24)   for *x* = John, he found a snake near the girl that *x* was talking with.

Since *he* c-commands *x* in this LF-representation as much as in (8.22), Condition C would apply and erroneously block coindexing of *he* and *x*. Therefore, trace theory with structured trace does not solve the problem under discussion.

Condition C as applied to the LF-representation derived from S-structures with structured trace seems to be based on the assumption that whatever is ill-formed before fronting is ill-formed after fronting, and whatever is well-formed before fronting is well-formed after fronting, also. I have shown the fallacies of the former assumption using (8.24). The following shows that the latter assumption is also wrong.

(8.25)   a.   John's mother adores him.
          b.   Him, John's mother adores.

Although (8.25a) allows for coreferential interpretation between *John('s)* and *him,* (8.25b) does not.

Chomsky (1981, p. 144, n. 79) observes that the depth of embedding appears to be a factor in determining permissible coindexing between a pronoun in S and a noun that appears in the specification of the category of a variable in the pre-S position in LF:

(8.26)   a.   Which pictures of John did he like?
          b.   Which picture of the woman John married did he like?
          c.   Which people who John liked did he meet?

He notes that it is much more natural to take *John* and *he* to be coreferential in (b) and (c) than in (a)—a fact that has long been known to those who are familiar with Lakoff's rule ordering paradox—but he does not attempt to find a solution to this problem.

Before showing how functional syntax can account for such sentences, let us first examine how sentences such as (8.14), (8.18), (8.21), and (8.23) would fare in the framework in which the binding conditions apply to S-structure rather than to LF-representation. In this framework, Condition C would apply to the following S-structures of (8.14) and (8.18):

(8.27)   a.   [$_\bar{s}$ Whose brother$_i$ [$_s$ he did see [e]$_i$]
          b.   [$_\bar{s}$ Which book that John likes$_i$ [$_s$ he did read [e]$_i$]

Chomsky stipulates that the binding conditions not apply between an NP in COMP position (i.e., a fronted NP) and an NP in S. Therefore, all that Condition C can do about (8.27) is to block coindexing of *he* with the trace *e* of the fronted NP. It cannot block coindexing of *he* with *whose* in (a).

Let us assume, temporarily, that the binding conditions are allowed to apply between an NP in COMP position and an NP in S. Then, in (8.27a) and (8.27b), the pronoun *he* c-commands *whose* and *John,* respectively, via an S to $\bar{S}$ projection. Therefore, Condition C would correctly block coindexing of *he* and *whose* for (a) and incorrectly block coindexing of *he* and *John* for (b). Next observe the following sentences:

(8.28)   a.   Whose brother do you think he saw?
          b.   Which book that John likes do you think he read?

Coreference possibilities of these sentences are exactly the same as those for (8.27a) and (8.27b). Example (8.28a) lacks an interpretation in which *he* is coreferential with *whose,* while (8.28b) allows for one in which *he* is coreferential with *John.* Here again, if Condition C is not allowed to apply between an NP in COMP position and an NP in S, all that it can do is to block coindexing of *he* with the trace of the fronted *wh*-expressions—it would allow for the coindexing of *he* and *whose* incorrectly for (a), and the coindexing of *he* and *John* correctly for (b). The situation is the same even if Condition C is allowed to apply between an NP in COMP position and an NP in S. In the S-structures of these sentences, the pronoun does not c-command *whose* and *John,* respectively. Therefore, Condition C would allow for a coreferential interpretation for both sentences, correctly for (8.28b) but incorrectly for (8.28a). The coreference facts of (8.14) and (8.18) remain unexplained in the framework in which the binding conditions apply to S-structure (with unstructured trace), regardless of whether they are allowed to apply between an NP in COMP position and an NP in S. Exactly the same situation holds for (8.21), (8.23), and their variation with *do you think* between the fronted element and the rest of the question.

Finally, for the sake of completeness, let us examine how the above sentences would fare in the framework in which the binding conditions apply to S-structure with structured trace. In this framework, Condition C would apply to the following S-structures of (8.14) and (8.18):

(8.29)   a.   [$_\bar{s}$ Whose brother$_i$ [$_s$ he did see [$_{NP}$, $_D$ whose brother]]
          b.   [$_\bar{s}$ Which book that John likes$_i$ [$_s$ he did read [$_{NP}$, $_D$ which book that John likes]]

It is clear that the situation that holds here is identical with that which holds in the framework in which the binding conditions apply to LF-representation:

Condition C, as it applies between *he* and *whose/John* in the structured trace, would block a coreferential interpretation both for (8.29a) and (8.29b). Likewise, Condition C would block a coreferential interpretation for (8.21), (8.23), (8.28a), and (8.28b). This would leave the acceptability of (8.18), (8.23), and (8.28b) totally unexplained.

The above observations show that GB theory still fails to account for a wide range of facts that have puzzled linguists for the past two decades, regardless of whether S-structure is assumed to have trace with or without inner structure and regardless of whether the binding conditions are assumed to apply to LF-representation or to S-structure.

2.9 Reflexives and Pronouns

Now that we have reviewed the earlier unacceptable accounts of pronominalization, I am ready to present my own account, beginning with a discussion of the relation between reflexivization and pronominalization. The standard account of reflexives in English includes a statement to the following effect:

(9.1)   *Reflexivization:* Given two coreferential clause-mate noun phrases NP_1 and NP_2 such that NP_1 precedes NP_2 and NP_1 is a major constituent of the clause, NP_2 must be a reflexive pronoun.

Given an S, the immediate daughter nodes of the S and those of its VP node are major constituents of that S. In addition, the object NPs of prepositional phrases that are the S's major constituents are major constituents of that S. This excludes possessive NPs from the major constituent category.

Observe the following sentences:

(9.2)   a. $John_i$ killed $himself_i$.
         b. *$John_i$ killed him_i.
(9.3)   a. $John_i$ talked to Mary about $himself_i$.
         b. *$John_i$ talked to Mary about him_i.

The use of reflexive pronouns is obligatory in (9.2) and (9.3) because $NP_1 = John$ is a major constituent of the sentence.

The above rule has no exception when NP_2 is either the direct or indirect object of a verb or when NP_2 is the object of the preposition in the "V + Preposition" complex. For example, observe the following sentences:

(9.4)   a. $John_i$ gave $himself_i$ a prize.
         b. *$John_i$ gave him_i a prize.
(9.5)   a. $John_i$ talked to $himself_i$.
         b. *$John_i$ talked to him_i.

It is inconceivable that we could find verbs that would appear in the context of (9.2), (9.4), and (9.5) which would allow use of nonreflexive pronouns.

However, there are many instances in which nonreflexive pronouns appear as objects of prepositions where reflexives are expected. For example, for many speakers the following sentences are better with a pronoun than with a reflexive:

(9.6)   a.   At the dinner, the host$_i$ seated me next to him$_i$/??himself$_i$.
        b.   John$_i$ heard strange noises behind him$_i$/*himself$_i$.
        c.   John$_i$ saw a plane above him$_i$/*himself$_i$.

Cases like (9.6) have been brushed aside as exceptions to (9.1) by casual statements such as ". . . NP$_2$ must reflexivize except when it is in certain prepositional phrases." As far as I know, no serious attempt has been made to account for the fact that pronouns are disallowed in (9.2)–(9.5) but are allowed or rather obligatory in (9.6).

Let us now consider carefully whether we can find some syntactic or semantic features that distinguish between the reflexive pattern and the pronominal pattern. I give below more examples of both patterns. In order to avoid the interpretation in which *himself* is used emphatically for contrast, both *himself* and *him* should be pronounced without stress.

(9.7)   a.   John$_i$ wrote to Mary about himself$_i$.
        b.   *John$_i$ wrote to Mary about him$_i$.
(9.8)   a.   John$_i$ referred Mary to himself$_i$.
        b.   *John$_i$ referred Mary to him$_i$.
(9.9)   a.   John$_i$ compared Bill with himself$_i$.
        b.   *John$_i$ compared Bill with him$_i$.
(9.10) a.   John$_i$ addressed the letter to himself$_i$.
        b.   *John$_i$ addressed the letter to him$_i$.
(9.11) a.   John$_i$ fell in love with himself$_i$.
        b.   *John$_i$ fell in love with him$_i$.
(9.12) a.   *John$_i$ left his$_i$ family behind himself$_i$.
        b.   John$_i$ left his$_i$ family behind him$_i$.
(9.13) a.   *John$_i$ has many friends around himself$_i$.
        b.   John$_i$ has many friends around him$_i$.
(9.14) a.   *John$_i$ has an air of aloofness about himself$_i$.
        b.   John$_i$ has an air of aloofness about him$_i$.
(9.15) a.   *John$_i$ has passion in himself$_i$.
        b.   John$_i$ has passion in him$_i$.
(9.16) a.   *John$_i$ has no gumption in himself$_i$.
        b.   John$_i$ has no gumption in him$_i$.[18]

In (9.7)–(9.11), *himself,* and not *him,* is used to refer to *John.* On the other hand, in (9.12)–(9.16), *him,* and not *himself,* is used (unless contrast is intended).

Pragmatically speaking, there is a difference between the role that the prepositional object plays in (9.7)–(9.11) and (9.12)–(9.16). In the former,

John, the referent of the prepositional object, is the direct recipient of the action represented by the rest of the verb phrase. For example, John is the target of the action of *wrote to Mary about* in (9.7). In contrast, in (9.12), the action *left his family (behind)* does not have John as a target of action. The semantic distinction between (9.7)–(9.11) and (9.12)–(9.16) becomes clearer when we observe the following sentences, in which both the reflexive and nonreflexive pronouns are allowable (at least for some speakers).

(9.17) a. John$_i$ hid the book behind himself$_i$.
        b. John$_i$ hid the book behind him$_i$.
(9.18) a. John$_i$ pulled the blanket over himself$_i$.
        b. John$_i$ pulled the blanket over him$_i$.
(9.19) a. John$_i$ put the blanket next to himself$_i$.
        b. John$_i$ put the blanket next to him$_i$.
(9.20) a. John$_i$ put the blanket under himself$_i$.
        b. John$_i$ put the blanket under him$_i$.
(9.21) a. John$_i$ pulled the rope toward himself$_i$ and won the game.
        b. John$_i$ pulled the rope toward him$_i$ and won the game.

Example (9.17a) implies that John held the book with his hand and put it behind his back. The book was directly touching him. On the other hand, (9.17b) implies that perhaps the book was on a chair, and he was standing in front of the chair so that the book could not be seen. In other words, it is most likely that there was no physical contact between John and the book. It might be possible to use (9.17b) to describe the first situation, in which John held the book in his hand behind his back, but the sentence would not be asserting this physical contact at all. Example (9.18a) implies that John put the blanket over his head and covered himself with it, perhaps intending to hide under it. On the other hand, (9.18b) does not imply such direct action with the whole body of John as target. If John was in bed under a comforter, and he pulled the blanket and put it over the comforter, only (9.18b) can be used to describe the situation. Similarly, even if John put the blanket directly over him, if his head was still sticking out, only (9.18b) can be used. Similarly, (9.19a) implies that the blanket was touching John or that he was anticipating that someone would grab it away from him, while there is no such implication in (9.19b). Likewise, (9.20a) implies that John was trying to hide the blanket by covering it with his body, while (9.20b) lacks any such implication. John might have been sitting on a chair and might have put the blanket under the chair. Example (9.21a) is acceptable, for example, in a tug-of-war situation in which John could keep pulling the rope toward his direction and gathering it up in his arms. On the other hand, in the same kind of tug-of-war situation, (9.21b) simply means that the rope moved a little bit in John's direction. This semantic contrast between (9.21a) and (9.21b) is confirmed by the following contrast, which was suggested by John Whitman (personal communication):

(9.22)   a.   John$_i$ pulled the rope in to himself$_i$.
          b.   *John$_i$ pulled the rope in to him$_i$.

The expression *pull x in to y* implies gathering *x* up in *y*'s arms. Hence, *y* is the direct target of the action represented by the expression and disallows the use of a nonreflexive pronoun, as indicated by the ungrammaticality of (9.22b). Similarly, observe the following sentences:

(9.23)   a.   John$_i$ strung the rope around himself$_i$.
          b.   John$_i$ strung the rope around him$_i$.
(9.24)   a.   John$_i$ spilled the gasoline all over himself$_i$.
          b.   John$_i$ spilled the gasoline all over him$_i$.
(9.25)   a.   John$_i$ poured the gasoline all over himself$_i$.
          b.   *John$_i$ poured the gasoline all over him$_i$.

Example (9.23a) means that John bound himself with the rope. On the other hand, (9.23b) means that John did not tie himself with the rope and that the rope perhaps did not even touch John. It implies that perhaps there were four poles standing around him, and he strung the rope around the poles so that he was inside the rope. The distinction between (9.24a) and (9.24b) is more subtle, but the former implies that there was much more action involved with the incident. It describes John as a victim of the incident. Perhaps he got drenched with gasoline. Example (9.24a) also has a strong intentional interpretation. This is only slightly affected by the unmarked nonintentional interpretation of "spill." On the other hand, (9.24b) is more stative. It does not assert that John's whole body was the recipient of the action. His body represents an incidental location where the spilled gasoline ended up.[19] In contrast, (9.25) represents an intentional action with a specific target. Therefore only *himself* can be used.

The above observations lead us to hypothesize the following semantic filter:

(9.26)   *Semantic Constraint on Reflexives:* Reflexive pronouns are used in English if and only if they are the direct recipients or targets of the actions represented by the sentences.[20]

The fact that reflexives are obligatory in (9.2)–(9.5) automatically follows from the fact that the direct and indirect object of verbs and the object of the "V + Preposition" always satisfy the above constraint.[21]

2.10 Resolution of Rule Ordering Paradoxes

In the preceding section, I have shown that, given two coreferential NPs as clause mates, whether the second NP is to be realized as a reflexive or nonreflexive pronoun is a matter that is semantically or pragmatically controlled. In particular, the contrast that can be seen in

(10.1)   a.   John$_i$ put the blanket under himself$_i$.
         b.   John$_i$ put the blanket under him$_i$.
(10.2)   a.   John$_i$ pulled the rope toward himself$_i$.
         b.   John$_i$ pulled the rope toward him$_i$.

shows that it is not possible to state the condition for the nonreflexive pronominal pattern by referring to the phrase structure configuration in which the
prepositional phrases under discussion appear.

Now I am ready to present a way to resolve Lakoff's rule ordering paradoxes. This proposal is identical with the one that I made in Kuno (1972c),
which was couched in a framework in which pronouns and reflexives are
transformationally derived. Here I present the same proposal in an interpretive framework. It is first necessary to assume that all nonnominative personal pronouns are ambiguous between [−reflexive] and [+reflexive].[22] Thus
we will start out with structures such as the following:

(10.3)   a.   [John put the blanket under himself [+reflexive]]
         b.   [John put the blanket under him [−reflexive]]
         c.   [John put the blanket under him [+reflexive]]

As the first approximation, I hypothesize the following two rules. The reflexive rule is an interpretive rule, while the semantic constraint on reflexives is a
semantic filter rule.

(10.4)   *Reflexive Rule:* A [+reflexive] NP must be coindexed with a clause-mate
         NP that k-commands it. A [−reflexive] NP must be marked for disjoint
         reference with a clause-mate NP that precedes and k-commands it.
(10.5)   *Semantic Constraint on Reflexives* (revised): A [+reflexive] NP that
         ends with *-self/selves* can be used in English if and only if its referent is
         the direct recipient or target of the actions or mental states represented
         by the sentences.

At this point I will leave unexplained why the concept of "k-command" is
used in (10.4) instead of "c-command." I will also leave unexplained why the
concept of "clause mate" (i.e., in the sense of S-mate) is used rather than that
of "S- or NP-mate." These two issues will be discussed in detail in the next
section.

Returning to the structures given in (10.3), the Reflexive Rule obligatorily
coindexes *himself [+reflexive]* of (a) and *him [+reflexive]* of (c) with *John.*
In the semantic component of the grammar, *John put the blanket under x* receives two interpretations: one in which *x* is the direct target of action represented by *John put the blanket under,* and the other in which it is not. The
Semantic Constraint on Reflexives allows *himself [+reflexive]* and disallows
him [+reflexive] for the first interpretation, and vice versa for the second.
Hence we derive (10.1a) and (10.1b) with their respective "target" and "non-
target" interpretations. The Reflexive Rule also applies to the structure shown

in (10.3b), and since *John* and *him* [−reflexive] are clause mates, it assigns disjoint reference to the two NPs:

(10.6) $John_i$ put the blanket under him_j.

Observe, further, the following structures:

(10.7)   a.   [John killed himself [+reflexive]]
           b.   [John killed him [−reflexive]]
           c.   [John killed him [+reflexive]]

The Reflexive Rule coindexes *himself [+reflexive]* of (a) and *him [+reflexive]* of (c) with *John,* and assigns distinct indices to *John* and *him [−reflexive]* of (b). The Semantic Constraint on Reflexives disallows (c) because the expression *John killed x* can receive only the interpretation in which x is the target of the action *John killed.* Thus, we obtain the following surface sentences:

(10.8)   a. $John_i$ killed $himself_i$.
           b. $John_i$ killed him_j. (*him* as [−reflexive])
           c.   *$John_i$ killed him_i. (*him* as [+reflexive])

For disjoint reference, I tentatively assume here Lasnik's "precede and k-command" analysis. I add $\overline{S}$ and $\overline{\overline{S}}$ to the k-command domain to take care of phrase structures that distinguish them from S. (In sec. 2.11, I will reexamine this analysis and propose that c-command, as well as k-command, is needed for the Disjoint Reference Rule.)

(10.9)   *Disjoint Reference Rule:* Mark NP_1 and NP_2 for disjoint reference if
           (i) NP_1 precedes and k-commands NP_2; and
           (ii) NP_2 is not a pronoun or reflexive.

It is stipulated that the Disjoint Reference Rule applies only between NPs which have not yet been marked for coreference or disjoint reference. For reasons that will be made clearer in the next section, I assume that the Reflexive Rule applies cyclically and the Disjoint Reference Rule to surface structure. This is the assumption that was also made in Kuno (1972c).

We now turn to our crucial examples, repeated here for ease of reference:

(10.10)   a. $John_i$ found a snake near him_i.
            b.   Near him_i, $John_i$ found a snake.
            c.   *Near $John_i$, he_i found a snake.
(10.11)   a. $John_i$ found a snake near the girl he_i was talking with.
            b.   Near the girl he_i was talking with, $John_i$ found a snake.
            c.   Near the girl $John_i$ was talking with, he_i found a snake.

For (10.10), we start out with the structures shown in (10.12):

(10.12)   a.   [John found a snake near him [+reflexive]]
           b.   [He found a snake near John [−reflexive]]

The Reflexive Rule coindexes *him [+reflexive]* of (a) with *John* and assigns distinct indices to *he* and *John [−reflexive]* of (b). If adverb preposing does not apply, we obtain (10.10a) from (10.12a). The Semantic Constraint on Reflexives marks *him [+reflexive]* as acceptable because the expression *John found a snake near x* does not have *x* as target of the action represented. If adverb preposing does apply, we obtain the following intermediate structures:

(10.13) a. [Near him_i, $John_i$ found a snake]
         b. [Near $John_i$, he_j found a snake]

The Disjoint Reference Rule does not apply between him_i and $John_i$ of (a) because they have already been marked for coreference. This structure yields (10.10b).[23] Since there is no intermediate structure of the pattern of (10.13b) in which *John* and *he* are coindexed, there is no deriving (10.10c). Hence the ungrammaticality of the sentence.

The relevant underlying structures for (10.11) are

(10.14) a. [John found a snake near the girl [he was talking with]]
         b. [He found a snake near the girl [John was talking with]]

The Reflexive Rule does not apply between *John* and *he* of (a) and between *he* and *John* of (b) because they are not clause mates. If adverb preposing does not apply, the Disjoint Reference Rule applies to the structures (10.14a) and (10.14b). In (a), *he* does not precede or k-command *John,* and therefore it can be coindexed with the latter, yielding (10.11a). On the other hand, in (b), *he* both precedes and k-commands *John,* and therefore the two NPs must be marked for disjoint reference.

If adverb preposing applies to the structures shown in (10.14), we obtain the following:

(10.15) a. [Near the girl [he was talking with], John found a snake]
         b. [Near the girl [John was talking with], he found a snake]

Since the two relevant NPs in each of the above structures have not yet been marked for or against coreference, the Disjoint Reference Rule applies to them. However, since neither structure satisfies the conditions requiring disjoint reference, the two NPs can be coindexed, yielding (10.11b) and (10.11c).

I have shown above that the combination of my cyclical Reflexive Rule and Lasnik's precede and k-command analysis of disjoint reference, coupled with the assumption that all nonnominative personal pronouns are ambiguous between [+reflexive] and [−reflexive], successfully resolves Lakoff's rule ordering paradox between pronominalization and adverb preposing. It also accounts for the following contrast:

(10.16) a. $John_i$'s mother loves him_i dearly.
         b. His_i mother loves $John_i$ dearly.

    c. *Him$_i$, John$_i$'s mother loves dearly.

    d. John$_i$, his$_i$ mother loves dearly.

We start out with the following underlying structures:

(10.17)   a. [John's mother loves him [−reflexive] dearly]

            b. [His [+reflexive] mother loves John dearly]

The Reflexive Rule marks *John's mother* and *him* of (a) for disjoint reference, but does not mark *John('s)* and *him* for either coreference or disjoint reference. If the object NP does not get fronted, *John('s)* and *him* are optionally marked for coreference, yielding (10.16a). In contrast, in (10.17b), the Reflexive Rule marks *his [+reflexive]* for obligatory coreference with *John* because the latter k-commands the former. This yields (10.16b). If adverb preposing applies, we obtain the following structures:

(10.18)   a. [Him [−reflexive], John's mother loves dearly]

            b. [John$_i$, his$_i$ [+reflexive] mother loves dearly]

In (10.18a), *him* both precedes and k-commands *John('s)*. Therefore, these two NPs are obligatorily marked for disjoint reference. Hence, the unacceptability of (10.16c). On the other hand, in (10.18b), *John* and *his* are already marked for coreference, and therefore the disjoint reference rule does not apply. Hence the acceptability of (10.16d).

    Observe now the following underlying structures:

(10.19)   a. [John found a snake near his [−reflexive] sister]

            b. [John found a snake near his [+reflexive] sister]

            c. [He found a snake near John's [−reflexive] sister]

The Reflexive Rule applies to the two relevant NPs in these structures and marks them for disjoint reference for (a) and (c) and for coreference for (b). Adverb preposing can then apply, yielding (10.20a, b, c), respectively:

(10.20)   a. [Near his$_j$ sister, John$_i$ found a snake]

            b. Near his$_i$ sister, John$_i$ found a snake]

            c. [Near John$_j$'s sister, he$_i$ found a snake]

The above derivations predict that only (a) below would be acceptable:

(10.21)   a. $^{P\vee}$Near his$_i$ sister, John$_i$ found a snake.

            b. ^{P*}Near John$_i$'s sister, he$_i$ found a snake.[24]

The above prediction is borne out by the observed acceptability of (10.21a) and the observed unacceptability of (10.21b).

    I have shown in the above that Lakoff's rule ordering paradox has been resolved by assuming that there are two separate rules for determining coreference and disjoint reference. The first is a cyclical rule that determines coreference or disjoint reference between clause-mate NPs in the reflexivization context, and the second is a surface structure rule that rules out coreference linkage under the "precede and k-command" condition. All the past efforts, including those of Ross, Langacker, Lakoff, Reinhart, Wasow, and Chomsky, which did not recognize the fact that

(10.22)   John$_i$ found a snake near him$_i$.

involves a reflexivization process, resulted in failure to state the condition for pronouns and reflexives. Similarly, all past efforts, including those of Lasnik, Reinhart, Wasow, and Chomsky, which assumed that the condition for pronominal reference can be determined on the basis of surface structure alone or on the basis of LF-representation alone, ran into difficulty accounting for sentences involving postcyclical movement transformations. It seems that there is no way to avoid two rules, one cyclical and the other postcyclical (applying to surface structure), for determining all the relevant facts of reference in the sentences that we have examined in this chapter.

2.11 GB Theory Reexamined

Let us now return to the GB theory of coreference and disjoint reference to see where it has gone wrong and to find out whether it can be made to work without affecting the foundation of the theory. In my view, the binding conditions that were outlined in Section 2.9 are based on the following five fundamental assumptions:

(11.1)   (a) *Governing category:* There is a syntactically well-definable domain called a "governing category" in which anaphors (reflexives and reciprocals) must find their antecedents; and NP, as well as S, constitutes such a domain.

(b) *C-command:* A single command concept controls binding, and it is that of c-command, rather than that of k-command or S-command.

(c) *Precedence:* Coreference or lack thereof can be determined without referring to the linear order of NPs.

(d) *Homogeneity:* Coreference or lack thereof can be determined by applying *all* of the binding conditions at the same time (to LF-representation, to S-structure, or to both).

(e) *Obligatoriness:* All of the binding conditions apply obligatorily.

In the course of reexamining binding conditions A, B, and C below, I will show that it is difficult to maintain any of these assumptions.

2.11.1 Condition A, Governing Category, and C-Command

Let us first observe Condition A:

(11.2)   *Condition A:* An anaphor is bound in its governing category.

The governing category of an anaphor (a reflexive for the purpose of the present discussion) is NP or S. The inclusion of NP in this set must have been motivated at least in part by the fact that while (11.3a) is acceptable, (11.3b) is not.

(11.3)   a.   John criticized himself.
          b.   *John looked at Mary's picture of himself.

According to Condition A, the reflexive in (11.3a) must be bound within the S (i.e., the reflexive's governing category) by an NP that c-commands it. The sentence is acceptable because *John* satisfies this condition. On the other hand, the reflexive in (11.3b) must be bound within the NP for *Mary's picture of himself* (the reflexive's governing category) and not within the S for the sentence. *Mary* c-commands *himself,* and thus satisfies this condition, but does not agree with *himself* in gender. Hence the unacceptability of the sentence.

As should have been obvious from the beginning, Condition A suffers from a critical failure if an NP's governing category is taken to be its closest parent NP or S. It fails to coindex the reflexive in the following sentences with the subject NP:

(11.4)   a.   John bought a portrait of himself at the studio.
          b.   John bought a reproduction of a portrait of himself at the studio.

The reflexive *himself* must be bound in the NP dominating *a portrait of himself.* But there is no possible antecedent for the reflexive in this NP, and therefore it is left free (uncoindexed), and the sentence would be erroneously judged unacceptable.

Similarly, observe the following examples, in which *each other,* an archetypical anaphor, appears without being bound within its minimal NP structure:

(11.5)   a.   John and Mary scratched each other's backs.
          b.   John and Mary put money in each other's piggy banks.[25]

In these sentences, *each other*'s governing category is the NP corresponding to *each other's backs* and *each other's piggy banks,* and therefore the anaphor would be left unbound within this category.

Chomsky is aware that examples such as (11.4) and (11.5) counterexemplify Condition A, as well as Condition B, and he circumvents it by modifying his definition of "governing category." Technical details aside, it now says that the governing category of an NP is its closest parent NP or S that has a SUBJECT, the most prominent nominal element, accessible to the NP. The concept of SUBJECT is not well defined, but we take it as referring to the subject of S and the possessive NP of picture nouns. Applying Condition A with this revised definition of the "governing category" to (11.3), we find that (11.3b) is unacceptable because the governing category of *himself* is still the NP dominating *Mary's picture of himself* because this NP has a SUBJECT (i.e., *Mary's*) accessible to the anaphor. On the other hand, (11.4a), for example, is acceptable because the NP dominating *a portrait of himself* does not constitute a governing category of *himself* for the reason that it lacks a SUBJECT accessible to the reflexive. It is the S for the whole sentence that has a SUBJECT, and within this category, *himself* is bound (i.e., coindexable, or rather, requiring coindexing, with *John,* which c-commands it).

Chomsky, as shown above, handles the problem represented in (11.4) and (11.5) by adding a requirement for "accessible SUBJECT" in the definition of the "governing category." What this requirement does is to expand the domain of anaphor binding. Later on in this section, I will bring up sentences which cast doubt on the basic assumption that anaphors must find antecedents in the minimal governing category, however it is to be defined, and will make a radical proposal which expands the domain of anaphor binding indefinitely by assuming that NPs can be bound by NPs in any Ss provided that a certain "command" relationship is met and that a set of semantico-syntactic conditions is fulfilled. Until then, I will attempt to stay as close as possible to the present formulation of binding conditions and discuss here the less radical alternative shown below:

(11.6)   Only S serves as a governing category of NP for the purpose of anaphor binding.

I am not able to discuss here the ramifications of such a modification in GB theory as a whole. The objective of the discussion here is to see whether the two alternatives make different predictions, and, if so, which represents the facts about anaphors more accurately. In the following, I will discuss ramifications of (11.6) on the binding conditions. Condition A refers to Chomsky's original Condition A with the revised definition of "governing category" including a requirement for an "accessible SUBJECT." Condition A' refers to the original Condition A with NP removed as governing category.

It is easy to see that the proposed removal of NP as governing category of an anaphor turns (11.4) and (11.5) into a nonproblem. In (11.4), the NP that dominates *a portrait of himself* no longer counts as the reflexive's governing category. Only the S for the whole sentence is relevant. Since *himself* is bound within this category (i.e., coindexed with *John*), these sentences present no problem. Similarly, in (11.5), the NP that contains the possessive NP *each other's* does not qualify as a governing category from the outset. Only the S for the whole sentence counts. Since *each other('s)* is bound within this category, there is no problem with these sentences.

However, Condition A' overcoindexes. It coindexes *himself* of (11.3b) with *John*. I hypothesize that the unacceptability of (11.3b) is due to the working of some kind of a chain-of-command constraint: note the following principle, taken from Langacker (1969):

(11.7) If (i)   two identical nodes A_1 and A_2 both command some other node B; and

(ii) A_1 commands A_2, and

(iii) A_2 does not command A_1; then

any transformational operation involving A and B can apply only with respect to A_2 and B and not A_1 and B. Thus, if there is a "chain of command" so that A_1 commands A_2, A_2 commands B, and A_2 does not command A_1 but is identical to it, A_2 "controls" B, protecting it from the influence of A_1, so to speak.

If we interpret "command" in the above principle as referring to "k-command" and not to "c-command," it is easy to see that the above principle serves pretty much the same function as the "accessible SUBJECT" requirement does for Condition A.[26] According to this principle, (11.3b) is unacceptable because *John* commands *himself*, *Mary* commands *himself*, and *John* commands *Mary*, but not vice versa. Therefore, *Mary* is the "controller" for the reflexive.

The two formulations described above begin to make different predictions if we interpret the chain-of-command principle as a semantico-syntactic constraint that is not absolute. For example, compare the following two sentences:

(11.8) a.   *Mary wouldn't care a bit about John's opinions of herself.

b.   ?Mary wouldn't care a bit about anybody's opinions of herself.

For many speakers, there is a significant difference between the above two sentences. Example (11.8a) is clearly unacceptable, but (11.8b) is "almost" acceptable, and if they hear (11.8b) actually used in conversation, they might not notice the "unusualness" of the sentence. In Chapter 4, I will show that an indefinite pronoun is a weak controller for reflexives. I assume that the fact that (11.8b) is nearly acceptable for many speakers is owing to the fact that the triggering power of *anybody* for reflexivization is weak, and it can be nearly superseded by the strong triggering power of *Mary*. Note that Condition A, which recognizes the NP dominating *anybody's opinion of herself* as the governing category of *herself*, does not allow for any possibility of acceptability for (11.8b) and predicts that (11.8a) and (11.8b) are equally unacceptable.

Observe, further, the following sentences:

(11.9) a.   John and Mary asked each other to draw portraits of themselves.

b.   John and Mary asked each other to write to themselves during the vacation.

Example (11.9a) means 'John asked Mary to draw a portrait of herself, and Mary asked John to draw a portrait of himself.' In other words, *themselves* is bound in the S for [*PRO to draw portraits of themselves*]. The sentence does not mean 'John asked Mary to draw a portrait of him and Mary asked John to draw a portrait of her' or 'John asked Mary to draw a portrait of John and

Mary, and Mary asked John to draw one, too.' Such an interpretation would have *themselves* free in the S for [*PRO to draw portraits of themselves*] and would constitute a violation of Condition A. Similarly, in spite of the fact that one usually does not write to oneself, (11.9b) still means that 'John asked Mary to write to herself, and Mary asked John to write to himself.' It does not allow a pragmatically more plausible interpretation to the effect that John asked Mary to write to him and Mary asked John to write to her. This sentence, too, shows that *themselves* is bound within its minimal S-node.

Now, observe the following sentence:

(11.10)   a.   John and Mary commissioned each other's portraits of themselves.
           b.   John and Mary traded each other's opinions of themselves.

It seems that it is much easier to obtain an interpretation for these sentences in which *themselves* is bound not by *each other*, but by *John and Mary*, than for (11.9). If there are enough speakers who share the same intuition, it supports the view that NP is not a governing category for anaphors.

Next observe the following sentences:

(11.11)   a.   *Mary had never been willing to listen to John's criticism of herself.
           b.   Mary had never been willing to listen to criticism from/by John of herself.
(11.12)   a.   Mary had never been willing to listen to John's criticism of himself.
           b.   ?Mary had never been willing to listen to criticism from/by John of himself.

The fact that (11.11b) is acceptable or nearly so shows that the structure that Condition A applies to does not have the picture noun agent in the possessive NP position. In other words, (11.11b) is derivable only if *from/by John* does not constitute an accessible SUBJECT for *herself*. On the other hand, (11.12b), which is acceptable or nearly acceptable depending upon the speaker, is derivable only if *from/by John* is an accessible SUBJECT for *himself*, or at the very least, only if *John* c-commands *himself*.[27] There does not seem to be any way to resolve this problem within GB theory. On the other hand, according to Condition A', both *Mary* and *John* can potentially bind the reflexive in any of the four sentences. The fact that (11.12b) is not as acceptable as (11.11b) can be accounted for by observing that a *by*-agentive NP is not a strong controller for reflexivization in general:[28]

(11.13)   a.   John spoke to Mary about himself.
           b.   ??Mary was spoken to by John about himself.

Let us use the expression $C(NP_1) > C(NP_2)$ to show that NP_1 is a stronger controller for reflexivization than NP_2 is. Now we can account for the degree of acceptability of the sentences in (11.11) and (11.12). In (11.11a) and (11.12a), the chain-of-command principle dictates that $C(John) > C(Mary)$. Since there is no factor that counteracts this and elevates *Mary*'s controlling power for reflexivization vis-à-vis that of *John*, only (11.12a) is deemed acceptable. In contrast, in (11.11b) and (11.12b), two counteracting forces are in operation. In both sentences, *Mary* and *John* k-command the reflexives, *Mary* k-commands *John*, but not vice versa. Therefore, the chain-of-command principle dictates that C(John) > C(Mary). On the other hand, the fact that *John*, but not *Mary*, is in a *by*-agentive position dictates that C(Mary) > C(John). The fact that (11.11b) is acceptable shows that the controlling power of *Mary* for reflexivization that is derived from C(subject) > C(*by*-agentive) is so strong that it can override the C(John) > C(Mary) relationship derived from the chain-of-command principle. The fact that (11.12b) is slightly awkward shows that the loss of control for reflexivization on the part of *(by) John* due to the C(subject) > C(*by*-agentive) hierarchy is so strong that it cannot be made up for totally by the fact that *John* wins over *Mary* via the chain-of-command principle. Later on in this section, I will have more to say about the kinds of factors that interact with the chain-of-command principle. Furthermore, in Chapter 4 I will develop a model in which the relative strength of potential controllers for reflexivization is much more fully explored. It is sufficient to mention here that the facts of (11.11) and (11.12) have a possibility of receiving an adequate explanation in the framework of Condition A′ but not in that of Condition A.

In the above discussion, I have shown that it is impossible to maintain GB theory's assumption that NP, as well as S, is a governing category for the purpose of determining anaphor binding, and that NP needs to be removed as a governing category. I will now proceed to the assumption shown in (11.1b), that is, the assumption that c-command, rather than k-command or S-command, is the "command" concept needed for determining anaphor binding. Condition A states that a reflexive must be coindexed with an NP (in its governing category) that c-commands it. This "c-command" requirement gets into difficulty with respect to sentences such as the following:

(11.14) a. Many people have talked with Mary about herself.
         b. Nobody has heard from Mary about herself.
         c. John has just received a letter from Mary about herself.
         d. In the mail, there was a letter from Mary about herself.
         e. (He has been talking with many people about many things.) He has talked, for example, with Mary about herself, and with Jane about his fiancee.
         f. He did talk, and will continue to talk, with Mary about herself.
         g. He had a rather lengthy discussion with Mary about herself in his office.

In the S-structures for the above sentences, *Mary* does not c-command *herself*. Likewise, in the LF-representation corresponding to the above sentences, x (= *Mary*) does not c-command *herself*. Therefore, Condition A does not allow coindexing of *herself* with *Mary* and the sentences are erroneously judged unacceptable. These examples clearly suggest that k-command, rather than c-command, should be used for the binding condition for anaphors.

It might be argued that in (11.14a, b), *talk with* and *hear from* constitute a single V such that *Mary* as an immediate daughter node of VP, c-commands *herself*.[29] Examples (11.14c)–(11.14g) show that, even if the above approach could be maintained for the first two sentences, it cannot be a general solution to the problem under discussion. Note that in (11.14c), *receive a letter from* would have to be restructured as a V. This would be a far-fetched analysis considering the fact that there is nothing idiomatic about the expression and that *a letter* can be freely modified by adjectival expressions, as in:

(11.14)   c′. John has just received a twenty-page single-spaced typewritten letter from Mary about herself.

If restructuring of such productively formed expressions as *received a twenty-page single-spaced typewritten letter from* into a single V could be allowed by a theory, that theory could not be making any serious claims about the phrase-structure configurations of its S-structures or LF-representations.

Similarly, observe (11.14d). In order for *Mary* to c-command *herself*, the preposition *from* would have to be incorporated into the noun *letter*. This kind of restructuring is difficult to motivate and is contrary to everything we know about the internal structure of noun phrases.

Likewise, observe (11.14e, f, g). A parenthetical adverbial in (e), a long pause after *talk* in (f), and the presence of an adjectival modifier of *discussion* in (g) make it impossible to treat *talk with* and *have a discussion with* as constituting a single V.

It might also be argued that the difficulty of the c-command analysis illustrated in (11.14) can be resolved by revising the definition of c-command in such a way as to extend the command domain beyond PP. This will make it possible to coindex *herself* with *Mary* in (11.14). Reinhart (1981, pp. 631–632), aware that her c-command analysis makes the wrong prediction for PP-domain NPs in VP, hinted at such a solution. But there is no denying that such a revision, coupled with the proviso, discussed in section 2.6, which allows for the extension of the domain of c-command via an S to $\overline{S}$ projection, would turn c-command into something that is far removed from the original concept of c(onstituent) command. Furthermore, recall that Reinhart depended upon the presence of a PP node in accounting for the acceptability of

(11.15)   Near him$_i$, John$_i$ found a snake.

In any case, if a revision of the kind discussed above is made, the difference between c-command and k-command seems to narrow down to whether VP is to be regarded as a category that sets the command domain. K-command is an NP/S command, while c-command, with the proposed revision, would be equivalent to NP/S//VP command. I will return to this comparison later on in this section.

Let us now discuss how *him* can be coindexed with *John* in the following sentences in the framework of Condition A':

(11.16)   a.   John found a snake near him.
          b.   John put a blanket under him.

Recall that it is necessary to consider personal pronouns that are not in the nominative case as ambiguous between [−reflexive] and [+reflexive]. It is the *[+reflexive] him* that receives coindexing with *John* in these sentences.[30] The Semantic Constraint on Reflexives determines for a given context whether *him [+reflexive]* (as opposed to *himself [+reflexive]*) is appropriate for that context. Thus, given

(11.17)   a.   John$_i$ killed him$_i$ [+reflexive].
          b.   John$_i$ talked to Mary about him$_i$ [+reflexive].

this filtering rule would rule the sentences unacceptable because the referent of the [+reflexive] NP is the target of action represented by the predicate, and therefore the NP should have been realized as *himself.*

2.11.2 Condition B and the Reflexive Rule

Let us now proceed to Condition B:

(11.18)   Condition B: A pronominal is free in its governing category.

This condition should receive the same kind of revision as Condition A, because it should cover the complement of the domain covered by Condition A'. I will refer to Condition B based on the concept of k-command and with NP removed as a governing category as Condition B'.

In GB theory it has been necessary to consider NP as a governing category of a pronominal in order to block Condition B from applying between *John* and *his* in (11.19):

(11.19)   John criticized his brother.

Now, with the revision of the concept of "governing category" in such a way as to require an accessible SUBJECT, (11.19) has become a liability for Condition B. Note that *his* does not have an accessible SUBJECT within the NP for *his brother,* and therefore its governing category must be the S for the whole sentence. But then, Condition B says that *his* must be free within this S and thus erroneously disallows the coindexing of *his* and *John.*

In order to solve the problem that the binding conditions have in establishing coreference between *John* and *his* in (11.19), Huang (1983) proposes that the accessibility of a SUBJECT be made irrelevant as far as pronouns are concerned. According to this proposal, the governing category of *his* in (11.19) is the NP dominating *his brother,* despite the fact that this NP does not have a SUBJECT accessible to *his,* because *his* in the GB framework is a pronominal and makes the "accessible SUBJECT" requirement inoperative. I will discuss the "accessible SUBJECT" requirement with Huang's proviso more fully later on in this section.

The coindexing of *his* with *John* in (11.19) is not a problem in the framework of my reflexive analysis. Observe that (11.19) has the following two structures:

(11.20)　a.　John criticized his [−reflexive] brother.
　　　　　b.　John criticized his [+reflexive] brother.

Condition B' establishes disjoint reference between *John* and *his* in (11.20a), while Condition A' establishes coreference between *John* and *his* in (11.20b).

Those who are familiar with GB theory might feel that the above analysis of a personal pronoun ambiguously as [+reflexive] (i.e., as anaphor) resembles Chomsky's observation (1982, p. 100) that "pronouns can (for some reason) be regarded as anaphors" in the context of NP determiners. He supports this observation by noting that there are idioms such as

(11.21)　John lost his way.

where the determiner (i.e., the possessive NP) of the NP must be interpreted as coreferent with the matrix subject, but no such idioms where the pronoun inside NP is not in determiner position, as in

(11.22)　John took a picture of him.

Chomsky's observation about personal pronouns in the context of NP determiners is similar to my analysis but seems to be fragmentary and is not incorporated into the binding theory systematically.[31] It is also different from mine in that it does not extend to personal pronouns in the accusative case such as *him* in (11.16) and (11.22). According to my analysis, *him [+reflexive]* is coindexed with *John* both in (11.16) and (11.22), but the Semantic Constraint on Reflexives determines that (11.22) is inappropriate on account of the fact that the referent of *him [+reflexive]* is the direct target of the action *took a picture of,* and therefore the *-self* spelling should have been used. In any case, the anaphor [+reflexive] analysis of personal pronouns in the NP determiner position, as well as in prepositional phrases as in (11.16), was first proposed in Kuno (1972c) explicitly and systematically. Condition B' described here is simply a possible GB rendition of this analysis.

It is now necessary to discuss how Conditions A' and B' apply to the following structures:

(11.23)　a.　[John looked at Mary's picture of him [+reflexive]]
　　　　　b.　[John looked at Mary's picture of him [−reflexive]]

Since NP is no longer a governing category, Condition A' allows for the coindexing of *him [+reflexive]* with *Mary('s),* or, alternatively, with *John.* The first possibility is later rejected on the basis of gender disagreement. The second possibility, on the other hand, is rejected by the chain-of-command principle, which dictates that in (a), only *Mary('s)* controls the reflexive. In the case of (b), Condition B' dictates that *him [−reflexive]* be marked for disjoint reference from both *Mary's* and *John*. Thus it might appear that Condition B' would make it impossible to coindex *John* and *him*. This difficulty can very easily be solved by assuming that what Condition B' represents is a disjoint indexing function, and that this function, just like the coindexing function represented by Condition A', is subject to the chain-of-command principle. This principle dictates that in (11.23b), *Mary('s)*, and not *John*, controls Condition B''s disjoint indexing function. Therefore, *him* is not marked for disjoint reference from *John*, thus allowing for the possibility for coindexing the two NPs.

2.11.3 Condition C

Let us move on to Condition C:

(11.24)   Condition C: An R-expression is free.

The above condition can be paraphrased as "an R-expression cannot be coindexed with an NP that c-commands it." There seem to be two major problems with this condition. First observe the following sentences:

(11.25)   a.   (Bill$_i$ regards Mary as a second-rate mathematician, and Jane as a third-rate philosopher.) Himself$_i$, he$_i$ regards as a first-rate psychologist.
              b.   (Bill$_i$ thinks that Mary is in love with Tóm, and Jane is in love with Jáck.) Hím$_i$, he$_i$ thinks Martha is in love with.

Most speakers consider (a) perfectly acceptable, and many speakers consider (b) acceptable also. This fact turns out to be unexplainable in GB theory. Recall that GB theory attempts to account for the unacceptability of (11.26) by applying Condition C to the trace (empty category) of the fronted *wh*-word:

(11.26)   a.   *Who$_i$ did he$_i$ criticize severely?
              b.   *Who$_i$ did he$_i$ say Mary kissed?
(11.27)   a.   *Who$_i$ [$_s$ he$_i$ did criticize [e]$_i$ severely]
              b.   *Who$_i$ [$_s$ he$_i$ did say Mary kissed [e]$_i$]

Traces are R-expressions. Condition C would bar the coindexing of the empty category with *he* in (11.27a) and (11.27b) because it is c-commanded by the latter.

Similarly, observe the following sentences:

(11.28)   a.   *John$_i$, he$_i$ criticized severely.
              b.   *John$_i$, he$_i$ said Mary kissed.

Regardless of what the derivational history is of these sentences in GB theory, their unacceptability is accounted for in the same fashion as that of

(11.26): Condition C disallows coindexing of the trace with *he,* which c-commands it:[32]

(11.29)   a.   *John$_i$ [$_s$ he$_i$ criticized [e]$_i$ severely]
          b.   *John$_i$ [$_s$ he$_i$ said Mary kissed [e]$_i$]

Now, the same condition would apply to the S-structure (or LF-representation) of (11.25a, b) and would erroneously disallow the coindexing of the trace with *he:*

(11.30)   a.   Himself$_i$ [$_s$ he$_i$ regards [e]$_i$ as a first-rate psychologist]
          b.   Him$_i$ [$_s$ he$_i$ thinks Martha is in love with [e]$_i$]

The contrast between (11.26, 28) and (11.25) is clearly attributable to the fact that while in the former, a full NP (a name, e.g., *John* or a *wh*-expression, e.g., *who*) has been moved crossing over a coreferential NP, in the latter, a pronominal or a reflexive has been moved crossing over a coreferential NP. But trace theory does not distinguish between the trace of a full NP and that of a pronominal or reflexive, and therefore is incapable of distinguishing the two situations. This casts a serious doubt on the very foundation of trace theory.

The second major problem with Condition C is the fact that it is the only rule in Chomsky's binding theory that applies to R-expressions. But before we discuss this problem, let us observe the following sentences:

(11.31)   a.   *John received a letter from her$_i$ about Mary$_i$.
          b.   *In the mail, there was a letter from her$_i$ about Mary$_i$.
          c.   *John has heard from her$_i$ about Mary$_i$.

Coreferential interpretation between *her* and *Mary* is impossible in any of these sentences. Condition C, as it is based on GB's definition of c-command, however, erroneously allows coindexing of *Mary* with *her* because *her* does not c-command *Mary.* It appears as if k-command, rather than c-command, should be the controlling condition for application of Condition C.

There are, however, conflicting pieces of evidence for the above hypothesis. First, observe the following sentences:

(11.32)   a.   *They interviewed her$_i$ about Mary$_i$'s latest discovery.
          b.   ?/??/*They talked with her$_i$ about Mary$_i$'s latest discovery.
(11.33)   a.   *John introduced her$_i$ to Mary$_i$'s new teachers.
          b.   ?/??/*John heard from her$_i$ about Mary$_i$'s new teachers.

The acceptability status of the (b) sentences is subject to wide idiolectal variations, but most speakers consider (b) considerably better than (a), and some consider (b) nearly acceptable. It seems as if this contrast would be explainable only if Condition C is based variably on k-command or c-command depending upon the speaker.[33]

Observe, further, the following sentences:

(11.34) a.   *Him$_i$, John$_i$'s father dislikes bitterly.

        b. $^\vee$/?/??Near him$_i$, John$_i$'s father found a snake.

(11.35) a.   *Him$_i$, John$_i$'s mother thinks Mary is in love with.

        b. $^\vee$/?/??In him$_i$, John$_i$ thinks Mary has full confidence.

Most speakers consider (11.34b) and (11.35b) considerably better than (11.32b) and (11.33b), and some consider them perfectly acceptable. This fact, contrary to (11.31), appears to suggest that c-command, rather than k-command, conditions application of Condition C in some idiolects.

It is clear that the above paradox cannot be resolved as long as we have a single binding condition applying to all occurrences of R-expressions. It can be resolved only if we assume that two different rules apply to R-expressions—one applying to R-expressions in reflexive contexts, as in (11.31), and the other applying to R-expressions in nonreflexive contexts, as in (11.34) and (11.35).[34] The former rule, operating under the k-command condition, marks *Mary* in (11.31a, b, c) for disjoint reference with *her* (as well as with *John* for (a) and (c)) because if it were coreferential with *her*, the reflexive *herself* should have been used. The latter rule, operating variably under the k-command or c-command condition, marks (11.34a) and (11.35a) unacceptable because *him* c-commands *John* in these sentences, but marks (11.34b) and (11.35b) acceptable in some idiolects because *him* does not c-command *John* in these sentences. This still does not explain the contrast between (a) and (b) in (11.32) and (11.33). I will discuss these sentences later on in this section.

2.11.4 Cyclical and S-Structure Binding Conditions

Now we are ready to examine the basic assumption of the binding conditions mentioned in (11.1c), that coreference or lack thereof can be determined by applying *all* of the binding conditions at the same time (to LF-representation, to S-structure, or to both). Observe the following sentences, which we already discussed in section 2.8:

(11.36) a.   *He$_i$ found a snake near John$_i$.

        b.   *Near John$_i$, he$_i$ found a snake.

(11.37) a.   *He$_i$ found a snake near the girl that John$_i$ was talking with.

        b.   Near the girl that John$_i$ was talking with, he$_i$ found a snake.

The above examples show clearly that coreference or disjoint reference should be dealt with at the prefronting stage for reflexive contexts (i.e., clause-mate contexts) and at the postfronting stage otherwise. This is consistent with the proposal given above that Condition C should be split into two parts—one dealing with R-expressions in reflexive contexts and the other dealing with R-expressions in nonreflexive contexts.[35] The former can be collapsed with Condition B'. Below I will restate the proposed revisions of Conditions A, B, and C in a self-contained fashion, not depending upon the concept of "binding" or "governing category," in order to avoid confusion that might arise from differences in the definitions of concepts and to make the formulation more intelligible to those who are not initiated into GB theory. It should be kept in mind that a more radical formulation of Condition A′ which rejects the assumption that anaphors must find antecedents in S will be presented later on in this section.

(11.38)	*Anaphor Rules*	(Cyclical) [Tentative Formulation]
	Condition A′:	A reflexive (as well as a reciprocal) is coindexed in S with a nonreflexive NP that k-commands it. (optional)
	N.B.	An S-structure that contains a reflexive (or a reciprocal) that is not coindexed with any other NP in it is unacceptable. (stranded reflexive rule)
	Condition B′:	A nonreflexive (pronominal or R-expression) is marked for disjoint reference in S with an NP that precedes and k-commands it. (obligatory)
	N.B.	Conditions A′ and B′ are subject to the chain-of-command principle.
(11.39)	*Nonanaphor Rule*	(Postcyclical—applying to the S-structure)[36]
	Condition C′:	An R-expression is variably marked for disjoint reference with an NP that precedes and k-commands it. An R-expression is invariably marked for disjoint reference with an NP that precedes and c-commands it.

I will discuss at the end of this section why Condition A′ must be formulated as an optional rule and why "precedence" must be specified in the conditions. It is assumed here that Conditions A′ and B′ apply cyclically to the structure before fronting, while Condition C′ applies to the S-structure (and not to the LF-representation), and only to the right-hand NP of a pair of NPs whose coreference or disjoint reference has not been established by Conditions A′ and B′.[37] For example, Condition B′ marks *John* of (11.36a) for disjoint reference with *he*. Hence the impossibility of coreferential interpretation of the sentence. Condition B′ also marks *John* of (11.36b) for disjoint reference with *he* at prefronting structure, and hence, Condition C′ cannot apply to this pair of NPs at the postfronting stage. Since there is no possibility for coindexing the two NPs, no coreferential interpretation exists for the sentence. In contrast, Condition B′ is inapplicable to (11.37) because *he* and *John* are not in the same S. Condition C′ applies to this pair at the postfronting stage because their coreference or disjoint reference has not been established. Since *John* is both preceded and k-/c-commanded by *he* in (11.37a), it is marked for disjoint reference with it. On the other hand, in (11.37b), the right-hand NP that is relevant is not an R-expression. Therefore, the coindexing of the two NPs is allowable.

The contrast between the (a) and (b) sentences in (11.34) and (11.35) is now readily explainable. Observe that *him* is not in a reflexive context vis-à-vis *John* at the prefronting stage in any of these sentences. Therefore, there is neither coindexing nor disjoint indexing between the two NPs. After fronting, Condition C' applies. Coindexing is disallowed for (11.34a) and (11.35a) because *him* both precedes and c-commands *John*. In contrast, in (11.34b) and (11.35b), *him* precedes and k-commands, but does not c-command, *John*. The sentences are acceptable or awkward/marginal subject to idiolectal variations in the strength of the k-command constraint for Condition C'.

The acceptability of (11.25a) and (11.25b) is also automatically accounted for now. At the prefronting stage, we have:

(11.40)   a.   He regards himself as a first-rate psychologist.
          b.   He thinks Martha is in love with him.

Condition B' applies to (a) and coindexes *himself* with *he*. Fronting of *himself* does not cancel this coindexing. Hence the acceptability of (11.25a). In contrast, Condition B' does not apply between *he* and *him* in (b) because they are not clause mates. After fronting of *him*, Condition C' applies, but it does not disallow the coindexing of the two NPs because *he*, the right-hand NP, is not an R-expression. Hence the acceptability of (11.25b).

Next observe the following sentences:

(11.41)   a.   John found a snake near him [+reflexive]
          b.   Near him [+reflexive], John found a snake.

Condition A' coindexes *him [+reflexive]* with *John* before fronting of the prepositional phrase. Condition C' does not apply to a pair of NPs which have already been marked for coreference or disjoint reference.

Observe, further, the following sentences:

(11.42)   a.   In a recent portrait of Mary, she found a scratch.
          b.   In a recent portrait of Mary, she looks terribly sick.

Disjoint reference is established between *Mary* and *she* of (11.42a) at the prefronting structure due to Condition B'. Hence, there is no coreferential interpretation of the two NPs for the sentence. In contrast, the prepositional phrase of (11.42b) is a sentential adverb that originates at sentence-initial position from the beginning.[38] Condition B' does not apply because *Mary* and *she* are not clause mates and *Mary* does not k-command *she*, either. Condition C' is inapplicable because the pronoun does not precede *Mary*. Hence the possibility of obtaining a coreferential interpretation between *Mary* and *she*.[39]

Condition B' applies to R-expressions with varying degrees of strength depending upon how deeply embedded they are in the NP structure. When they are not embedded, the obligatoriness of disjoint indexing is absolute. For example, observe the following sentences:

(11.43)   a.   *She$_i$ found a snake near Mary$_i$.
          b.   *Near Mary$_i$, she$_i$ found a snake.
(11.44)   a.   *They interviewed her$_i$ about Mary$_i$ for three hours.
          b.   *About Mary$_i$, they interviewed her$_i$ for three hours.

The unacceptability of (b) shows that the coindexing of *Mary* with *she/her* is marked unacceptable before the fronting of the prepositional phrases, namely, at the stage represented by (a). Similarly, when R-expressions are embedded in nondeterminer position in larger NPs, Condition B′ seems to apply with full force. Observe the following sentences:

(11.45)   a.   Which pictures of John did he like?
          b.   Which picture of the woman John married did he like?
          c.   Which people who John liked did he meet?

As discussed in section 2.8, Chomsky notes that it is much more natural to take *John* and *he* to be coreferential in (b) and (c) than in (a). This fact follows automatically from Condition B′. The two NPs under discussion, *he* and *John,* are not clause mates in (b) and (c), and therefore there is no disjoint indexing at the prefronting stage. Hence the possibility of coreferential interpretation for these sentences. In contrast, they are clause mates in (a), and therefore *John* is obligatorily marked for disjoint reference with *he* at the prefronting stage. If there are speakers who can get a coreferential interpretation for (a), application of Condition B′ is not obligatory for these speakers when the target NP is embedded in nondeterminer position in a larger NP.

When R-expressions are in determiner position of an NP that is embedded in a larger NP, Condition B′ seems to apply optionally for most speakers. For example, observe the following sentences:

(11.46)   a.   *I think she$_i$ liked some of Betty$_i$'s dates.
          b.   Which of Betty$_i$'s dates do you think she$_i$ liked most?

Sentence (b) is acceptable to most speakers. In order to deal systematically with the contrast among (11.43)–(11.46), it is necessary to assume that Condition B′, when it applies to pairs of NPs, assigns an index that represents the "strength" of the disjoint indexing. The more deeply embedded the target NP is within larger NPs, the weaker the strength of disjoint indexing. Condition C′, which applies to S-structure after the fronting of elements that contain the target NPs, would then be allowed to ignore weak disjoint indexing and could assign coindices as long as the "precedence and k-command" constraint is not violated. For example, Condition B′ applies to the embedded clause of (11.46a) and marks *Betty('s)* for disjoint reference with *she*. However, the index that the condition assigns to these NPs indicates that the force of disjoint indexing is weak. After the fronting of *which of Betty's dates,* Condition C′ applies, and is allowed to coindex the two NPs by ignoring the weak disjoint indexing. It goes without saying that if a constituent that contains *Betty('s)* is not fronted, as in (a), Condition C′ is again allowed to apply to the two NPs ignoring the weak disjoint indexing, but it totally disallows coindexing of *Betty('s)* with *she* because the latter both precedes and c-commands the former.

When R-expressions are in determiner position of the largest NP, it seems that there are wide idiolectal variations with respect to the strength of Condition B′. For example, observe the following sentences:

(11.47) a.   *I think he$_i$ dislikes John$_i$'s father bitterly.
         b. $\sqrt{}$/?/??John$_i$'s father, I think he$_i$ dislikes bitterly.
(11.48) a.   *He$_i$ found a snake near John$_i$'s father.
         b. $\sqrt{}$/?/??Near John$_i$'s father, he$_i$ found a snake.
(11.49) a.   *Mary introduced him$_i$ to John$_i$'s new teachers.
         b. $\sqrt{}$/?/??To John$_i$'s new teachers, Mary introduced him$_i$ (with a brief summary of his academic records).

There are speakers who consider the (b) sentences perfectly acceptable and those who consider them as marginal.[40] I attribute these idiolectal variations to idiolectal differences in the strength with which Condition B′ applies to R-expressions when they are in determiner position of major NPs.

In the above examples, if the R-expressions remain in their original position, Condition C′ invariably disallows their coindexing with *he,* which both precedes and c-commands them. This fact stands in marked contrast with the fact that the following (a) sentence is acceptable for some speakers:

(11.50) a.   ?/??/*They talked with her$_i$ about Mary$_i$'s latest discovery for three hours.
         b. $\sqrt{}$/?About Mary$_i$'s latest discovery, they talked with her$_i$ for three hours.

As mentioned already, most speakers consider (11.50a) much better than (11.44a) or (11.49a). This is attributable to the fact that in (11.50a) *her* does not c-command *Mary('s).* Most speakers consider (11.50b) more acceptable than (11.50a). This must be attributable to the fact that while (11.50a) potentially involves violations of two constraints, (11.50b) involves only one. Observe that (11.50b) does not violate Condition C′ at all because the right-hand NP that is relevant is a pronoun and not an R-expression. Therefore, the sentence contains only one possible violation—that of Condition B′ at the prefronting stage for speakers for whom disjoint indexing is (weakly) obligatory for NPs in determiner position of major NPs. In contrast, (11.50a) involves a violation of the k-command constraint of Condition C′ (for speakers who have the constraint), as well as the same violation of Condition B′ that (11.50b) might involve.

The assumption that Condition B′ may not apply obligatorily to R-expressions in determiner position, subject to ideolectal variations, might appear to have difficulty in accounting for the impossibility of coreferential interpretation between *whose* and *he* in the following sentence:

(11.51)   Whose brother did he see?

At the prefronting stage, we have the following structure:

(11.52)   [Q [he did see whose brother]]

Since the R-expression *whose* is in determiner position, it should be the case that Condition B′ need not obligatorily assign disjoint indices between *he* and *whose,* at least in some idiolects. More particularly, those speakers who accept

(11.53)   John$_i$'s father, he$_i$ dislikes bitterly.

should be able to consider (11.51) acceptable, but as far as I know, there are no speakers who do.

I attribute the unacceptability of (11.51) on the coreferential reading partly to the fact that interrogative *wh*-expressions in determiner position cannot ordinarily trigger forward pronominalization. Observe the following sentence:

(11.54)   *Whose$_i$ brother saw him$_i$?

I hypothesize that the unacceptability of (11.54) in turn can be attributable, at least in part, to the constraint that NPs in determiner position, even when they are definite, can trigger pronominalization (forward as well as backward) only when their referents are the topics of the preceding discourse. Justification for this constraint is given in Kuno (1975a). In (11.51) and (11.54), the NPs in determiner position are indefinite, and therefore their referents could not have been the topics of the preceding discourse. Thus, they cannot serve as antecedents for the pronouns that follow them. This fact, together with the fact that (11.53) is unacceptable for many speakers, accounts for the general unacceptability of (11.51).

The above account of the unacceptability of (11.51) receives strong support from the fact that those speakers who accept (11.53) also consider the following sentences acceptable:

(11.55)   a.   Mary$_i$, whose$_i$ mother she$_i$ hated bitterly, decided to leave home.
           b.   The girl$_i$ I am talking about, whose$_i$ little brothers and sisters she$_i$ supports by working as a waitress after school, has told me that she$_i$ does not want to go to college.

These sentences are acceptable to the extent that the head noun can be interpreted as referring to the topic of the preceding discourse. The above fact shows that the unacceptability of (11.51) is primarily a discourse phenomenon, at least for those speakers who accept (11.53), and should not and cannot be accounted for by binding conditions.

2.11.5 **Precedence**

In the above discussion, I have shown that it is not possible to maintain that coreference or lack thereof can be determined by applying all the binding conditions homogeneously at the same time (either to S-structure or to LF-representation). I have shown that Condition B' must apply at the prefronting structure, while Condition C' must apply at the postfronting structure (i.e., at S-structure). Let us now address ourselves to GB's basic assumption, mentioned in (11.1d), that coreference or lack thereof can be determined without reference to the concept of "precedence." Observe, first, the following sentences:

(11.56)   a.   John took out a mirror, and he showed Mary$_i$ herself$_i$.
          b.   *John took out a mirror, and he showed herself$_i$ Mary$_i$.
(11.57)   a.   ?John took out a mirror, and he showed her$_i$ herself$_i$.
          b.   *John took out a mirror, and he showed herself$_i$ herself$_i$.

According to Chomsky's binding conditions, a reflexive is coindexed with an NP that c-commands it within the minimal governing category regardless of whether the latter precedes the reflexive or follows it. Therefore, as far as Condition A is concerned, there is nothing wrong with the coindexing shown in (11.56) and (11.57). What rules out (11.56b) is Condition C, which prevents an R-expression (i.e., *Mary* in this sentence) from being coindexed with an NP that c-commands it (i.e., *herself*). But this latter condition, too, applies whether the NP that c-commands the R-expression precedes or follows it. Therefore, Condition C also blocks the acceptable sentence (11.56a), in which the R-expression *Mary* is c-commanded by *herself*. Similarly, Condition B blocks the coindexing of *her* with *herself* in (11.57a) because the condition dictates that the pronominal *her* must be free from *herself*, which c-commands it within the minimal governing category of the former. In fact, (11.57b) is the only sentence among (11.56a, b) and (11.57a, b) which does not violate any of the binding conditions, but the sentence is totally unacceptable. (An additional stipulation to the effect that an anaphor cannot bind another anaphor would be needed to rule out (11.57b).)

The above observations make clear that the order of the two relevant NPs that are under examination for coindexing or disjoint indexing is significant. The fact that (11.56a) is perfectly acceptable shows that Condition C should apply only when an R-expression is "preceded" by the potential antecedent NP, as in (11.56b), and not when it is followed by the latter. The acceptability or near acceptability of (11.57a) indicates that Condition B should apply only when the pronominal under examination is "preceded" by its potential antecedent, and not when it is followed by the latter.[41]

In my formulations of the binding conditions, (11.56a) is acceptable because the reflexive *herself* is k-commanded by the coindexed clause-mate NP *Mary* (Condition A'), and *Mary*, although it is k-commanded by the coindexed clause-mate NP *herself,* is *not preceded* by it (Condition B'). Example (11.57a) is acceptable or nearly acceptable for the same reasons. On the other hand, (11.56b) is unacceptable, in spite of the fact that the reflexive *herself* is k-commanded by the coindexed clause-mate NP *Mary* (Condition A'), because the nonreflexive *Mary* is both *preceded* and k-commanded by the coindexed clause-mate NP *herself* (Condition B'). Lastly, (11.57b) is unacceptable because the reflexives do not have an independent NP that binds them.[42]

The order-free formulation of Condition A' is justified by the fact that a reflexive can precede its antecedent as long as it does not k-command the latter:

(11.58)   a.   A picture of himself in the morning paper shocked John.
           b.   A rumor about himself that was going around disgusted John.

Note that Condition B' does not block these sentences because the nonreflexive *John,* although it is preceded by the coindexed *himself,* is not k-commanded by it. Incidentally, Chomsky's Condition A, which is based on c-command, is unable to deal with sentences such as the above because the reflexive is not c-commanded by *John.*[43]

Continuing our discussion on whether the binding conditions can be stated without using the concept of "precedence," observe the following sentences:

(11.59)   a.   John received a letter from her$_i$ about herself$_i$ and about Jane.
           b.   John received a letter not in Mary$_i$'s handwriting from her$_i$.
           c.   John received a letter not in Mary$_i$'s handwriting from her$_i$ about herself$_i$ and about Jane.

In order for *herself* to be c-commanded by *her* in (a), it is necessary to get rid of the PP node dominating *from her* either by assuming that PP nodes do not count or by restructuring *receive a letter from* into a V.[44] At the same time, in order to prevent *her* from c-commanding *Mary's* in (b), lest Condition C should block the coindexing of the two NPs, it is necessary to retain the PP node dominating *from her.* It would not do to assume that restructuring is optional and that (b) derives from the structure that has not undergone restructuring because (c), although awkward, seems to be acceptable. Sentence (c) would require restructuring with respect to the coindexing of *her* and *herself* and exclude the possibility for restructuring with respect to the coindexing of *Mary's* and *her.*

Observe that (11.59) poses no difficulty to my formulation of the binding conditions, which are based on "k-command" and "precedence." In (a), *her* and *herself* are clause mates, and the latter is k-commanded by the former. Therefore, Condition A' can coindex the two NPs. In this structure, *herself* k-commands the left-hand *her* but Condition B' does not block the coindexing because *her* is *not preceded by herself.* In (b), *Mary* is not preceded by *her.* Therefore, Condition C' does not block the coindexing of the two NPs. The same coindexing procedure applies to (c). In all the above, there is no need for ad hoc restructuring, and therefore no conflict in the assumptions for restructuring. The above observations disconfirm GB theory's claim that reference can be determined irrespective of the linear order of NPs and firmly establish the need for utilizing the concept of "precedence" in binding conditions.

2.11.6 Optionality of the Anaphor Rule

Finally, let us examine how the proposed Conditions A', B', and C' apply to block a coreferential interpretation between *who* and *he* in the following sentence:

(11.60)   Who did he say Mary kissed?

The underlying structure of the sentence is as shown in (11.61):

(11.61)   [$_{\bar{S}}$ COMP [$_S$ he did say [$_{\bar{S}}$ COMP [$_S$ Mary kissed who]]]]

The fronting of *who* into the COMP position takes place in successive cycles, yielding:

(11.62)   a.   At the end of the lower $\bar{S}$ cycle
                 [$_{\bar{S}}$ COMP [$_S$ he did say [$_{\bar{S}}$ who$_i$ [$_S$ Mary kissed [e]$_i$]]]]
            b.   At the end of the higher $\bar{S}$ cycle
                 [$_{\bar{S}}$ who$_i$ [$_S$ he did say [$_{\bar{S}}$ [e]$_i$ [$_S$ Mary kissed [e]$_i$]]]]

The anaphor rules, being cyclical, apply at each S or $\bar{S}$ cycle, starting from the lower S. When they apply at the higher S structure of (11.62a), they mark *he* and *who* for disjoint reference because the latter is k-commanded by the former and they are in the same simplex S.[45] I here assume that $\bar{S}$ is not a domain-limiting node with respect to binding, and that therefore Condition B' applies to *who* in (11.62a) with *he* in the higher S as its potential antecedent. I will show below that this assumption that $\bar{S}$ is not a domain-limiting node with respect to binding is needed on independent grounds.

First observe the following sentences:

(11.63)   a.   *John$_i$ knew that Mary liked that picture of himself$_i$.
            b.   John$_i$ asked which pictures of himself$_i$ Mary liked most.

Example (11.63a) is clearly unacceptable, but (11.63b) is at least nearly acceptable, and to many speakers it is perfectly acceptable.[46] Let us examine the structure of (11.63b) at two stages of its derivation:

(11.64)   a.   Underlying structure
                 [$_S$ John asked [$_{\bar{S}}$ COMP [$_S$ Mary liked which pictures of himself]]]

   b.   At the end of the $\bar{\text{S}}$-cycle
        [$_S$ John asked [$_{\bar{S}}$ [which pictures of himself]$_i$ [$_S$ Mary liked [e]$_i$]]]

If Condition A′ were to apply obligatorily, it would apply to the lower S cycle
and mark *himself* for coreference with *Mary,* and a later filtering rule would
mark the derived sentence as unacceptable because of gender disagreement.
Condition A′, however, is formulated as an optional condition. Therefore, it
leaves a possibility for not marking *Mary* and *himself* either for coreference or
disjoint reference in this cycle. In the $\bar{\text{S}}$ cycle, the *wh*-expression gets fronted
into the COMP position. In the higher S cycle, Condition A′ applies and optionally coindexes *himself* with *John* because *John* precedes and k-commands
himself in (11.64b). Hence arises a coreferential interpretation between the
two NPs in (11.63b). Note that if $\bar{\text{S}}$ were the absolute boundary for binding, it
would not be possible to coindex *himself* with *John* in (11.64b), and sentence
(11.63b) would be erroneously predicted to be unacceptable.
   Observe, next, the following sentence:

(11.65)   a.   *John$_i$ thought that Mary sold pictures of himself$_i$ to the newspaper.
          b.   Which pictures of himself$_i$ did John$_i$ think that Mary sold to the
               newspaper?

Sentence (11.65a) is clearly unacceptable, but (11.65b) is at least nearly acceptable, and again for many speakers it is perfectly acceptable. Let us examine the structure of (11.65b) at various stages of its derivation:

(11.66)   a.   Underlying structure
               [$_{\bar{S}}$ COMP [$_S$ John did think [$_{\bar{S}}$ COMP [$_S$ Mary sold which pictures of
               himself to the newspaper]]]]
          b.   At the end of the lower $\bar{\text{S}}$ cycle
               [$_{\bar{S}}$ COMP [$_S$ John did think [$_{\bar{S}}$ [which pictures of himself]$_i$ [$_S$ Mary
               sold [e]$_i$ to the newspaper]]]]
          c.   At the end of the higher $\bar{\text{S}}$ cycle
               [$_{\bar{S}}$ [which pictures of himself]$_i$ [$_S$ John did think [$_{\bar{S}}$ [e]$_i$ [$_S$ Mary sold
               [e]$_i$ to the newspaper]]]]

If Condition A′ is optionally not applied to the lower S cycle, *himself* remains
uncoindexed with *Mary.* In the lower $\bar{\text{S}}$ cycle, the successive-cyclical fronting
of the *wh*-expression takes place, yielding the structure shown in (b). In the
higher S cycle, Condition A′ applies, and (optionally) coindexes *himself* with
John because the latter precedes and k-commands the former in (b). Hence
arises a coreferential interpretation of the two NPs in (11.65b). Here again, if
$\bar{\text{S}}$ were the absolute boundary for binding, the acceptability of (11.65b) would
not be explainable.
   The acceptability of (11.63b) and (11.65b) raises two serious problems
with GB theory. First, there is no way in the current formulation of the bind-

ing conditions to account for the acceptability of (11.63b) and (11.65b) and for that of (11.67a, b) at the same time.

(11.67) a. John asked which pictures of herself$_i$ Mary$_i$ liked most.
       b. Which pictures of herself$_i$ did John think that Mary$_i$ sold to the newspaper?

In order for Condition A to be able to coindex *herself* to *Mary*, the rule must apply to the structure in which we have

(11.68) a. [Mary liked which pictures of herself most]
       b. [Mary sold which pictures of herself to the newspaper]

At the same time, in order for Condition A to be able to coindex *himself* to *John* in (11.63b) and (11.65b), the rule must apply to the structure in which the *wh*-expressions have been fronted out of the above S structures. It seems that the above two apparently conflicting requirements can be satisfied only by assuming that Condition A applies *cyclically* and *optionally*.

However, Condition B', which is a disjoint reference rule for clause-mate contexts, still needs to be made to apply obligatorily. To see this, observe the following structures:

(11.69) a. [Q [$_S$ John does think [COMP [$_S$ she sold which pictures of Mary to . . .]]
       b. [Q [$_S$ John does think [which pictures of Mary [$_S$ she sold e . . .]]]]
       c. *Which pictures of Mary$_i$ does John think she$_i$ sold to the newspaper?

Condition B', when it applies to the lower S of (a), marks *she* and *Mary* for disjoint reference. But if this rule were to apply optionally, we would obtain the structure (b), in which *Mary* and *she* are not yet marked for disjoint reference. From here on, no rule would be able to mark the two NPs for disjoint reference. Therefore, it is important that Condition B' be made to apply obligatorily on the first opportunity that it is applicable.

The optionality of Condition A' proposed above requires one important proviso. Hasegawa (1983) contrasts (11.63b) and (11.65b) with sentences of the following type:[47]

(11.70) a. *How fond of himself did George think that Susan was?
       b. *Proud of himself though George knows that Susan is, . . .

He observes that the difference between (11.63b, 65b) and (11.70a, b) lies in the fact that in the latter the reflexive and its possible antecedent were "cycle mates." Observe the following lower S structure for (11.65b) and (11.70a):

(11.71) a. . . . [$_S$ Mary sold [$_{NP}$ which pictures of himself] to the newspaper]
       b. . . . [$_S$ Susan was [$_{AP}$ how fond of himself]]

Hasegawa then proposes the following hypothesis:

(11.72)   The reflexive interpretive rule, which generally applies optionally, must apply obligatorily when the reflexive is a "cycle mate" of a possible controller.

Note that in (11.71a) *Mary* and *himself* are not cycle mates because the latter is under the cyclical node NP, while in (11.71b), *Susan* and *himself* are cycle mates because AP is not a cyclical node. It seems clear that Hasegawa's condition needs to be incorporated into Condition A'.

The second point that the above discussion has made clear is the necessity to make the COMP position under $\bar{S}$ a clause-mate (S mate) position to the constituents of the immediately higher S. This assumption makes it possible to mark *he* and *who* of (11.62a) for disjoint reference (via Condition B') at the higher S cycle, and makes it possible to account for the impossibility of a coreferential interpretation between *who* and *he* of (11.60). It also makes it possible to coindex *himself* with *John* in (11.64b) and (11.66b).

The assumption that $\bar{S}$ is not a domain-limiting category for the purpose of defining governing category is implicit in Chomsky (1981) in spite of his explicit claim that "NP and $\bar{S}$ are absolute boundaries to government" (1981, p. 163). Observe the following sentences, which are patterned after Chomsky's examples:

(11.73)   a.   *They made sure $[_{\bar{S}}$ that $[_S$ Mary would pay for $[_{NP}$ pictures of themselves]]].
          b.   They made sure $[_{\bar{S}}$ that $[_S$ $[_{NP}$ pictures of themselves] would be printed in the newspaper]].

Chomsky argues that the acceptability status of (a) and (b) can be explained by the "accessible SUBJECT" requirement for the definition of "governing category" for anaphors. That is, the governing category of *themselves* in (a) is not the NP that dominates the picture noun because this NP does not have an accessible SUBJECT but the S for the complement clause, in which *Mary* is a SUBJECT that is accessible to the reflexive. Condition A dictates that the reflexive be bound within this S, and thus forces the reflexive to be coindexed with *Mary*. Hence, (11.73a) is ungrammatical. In contrast in (b), the S that dominates the complement clause does not have a SUBJECT that is accessible to *themselves* due to the i-within-i condition against coindexing:

(11.74) $[\gamma \ldots \delta]$, where γ and δ bear the same index, is ungrammatical. (Chomsky 1981, p. 212)

Therefore, the governing category for the reflexive in (11.73b) is neither the NP that dominates the picture noun, nor the S that dominates the complement clause, but it is the S for the main clause. It is argued that the sentence is acceptable because the reflexive is bound within this main clause S. The same explanation has been given for the acceptability of sentences such as the following:

(11.75)   They made sure that pictures of each other would be printed in the newspaper.

Implicit in the above explanation is the assumption that $\overline{S}$ does not constitute an absolute boundary to government. Observe, further, the following sentences:

(11.76)   a. *They think (that) it bothered each other that . . .
          b. They think it is a pity that pictures of each other are hanging on the wall.

Chomsky (1981, pp. 214–215) attempts to explain the above contrast by claiming that in (a), *it* is a SUBJECT that is accessible to the reciprocal, which it is not in (b). That is, Chomsky argues that if *it* were accessible to *each other* in (b), and were coindexed with it, a violation of the i-within-i principle stated in (11.74) would result:

(11.77)   *They think [it$_i$ is a pity [$_i$ that pictures of each other$_i$ are hanging on the wall]]

Thus, in (11.76b), the governing category of *each other* is not the S for the complement clause but the S for the main clause.

The above explanation of (11.73), (11.75), and (11.76) might appear to demonstrate the explanatory power of the binding theory especially as it relates to the concepts of "accessible SUBJECT" and the i-within-i condition against coindexing. However, further examination of related facts shows that it has not captured the essence of what is going on in these sentences. To see this, observe the following sentences:

(11.78)   a. They made sure that it was clear to each other that this needed to be done immediately.
          b. They made sure that nothing would prevent each other's pictures from being put on sale.
          c. They made sure that that wouldn't prevent each other's pictures from being put on sale.[48]

It seems that these sentences are acceptable to most speakers. In (a), the dummy subject *it* is an accessible SUBJECT for *each other* because the latter is not contained in the that-clause. In this respect, the sentence has the same structure as (11.76a), which is unacceptable. This shows that Chomsky's explanation of the unacceptability of (11.76a) cannot be maintained. Similarly, in (11.78b), *nothing* is clearly a SUBJECT that is accessible to the reciprocal. The fact that the sentence is acceptable shows that the extension of the domain of governing category based on the "accessible SUBJECT" requirement does

not go far enough. Likewise, in (11.78c), the demonstrative *that*, which refers to a previously mentioned event or state, clearly constitutes an accessible
SUBJECT, but *each other* need not be bound within this complement S.

2.11.7 Extension of the Domain of Anaphor Binding

Now I am ready to present a radical proposal that replaces the clause-mate
condition for anaphors that is embodied in Condition A'. The fact that (11.78a,
b, c) are acceptable shows that neither purely syntactic attempt—GB's to extend the domain of anaphor binding by adding an "accessible SUBJECT" requirement for governing category nor that represented in Condition A' to extend the domain by removing NP from the set of governing categories—has
gone far enough. It seems necessary to extend the domain of anaphor binding extensively by letting an anaphor be coindexed freely with NPs that
(k-)command it. According to this approach, the reflexives and reciprocals in
(11.73a, b), (11.75), (11.76a), and (11.78a, b, c) are all coindexable to the
main clause subject *they*.[49] Then a semantico-syntactic chain-of-command
principle will apply to filter out sentences in which a weak controller for control of anaphors has been chosen over a much stronger potential controller for
coindexing. It seems that at least the following two scales for control are
needed:

(11.79)   A.   *Syntactic Scale*
                The control of the subject of a verb for anaphor binding varies in
                strength according to the syntactic role of the anaphor:
                    Strongest: The verb's direct object anaphor
                    Middle: Object-of-preposition anaphor
                    Weakest: Picture noun anaphor
          B.   *Semantic Scale*
                The control of an NP for anaphor binding varies in strength ac-
                cording to the semantic/discourse nature of that potential con-
                troller NP:
                    Strongest: Definite animate NP
                    Middle: Definite inanimate NP
                    Weakest: Dummy *it*, indefinite unspecific pronouns (e.g.,
                                 nothing, anything, nobody, anybody), *that* for
                                 previously mentioned event/state

The above scales are crude first approximations, and much further work is
clearly needed. And I am not excluding the possibility that there might be
other scales of different planes. I can only show here the general direction of
the approach that must be taken in order to account for the facts observed
above.

Now I am ready to reexamine our crucial sentences. Sentence (11.73a)

(11.73)   a.   *They made sure [s̄ that [s Mary would pay for [NP pictures of themselves]]].

is unacceptable because the chain-of-command principle dictates that *Mary* be the controller for the reflexive: note that *Mary,* as a definite animate NP, is a strong controller for the reflexives. Sentence (11.76a)

(11.76)   a.   *They think (that) it bothered each other that . . .

is unacceptable because the dummy subject *it* strongly controls an anaphor in the direct object position. On the other hand, (11.78a) is acceptable partly because the dummy subject *it* does not strongly control an anaphor in the object-of-preposition position, and partly because the dummy *it* in itself is an extremely weak controller. Sentences (11.78b, c) are acceptable partly because the lower subject only weakly controls picture noun anaphors and partly because *nothing* and *that* are weak controllers for anaphor binding in themselves.

There are at least two other factors that seem to interact with the anaphor-binding phenomenon under discussion. First, as already mentioned (cf. n. 25 of this section), sentences involving reciprocals are the best when they represent actions or states involving reciprocal interactions. For example, compare the following pairs of sentences:

(11.80)   a.   They agreed to commit suicide on each other's birthdays.
          b.   ??They passed away on each other's birthdays.
(11.81)   a.   They went to each other's prospective funeral homes.
          b.   *After the autopsy, they were taken to each other's funeral homes by mistake.

The (a) sentences involve reciprocal interactions between the referents of the antecedents of *each other,* while the (b) sentences do not. In other words, in the (b) sentences, the referents of *they* were not aware that an event took place that involved the two reciprocally. Now, sentences involving reciprocals in embedded clauses seem to be acceptable to the extent that they readily imply "awareness," on the part of the referents of the antecedents of *each other,* of the reciprocity of the actions represented. For example, (11.76b) seems to predominantly imply either that (i) the speaker hears a conversation between A and B—"A: I think it is a pity that your picture is hanging on the wall. B: I think it is a pity that YOUR picture is hanging on the wall."—or (ii) that A and B were both present when they said to the speaker, "A: I think it is a pity that B's picture is hanging on the wall. B: I think it is a pity that A's picture is hanging on the wall." The sentence does not seem to imply that A has told the speaker that it is a pity that B's picture is hanging on the wall, and B, that it is a pity that A's picture is hanging on the wall, with A and B not knowing that the other has an opposite view about the pictures. Thus, compare the following two sentences:

(11.82) a.   They made sure that it was clear to each other that this needed to be done immediately.
         b.   ??They think it is clear to each other that this needs to be done.

For many speakers, (b) is considerably less acceptable than (a). This must be owing to the fact that there is no hint in (b) that indicates awareness, on the part of the referent of *they*, of the reciprocity of the thinking. From this point of view, there is no wonder that (11.76a), which is Chomsky's, is totally unacceptable. Compare the sentence with (11.83b):

(11.83) a.   *They think (that) it bothered each other that . . . (= 11.76a)
         b.   ?/??They made sure that it wouldn't bother each other to invite their respective friends to dinner.

Although (b) is still marginal (due to the fact that *it* strongly controls the direct object anaphor), it is considerably better than (a).[50]

The "awareness" or "mutual interaction" constraint that reciprocals are subject to seems to be a key to accounting for some of the facts that have mystified researchers or that have received imperfect analysis. Observe, for example, the following sentences:

(11.84) a.   They told us about each other.
         b.   They told us that each other's pictures were in the newspapers.

It is claimed that it is difficult to obtain the interpretation for each of the above sentences in which the object *us* binds the reciprocal. On the basis of such sentences, it has been observed that the subject is a much stronger controller for anaphors than the object. I do not deny this generalization because I have been claiming the same since Kuno and Kaburaki (1975). However, the difficulty of obtaining the object reference interpretation for (11.84) is far more pronounced than the difficulty for obtaining the object reference interpretation (i.e., "himself = Bill") for the following sentences:

(11.85) a.   John talked to Bill about himself.
         b.   John told Bill that there was a picture of himself in the morning paper.

Therefore, there must be another, stronger reason for the difficulty in obtaining the object reference interpretation for *each other* in (11.84a, b). I attribute it to the fact that the "awareness" or "mutual interaction" constraint is easily fulfilled when the reciprocal refers to the *subject* because a "reciprocal action by mutual consent" interpretation is readily available, while it is not easily fulfilled when the reciprocal refers to the object because the referents of the object do not ordinarily control the agent's action. Therefore, one has to come up with a more complex context in which the action represented is reciprocal, and that reciprocity is recognized as such by the referents of the reciprocal. To see this point, compare (11.84a, b) with the following sentences:

(11.86) a. They reminded the twins of each other's need for independence.
         b. They told the twins that each other's contributions should not be forgotten.

Now, it is very easy to obtain the object reference interpretation (i.e., *each other* = *the twins*) for these sentences. The reason for this seems to be clear: it is easy to visualize the situation for (11.86a, b) in which the referents of *they* were addressing the twins in such a way as to produce a mutual interaction between the two. For example, imagine the following conversation:

(11.87) (The counselors are talking to the twins John and Bill.)
         John, you have to honor Bill's need for independence, and you, Bill, you have to honor John's need for independence.

In such a context, the referents of the reciprocal are aware of the reciprocity of the action represented by the sentence. Hence the acceptability of (11.86a) with *each other* referring to *the twins*. The same explanation applies to the acceptability of (11.86b) with the object reference interpretation of the reciprocal. But then, the fact that the object reference interpretation of the reciprocal is difficult or impossible for some speakers for (11.84a, b) must be attributed primarily to the fact that there is little in the sentences which implies that the "awareness" or "mutual interaction" constraint was fulfilled by the events that are described by the sentences.[51]

I have shown above that one of the factors that control anaphor binding is the "awareness" or "mutual interaction" constraint for reciprocals. The second factor that interacts with anaphor binding is the fact that anaphors are not a unitary phenomenon with respect to the strength of the chain-of-command principle; the reflexives are subject to it more rigidly than are the reciprocals. For example, compare the following pairs of sentences:

(11.88) a. They made sure that it was clear to each other that this needed to be done.
         b. ?They made sure that it was clear to themselves that this needed to be done.
(11.89) a. ?/??They made sure that it wouldn't bother each other to invite their respective friends to dinner. (= 11.83b)
         b. *They made sure that it wouldn't wear themselves out to invite their friends to dinner.

All of the above observations point to the conclusion that the phenomenon under discussion can be dealt with best by overgenerating first and filtering out unacceptable sentences via the chain-of-command principle and other semantico-syntactic constraints. It seems that it is a mistake to treat it as an all-or-nothing phenomenon, as the present GB treatment seems to. Of course, if the concept of "accessible SUBJECT" is modified in such a way as to make it possible to talk about "degrees of accessibility," and if Condition A is modified in such a way as to make it possible to go up to a higher governing category if the SUBJECT of the minimal governing category is only weakly accessible, then the difference between the GB analysis and the one proposed here disappears. But this would be a significant departure from the current position taken in binding theory.

The above discussion leads to the following reformulation of Condition A':

(11.90)   *Condition A'* (Revised):   An anaphor is coindexed with a nonreflexive NP that k-commands it. (optional)

        N.B.1:   An S-structure that contains an anaphor that has not been coindexed with any other NP in it is unacceptable. (stranded anaphor (reflexive) rule)

        N.B.2:   Anaphors are subject to the semantico-syntactic chain-of-command principle (as outlined in (11.79)), with the principle applying more strongly to reflexives than to reciprocals.

In the above formulation, Hasegawa's requirement for obligatory application of the reflexive interpretive rule when the reflexive is a "cycle mate" of a possible controller (as stated in (11.72)) has been subsumed under the chain-of-command principle. Note that if *fond of* can be regarded as a composite transitive adjective such that the object of preposition *of* can be reinterpreted as its "direct object," then the obligatory application of Condition A' between *Susan* and *himself* in

(11.91)   . . . [$_S$ Susan was [$_{AP}$ how fond of himself]]

can be explained by the fact that *Susan*, as the subject of *be fond-of*, controls the direct object anaphor *himself* to the strongest degree (cf. 11.79A).

It is only the domain of application of Condition A' that is extended. The domain of application of Condition B', which obligatorily marks a nonreflexive for disjoint reference with an NP that precedes and k-commands it, must be limited to the minimal S that contains the nonreflexive. This is because of sentences such as the following:

(11.92)   a.   John$_i$ liked the girl he$_i$ met at the party.
        b.   John$_i$ remembered the day when he$_i$ met Mary for the first time.

If the domain of application of Condition B' were made as open-ended as that of Condition A', Condition B' would apply to *he* in the above sentences and mark it for disjoint reference from *John* in the absence of an NP that would block this disjoint indexing on the basis of the chain-of-command principle. It is necessary to limit the domain of Condition B' so that the pronoun in these sentences can be left free within the relative clause. The ensuing asymmetry between the domain of Condition A' and that of Condition B' partly reflects the fact that pronouns and reflexives do not in fact show complementary distributions.[52]

In this section, I have shown that each of the five assumptions in GB's binding theory needs to be abandoned and be replaced by assumptions that better reflect the coreference facts in language. More particularly, I have made the following proposals:

(11.93)   (a) *Governing category:* The assumption that there is a syntactically well-definable domain called "governing category" in which anaphors must find their antecedents must be abandoned. It is necessary to make the domain of anaphor binding open-ended, and let a semantico-syntactic chain-of-command principle yield an "NP-mate" and "clause-mate" effect.

      (b) *C-command:* It is not possible to claim that c-command is the only command concept needed for determining coreference or disjoint reference. While c-command is needed for a nonanaphor rule (Condition C'), k-command is needed both for anaphor rules (Conditions A' and B'), and for a nonanaphor rule (Condition C').

      (c) *Precedence:* It is not possible to determine coreference or lack thereof without referring to the linear order of NPs.

      (d) *Homogeneity:* It is not possible to maintain that all of the binding conditions apply at the same time to S-structure, to LF-representation, or to both. It is necessary to let anaphor rules (Conditions A' and B') apply cyclically and a nonanaphor rule (Condition C') apply to S-structure.

      (e) *Obligatoriness:* It is necessary to assume that the anaphor-binding rule applies optionally.

The above proposals, if adopted, constitute a major revision to GB theory. If some of the suggestions cannot be accommodated in GB theory as they are, alternative ways to handle them that are consistent with the basic foundation of the theory must be sought.

3 Direct Discourse Perspective

3.1 **A New Rule Ordering Paradox**

We saw in the preceding chapter that Lakoff's rule ordering paradox can be solved by assuming that clause-mate rules for reflexivization apply cyclically and blindly, so that given

(1.1) a.   [He saw a snake near John]
       b.   [He saw a snake near the girl [John was talking with]]

Condition B', which marks a pronominal or R-expression for disjoint reference with an NP within the same S that precedes and k-commands it, disallows coindexing of *he* and *John* in (1.1a) because they are clause mates, but the condition does not apply between *he* and *John* in (1.1b) because they are not clause mates. After adverb fronting, we obtain

(1.2) a.   *[Near John$_i$, he$_i$ saw a snake]
       b.   [Near the girl John was talking with, he saw a snake]

There is no possibility of interpreting *John* and *he* of (1.2a) as coreferential, but it is possible to coindex *John* and *he* of (1.2b) because Condition C', which marks an R-expression (e.g., a full NP) for disjoint reference with an NP that precedes and k-commands it, does not apply to (1.2b).

There are, however, some rule ordering paradoxes that cannot be solved in the same way. Observe the following set of sentences:

(1.3) a.   The students who studied with John$_i$ adored him$_i$.
       b.   The students who studied with him$_i$ adored John$_i$.
(1.4) a.   John$_i$ was adored by the students who studied with him$_i$.
       b.   *He$_i$ was adored by the students who studied with John$_i$.

The above sentences can be accounted for by assuming that Condition C' applies, as it should, to the surface structure (i.e., to the S-structure in GB theory) of these sentences. That is, (1.4b) is ruled out because *he* both precedes and k-commands *John,* but (1.3a), (1.3b), and (1.4a) are allowed because the precede/k-command condition is not met in these sentences.

Similarly, observe the following sentences:

(1.5) a.   John$_i$ repeatedly betrayed those who trusted him$_i$.
       b.   *He$_i$ repeatedly betrayed those who trusted John$_i$.

(1.6)   a.   Those who trusted him$_i$ were betrayed by John$_i$ repeatedly.
      b.   Those who trusted John$_i$ were betrayed by him$_i$ repeatedly.

The acceptability of (1.5a, 1.6a, b) and the unacceptability of (1.5b) is consistent with the hypothesis that Condition C′ (a pronominalization rule) applies to the surface structure of passive sentences: in the above sentences, only (1.5b) has a pronoun that both precedes and k-commands *John* in the surface structure.

The above two sets of data firmly establish that pronominalization (Condition C′) applies to the surface structure. With this in mind, let us now examine the following sentences:

(1.7)   a.   Ali$_i$ repeatedly claimed that he$_i$ was the best boxer in the world.   *that*
      b.   *He$_i$ repeatedly claimed that Ali$_i$ was the best boxer in the world.
(1.8)   a.   ??That Ali$_i$ was the best boxer in the world was claimed by him$_i$ repeatedly.
      b.   (?)That he$_i$ was the best boxer in the world was claimed by Ali$_i$ repeatedly.   — *attributed to heavy sentential subjects*

If pronominalization applies to the surface structure of passive sentences, (1.8a) should be acceptable because *he* does not even precede *Ali* in this sentence. But the sentence is marginal at best, and unacceptable for most speakers. In contrast, (1.8b), although not impeccable, is considerably better than (1.8a).[1] This suggests that passive sentences involving pronouns and full NPs are acceptable or unacceptable depending upon whether the corresponding active sentences are acceptable or unacceptable. But this hypothesis diametrically opposes the hypothesis arrived at before on the basis of (1.3)–(1.6)— that is, passive sentences involving pronouns and full NPs are unacceptable or acceptable depending upon whether the pronoun does or does not both precede and k-command the full NP in the surface structure.

Similarly, observe the following sentences:

(1.9)   a.   John mentioned to Mary$_i$ that she$_i$ was in line for promotion.
      b.   *John mentioned to her$_i$ that Mary$_i$ was in line for promotion.
(1.10) a.   ?*That Mary$_i$ was in line for promotion was mentioned to her$_i$ by John.   *on several occasions*
      b.   ?That she$_i$ was in line for promotion was mentioned to Mary$_i$ by John.

Example (1.10b) is awkward, but it is considerably better than (1.10a). Again, if pronominalization applies to the surface structure, (1.10a) should be acceptable because *she* does not precede *Mary*.

Here we have what appears to be a new rule ordering paradox. The facts of (1.3)–(1.6) dictate that pronominalization (i.e., Condition C′) apply to the surface structure of passive sentences. On the other hand, the facts of (1.7)–(1.10) dictate that pronominalization apply not to the surface structure of passive sentences but to the structure of the corresponding active sentences. Furthermore, this paradox does not seem to have anything to do with Lakoff's paradox, which originated with the contrast between simplex sentence structures (e.g., *near him/John*) and complex sentence structures (e.g., *near the girl he/John was talking with*).

The same kind of rule ordering paradox can be constructed with pronominalization and topicalization sentence patterns. First observe the following sentences:

(1.11) a. The students who have studied with this professor$_i$ all praise him$_i$ lavishly.
        b. The students who have studied with him$_i$ all praise this professor$_i$ lavishly.
(1.12) a. This professor$_i$, the students who have studied with him$_i$ all praise lavishly.
        b. *Him$_i$, the students who have studied with this professor$_i$ all praise lavishly.

The unacceptability of (1.12b) can be accounted for if we assume that pronominalization applies to the surface structure of the topicalization sentence pattern. Likewise, observe the following sentences:

(1.13) a. This professor$_i$ always lavishly recommends for teaching appointments the students that he$_i$ has personally taught.
        b. *He$_i$ always lavishly recommends for teaching appointments the students that this professor$_i$ has personally taught.
(1.14) a. The students that this professor$_i$ has personally taught, he$_i$ lavishly recommends for teaching appointments.
        b. The students that he$_i$ has personally taught, this professor$_i$ lavishly recommends for teaching appointments.

The acceptability of both (1.14a) and (1.14b) shows again that pronominalization applies to the surface structure of the topicalization sentences.

But now observe the following sentences:

(1.15) a. Bill$_i$ revealed for the first time that he$_i$ had cancer.
        b. *He$_i$ revealed for the first time that Bill$_i$ had cancer.
(1.16) a. *That Bill$_i$ had cancer, he$_i$ revealed for the first time.
        b. That he$_i$ had cancer, Bill$_i$ revealed for the first time.

If pronominalization applies to the surface structure of the topicalization sentences, (1.16a) should be acceptable because the pronoun does not precede the full NP in this sentence. The fact that this sentence is unacceptable suggests that pronominalization applies to the pretopicalization structure. Observe that the acceptability status of the topicalization sentences of (1.16) exactly parallels that of the corresponding sentences without topicalization in (1.15).

We have here what appears to be another rule ordering paradox. As we have seen, the data given in (1.11)–(1.14) lead us to hypothesize that pronominalization should apply to the surface structure of topicalization sentences. On the other hand, the data given in (1.15) and (1.16) lead us to hypothesize that it should apply to the corresponding structures without topicalization.

In the following sections of this chapter, I will attempt to give a functional explanation of why (1.8a), (1.10a), and (1.16a) are unacceptable and propose a mechanism for incorporating this functional explanation into the theory of grammar.

3.2 Direct Discourse Perspective

It has long been recognized that pronominal and reflexive forms show peculiar behavior in indirect discourse clauses. For example, in Latin, a reflexive pronoun, instead of a personal pronoun, appears in a subordinate clause in indirect discourse representations:

(2.1)   Petiērunt ut   *sibi*   licēret.
          begged   so-that to-self be-allowed
          'They begged that it might be allowed them.'
(2.2)   Iccius nūntium mittit, nisi   subsidium *sibi*   submittātur . . .
                message sends   unless support   to-self is-furnished
          'Iccius sends a message that unless relief be furnished him, . . .'

Allen and Greenough (1883/1903, p. 181) characterize the condition for the use of reflexive pronouns in subordinate clauses in the following way:

> If the subordinate clause expresses the words or thought of the subject of the main clause, the reflexive is regularly used to refer to the subject . . . Sometimes the person or thing to which the reflexive refers is not the grammatical subject of the main clause, though it is in effect the subject of discourse . . . If the subordinate clause does not express the words or thought of the main subject, the reflexive is not regularly used, though it is occasionally found.

As we will see later, there are many other languages which show similar characteristics with respect to the use of reflexive pronouns.

I have shown in the preceding section that the following contrast exists:

(2.3)   a.   Those who trusted John$_i$ were betrayed by him$_i$ repeatedly.
          b.   Those who trusted him$_i$ were betrayed by John$_i$ repeatedly.
(2.4)   a.   ??That Ali$_i$ was the best boxer in the world was claimed by him$_i$ repeatedly.
          b.   (?)That he$_i$ was the best boxer in the world was claimed by Ali$_i$ repeatedly.

We can note here that the subordinate clause in (2.3) has nothing to do with anything that John said, while in (2.4) the subordinate clause is the indirect discourse representation of what Ali said, which could have been:

(2.5)   "I am the best boxer in the world."

I hypothesized in Kuno (1972b) that the underlying structures of sentences such as (2.4) have their complement clauses in a direct discourse representation. Thus, I hypothesized that the derivation of (2.4) would start with the following underlying structure:

(2.6)   [Ali claimed ["I am the best boxer in the world"]]

Rules for indirect discourse formation apply and take care of the tense and person agreements:

(2.7)   Ali claimed that *he was* the best boxer in the world.

As shown in (2.7), the first-person pronoun *I* gets changed into *he* in agreement with *Ali,* the main clause subject. There are no transformations which would change *I* to *Ali,* and hence there is no way to use *Ali* in this position. This explains the ungrammaticality of (2.4a).

Observe, next, the following sentences:

(2.8)   a. ??The statement that Churchill$_i$ was vain was often made to him$_i$.
         b. The statement that he$_i$ was vain was often made to Churchill$_i$.
(2.9)   a. The statement that Churchill$_i$ was vain has often been made about him$_i$.
         b. The statement that he$_i$ was vain has often been made about Churchill$_i$.

The above two sets of sentences have identical surface structures. In spite of this fact, (2.8a) is marginal or unacceptable, while (2.9a) is perfectly acceptable. From the point of view of what was actually said to or about Churchill, these two sets of sentences have very different structures. Examples (2.8) and (2.9) would correspond to (2.10a) and (2.10b), respectively.

(2.10)   a. [People often made to Churchill the statement ["*You* are vain"]]
          b. [People have often made about Churchill$_i$ the statement ["Churchill$_i$ is vain"]]

In (2.10a), indirect discourse formation will change *you* to *he* in agreement with *Churchill.* There are no transformations for changing *you* to unpronominal *Churchill.* Thus, (2.8a) is underivable, and hence the marginality/unacceptability of the sentence. On the other hand, *Churchill,* the subject of the complement in (2.10b), may or may not be pronominalized, depending upon what later word order change might take place. This accounts for the acceptability of (2.9a).

Likewise, observe the following sentences:

(2.11)   a.   John$_i$ anticipated that he$_i$ would be elected.
          b.   *He$_i$ anticipated that John$_i$ would be elected.
          c.   *That John$_i$ would be elected was anticipated by him$_i$.
          d.   (?)That he$_i$ would be elected was anticipated by John$_i$.

I hypothesized in Kuno (1972) that these sentences, too, were derived from an underlying structure that contained a direct discourse complement:

(2.12)   [John anticipated ["*I* will be elected"]]

This structure obligatorily undergoes indirect discourse formation. *I* becomes *he* due to person agreement. There is no way for it to be realized as *John*. Hence the unacceptability of (c). Whether a given verb must or need not undergo indirect discourse formation is an idiosyncratic feature that must be specified in the lexicon. For example, according to the analysis under discussion, verbs such as the following would require obligatory indirect discourse formation:

(2.13)   a.   John anticipates that he will be elected.
          b.   *John anticipates, "I will be elected."
(2.14)   a.   John claims that he is the best carpenter around.
          b.   *John claims, "I am the best carpenter around."
(2.15)   a.   John feels that he has been cheated.
          b.   *John feels, "I have been cheated."

In contrast, in the analytical framework under discussion, the following would allow optional inapplication of indirect discourse formation:

(2.16)   a.   John said to Mary that he loved her.
          b.   John said to Mary, "I love you."
(2.17)   a.   John answered that he was not feeling well.
          b.   John answered, "I am not feeling well."
(2.18)   a.   John wonders whether this is correct.
          b.   John wonders, "Is this correct?"

The explanation for the unacceptability of (2.4a), (2.8a), and (2.11c) and for the acceptability of (2.4b), (2.8b), and (2.11d) that I have presented above can be informally formulated as in the following:

(2.19)   *Logophoric Pronoun Rule* (tentative): When a given complement clause represents the thought of a main clause constituent NP, or the utterance transmitted by or to such an NP, an NP in that complement clause cannot be realized as a nonpronominal (nonreflexive) NP if it corresponds to the first or second person in the direct discourse representation of the complement clause.

The term "logophoric" can be taken as meaning "pertaining to the speaker/hearer."

The direct discourse analysis outlined above gets into difficulty in accounting for sentences such as the following:

(2.20) a.   John$_i$ claimed that Mary$_j$ believed that he$_i$ was in love with her$_j$.
        b.   *That John$_i$ was in love with her$_j$, he$_i$ claimed that Mary$_j$ believed.
        c.   ??That he$_i$ was in love with Mary$_j$, John$_i$ claimed that she$_j$ believed.

The complement clause of *John claimed,* from John's point of view, is

(2.21) [John claimed, "[Mary$_j$ believes that I am in love with her$_j$]"]

However, *believes* in the complement clause of (2.21) is also a direct discourse verb, and therefore its complement clause must be in direct discourse representation, as shown below:

(2.22) [John$_i$ claimed, "[Mary$_j$ believes, "[John$_i$ is in love with me$_j$]"]"]

Now, in order to account for the unacceptability of (2.20b), we need to refer to the putative underlying structure shown in (2.21), in which the first-person pronoun *I* appears in reference to *John.* But in order to account for the unacceptability of (2.20c), we need to refer to the underlying structure shown in (2.22), in which the first-person *me* appears in reference to *Mary.* But since (2.22) has *John,* instead of *I,* as the subject of the most deeply embedded clause, it would not be able to block the derivation of (2.20b).

It seems that the way to solve the above problem is to hypothesize that relevant NP arguments (e.g., the subject, direct object, indirect object, etc.) of direct discourse verbs are marked with respect to whether they represent the speaker or the experiencer of the words or thoughts represented by the complement clause, and in the case that the verbs involve actual speech, with respect to whether they represent the addressee of the utterance. Let us use the symbol [+logo-1] to mark the NP that represents the speaker or experiencer (i.e., first person), and the symbol [+logo-2] to mark the NP that represents the addressee (i.e., second person). I will use the expression "logophoric verbs" to refer to verbs that take such NPs. The subjects of verbs such as *say, tell, ask, complain, scream, realize, feel, know, expect,* and so on, and the objects of verbs such as *worry, bother, disturb, please,* and so on, are marked in underlying structure as [+logo-1]. The dative objects of verbs such as *say, tell, ask, complain, scream,* are marked as [+logo-2]. According to this analysis, the underlying structure of (2.24a) below will be something like (2.24b):

(2.24) a.   John$_i$ told Mary$_j$ that he$_i$ loved her$_j$.
        b.   [John [+logo-1] told Mary [+logo-2] [he loved her]]

John told the story to Mary

The verb *told* is a logophoric verb that takes a [+logo-1] NP as subject and a [+logo-2] NP as dative object. We can now restate the Logophoric Pronoun Rule as follows:

(2.25)   *Logophoric Pronoun Rule* (revised): Given a verb that takes [+logo-1/2] NPs and a logophoric complement clause, a full (nonpronominal, non-reflexive) NP in that complement cannot be coindexed with the [+logo-1/2] NPs in the main clause.

In (2.24b), the Logophoric Pronoun Rule does not block coindexing of *he* and *her* with *John* and *Mary*, respectively. Hence the acceptability of (2.24a). On the other hand, observe the following:

(2.26)   a.   ??That Ali$_i$ was the best boxer in the world was claimed by him$_i$ repeatedly.
         b.   [He [+logo-1] claimed repeatedly [Ali was the best boxer in the world]]

The Logophoric Pronoun Rule blocks the coindexing of *Ali*, a full NP, in the complement clause with the main clause *he*, which is marked as [+logo-1]. Hence the marginality or unacceptability of (2.26a). This situation contrasts with the fact that (2.27a) is acceptable:

(2.27)   a.   Those who trusted John$_i$ were betrayed by him$_i$ repeatedly.
         b.   [He betrayed those who trusted John repeatedly]

The verb *betrayed* as it is used in the above with a nonclausal object is not a logophoric verb. The coindexing of *John* with *him* is allowed in (a) because the latter does not precede and k-command the former in the surface structure. Hence the acceptability of the sentence.

In the rest of this chapter, I will discuss many sentence patterns in English all of which require the Logophoric Pronoun Rule or its further elaborated version.

3.3 Passive Sentences

Let us return to our analysis of sentences like (2.8) and (2.9).

(3.1)   a.   That he$_i$ was the greatest boxer in the world was repeatedly claimed by Ali$_i$.
        b.   ??That Ali$_i$ was the greatest boxer in the world was repeatedly claimed by him$_i$.
(3.2)   a.   That he$_i$ was the greatest boxer in the world was explicitly denied by Ali$_i$.
        b.   (?)That Ali$_i$ was the greatest boxer in the world was explicitly denied by him$_i$.

For many speakers, (3.2b), although awkward, is considerably better than (3.1b). This contrast can be explained by assuming that while *claim* is obligatorily a logophoric verb when it takes a clausal object, *deny* is ambiguous between logophoric and nonlogophoric uses. That is, (3.3a) is ambiguous between (3.3b) and (3.3c):

(3.3)   a. Ali_i denied that he_i was the greatest boxer in the world.
         b.   *Logophoric:* Ali said, "I am not the greatest boxer in the world."
         c.   *Nonlogophoric:* Ali denied someone else's statement "Ali is the greatest."[2]

The main clause subject *Ali* is [+logo-1] in interpretation (b), but it is not in interpretation (c). It seems that (3.2b) has only interpretation (3.3c). This must be due to the fact that (3.2b) in interpretation (3.3b) has *(by) him* as a [+logo-1] NP, and the Logophoric Pronoun Rule would block the coindexing of *Ali* in the logophoric complement with this NP. On the other hand, (3.2b) in interpretation (3.3c) is not subject to the application of the Logophoric Pronoun Rule because the sentence on this reading does not have *(by) him* as a [+logo-1] NP. Naturally, (3.1b) is unacceptable because *Ali* has been coindexed with the [+logo-1] *him* in violation of the Logophoric Pronoun Rule.
    Similarly, compare the following sentences:

(3.4)   a.   *The rumor that $John_i$ would become the President of the Corporation was spread by him_i.[3]
         b.   The rumor that $John_i$ would become the President of the Corporation was denied by him_i.
(3.5)   a.   *The claim that $John_i$ was dying of cancer was made by him_i.
         b.   The claim that $John_i$ was dying of cancer was denied by him_i.[4]

In (3.4a) and (3.5a), John is the instigator (i.e., speaker) of the rumor and the claim. Therefore, these sentences are derived from the underlying structure in which the by-agentive *him* is marked as [+logo-1]. They are unacceptable because *John,* a full NP, has been coindexed with this [+logo-1] NP in violation of the Logophoric Pronoun Rule. On the other hand, in (3.4b) and (3.5b), John denied someone else's rumor or claim. Therefore, the underlying structures of these sentences do not have *him* marked as [+logo-1]. Hence, the Logophoric Pronoun Rule does not block the derivation of these sentences.

3.4 Clefting of *That*-Clauses

Observe the following sentences:

(4.1)   a.   *That $John_i$ was crazy was just one of the things Mary said to him_i.
         b.   That $John_i$ was crazy was just one of the things Mary said about him_i.

unlikely that Mary would use "John" to his face.

(4.2)   a.   *That John$_i$ had a medical appointment that afternoon was one of the things he$_i$ remembered.

      b.   That John$_i$ had a medical appointment that afternoon was one of the things he$_i$ forgot.

In (4.1a), John is the addressee of the statement represented by the subject *that*-clause. Therefore, the dative *him* is marked as [+logo-2] in underlying structure. Hence the impossibility of coindexing *John,* a full NP in the logophoric complement clause, with this [+logo-2] NP. On the other hand, in (4.1b), John is neither the speaker nor the addressee, and therefore, the oblique-case *him* is neither [+logo-1] nor [+logo-2]. Therefore, the Logophoric Pronoun Rule does not apply, and the sentence is acceptable.

The contrast between (4.2a) and (4.2b) is clearly due to the fact that *remember* is an obligatory logophoric verb when it takes complement clauses, but *forget* is ambiguous between logophoric and nonlogophoric:

(4.3)   a.   John forgot that he had a medical appointment that afternoon.

      b.   "John forgot, but later realized, that he had a medical appointment that afternoon."

      c.   "John forgot and never realized that he had a medical appointment that afternoon."

Sentence (4.3a) in interpretation (4.3b) has *forgot* as a logophoric verb because its complement clause represents the subject's thought. On the other hand, the same sentence in interpretation (4.3c) has *forgot* as a nonlogophoric verb because what the complement clause represents has nothing to do with John's thought or utterance. I assume that (4.2b) is acceptable on this reading.[5]

The following examples, which are due to John Goldsmith (personal communication, 1985), show that the Logophoric Pronoun Rule applies even when the [+logo-1/2] NP is only implied and is not overtly present in the sentence:

(4.4)   a.   Mary$_i$ spoke to the school doctor about her$_i$ ever-worsening depression. He gave her$_i$ some excellent advice; that she$_i$/*Mary$_i$ might consider a different major was perhaps his most important suggestion.

      b.   Mary$_i$'s mother spoke to the school doctor about her daughter$_i$'s ever-worsening depression. He gave her some excellent advice; that she$_i$/Mary$_i$ might consider a different major was perhaps his most important suggestion.

In the last sentence of (4.4a) and (4.4b), *that she/Mary might consider a different major* is a logophoric complement of *suggest(ion)* and *his* a [+logo-1] NP. But the sentence lacks an overt [+logo-2] NP for *suggest(ion).* In spite of this fact, the Logophoric Pronoun Rule still has its effect: the unacceptability of (4.4a) can be attributed to the fact that the full NP *Mary* is coindexed with the implied [+logo-2] NP *Mary* in violation of the Logophoric Pronoun Rule. In contrast, (4.4b) with the full NP *Mary* is acceptable because it is not co-indexed with the implied [+logo-2] NP *Mary's mother*.

3.5 The Subject's Direct Feeling and the Speaker's Knowledge

As Ross (1967) noted, when verbs such as *worry, disturb, bother, please,* and *amuse* take a sentential subject, they allow both backward and forward pro-nominalization. For example, observe the following sentences:

(5.1)   a.   That he$_i$ was blond worried John$_i$.
         b.   That John$_i$ was blond worried him$_i$.
(5.2)   a.   That he$_i$ was unpopular didn't disturb Oscar$_i$ at all.
         b.   That Oscar$_i$ was unpopular didn't disturb him$_i$ at all.

The (b) sentences are incompatible with the direct discourse analysis of these sentential subjects and thus suggest that these verbs are ambiguous between logophoric and nonlogophoric uses. For example, corresponding to (5.1), we can assume the following underlying structures:

(5.3)   a.   [[That he was blond] worried John [+logo-1]]
         b.   [[That he was blond] worried John [−logo-1/2]]
(5.4)   a.   [[That John was blond] worried him [+logo-1]]
         b.   [[That John was blond] worried him [−logo-1/2]]

The Logophoric Pronoun Rule does not apply to (5.3b) or (5.4b). Since these structures do not violate the precede and k-command constraint dictated by Condition C', the coindexing of *he* and *John* in (5.3b) and that of *John* and *him* are allowed. Hence the acceptability of (5.1a) and (5.1b) as sentences derived from these two sources. In contrast, in (5.3a) and (5.4a), we have logophoric complements. The Logophoric Pronoun Rule blocks the coindex-ing of *John,* a full NP, with *him [+logo-1]* in (5.4a), but it allows for the coindexing of *he* with *John [+logo-1]* in (5.3a).

The above analysis suggests that (5.1a) and (5.1b) are not exactly synony-mous. The primary interpretation of the former is that the sentential subject represents John's internal feeling directly. On the other hand, the sentential subject of (5.1b) represents the speaker's knowledge of John's feelings. This analysis should predict that if the sentential subject of, say, *worried John* rep-resents an internal feeling of John's that is not usually observable by third par-ties, the pattern of (5.1b) would have a lower degree of acceptability. It seems that this prediction is borne out, albeit very subtly, as shown by the following:

(5.5)   a.   ?That John$_i$ was utterly terrified of Mary worried him$_i$.
         b.   That he$_i$ was utterly terrified of Mary worried John$_i$.

(5.6)   a.   ?That John$_i$ was always unhappy worried him$_i$.
        b.   That he$_i$ was always unhappy worried John$_i$.
(5.7)   a.   ?That John$_i$ felt hungry all the time worried him$_i$.
        b.   That he$_i$ felt hungry all the time worried John$_i$.

Similarly, observe the following four sentences:

(5.8)   a.   ?That John$_i$ was sick worried him$_i$.
        b.   That he$_i$ was sick worried John$_i$.
(5.9)   a.   That John$_i$ was as sick as the tests indicated apparently worried him$_i$.
        b.   That he$_i$ was as sick as the tests indicated apparently worried John$_i$.

Even a state that is relatively objective, such as being sick, tends to be looked at from the experiencer's point of view unless there is enough information in the sentence that makes it clear that it represents an objective fact. It seems to be for this reason that sentences such as (5.8a) are less than perfect for many speakers. For these speakers, (5.9a) is considerably better than (5.8a) because the addition of *(as sick) as the tests indicated* objectifies the subject clause, and the adverb *apparently* also makes it clear that the speaker is describing John's sickness as a known fact rather than as something perceived by John.

What the above observation shows is that emotive verbs such as *worry* and *bother* are primarily direct discourse verbs, and their use as regular non–direct discourse verbs in an underlying structure of the type shown in (5.3b) and (5.4b) requires ample justification. Thus, the forward pronominalization pattern requires that the sentential subject represent a state or action that is observable from outside, and which has acquired the status of common knowledge. In other words, the sentential subject in this sentence pattern must represent something that everybody is talking about or aware of. For example, the following sentences, as well as (5.1b) and (5.2b), all seem to be acceptable for this same reason.

(5.10)   a.   That John$_i$ was overweight worried him$_i$.
         b.   That John$_i$ had been indicted didn't bother him$_i$ at all.
         c.   That the President$_i$ didn't receive a majority in the popular vote didn't worry him$_i$ at all.
         d.   That Nixon$_i$ fell below a 25% approval rating didn't seem to have bothered him$_i$ at all.

On the other hand, the following sentences, as well as those of (5.5a), (5.6a), (5.7a), and (5.8a), are less than perfect because the sentential subject represents an action or state that is difficult to imagine as known to everybody, because there is no explicit indication in the sentences to show that the action or state represented by the sentential subject is common knowledge.

(5.11)   a.   ??That John$_i$ was late worried him$_i$.
         b.   ??That John$_i$ wasn't feeling hungry after skipping two meals worried him$_i$.
         c.   ?That Mary didn't say hello to John$_i$ worried him$_i$.[6]

Now, with the above understanding that the forward pronominalization pattern is in general difficult for emotive verbs, let us proceed to the following two pairs of sentences:

(5.12)   a. ??That Mary had the nerve to call John$_i$ crazy to his$_i$ face bothered him$_i$.
         b.   That Mary had the nerve to call him$_i$ crazy to his$_i$ face bothered John$_i$.
(5.13)   a.   ?That Mary had the nerve to call John$_i$ crazy behind his$_i$ back bothered him$_i$.
         b.   That Mary had the nerve to call him$_i$ crazy behind his$_i$ back bothered John$_i$.

For many speakers, (5.13a) might be less than perfect for the reason mentioned above, but is considerably better than (5.12a). The fact that (5.12a) is marginal must be due to the fact that since John was the addressee of the statement, "You are crazy," it is most natural to interpret the sentential subject as representing John's internal feeling rather than the speaker's knowledge of the situation. On the other hand, in (5.13), John was not the addressee of the statement, and for this reason, the speaker of (5.13) can intervene between this statement and John and represent the content of the sentential subject as his own knowledge or as a well-established fact.

Similarly, observe the following sentences:[7]

(5.14)   a. ?/??That Mary had the nerve to call John$_i$ crazy in front of his$_i$ friends bothered him$_i$.
         b.   That Mary had the nerve to call him$_i$ crazy in front of his$_i$ friends bothered John$_i$.
(5.15)   a.   That Mary had described John$_i$ as crazy in front of his friends bothered him$_i$.
         b.   That Mary had described him$_i$ as crazy in front of his friends bothered John$_i$.

Example (5.14a) is not as acceptable as (5.13a), but it is still better than (5.12a) in spite of the fact that John was the direct addressee of the statement, "You are crazy." This seems to be owing to the fact that the explicit mention of the presence of John's friends at the place of utterance as witnesses adds to the objectivity of the statement and makes it easier, relatively speaking, for the speaker to present it as a fact, rather than as John's perception of what happened. Example (5.15a) is acceptable because the verb *described* more readily allows for John not to be the direct addressee of the statement represented by the complement clause.

The contrast among (5.12a), (5.13a), (5.14a), and (5.15a) is clearly unexplainable on any purely syntactic grounds because these sentences have identical phrase structure configurations. This shows that the problem of pronominalization under discussion here is basically a semantic and pragmatic phenomenon having to do with how difficult, or how easy, it is for the speaker to represent a third party's internal feelings as if in quotation marks (i.e., as logophoric complements vis-à-vis the experiencer NP) or to represent it as his (i.e., the speaker's) own knowledge (i.e., as nonlogophoric complements).

Likewise, compare the following pairs of sentences:

(5.16) a. *That the defendant$_i$ did not know the victim was claimed by him$_i$ at the court yesterday.

 b. (?)That the defendant$_i$ knew the victim was acknowledged by him$_i$ at the court yesterday.

(5.17) a. *That John$_i$ would take custody of the child was proposed by him$_i$ yesterday.

 b. (?)That John$_i$ would be the next president of the company was confirmed by him$_i$ at the staff meeting yesterday.

For many speakers, the (b) sentences are considerably better than the (a) sentences. This must be owing to the fact that the verbs *acknowledge* and *confirm* suggest that the propositions represented by the sentential subjects had existed as common knowledge outside the defendant's and John's internal feeling. The speaker of (5.16b) and (5.17b), by using a full NP in the sentential subjects, is implying that the propositions represented by them had been common knowledge even before the defendant's acknowledgment and John's confirmation.

Similarly, observe the following sentences:[8]

(5.18) a. That the Rolling Stones$_i$ weren't as popular as before worried all of them$_i$.

 b. That John$_i$ was sick worried only him$_i$.

These sentences clearly imply that the propositions that are represented by the sentential subjects were common knowledge. This implication derives partly from the fact that the main clause objects are quantified. Thus, it is easy to imagine that these sentences are answers to implicit or explicit questions of the following sort:

(5.19) a. Who did it worry that the Rolling Stones weren't as popular as before?

 b. Who did it worry that John was sick?

The answers (5.18a) and (5.18b) are acceptable because the sentential subjects have been established in (5.19), not as logophoric complements with respect to the Rolling Stones and John, but as complements that represent common knowledge.

3.6 *Say To* and *Say About*

Observe the following sentences:

(6.1) a. People often said to Mary$_i$ that she$_i$ was a lunatic.
     b. *People often said to her$_i$ that Mary$_i$ was a lunatic.
(6.2) a. People often said about Mary$_i$ that she$_i$ was a lunatic.
     b. $^\vee$/?/??People often said about her$_i$ that Mary$_i$ was a lunatic.

There are some speakers who consider (6.2b) nearly acceptable; almost all speakers consider it better than (6.1b). This must be due to the fact that while *her* in (6.1b) is [+logo-2], *her* in (6.2b) is not:

(6.3) a. *[People often said to her$_i$ [+logo-2] [Mary$_i$ is a lunatic]]
     b. [People often said about her$_i$ [−logo-1/2] [Mary$_i$ is a lunatic]

The Logophoric Pronoun Rule disallows coindexing of *Mary* in the complement clause with the [+logo-2] *her* in the main clause in (6.3a), but the rule is inapplicable to (6.3b).[9]

The following examples parallel (6.1) and (6.2):

(6.4) a. People often made the statement to Mary$_i$ that she$_i$ was a lunatic.
     b. *People often made the statement to her$_i$ that Mary$_i$ was a lunatic.
(6.5) a. People often made the remark about Mary$_i$ that she$_i$ was a lunatic.
     b. $^\vee$/?/??People often made the remark about her$_i$ that Mary$_i$ was a lunatic.

Here again, the direct discourse perspective can automatically explain why (6.5b) is considerably more acceptable than (6.4b). A theory of syntax which does not have a direct discourse perspective would erroneously predict that (6.4b) and (6.5b) would have the same degree of acceptability.[10]

3.7 *Expect* and *Expect Of*

Compare the following sentences:

(7.1) a. Mary$_i$ expected that she$_i$ would win.
     b. They expected of Mary$_i$ that she$_i$ would do it.
(7.2) a. *That Mary$_i$ would win was expected by her$_i$.
     b. That Mary$_i$ would do it was expected of her$_i$.

The above contrast is clearly attributable to the fact that, while the subject of *expect* is a [+logo-1] NP (as an experiencer of the expectation), the object of *expect of* is neither [+logo-2] nor [+logo-1]. The same contrast holds for the following sentence patterns as well.

(7.3)   a. ??That Mary$_i$ would win, she$_i$ expected.
      b.   That Mary$_i$ would do it, they expected of her$_i$.
(7.4)   a. ??That Mary$_i$ would win was one of the things that she$_i$ expected.
      b.   That Mary$_i$ would do it was one of the things that they expected of her$_i$.

3.8   Quasi-Indirect Discourse

Observe the following sentences:

(8.1)   a.   He$_i$ would be late, John$_i$ said.
      b.   *John$_i$ would be late, he$_i$ said.

Reinhart (1975) correctly observes that the above phenomenon belongs to the same class of phenomena that I discussed in Kuno (1972b) under the rubric of direct discourse perspective. The underlying representations for (8.1a) and (8.1b), according to the interpretive framework adopted here, are:

(8.2)   a.   [John [+logo-1] said [he would be late]]
      b.   [He [+logo-1] said [John would be late]]

Example (8.1b) is unacceptable because *John,* a full NP in the logophoric complement, has been coindexed with the logophoric *he* in the main clause.

    The same direct discourse perspective can explain the unacceptability of (8.3b) below:

(8.3)   a.   Did she$_j$ love him$_i$, John$_i$ [+logo-1] asked Mary$_j$ [+logo-2].
      b.   *Did Mary$_j$ love John$_i$, he$_i$ [+logo-1] asked her$_j$ [+logo-2].

The Logophoric Pronoun Rule marks (8.3b) unacceptable because *John* and *Mary,* full NPs in the complement clause, are coindexed with logophoric *he* and *her* in the main clause.

    Reinhart (1975) contrasts the sentences of (8.1) with the following:

(8.4)   John$_i$ will be late, he$_i$ said.

Reinhart hypothesizes that *John will be late* in this sentence represents the speaker's (and not John's) point of view and that it is the main clause of the sentence from the level of underlying structure to that of surface structure. According to this analysis, *he said* of (8.4) is a subordinate parenthetical expression. The fact that *John will be late* is the main clause of the sentence, and not a complement clause of *he said,* can be seen not only by the fact that there is no tense agreement between *said* and *will* but also by the following tests devised by Reinhart:

(8.5)   a.   John$_i$ will be late, or so he$_i$ said.
         b.   *He$_i$ would be late, or so John$_i$ said.
(8.6)   a.   John$_i$ will be late, or at least that's what he$_i$ said.
         b.   *He$_i$ would be late, or at least that's what John$_i$ said.
(8.7)   a.   We hired Mary because [the chairman$_i$ likes her, he$_i$ said].
         b.   *We hired Mary because [he$_i$ liked her, the chairman$_i$ said].

The preposed clauses in (8.5a) and (8.6a), and one in the *because* clause of (8.7a), are main clauses, according to Reinhart's analysis. In contrast, the (b) sentences in (8.5)–(8.7) represent proposed quasi–direct discourse complements (as can be witnessed by the fact that *will* is realized as *would* by tense agreement). Examples (8.5a), (8.6a), and (8.7a) show that the speaker can soften his own assertion by shifting the responsibility for the assertion to the source of information. On the other hand, the unacceptability of (8.5b) and (8.6b) shows that a quasi–indirect discourse complement cannot stand alone. The unacceptability of (8.7b) shows that a preposed indirect discourse complement clause cannot be embedded in a *because* clause.

The above observation shows that the acceptability of (8.4) is not a counterexample to my direct discourse analysis of the complement clause of saying verbs, and that the direct discourse analysis explanation of the acceptability of (8.1a) and (8.3a) and the unacceptability of (8.1b) and (8.3b) is still valid. A grammatical theory which does not contain a direct discourse perspective would have a hard time accounting for these facts.

3.9 Emphatic Reflexives

Ross (1970, pp. 226–229) assumes that there is a rule which can delete an anaphoric pronoun when this pronoun is followed by an emphatic reflexive. Example (9.1a) below is acceptable in Ross's idiolect, although there are many speakers who consider it unacceptable. In the following, I record Ross's judgments only:

(9.1)   a.   Tom$_i$ believed that the paper had been written by Ann and him$_i$ himself$_i$.
         b.   Tom$_i$ believed that the paper had been written by Ann and himself$_i$.

He hypothesizes that this deletion rule is subject to the following constraint:

(9.2)   *Anaphoric Pronoun Deletion (Ross):* If an anaphoric pronoun precedes an emphatic reflexive, the former may be deleted, if it is commanded (i.e., S-commanded) by the NP with which it stands in an anaphoric relationship.

For example, in (9.1a), *him* is commanded by *Tom,* with which it is anaphoric, and therefore (9.1b) is grammatical. Similarly, in (9.3a) and (9.4a) below, *him* is commanded by *Tom* although the latter is not the subject of the main sentence: hence the grammaticality of the corresponding (b) sentences:

(9.3)   a.   I told Tom$_i$ that the entries should be designed by Ann and him$_i$ himself$_i$. (acceptable in Ross's idiolect)
        b.   I told Tom$_i$ that the entries should be designed by Ann and himself$_i$.
(9.4)   a.   That the paper would have to be written by Ann and him$_i$ himself$_i$ was obvious to Tom$_i$. (acceptable in Ross's idiolect)
        b.   That the paper would have to be written by Ann and himself$_i$ was obvious to Tom$_i$.

On the other hand, in (9.5) the anaphoric pronoun is not commanded by the antecedent, and hence the deletion of the pronoun results in ungrammaticality:

(9.5)   a.   Tom$_i$ was not present, and many of the girls believed that the paper had been written by Ann and him$_i$ himself$_i$. (acceptable in Ross's idiolect)
        b.   *Tom$_i$ was not present, and many of the girls believed that the paper had been written by Ann and himself$_i$.[11]

Ross further notes that (9.6) is grammatical,

(9.6)   This paper was written by Ann and myself.

and uses this fact as one of his arguments for hypothesizing the presence of an underlying performative verb for declarative sentences. That is, he assumes that (9.6) is derived from the deep structure that corresponds to

(9.7)   [I SAY TO YOU THAT [this paper was written by Ann and me myself]]

The Anaphoric Pronoun Deletion Rule given in (9.2) can apply to delete the anaphoric pronoun *me*, he argues, because it is commanded by the main clause *I*, which later gets deleted together with the performative verb (i.e., SAY) and the second-person dative object.

The following examples, however, show that something much more semantic than Ross's constraint is controlling the phenomenon under discussion:

(9.8)   a.   Mary said to John$_i$ that an obscene paper supposedly written by Ann and himself$_i$ was being circulated.
        b.   *Mary said about/of John$_i$ that an obscene paper supposedly written by Ann and himself$_i$ was being circulated.
(9.9)   a.   Mary whispered to John$_i$ that the paper must have been written by Ann and himself$_i$.
        b.   ??Mary knew from John$_i$ that an important paper had been written by Ann and himself$_i$.

What makes (9.8b) and (9.9b) marginal? Both sentences have the same structure as the corresponding (a) sentences in terms of the command relationship.

The underlying *him* to the left of *himself* in (b), as in (a), is commanded by the matrix clause *John*. Therefore, Ross's condition on Anaphoric Pronoun Deletion predicts that they should be as grammatical as the (a) sentences. One cannot attribute the difference in judgments to the fact that the antecedent *John* in (a) is the (indirect) object of the main verb, while it is not in (b) because the following sentence, which has the same syntactic structure as (9.9b) for all practical purposes, is grammatical for many speakers:

(9.10)   Mary heard from John$_i$ that the paper had been written by Ann and himself$_i$.

Only the direct discourse perspective provides an obvious explanation of these facts:

(9.11)   *Semantic Condition on Emphatic Reflexives:* An emphatic reflexive in a subordinate clause is acceptable only if it is in a logophoric clause, and its antecedent is [+logo-1/2] with respect to the logophoric verb that takes the complement.[12]

In (9.1b) and (9.4b), *Tom*, the antecedent of the emphatic reflexive *himself*, is [+logo-1], while in (9.3b), it is [+logo-2]. These sentences thus all fulfill the above condition and are hence acceptable. The contrast between (9.8a) and (9.8b) is obviously due to the fact that while *John*, the antecedent of the emphatic reflexive *himself*, is [+logo-2] in the former, it is [−logo-1/2] in the latter. Similarly, the contrast between (9.9a) and (9.9b) is due to the fact that *John* as the object of *whisper to* is [+logo-2] but *John* as the object of *know from* is not. The fact that (9.10) is acceptable for most speakers is owing to the fact that the object of *hear from* is the *speaker* of the content of the complement clause: *John* in this sentence is a [+logo-1] NP. Finally, the fact that (9.9b) has a status between (9.10) and (9.8b) can be attributable to the fact that, although it is totally impossible to interpret *John* of (9.8b) as [+logo-1], it is remotely possible to interpret *John* of (9.9b) as [+logo-1]—the expression *Mary knew from John that S* generally implies that John did not say S (and hence the nonlogophoric nature of *John*), but at the same time, it can imply that John said something close to S. The sentence (9.9b) is acceptable to the extent that one can interpret *John* of this sentence as a [+logo-1] NP.[13]

The fact that the emphatic reflexives coreferent with upstairs oblique NPs are allowable only if their antecedent NPs are [+logo-1/2] can be seen clearly by observing the following examples (due to John Whitman), also.

(9.12)   a.   Mary heard from John$_i$ that an obscene paper supposedly written by Ann and himself$_i$ was being circulated.
             b.??Mary surmised from John$_i$ that an obscene paper supposedly written by Ann and himself$_i$ was being circulated.
             c. *Mary concealed from John$_i$ that an obscene paper supposedly written by Ann and himself$_i$ was being circulated.

(9.13)   a.   Mary agreed/concurred with John$_i$ that an obscene paper sup-
         posedly written by Ann and himself$_i$ was being circulated.
         b. ??Mary sympathized with John$_i$ that an obscene paper supposedly
            written by Ann and himself$_i$ was being circulated.
(9.14)   a. ?Mary informed the authorities for John$_i$ that an obscene paper
            supposedly written by Ann and himself$_i$ was being circulated.
         b. *Mary lied to the authorities for John$_i$ that an obscene paper sup-
            posedly written by Ann and himself$_i$ was being circulated.

The above examples show that the degree of acceptability of the sentences
directly parallels the ease with which it is possible to interpret *John*, the antecedent of the emphatic reflexive *himself*, as [+logo-1]. For example, in
(9.13), the expression *Mary agreed/concurred with John that S* implies that
John did say S. Hence the acceptability of the (a) sentence. On the other hand,
the expression *Mary sympathized with John that S* only remotely indicates
that John might have said S. Hence the marginality of the (b) sentence. In
(9.14), the expression *Mary informed the authorities for John that S* indicates, albeit indirectly, that it was most likely that John said S, and hence the
near acceptability of the (a) sentence. On the other hand, the expression *Mary
lied to the authorities for John that S* does not imply at all that John said S,
and hence the total unacceptability of the (b) sentence.
    Observe, next, the following sentences:

(9.15)   a. *Mary didn't hear from JOHN$_i$ that the paper had been written by
            Ann and himself$_j$. She heard it from BILL.
         b.   MARY didn't hear from John$_i$ that—you know—that the paper had
            been written by Ann and himself$_i$. JANE heard it from him$_i$.

In (a), since Mary didn't hear it from John, but from Bill, John could not have
uttered the content of the complement clause. Therefore, *John* in this sentence
is semantically not a [+logo-1] NP. Hence the unacceptability of the sentence
for most speakers. In contrast, there are speakers who regard (b) as acceptable, and most speakers regard it as considerably better than (a). This must be
due to the fact that in (b), John can be interpreted as having uttered the content
of the complement clause. Therefore, the emphatic reflexive *himself* in this
sentence has a [+logo-1] antecedent, and hence, the acceptability of the
sentence.[14]
    Observe, further, the following sentences:

(9.16)   a. *Speaking of John$_i$, the article was written by Ann and himself$_i$.
         b.   According to John$_i$, the article was written by Ann and himself$_i$.[15]

The above two sentences have an identical constituent structure, but only (b)
is acceptable. This is undoubtedly due to the fact that *John*, the antecedent of
the emphatic reflexive, is semantically a [+logo-1] NP in (b) but not in (a).
    It should be clear by now that the conditions on the use of emphatic reflex-

ives are basically semantic or pragmatic, rather than syntactic in the narrow sense, and also that the nature of direct discourse perspective and its role in linguistic explanation are basically semantic or pragmatic. The latter point will come up repeatedly in my discussion of other syntactic phenomena that bear on this role.

Finally, the following examples show that the emphatic reflexive pattern is subject to the chain-of-command principle, which we discussed in some detail in Chapter 2:

(9.17)   a.   ?/*John$_i$ said to Mary that Jane was sure that the paper had been written by Ann and himself$_i$.
         b. $^\vee$/?John$_i$ said to Mary that someone might guess that the paper had been written by Ann and himself$_i$.
         c. $^\vee$/?John$_i$ said to Mary that nobody would doubt that the paper had been written by Ann and himself$_i$.

For ease of reference, I will restate Langacker's chain-of-command principle, with "command" replaced with "k-command":

(9.18)   *Chain-of-Command Principle*
         If (i)   two identical nodes A$_1$ and A$_2$ both k-command some other node B;
             (ii)   A$_1$ k-commands A$_2$; and
             (iii) A$_2$ does not k-command A$_1$; then
         any transformational operation involving A and B can apply only with respect to A$_2$ and B, and not A$_1$ and B. Thus, if there is a "chain of command" so that A$_1$ k-commands A$_2$, A$_2$ k-commands B, and A$_2$ does not k-command A$_1$ but is identical to it, A$_2$ "controls" B, protecting it from the influence of A$_1$, so to speak.

In (9.17a), both A$_1$ (= *John*) and A$_2$ (= *Mary*) k-command the emphatic reflexive, and A$_1$ k-commands A$_2$, but not vice versa. Thus, the chain-of-command principle dictates that only A$_2$ "controls" the reflexive. The fact that (9.16b, c) are acceptable or nearly so depending upon the speaker shows that the chain-of-command principle, as it interacts with the emphatic reflexive pattern, is not an absolute constraint, but applies with varying degrees of strength, depending upon the relative strength of A$_1$ and A$_2$, as "controller" for reflexives. Indefinite NPs, especially indefinite nonspecific NPs such as *someone* and *nobody,* are weak antecedents for reflexives in general. Therefore, the "protecting" or insulating power of A$_2$ (= *someone/nobody*) from the influence of A$_1$ (= *John*) for control of the emphatic reflexive is rather weak. Hence the acceptability or near acceptability of these sentences. We will see in the following sections that several other patterns that are relevant to the direct discourse perspective share the same characteristic vis-à-vis the chain-of-command principle.

3.10 *Physicists Like Himself*

Observe the following sentences, which are also taken from Ross (1970, pp. 229–230) and are accompanied with his own acceptability judgments.

(10.1) a. Physicists like $\left\{\begin{array}{c}\text{Albert}\\\text{him}\end{array}\right\}$ don't often make mistakes.

  b. *Physicists like himself don't often make mistakes.

(10.2) a. I told Albert$_i$ that physicists like him$_i$ were a godsend.

  b. I told Albert$_i$ that physicists like himself$_i$ were a godsend.

(10.3) a. Physicists like me were never too happy with the parity principle.

  b. Physicists like myself were never too happy with the parity principle.

Ross hypothesizes that the following constraint holds for the use of reflexives in the pattern under discussion:

(10.4) *Constraint on Like-phrase Reflexives* (Ross): *Like*-phrases containing reflexives must be commanded by the NP to which they refer.

According to this constraint, (10.2b) is grammatical because *physicists like himself* is commanded by the matrix clause *Albert*, which is coreferential with *himself*. On the other hand, (10.1b) is ungrammatical because the same expression is not commanded by an NP that is coreferential with the reflexive.

The following examples show that the phenomenon under discussion is in fact conditioned by whether the antecedent of the reflexive is logophoric or not:

(10.5) a. John said to Mary that physicists like himself were a godsend.

  b.$^{\vee}$/?Mary said to John that physicists like himself were a godsend.

  c.$^{\vee}$/?Mary heard from John that physicists like himself were a godsend.

  d. *Mary heard about John that physicists like himself were a godsend.

  e. *Mary said about/of John that physicists like himself were a godsend. *not to J.*

As far as I know, (a) is acceptable to all speakers. Some speakers consider (b) and (c) perfectly acceptable, and others consider them awkward and less than perfect. I will return to this problem shortly. Now, (d, e), like (b, c), have *John* commanding *physicists like himself*, and therefore Ross's constraint as stated in (10.4) predicts that they would be grammatical. But in actuality, as far as I know, all speakers reject these sentences. The direct discourse perspective readily explains why these sentences are ungrammatical:

(10.6) *Constraint on NP Like X-self:* The *NP like x-self* pattern in a subordinate clause is acceptable if it is in a logophoric complement clause and if the antecedent of the reflexive is [+logo-1] with respect to the logophoric verb that takes the complement clause. It is acceptable, awkward, or marginal, subject to idiolectal variation, if the antecedent is [+logo-2]. Otherwise it is unacceptable.

The following examples show that whether a given NP is [+logo-1/2] or not is not determinable simply on the basis of selectional restrictions on verbs (with respect to whether they take logophoric NPs as their arguments), but must be determined on the basis of what the sentences in which they appear mean:

(10.7)   a. *Mary didn't hear from JOHN$_i$ that physicists like himself$_i$ were a godsend. She heard it from BILL.

   b. MARY didn't hear from John$_i$ that physicists like himself$_i$ were a godsend. JANE heard it from him$_j$.

Sentence (10.7a) implies that John was not the speaker of the complement clause that contains an *NP like x-self* expression. Hence the unacceptability of the sentence. In contrast, (10.7b) implies that John was the speaker. Hence the acceptability of the sentence.

The claim that the *NP like x-self* pattern is acceptable to the extent that the hearer can interpret its antecedent as [+logo-1] is also supported by the fact that the acceptability status of sentences such as (10.5c) improves when they are modified in such a way as to make it clear that John was the speaker of the content of the complement clauses. For example, observe the following sentence:

(10.8)   Mary is always hearing from John that physicists like himself are a godsend.

For many speakers, (10.8) is considerably better than (10.5c). This must be owing to the fact that the repeated nature of the action makes it easier for the hearer to imagine that John is the speaker.

The above phenomenon presents an interesting contrast with the fact that the acceptability status of (10.5b) does not seem to improve even if it is modified in such a way as to make it clear that John was the hearer of the content of the complement clause:

(10.9) $^\vee$/?Mary is always saying to John that physicists like himself are a godsend.

For those speakers who consider (10.5b) as less than perfect, the use of the progressive form and of *always* does not improve the acceptability status of the sentence. This is because the awkwardness of marginality of (10.5b) is due to the fact that the antecedent of the reflexive is [+logo-2], and this situation does not change even when the progressive form is used.[16]

The following examples, which I owe to John Goldsmith (personal communication, 1985), show that the Constraint on *NP Like X-self* applies even when the [+logo-1/2] NP is only implied, and not overtly present, in the following sentence:

(10.10) a.   Mary$_i$ spoke to the school doctor about her$_i$ ever-worsening depression. He gave her$_i$ some excellent advice; that she$_i$ might consider a different major was perhaps his most important suggestion. He then noted that it was not uncommon for students like her$_i$/herself$_i$ to try several fields before making a decision.

         b.   Mary$_i$'s mother$_j$ spoke to the school doctor about her$_j$ daughter$_i$'s ever-worsening depression. He gave her$_j$ some excellent advice; that Mary$_i$ might consider a different major was perhaps his most important suggestion. He then noted that it was not uncommon for students like her$_i$/*herself$_i$ to try several fields before making a decision.

In the last sentence of (10.10a) and (10.10b), the *that*-clause is a logophoric complement of *noted,* with *he* as a [+logo-1] NP. The implied [+logo-2] NP for (10.10a) is *Mary,* thus making *students like herself* acceptable, awkward, or marginal depending upon the speaker. In contrast, in (10.10b) the implied [+logo-2] NP is *Mary's mother,* and not *Mary,* which makes *students like herself (= Mary)* totally unacceptable for all speakers.

Like the emphatic reflexive pattern, the *NP like x-self* pattern is subject to the chain-of-command principle. Observe the following sentences:

(10.10) a.   ?/*John$_i$ said to Mary that Jane was sure that physicists like himself$_i$ were a godsend.

         b. $^\vee$/?John$_i$ said to Mary that nobody would doubt that physicists like himself$_i$ were a godsend.

In (a), *Jane* blocks, or nearly blocks, *John* from controlling the reflexive. In contrast, in (b), *nobody,* which is an indefinite nonspecific pronoun, is a weak antecedent for the reflexive and does not have such a strong blocking power. Hence the acceptability or near acceptability of the sentence.

3.11 Picture Noun Reflexives

In section 2.11, we saw that picture noun reflexives can appear in subordinate clauses with their k-commanding antecedents in the main clauses as long as the syntactico-semantic chain-of-command principle does not disqualify the antecedents from controlling the reflexives. Thus, we have the following kind of contrast:

(11.1)   a.   John$_i$ said that there was a picture of himself$_i$ in the post office.

         b.   ??/*John$_i$ said to Mary that Jane was sure that there was a picture of himself$_i$ in the post office.

    c.   √/?John$_i$ said to Mary that someone might notice that there was a picture of himself$_i$ in the post office.

Example (a) shows that a picture noun reflexive can appear in a subordinate clause. Example (b) is unacceptable because the chain-of-command principle dictates that *Jane,* rather than *John,* control the reflexive. Example (c), on the other hand, is acceptable or nearly acceptable, depending upon the speaker, because *someone,* as an indefinite nonspecific pronoun, is not a strong controller for reflexives.

Observe the following examples:

(11.2)   a.   John$_i$ knew that there was a picture of himself$_i$ in the post office.

         b.   That there was a picture of himself$_i$ in the post office surprised John$_i$.

         c.   John$_i$ said to Mary that there was a picture of himself$_i$ in the po office.

(11.3)   a.   √/?Mary said to John$_i$ that there was a picture of himself$_i$ in the post office.

         b.   √/?Mary revealed to John$_i$ that there was a picture of himself$_i$ in the post office.

(11.4)   a.   *Mary said about/of John$_i$ that there was a picture of himself$_i$ in the post office.

         b.   *His$_i$ parents expected of John$_i$ that there would be a picture of himself$_i$ with a winning trophy in all the papers in the world.

It seems clear from the above examples that picture noun reflexives in complement clauses are subject to a constraint that is similar to that for the *NP like x-self* pattern:

(11.5)   *Constraint on Picture Noun Reflexives:* The reflexive pronoun in a picture noun construction in a logophoric complement clause is acceptable if its antecedent is [+logo-1] with respect to the logophoric verb that takes the complement clause and acceptable, or marginal, depending upon the speaker, if the antecedent is [+logo-2]. Otherwise it is unacceptable.

As is the case with the emphatic reflexives and the *NP like x-self* pattern, the easier it is to establish that the antecedent of the reflexive is the speaker of the content of the complement clause, the more acceptable the sentence becomes. Observe, in the following, that the degree of acceptability decreases as we go down the list.

(11.6)   a.   √/?Mary heard from John$_i$ that there was a picture of himself$_i$ in the post office.

         b.   ??Mary learned from John$_i$ that there was a picture of himself$_i$ in the post office.

     c.   *Mary said about/of John$_i$ that there was a picture of himself$_i$ in the post office.

     d.   *Mary didn't hear from JOHN$_i$ that—you know—that there was a picture of himself$_i$ in the post office. She heard it from BILL.

     e.   cf. $^\surd$/?MARY didn't hear from John$_i$ that—you know—that there was a picture of himself$_i$ in the post office. JANE heard it from him$_i$.

Many speakers consider (11.6b) less acceptable than (11.6a). It must be that for these speakers, it is more difficult to imagine that John did indeed utter the content of the complement clause when *learned from John* is used than when *heard from John* is used. This is because *learning something from someone* describes an agent's acquisition of knowledge from that agent's point of view: in other words, while one hears from someone exactly what that someone tells him, one does not necessarily learn from someone exactly what that someone teaches him—one can learn less, or sometimes more. Example (11.6c) is ungrammatical because saying something about someone is a process that is completely independent of that someone, and the sentence does not imply in any way that John said that there was a picture of himself in the post office.

In (11.6d) we see the behavior of *hear from* under negation. This is not an isolated phenomenon, as we have observed a similar effect with emphatic reflexives and the *NP like x-self* pattern: if negation prevents an antecedent of a reflexive from meeting the logophoric requirements of a verb, unacceptability results. It seems that this is a general characteristic of logophoric verbs. For example, observe the following sentences:

(11.7)   a.   John$_i$ told Mary that there was a picture of himself$_i$ in the morning paper.

     b.   John$_i$ didn't tell MARY that there was a picture of himself$_i$ in the morning paper. He$_i$ told it to JANE.

     c. ??JOHN$_i$ didn't tell Mary that there was a picture of himself$_i$ in the morning paper. BILL did.

Example (11.7b) implies that John uttered the content of the complement clause. Hence the acceptability of the sentence. On the other hand, (11.7c) implies that John did not utter the content of the complement clause. Hence the relative unacceptability of the sentence.[17] Let us now see what happens when neither *John* nor *Mary* receives contrastive stress in (11.7):

(11.8)   John$_i$ didn't tell Mary that there was a picture of himself$_i$ in the morning paper.

Most speakers feel that (11.8) implies that John knew that there was a picture of himself in the morning paper. This is confirmed by the fact that the following sentence is not as good as (11.8):

(11.9)   ??John$_i$ didn't tell Mary that there was a picture of himself$_i$ in the morning paper because he$_i$ never knew about it.

The following sentence shows an interesting contrast with (11.9):

(11.10)   John$_i$ didn't tell Mary that there was a picture of himself$_i$ in the morning paper because he$_i$ didn't know about it yet.

It seems that (11.10) is acceptable because it is very easy to imagine that John later came to know about it.

Similarly, observe the following sentences:

(11.11)   a.   John$_i$ knew that there was a picture of himself$_i$ in the morning paper.
        b.   John$_i$ didn't know that there was a picture of himself$_i$ in the morning paper.
        c.   ?John$_i$ never knew that there was a picture of himself$_i$ in the morning paper.
        d.   cf. ??John$_i$ never found out that there was a picture of himself$_i$ in the morning paper.
        e. ??John$_i$ still doesn't know that there is a picture of himself$_i$ in the morning paper.[18]

For most speakers, (b) implies that John later came to know about it or that he now knows about it. The near acceptability of (c) might appear to be a problem for the assumption that the use of a picture noun reflexive in a complement clause requires that its antecedent be an actual speaker/perceiver. However, it seems that this sentence is nearly acceptable only in the interpretation in which the speaker has strongly identified himself with John. As I will show in the next chapter, the speaker identification is one of the factors that facilitate the use of reflexives in picture nouns. From this point of view, it is interesting to note that (d) is not as good as (c). This seems to be owing to the fact that, while *knew* describes an internal state, *found out* describes a more objective state and is less readily amenable to the speaker-identification interpretation of the sentence. The fact that (e) is marginal for many speakers seems to be owing to the same reason—a present-tense sentence is not readily interpretable as one that involves the speaker's strong identification of himself with a person that is being described.[19]

The following examples are also such that they can be explained only in a theory which has a direct discourse perspective:

(11.12)   a.   ?The minister$_i$ was worried by the fact that there were pictures of himself$_i$ with a prostitute in circulation.
        b.   *The minister$_i$ was implicated by the fact that there were pictures of himself$_i$ with a prostitute in circulation.

Example (11.12a) has as its matrix verb a psychological verb that takes an experiencer NP (i.e., "thinker/feeler" NP) as its object. Therefore, this sentence satisfies the Constraint on Picture Noun Reflexives stated in (11.5). The awkwardness or marginality of the sentence must have arisen from the fact that the content of the complement clause is presented in this sentence, not as his thought, but as an independently established fact. On the other hand, the matrix verb of (11.12b) has nothing to do with a psychological process on the part of the minister. Thus, the antecedent of the reflexive in this sentence is neither [+logo-1] nor [+logo-2]. It seems that this difference accounts for the difference in acceptability of these two sentences.

3.12 *As For X-Self*

Observe the following sentences:

(12.1) a. As for myself, I won't be invited.
  b. ??As for yourself, you won't be invited.
  c. *As for herself, she won't be invited.
(12.2) a. John told Mary that as for himself, he wouldn't be invited.
  b. ??John told Mary that as for herself, she wouldn't be invited.
  c. *John told me (in reference to Mary) that as for herself, she wouldn't be invited.

Ross (1970, pp. 230–232) attempts to account for the ungrammaticality of (12.2c) in the following manner:

(12.3) *Constraint on "As For X-Self" (Ross):* The reflexive pronoun may occur following *as for* only if its antecedent is the *subject* of the next higher sentence.

He uses the same hypothesis for justifying the presence of the abstract matrix sentence corresponding to *I SAY TO YOU* for declarative sentences. Examples (12.1a) and (12.1b), he claims, are derived from (12.4a) and (12.4b), respectively:

(12.4) a. *I* SAY TO YOU THAT as for *myself,* I won't be invited.
  b. **I* SAY TO YOU THAT as for *herself,* she won't be invited.

Example (12.4a), which is the source for (12.1a), is a well-formed underlying structure, according to Ross, because *I,* the antecedent of *myself,* is the subject of the next higher sentence, while (12.4b), which is the source structure for (12.1b), is ungrammatical because there is no antecedent of *herself* in the higher sentence.

Ross's explanation would fail to account for the fact that for many speakers, (12.5b) is more acceptable than (12.5a):

(12.5) a.   ??John heard from Mary that, as for himself, he wouldn't have to move.

     b.   √/?John heard from Mary that, as for herself, she wouldn't have to move.

This can, however, be accounted for in the direct discourse perspective by assuming that the following constraint holds:

(12.6) *Constraint on "As For X-Self"*: The reflexive pronoun following *as for* in a subordinate clause is acceptable if it is in a logophoric complement clause, and if its antecedent is [+logo-1] with respect to the logophoric verb that takes the complement clause. It is marginal if its antecedent is [+logo-2]. Otherwise, it is unacceptable.

In the expression *x hears z from y, x* is [+logo-2]. Hence the marginality of (12.5a). Example (12.5b) is acceptable to the extent that the hearer can identify *Mary,* the object of *heard from,* as a [+logo-1] NP.

Of course, once John heard from Mary that he wouldn't be invited, he must have formed an internal feeling to the effect that "as for myself, I won't be invited." The fact that many speakers regard (12.5a) as less acceptable than (12.5b) seems to suggest that the expression *x hears z from y* implies that "y said z" more strongly and more readily than it implies that "x feels/knows z." On the other hand, a minority of speakers who regard (12.5b) as less acceptable than (12.5a) must be those for whom *x hears z from y* implies that "x feels/knows z" more strongly than it implies that "y said x."

Support for my explanation of the variable interpretation of *hear from* can be derived from examples like the following:

(12.7) a. ??John$_i$ heard from Mary that, as for himself$_i$, he$_i$ wouldn't have to move.

     b.   ?John$_i$ heard from someone that, as for himself$_i$, he$_i$ wouldn't have to move.

     c.   John$_i$ heard that as for himself$_i$, he$_i$ wouldn't have to move.

When the subject of the sentence is definite and the source NP is indefinite, it becomes easier to interpret the complement clause of *hear from* as representing the internal feeling of the referent of the subject rather than as an utterance by a faceless speaker. Hence, (12.7b) is more acceptable than (12.7a). When the source NP is omitted completely, as in (12.7c), there is no problem interpreting the complement clause as the subject's internal feeling. Hence the total acceptability of (12.7c).

In order to formally state the above intuitive explanation for the contrast between (12.7a) and (12.7c) in the proposed direct discourse perspective, it is necessary to distinguish between a [+logo-1] NP that represents a speaker and a [+logo-1] NP that represents an experiencer/thinker/feeler. I will use the notation [+logo-1a] for the former and the notation [+logo-1b] for the latter. We need a rule that adds a logophoric feature to a subject NP.

(12.8)   *Logophoric Feature Assignment Rule:* If an NP is in the subject position and if it is marked as [+logo-1a] or [+logo-2], optionally mark it as [+logo-1b].

Given *x [+logo-1a] told y [+logo-2] that . . .* , the above rule adds a [+logo-1b] feature to *x* specifying that a speaker is also an experiencer/ feeler. It does not add a [+logo-1b] feature to *y*, however, because *y* is not in subject position. Given *y [+logo-2] is told by x [+logo-1a] that . . .* , the above rule adds a [+logo-1b] feature to *y* because it is a [+logo-2] NP in subject position. It does not add a [+logo-1b] feature to *x* because it is not in subject position. Likewise, given *y [+logo-2] heard from x [+logo-1a] that . . .* , a [+logo-1b] feature is added to *y* because it is in subject position, but not to *x* because the latter is not in subject position.

We restate the condition for the use of the *as for x-self* pattern in the following way:

(12.9)   *Constraint on "As for X-Self"* (revised): The reflexive pronoun in the *as for x-self* pattern in a subordinate clause requires that the clause be a logophoric complement. It is
   (i)   √ if its antecedent is [+logo-1b] with respect to the logophoric verb that takes the complement clause and if there is no [+logo-1a] NP elsewhere in the same clause;
   (ii)   ? if it is [+logo-1a] but not [+logo-1b];
   (iii) ?? if it is [+logo-2], or if it is [+logo-1b] but there is a [+logo-1a] NP elsewhere in the same clause; and
   (iv)   * otherwise.

What the above constraint captures is the generalization that the pattern under discussion is best used only when its antecedent is an experiencer NP, but that if there is a "speaker" NP elsewhere in the same clause, that [+logo-1a] NP wins over the experiencer NP and forces a [+logo-2] interpretation (i.e., "??as for yourself") on the reflexive.

We are now ready to apply the above constraint to our crucial sentences:

(12.10)   a.   √*John* told Mary that, as for *himself,* he wouldn't have to move.
               $\left\{ \begin{array}{l} [+\text{logo-1a}] \\ [+\text{logo-1b}] \end{array} \right\}$
          b.   ??John told *Mary* that, as for *herself,* she wouldn't have to move.
               [+logo-2]
          c.   ?John heard from *Mary* that, as for *herself,* she wouldn't have to
               [+logo-1a]
               move.

    d.   ??*John* heard from Mary that, as for *himself,* he wouldn't have
$\begin{Bmatrix} [+\text{logo-2}] \\ [+\text{logo-1b}] \end{Bmatrix}$ $[+\text{logo-1a}]$
to move.

    e. $^{\vee}$*John* heard that, as for *himself,* he wouldn't have to move.
$\begin{Bmatrix} [+\text{logo-2}] \\ [+\text{logo-1b}] \end{Bmatrix}$

In (a), *John* receives a [+logo-1b] feature via application of the Logophoric Feature Assignment Rule. The sentence is acceptable because the antecedent of the reflexive is [+logo-1b]. In (b), *Mary,* the antecedent of *herself,* does not receive a [+logo-1b] feature because it is not in subject position. The sentence is marginal because the antecedent of the reflexive is [+logo-2]. In (c), *Mary,* the antecedent of the reflexive, does not receive a [+logo-1b] feature because it is not in subject position. The sentence is awkward because the antecedent of the reflexive is only [+logo-1a]. In (d), *John,* the antecedent of the reflexive, receives a [+logo-1b] feature, but (12.9i) does not apply because there is another NP (i.e., *Mary*) in the same clause that is [+logo-1a]. Rule (12.9iii) applies instead and marks the sentence as marginal. Finally, in (e), the antecedent of *himself* receives a [+logo-1b] feature because it is a [+logo-2] NP in subject position. Rule (12.9i) applies and marks the sentence as acceptable.

The Logophoric Feature Assignment Rule receives independent support from contrasts such as the following:

(12.11)   a.   ??Mary told John that, as for himself, he wouldn't have to move.

           b.   ??John was told by Mary that, as for himself, he wouldn't have to move.

           c.   John was told in no uncertain terms that, as for himself, he would have to move.

Example (a) is marginal because the antecedent of the reflexive is [+logo-2]. In (b), *John [+logo-2]* is in subject position and receives a [+logo-1b] feature, but the presence of a [+logo-1a] NP (i.e., *(by) Mary*) elsewhere in the same clause blocks application of (12.9i) and the sentence is marginal. In contrast, in (c), *John* [+logo-1b] satisfies (12.9i) because the speaker NP is missing in the sentence. This explains the contrast among (a), (b), and (c).

The constraint on the *as for x-self* pattern given in (12.9) undoubtedly derives from the fact that it is used to represent contrast, and therefore the sentence that contains the expression must represent a chain of thought on the part of the referent of the reflexive, concerning a group of people of which he is a member. For example, (12.10e) would require a context like the following:

(12.12)   John found out that Mary would have to move to California, and that Bill would be transferred to Texas, but he heard that, as for himself, he wouldn't have to move.

In the above example, the person who is making a comparison is John, the referent of the reflexive. The unacceptability of (12.11a, b) and (12.10d) seems to be owing to the fact that these sentences give the impression that someone else (namely, Mary) is making the comparison.[20]

Let us examine some more sentences that can only be accounted for by the proposed direct discourse perspective:

(12.13) a. *John said about Mary that, as for herself, she wouldn't be invited.
         b. *John expected of Mary that, as for herself, she would do it.
(12.14) a. It relieved Mary that, as for herself, she didn't have to move.
         b. It worried Mary that, as for herself, she hadn't been invited.

Examples (12.13a) and (12.13b) are totally unacceptable because the antecedent of the reflexive is neither [+logo-1] nor [+logo-2]. In contrast, (12.14a) and (12.14b) are completely acceptable because *Mary,* as the object of emotive verbs, is marked as [+logo-1b] from the beginning.

Next observe the following sentences:

(12.15) a. *John knew that, as for myself, I wouldn't have to move.
         b. ?John agreed with me that, as for myself, I wouldn't have to move.

Example (12.15a) is unacceptable, in spite of the fact that the complement clause in isolation is acceptable, as shown in (12.1a). This is because the reflexive *myself* in (12.15a) does not have a [+logo-1/2] antecedent. Of course, if Ross's performative analysis or an analysis similar to it were to be adopted, we would have underlying structures that would look like the following for (12.1a), (12.15a), and (12.15b):

(12.16) a. [I$_i$ [+logo-1a] SAY TO YOU [+logo-2] THAT [as for myself$_i$, I$_i$ wouldn't have to move]]
         b. [I$_i$ [+logo-1a] SAY TO YOU [+logo-2] THAT [John [+logo-1b] knew that [as for myself$_i$, I$_i$ wouldn't have to move]]]
         c. [I$_i$ [+logo-1a] SAY TO YOU [+logo-2] THAT [John agreed with me$_i$ [+logo-1a] that [as for myself$_i$, I$_i$ wouldn't have to move]]]

The chain-of-command principle would block the main clause *I* of (12.16b) from controlling the reflexive in the *as for x-self* pattern due to the presence of *John.* This would explain why (12.15a) is unacceptable. In contrast, there is no such problem with (12.16c). The sentence satisfies the constraint on the *as for x-self* pattern to the extent that *me* as the object of *agreed with* can be interpreted as representing the speaker of the content of the complement clause. Hence the acceptability of (12.15b).

All the facts discussed in this section point to the need to incorporate into any theory of grammar mechanisms that give a special status to NPs in logophoric complements that are coreferential with the speaker/hearer NPs in the main clauses.

3.13 "Super Equi-NP Deletion"

Super Equi-NP Deletion is a putative transformation that was hypothesized by Grinder (1970) to account for the correspondence between (a) and (b) in the following pairs of sentences:

(13.1) a. John$_i$ told Mary that his$_i$ preparing himself$_i$ for the exam would be impossible.

   b. John$_i$ told Mary that $\emptyset$ preparing himself$_i$ for the exam would be impossible.

(13.2) a. John told Mary$_i$ that her$_i$ preparing herself$_i$ for the exam would be impossible.

   b. John told Mary$_i$ that $\emptyset$ preparing herself$_i$ for the exam would be impossible.

(13.3) a. John$_i$ told Mary that it would be easy for him$_i$ to prepare himself$_i$ for the exam.

   b. John$_i$ told Mary that it would be easy $\emptyset$ to prepare himself$_i$ for the exam.

(13.4) a. John told Mary$_i$ that it would be easy for her$_i$ to prepare herself$_i$ for the exam.

   b. John told Mary$_i$ that it would be easy $\emptyset$ to prepare herself$_i$ for the exam.

This transformation must be constrained in such a way as to not apply to (13.5a) because (13.5b) is ungrammatical for many speakers.

(13.5) a. John$_i$ believes that Mary has told Jane that it is easy for him$_i$ to prepare himself$_i$ for the exam.

   b. *John$_i$ believes that Mary has told Jane that it is easy $\emptyset$ to prepare himself$_i$ for the exam.

It has generally been assumed that Super Equi-NP Deletion applies regularly with a matrix NP as trigger, regardless of its semantic role, unless there is an intervening noncoreferential NP between the trigger and the target, with the understanding that an NP in the same clause as the matrix trigger would not be regarded as an intervening NP.[21]

I have shown in Kuno (1974b, 1976c) that the Super Equi-NP Deletion phenomenon cannot be accounted for without recourse to the direct discourse analysis of complement clauses. Observe the following sentences:

(13.6) a. Mary$_i$ said that it would be easy to prepare herself$_i$ for the exam.

   b. John told Mary$_i$ that it would be easy to prepare herself$_i$ for the exam.

   c. $\checkmark$/?John heard from Mary$_i$ that it would be easy to prepare herself$_i$ for the exam.

d.   *John didn't hear from MARY$_i$ that it would be easy to prepare her-
self$_i$ for the exam. He heard it from JANE.

e. $\sqrt{}$/?JOHN didn't hear from Mary$_i$ that it would be easy to prepare
herself$_i$ for the exam. BILL heard it from her$_i$.

f.   *John said about Mary$_i$ that it would be easy to prepare herself$_i$ for
the exam.

The above sentences are acceptable or nearly acceptable if the direct discourse
representation of the complement clauses is (13.7a) or (13.7b), both of which
are acceptable, and they are unacceptable if the direct discourse representation
is (13.7c), which is unacceptable:

(13.7)   a.   "It will be easy to prepare myself for the exam."
         b.   "It will be easy to prepare yourself for the exam."
         c.   "*It will be easy to prepare himself/herself for the exam." [22]

In the interpretive framework that is being used in this chapter, the above
constraint can be stated in the following way:

(13.8)   *Constraint on Super Equi-NP Deletion Pattern:* The Super Equi-NP Deletion pattern in a subordinate clause is acceptable only if it appears in a
logophoric complement and if the antecedent of the PRO subject of the
infinitival or gerundive construction is [+logo-1/2] with respect to the
logophoric verb that takes the complement clause. It is unacceptable
otherwise.

We can now attribute the awkwardness of (13.6c) and (13.6e) in some idiolects
to a certain degree of difficulty that might accompany the effort to interpret
the main clause *Mary* as a [+logo-1] NP with respect to *hear from*.

The antecedent of the Super Equi-NP Deletion pattern does not have to be
in the immediately higher clause. Observe the following sentences:

(13.9)   a.   John$_i$ said to Mary that it was obvious that Ø preparing himself$_i$ for
the exam would be impossible.
         b.   ?/*John$_i$ said to Mary that Jane thought that Ø preparing himself$_i$
for the exam would be impossible.
         c. $\sqrt{}$/?John$_i$ said to Mary that some people thought that Ø preparing
himself$_i$ for the exam would be impossible.

There are wide idiolectal variations on the acceptability status of (b) and (c),
but most speakers consider (b) marginal or unacceptable and (c) acceptable or
nearly acceptable. This phenomenon can be accounted for by assuming that
the Super Equi-NP Deletion pattern is subject to the semantico-syntactic
chain-of-command principle, which applies strongly if the intervening NP is a
strong potential antecedent for PRO but only weakly if it is a weak antecedent.

3.14 **Direct Discourse Phenomena in Other Languages**

I have shown in this chapter that NPs in a logophoric complement that are coreferential with [+logo-1/2] NPs display characteristic behaviors: first, they cannot be realized in surface sentences as unpronominalized NPs; and second, they show up as reflexive pronouns in certain patterns (i.e., in patterns such as *as for himself, by Ann and himself, physicists like himself,* and *a picture of himself*). What this means is that English uses for logophoric reference a series of pronominal forms that have independent functions (personal pronouns for regular nonlogophoric reference and reflexive pronouns for regular clause-mate coreference):

(14.1) a. $John_i$ thinks that he_i (logophoric) is sick.
        b. $John_i$ thinks that he_j (nonlogophoric) is sick.
        c.   He (nonlogophoric) is sick.
(14.2) a. $John_i$ knows that there is a picture of $himself_i$ (logophoric) in the post office.
        b. $John_i$ knows that there is a picture of him_j (nonlogophoric) in the post office.
        c. $John_i$ criticized $himself_i$ (nonlogophoric) in public.

English does not regularly distinguish between logophoric and nonlogophoric pronouns, and even when it does, as in (14.2a) and (14.2b), it uses a reflexive pronoun for logophoric use, which has its independent function for specifying a "clause-mate" coreference, as shown in (14.2c).

The status of logophoric pronouns in Latin and Greek is similar. Let us first reexamine Allen and Greenough's characterization, quoted in section 3.2, of the condition for the use of indirect reflexives (i.e., reflexive pronouns in subordinate clauses with their antecedents in main clauses) in Latin.

(14.3) a.   If the subordinate clause expresses the words or thought of the subject of the main clause, the reflexive is regularly used to refer to the subject.
        b.   Sometimes the person or thing to which the reflexive refers is not the grammatical subject of the main clause, though it is in effect the subject of discourse.
             (Allen and Greenough 1883/1903, pp. 180–183)

In the framework of our direct discourse perspective, the above condition can be restated as follows:

(14.4) *Indirect Reflexives in Latin:* A reflexive pronoun can be used in a subordinate clause in Latin with a main clause antecedent only if the latter is marked as [+logo-1].

With the above generalization in mind, let us examine some sentences that Allen and Greenough use as illustrations of their observations. First observe the following two sentences:

(14.5) Petiērunt ut *sibi* licēret.
begged   that refl. be-allowed (subjunctive imperf.)
'They begged that it might be allowed them(selves).'

(14.6) Iccius nūntium mittit, nisi   subsium *sibi* submittātur . . .
message sends   unless relief   refl. is-furnished
'Iccius sends a message that unless relief be furnished him(self), . . .'

The subject of *petiērunt* '(they) begged' and that of *nūntium mittit* '(he) sends a message' are both [+logo-1a], and they serve as the antecedents of *sibi* in these two sentences. Similarly, observe the following sentence:

(14.7) Cum ipsī deō   nihil   minus grātum   futūrum   sit quam nōn
since self to-god nothing less   pleasing   about-to-be be than   not
omnibus patēre   ad *sē*   plācandum viam . . .
to-all   lie-open to refl. appeasing way
'Since to God himself nothing will be less pleasing than that the way to appease him(self) should not be open to all men . . .'

The antecedent of the reflexive *sē* is the dative-case noun *deō* 'to God.' It can trigger reflexivization because, as an experiencer dative of *plācandum* 'pleasing,' it is marked as [+logo-1b].

Compare the above sentences with the following:

(14.8) a. Sunt ita multī ut   *eōs*   carcer capere nōn
are   so many that them prison hold   not
possit.
be-possible (subjunctive)
'There are so many that the prison cannot hold them.'

   b. Ibi in proximīs villīs   ita bipartītō   fuērunt, ut Tiberis
there nearest   country-houses so in-two-parts were   that
inter eōs   et   pōns   interesset.
them and bridge lay-between (subjunctive imperf.)
'They stationed themselves in the nearest farmhouses, in two divisions, in such a manner that the Tiber and the bridge were between them.'

The antecedent of *eōs* 'them' in the *ut*-clause of (14.8a) is not a [+logo-1a/1b] noun phrase. Therefore, the use of *sē* in the place of *eōs* would have been impossible. Similarly, the antecedent of *eōs* of (14.8b), which is the subject of *fuērunt* '(they) were,' is neither [+logo-1a] nor [+logo-1b]. Hence, here too, *sē* would have been inappropriate.

It seems that a reflexive pronoun in subordinate clauses in Greek also requires that its antecedent be [+logo-1a/1b]. Smyth (1920/1956/1973) makes the following observations:

(14.9)   (i)   The reflexives of the first and second persons are not used in subordinate clauses when they refer to the subject of the main clause.

(ii)   Third-person reflexive pronouns (*heautón, heautễn, heautó* 'himself, herself, itself') can be used in subordinate clauses when they refer to the subject of the main clause.

(iii) Third-person reflexives are rarely used as indirect reflexives in adjectival clauses.

(iv)   Forms other than the reflexive pronouns are used when the subordinate clause does not form a part of the thought of the principal subject.

The above observations are very similar to those made by Allen and Greenough for Latin. Observation (iii) can be accounted for by the fact that the antecedent of the reflexive in adjectival clauses is usually not [+logo-1a/1b]. Even when a noun phrase containing a relative clause is embedded in a complement clause of saying and thinking verbs, it usually represents the speaker/narrator's characterization of the referent of the noun phrase, and therefore, if a reflexive pronoun were used in the adjectival clause, it would not correspond to the first-person pronoun in the direct discourse representation of the complement clause.

I have shown above that reflexive pronouns in Latin and Greek, whose primary function is for clause-mate reflexivization, are used as logophoric pronouns in complement clauses. There are many other languages which resort to their ready-made reflexive pronouns for logophoric functions. For example, observe the following sentences in Japanese:

(14.10)   a.   Taroo$_i$ wa *zibun$_i$* ga tensai da to   omotte   iru.
                      refl.   genius is that thinking is
          'Taroo thinks that he is a genius.'

          b. ??Taroo$_i$ wa *kare$_i$* ga tensai da to   omotte   iru.
                      he   genius is that thinking is

Facts about reflexive pronouns in Japanese are extremely complex, and the above examples grossly oversimplify them. However, it would not be too inaccurate to state that in complement clauses of saying and thinking verbs, reflexive pronouns are the unmarked [+logo-1] pronouns at least in subject position.

Similarly, observe the following sentences in Turkish:

(14.11)   a.   Ayşe Ali'ye$_i$ bugünkü gazetede *kendisinin$_i$* bir resmi olduğunu
                            dat. today's   paper-in self's   one picture being
          söyledi.
          said

'Ayshe told Ali$_i$ that there is a picture of himself$_i$ in today's paper.'

b. $^\sqrt{}$/?Ayşe Ali'den$_i$ bugünkü gazetede *kendisinin*$_i$ bir resmi
           from today's   paper-in self's   one picture
      olduğunu öğrendi.
      being   learned
      'Ayshe learned/heard from Ali$_i$ that there is a picture of (him)self$_i$
      in today's paper.'

c.   ??Ayşe Ali'den$_i$ bugünkü gazetede *kendisinin*$_i$ bir resmi
           from today's   paper-in self's   one picture
      olduğunu sakladı.
      being   concealed
      'Ayshe concealed from Ali$_i$ that there is a picture of (him)self$_i$ in
      today's paper.'

Ali, the antecedent of the reflexive, is [+logo-2] in (a) and [+logo-1] in
(b). Note that (b) is nearly acceptable—or acceptable, depending upon the
speaker—in spite of the fact that *Ali* is in an oblique case. Example (c), in
which *Ali,* the antecedent of the reflexive, is in the same ablative case, is considerably worse than (b). This must be owing to the fact that in this sentence
Ali is neither [+logo-1] nor [+logo-2]. This shows that the Turkish reflexive
also serves to some degree as a logophoric pronoun.
     Likewise, observe the following sentences in Korean:

(14.12)   a.   John$_i$-i Bill$_j$-eykey *caki*$_{i, *j}$-ka   am-i-la-ko   malhayssta.
                 Nom. Dat. self   Nom. cancer-be-that said
           'John$_i$ told Bill$_j$ that he (= John, ≠ Bill) had cancer.'

           b.   John$_i$-i Bill$_j$-hantheyse *caki*$_{i, j}$-ka   am-i-la-ko   tul-ess-ta.
                 Nom. from   self   Nom. cancer-be-that heard
           'John heard from Bill that he (= John, or Bill) had cancer.'

           c.   John$_i$-i Bill$_j$-eytayhayse *caki*$_{*i, *j}$-ka   am-i-la-ko   malhayssta.
                 Nom. about   self   Nom. cancer-be-that said
           'John said about Bill that he (≠ John, ≠ Bill) had cancer.'

Example (14.12a) shows that ordinarily, only the subject triggers reflexivization. The fact that (14.12b) is grammatical, with *caki* 'self' referring to the
oblique case NP *Bill,* can be accounted for only if we recognize the fact that
Bill is a [+logo-1] NP. In contrast, (14.12c) is unacceptable because the
oblique case NP *Bill* in this sentence is not a logophoric NP at all. These sentences show that the reflexive pronoun in Korean can be used only when its
antecedent is the subject of the sentence or is a [+logo-1] NP. Incidentally, the
fact that (14.12c) is unacceptable on the *caki = John* interpretation is owing
to semantic reasons. On this interpretation, the complement clause is not a
statement about Bill at all, and therefore it would be incompatible with what
the main clause says.
     Icelandic offers fascinating sets of data concerning the use of reflexives as

logophoric (more specifically, as [+logo-1] pronouns) in complement clauses. Thráinsson (1975) observes that reflexive pronouns *sig* (acc.), *ser* (dat.), and *sin* (gen.) show up in subordinate *that*-clauses containing subjunctive verbs but not in those containing indicative verbs:

(14.13) a. *Jón₁ veit   að María *elskar*   *sig*₁.
             knows that   loves (indic.) refl.
             'John₁ knows that Mary loves him₁.'
         b. Jón₁ segir að María *elski*   *sig*₁.
             says that   loves (subjunc.) refl.

The verb *veit* takes complement clauses with verbs in the indicative. Note that (14.13a) is unacceptable. In contrast, the verb *segir* 'says' takes complement clauses with verbs in the subjunctive. Note in (14.13b) that the reflexive *sig* can be coreferential with the main clause subject *Jón*. According to Thráinsson, verbs that typically take subjunctive in their *that*-clause complements include *telja* 'believe,' *vilja* 'want,' *neita* 'deny,' *halda fram* 'claim,' and *ímynda sér* 'imagine.'

Although the choice between indicative and subjunctive in complement clauses is mostly predetermined by the verbs that govern the complement clauses, there are certain verbs or predicates that allow both indicative and subjunctive complement clauses. Observe the following sentences:

(14.14) a. Jón las það í blaðinu   að María *hafði*   komið heim.
             read it   in newspaper that   had (indic.) come home
             'John read it in the newspaper that Mary had come home.'
         b. Jón las það í blaðinu að *hefði* komið heim.
             had (subj.)

Thráinsson observes that the indicative states a fact, whereas the subjunctive reports what John read and the speaker doesn't commit himself to the truth of that material.

The following examples show that it is not possible to say that the subjunctive controls indirect reflexivization because the subjunctive mode alone does not justify reflexivization:

(14.15) a. Jón₁ væri   glaður ef María *kyssti* hann₁/*sig₁.
             would be glad if María   would-kiss (subj.)
             'John₁ would be glad if Mary would kiss him(self)₁.'
         b. Jón₁ kemur ekki nema María *kyssi* hann₁/*sig₁.
             won't come unless   kiss (subj.)
             'John₁ won't come unless Mary kisses him(self)₁.'

In the above, reflexivization is not allowable in spite of the fact that subjunctive verbs are used in the adverbial clauses.[23]

So, occurrence in subjunctive subordinate clauses is not in fact a sufficient condition for third-person reflexives. Reflexivization into subordinate clauses in Icelandic is allowable only if the subordinate clauses are logophoric complements, and only if the reflexives are coreferential with [+logo-1] NPs in the main clause. This leads to the following formulation:

(14.16)   *Indirect Reflexives in Icelandic:* A reflexive pronoun can be used in a complement clause in Icelandic if it is coreferential with a [+logo-1] NP of the main clause, *and* if the complement clause is an expression of the logophoric NP's point of view rather than the speaker's rendition of it.[24]

Indirect reflexivization can go down into indefinitely deep complement clauses as long as (14.16) is observed. For example, compare the following sentences:

(14.17)   a.   Jón$_i$ segir að Haraldur *viti*   að María *elski sig$_i$*.
                          says that   knows (subj.) that   loves (subj.)
                 'John$_i$ says that Harold knows that Mary loves him(self)$_i$.
            b.   Jón$_i$ segir að Haraldur *viti* að María   *elskar hann$_i$/*sig$_i$*.
                                                 knows (subj.) loves (indic.)

In (a), the verb 'knows,' which ordinarily takes indicative complement clauses, appears with a subjunctive complement. This is because the complement clause represents part of John's point of view. Note that reflexivization into this deeply embedded clause is possible.[25] In (b), on the other hand, the most deeply embedded clause is in the indicative, indicating that the speaker presupposes that it is true that Mary loves John. Note that a reflexive pronoun cannot be used to refer to the main clause *Jón.*[26]

Observe, further, the following sentence:

(14.18)   Jón$_i$ segir að María$_j$ *viti*   að Haraldur$_k$ *vill*   að
                       says that   knows(subj.) that   wants(indic.) that
            Billi *heimsæki sig$_{k (*i, *j)}$*
                  visits (subj.)
            'John says that Mary knows that Harold wants that Bill visits him(self).'

Thráinsson observes that *sig* can be coreferential only with *Haraldur*. This is because the use of the indicative *vill* 'wants' signals that the content of this clause (i.e., 'Harold wants . . .') represents the speaker's point of view and not John's or Mary's. That is to say, the speaker takes it for granted that Harold wants something. The most deeply embedded clause is in the subjunctive because the verb *vilja* 'want,' as a nonfactive verb, requires a subjunctive complement clause. The reflexive *sig* can be used in this clause in reference to the subject *Haraldur* because the complement clause is an expression of Harold's wish from Harold's point of view.

The facts described above all seem to support the hypothesis that indirect reflexives in Icelandic are logophoric pronouns (more specifically, [+logo-1] pronouns), with an added requirement to the effect that the entire complement clause, of which the reflexive pronoun's antecedent is either the speaker or experiencer, be stated from his point of view (i.e., in the subjunctive). Thráinsson rejects such a characterization because of the use of reflexives in nonlogophoric contexts. For example, observe the following:

(14.19)   Jón$_i$ komþví til leiðar að María kæmi   til *sín*$_i$.
           brought it about   that   come (subj.) to refl. gen.
           'John$_i$ brought it about that Mary came to him(self)$_i$.'

Thráinsson hypothesizes that what is responsible for the use of a reflexive pronoun in (14.19) is the "intentionality" on the part of the referent of the reflexive that the sentence expresses. Compare the following two sentences:

(14.20)   a.   Jón$_i$ komþvi til leiðar að María *kom*   heim.
                brought it about   that   came (indic.) home
                'John brought it about that Mary came home.'
           b.   Jón$_i$ komþvi til leiðar að María *kæmi* heim.
                                                would-come (subj.)
                'John brought it about that Mary (lit.) would come home.'

While (b), which uses a subjunctive verb in the *that*-clause, clearly indicates that John wanted Mary to come, and he intentionally brought it about that she would, (a) lacks such an "intentionality" implication—John might not have wanted Mary to come home, or he might not have been aware that his action would and did result in Mary's coming home. Thráinsson does not try to find the common denominator between the use of indirect reflexives in complement clauses of saying and thinking verbs (for which he rejects the direct discourse analysis) and the use of reflexives exemplified in (14.19). He simply states that the common denominator, which he speculates must be a semantic one, must include concepts like "intentionality." But there does not seem to be any need for giving up the direct discourse analysis of indirect reflexives in Icelandic. The fact that the *that*-clauses of (14.19) and (14.20a) represent the content of the main clause subject's wish suggests that the *that*-clauses in these sentences function as logophoric complements, with the main clause subjects as [+logo-1b] NPs.

Napoli (1979) reports that there are speakers of Italian who allow the use of a reflexive pronoun in a subordinate clause with a main clause antecedent. She observes that reflexives of this kind are allowable for these speakers only when the verb of the subordinate clause is in the subjunctive mood. This restriction is similar to the one that we have observed for Icelandic.

(14.21)   a.   La signora$_i$ dice che io giaccia   presso di sè$_i$.
              the woman tells that I lie (subj.) near   self
              'The woman orders that I lie near (lit.) herself.'
         b.   *La signora$_i$ dice che io giaccio presso di sè$_i$.
                                    lie (indic.)
              'The woman says (states/asserts) that I am lying near (lit.) herself.'

In (a), the verb *dire* is used in the sense of 'tell, order' with a subjunctive complement, while in (b) it is used in the sense of 'say, report' with an indicative mood complement. Note that the reflexive *sè* with the main clause *la signora* as its antecedent is acceptable in (a) but unacceptable in (b).[27]

Napoli states that even when the "subjunctive mood" condition is fulfilled, different degrees of acceptability arise depending upon how clear the desires of the antecedent are with respect to the content of the target clause. She reports that the acceptability of the following sentences, for some speakers, declines as we go down the list:

(14.22)   a.   La signora ha lasciato che io restassi   ancora
              the woman has allowed that I remain (subj.) still
              presso di sè.
              beside   self
              'The woman allowed that I remain beside (lit.) herself still.'
         b.   La signora ha preteso che io restassi ancora presso di sè.
              'The woman insisted that I remain beside (lit.) herself still.'
         c.   La signora ha ordinato che io restassi ancora presso di sè.
              'The woman ordered that I remain beside (lit.) herself still.'
         d.   La signora ha permesso che io restassi ancora presso di sè.
              'The woman permitted that I remain beside (lit.) herself still.'
         e.   La signora ha negato che io fossi restato presso di sè.
                               negated   had (subj.) remained
              'The woman denied that I had remained beside herself.'

Napoli observes that the speakers who see a gradation in acceptability from best to worst in (a) through (e) use an indirect reflexive more readily when the desires of antecedents with respect to the complement clause are clear from the choice of the verb. Those desires are clearest in (a) and totally unknown in (e), according to her informants. According to her, such speakers accept the indirect reflexives in (14.23a) but not in (14.23b):

(14.23)   a.   Ho detto che Gesù voleva che noi bambini andassimo con sè
              have said that Jesus wanted   we children go (subj.) with self
              perchè me l'ha   detto proprio lui.
              because me it-has said he-himself
              'I said that Jesus wanted us children to go with himself, because he himself told me so.'

b. *Ho detto che Gesù voleva che noi bambini andassimo con sè,
   have said   Jesus wanted   we children go (subj.) with self
   ma mi sono sbagliato.
   but me am mistaken
   'I said that Jesus wanted us children to go with himself, but I was
   wrong.'

The above contrast reminds us of the contrast in English that we have observed between sentence pairs such as the following:

(14.24)   a. John$_i$ didn't tell MARY that there was a picture of himself$_i$ in the
             morning paper. He$_i$ told it to JANE.
         b. ??JOHN$_i$ didn't tell Mary that there was a picture of himself$_i$ in the
             morning paper. BILL did.

I have explained the above contrast by stating that *John,* the antecedent of the
reflexive *himself* in the picture noun in the subordinate clause, is a logophoric
(more exactly, a [+logo-1]) NP in (a), but not in (b), semantically speaking.
In (14.23a), *Gesù,* the antecedent of *sè,* is a real logophoric NP. In contrast, it
is not in (b), semantically speaking, because Jesus did not have the wish represented by the complement clause.

Although the exact conditions for the use of the indirect reflexive in Italian
in these idiolects are not clear, it seems that when it appears in a logophoric
complement, it must be, as Napoli has observed, that the logophoric complement is in the subjunctive mood, that the main clause verb expresses the desires of the main clause agent (i.e., the antecedent of the reflexive), and that
its antecedent is a real [+logo-1] NP.

I have shown above that languages such as English, Latin, classical Greek,
Japanese, Icelandic, and some idiolects of Italian use reflexive pronouns,
whose primary function is for marking coreference with clause-mate NPs, as
logophoric pronouns. In contrast, there are languages which use first- and
second-person pronouns in complement clauses of saying and thinking verbs in
reference to [+logo-1] and [+logo-2] noun phrases in the main clause. In other
words, these languages lack (obligatory) person agreement in indirect speech.
Observe, for example, the following sentences in Navajo from Akmajian and
Anderson (1970):

(14.25)   a. Jáan be'esdzą́ą́ 'áyóí yó'ní ńt'éé' Bill *hatsi'*   *'ayóí 'ájó'ní*
             John his-wife loves   but   Bill his-daughter loves
             hałní.
             told
             'John$_i$ loves his$_i$ wife, but Bill told (someone) that he$_i$ loves his$_i$
             daughter.'

b. Jáan be'esdzą́ą́   'áyóí yó'ní ńt'éé' Bill 'éi *nitsi'*
    John his-wife   loves   but Bill him your-daughter
    'ayóí 'ííní' haɬní.
    (you)-love told

In (b), the subject of the embedded verb and the genitive NP are intended to be coreferential with the main clause [+logo-2] NP (i.e., the hearer NP). Note that they are realized as second-person pronouns. In contrast, in (a), the subject of the embedded verb and the genitive NP are not intended to be coreferential with the main clause [+logo-2] NP, but with *John* of the preceding clause. Here, third-person pronouns show up.[28]

Likewise, observe the following sentences in Amharic, which I owe to Bach (personal communication, 1968; discussed in Kuno 1972b):

(14.26) a. yohannis habtam nəw.
             John   rich   is (third-person singular)
             'John is rich.'
         b. yohannis ine habtam nəñ alə.
             John   I   rich   am said
             'John$_i$ said he$_i$ was rich.'
         c. yohannis rasum habtam nəñ alə.
             John   himself rich am said
             'John$_i$ said he$_i$ was rich.'

Note that in both (b) and (c), the verb of the embedded sentence is in the first person. Bach observes that if the third-person pronoun is used in the embedded clause, the sentence means 'John said that he was rich,' where *John* and *he* are not coreferential. Thus, Amharic also lacks indirect discourse formation. In this language, 'John said that I was rich,' where *I* refers to the speaker of the sentence, is represented using the construction with the accusative pronoun:

(14.27) yohannis inen habtam nəw alə.
         John   me   rich   is   said (third person)
         '(Lit.) John said me is rich; John said I was rich.'

Similarly, observe the following example in Coptic taken from "The Martyrdom of St. Claude of Antioch":[29]

(14.28) Tenouče   on   afshai   nai   jeakti   ntekpsukhe
         so-now   moreover he-has-written to-me   that-you-gave your-life
         hatōi   hmppolumos.
         for-me   in-the-war
         'So now moreover, he has written to me that you gave your life *for him* in the war.'

The above sentence has an interesting mixture of indirect and direct discourse formation. The context of the sentence makes clear that the second person in the embedded clause refers, not to the utterer of this sentence, but to its addressee. That is, the second person here is the result of indirect discourse formation. At the same time, *hatōi* 'for me' refers, not to the utterer of the sentence, but to the grammatical subject (i.e., *he*) of the sentence. In other words, indirect discourse formation has not applied to *hatōi*. To put it differently, the first-person pronoun in the above example is intended to be coreferential with the main clause [+logo-1] NP.

Thus far, I have discussed languages which use regular reflexive pronouns or personal pronouns as logophoric pronouns. There are languages which have a special series of pronouns exclusively reserved for logophoric use. For example, observe the following sentences in Ewe:[30]

(14.29) a. Kofi be yè-dzo.
             say LOG-leave
             'Kofi said that he (= Kofi) left.'
         b. Kofi be me-dzo.
             'Kofi said that I left.'
         c. Kofi be e-dzo.
             'Kofi said that he/she (≠ Kofi) left.'

As the translation of (c) shows, a regular third-person pronoun in the complement clause of *be* 'say' cannot be coreferential with the subject of the main clause. If coreference is intended, the logophoric pronoun *yè* must be used. This is true even when the main clause subject is a first- or second-person pronoun:

(14.30) a. è-be   yè-a-va.
             you-say LOG-T-come
             'You$_i$ said you$_i$ (singular) would come.'
         b. è-be   yèwo-a-va.
             you-say LOG-T-come
             'You$_i$ said you$_{i+j}$ (plural) would come.'

Note that (a) has a singular logophoric pronoun *ye,* while (b) has a plural logophoric form *yewo.*

There are numerous other direct discourse phenomena in many languages, but they usually show up interacting with point-of-view factors, as is the case with Icelandic indirect reflexivization. We will observe some of these phenomena in Chapter 5 where I discuss point-of-view or empathy phenomena in English and other languages.

3.15 **Direct Discourse Perspective and GB Theory**

The discussions in this chapter must have made it clear that some kind of a logophoric rule is needed in GB theory, as well. For example, observe the following contrast, which was discussed in section 3.1.

(15.1)   a. *He$_i$ always lavishly recommends for teaching appointments the students that this professor$_i$ has personally taught.

      b. The students that this professor$_i$ has personally taught, he$_i$ always lavishly recommends for teaching appointments.

(15.2)   a. *He$_i$ admitted without any hesitation that John$_i$ was the child's father.

      b. *That John$_i$ was the child's father, he$_i$ admitted without any hesitation.

As discussed in section 2.8 and section 2.11, GB theory does not make clear at what stage and to what kind of structure its binding conditions apply. However, regardless of whether they apply to LF-representations constructed from empty trace or structured trace, and regardless of whether they apply to LF-representations only or to S-structure as well, binding conditions cannot distinguish between (15.1) and (15.2), and therefore they will mark (15.1b) and (15.2b) either as both acceptable or as both unacceptable.

In section 2.11, I stated that GB theory will need the following two sets of binding conditions in the place of Conditions A, B, and C in order to account for the facts discussed in that chapter:

(15.3)   Anaphor rules (Cyclical)

    Condition A': An anaphor is coindexed with a nonreflexive NP that k-commands it. (optional)

    N.B.1: An S-structure that contains an anaphor that has not been coindexed with any other NP in it is unacceptable.

    N.B.2: Anaphors are subject to the semantico-syntactic chain-of-command principle.

    Condition B': A nonreflexive (pronominal or R-expression) is marked for disjoint reference in S with an NP that precedes and k-commands it. (obligatory)

    N.B.: This condition applies subject to the chain-of-command principle.

(15.4)   *Nonanaphor Rule* (Postcyclical—applying to the S-structure)

    Condition C': An R-expression is variably marked for disjoint reference with an NP that precedes and k-commands it. An R-expression is invariably marked for disjoint reference with an NP that precedes and c-commands it.

The anaphor rules apply cyclically with S and $\bar{S}$ as cyclical nodes, while the nonanaphor rule applies postcyclically. Note also that the nonanaphor rule does not apply to a pair of NPs (the latter being an R-expression) that have already been marked for joint or disjoint reference by the anaphor rules.

It is clear that GB theory needs a logophoric rule that applies to the prefronting structure in order to account for facts such as (15.1)–(15.2). The rule would be something like the following:

(15.5)   *Logophoric Rule* (cyclical)

   Condition D':   Given a verb that takes [+logo-1/2] NPs and a logophoric complement clause, an R-expression in that complement clause must be marked for disjoint reference with the [+logo-1/2] NPs.

The subject of the verb *recommend,* as it is used with a nonsentential object, is neither [+logo-1] nor [+logo-2]. Therefore, the Logophoric Rule does not apply between *he* and *this professor* in (15.1a) so as to mark them for disjoint reference. After the fronting of *the students that this professor has personally taught,* Condition C' applies, but since the right-hand NP is a pronoun, the rule does not mark the two NPs for disjoint reference. Hence arises the possibility for a coreferential interpretation between the two NPs. On the other hand, the verb *admit* with a sentential object takes a [+logo-1] NP as its subject. Therefore, in (15.2a), *he* is marked as [+logo-1]. The logophoric rule applies to this structure and marks *John* for disjoint reference with *he.* After the fronting of the sentential object, Condition C' cannot apply to these two NPs to establish joint reference because they have already been marked for disjoint reference.

Observe, further, the following sentences:

(15.6)   a.   It's been claimed by John that he is the best lawyer around.
         b.   It's been claimed by him that John is the best lawyer around.

While a coreferential interpretation between *John* and *he/him* is possible for (15.6a), it is impossible for (15.6b). Even assuming that the *that*-clause is a constituent of a VP—which is a questionable assumption in itself—Chomsky's binding conditions as they are stated now cannot block a coreferential interpretation from (16.5b). Note that *John* is c-commanded by *him* neither in the S-structure nor in the LF-representation of the sentence, and therefore, co-indexing of the two is not ruled out. Furthermore, even if c-command is replaced by k-command, or modified in such a way as to be able to ignore a PP node, the binding conditions can still not explain why (15.7a) can have a coreferential interpretation while (15.7b) cannot.[31]

(15.7)   a.   Those who trusted John were betrayed by him repeatedly.
         b.   That John is the best lawyer around has often been claimed by him.

The Logophoric Rule is needed to block a coreferential interpretation of *John* and *he/him* from (15.6b) and (15.7b).

In section 2.11, I discussed how a coreferential interpretation can be blocked by the proposed anaphor rules (Conditions A' and B') from sentences such as the following:

(15.8)   Who did he say Mary kissed?

I hypothesized that Conditions A' and B' apply cyclically, and that they crucially apply to the higher S of the following intermediate structure:

(15.9)   [$_\bar{S}$ COMP [$_S$ he did say [$_\bar{S}$ who$_i$ [$_S$ Mary kissed [e]$_i$]]]

In the higher S-structure, the R-expression *who* is k-commanded by *he*. Therefore, they are marked for disjoint reference by Condition B'. In fact, there is another reason for the impossibility of a coreferential interpretation for *who* and *he* in (15.8). Observe the following underlying structure:

(15.10)   [he [+logo-1a] did say [Mary kissed who]]

The Logophoric Rule (Condition D') marks *who* for disjoint reference with *he* because the latter is [+logo-1]. Observe, also, the following sentence:

(15.11)   Whose brother did he say Mary kissed?

It is not possible to assign a coreferential interpretation to *whose* and *he* in the above sentence, either. This also can be accounted for by the Logophoric Rule, as well as by Condition B'.

The reason for an explanation of the sort that was given in Chapter 2, using the intermediate structure of (15.9), is that the absence of a coreferential interpretation for sentences of the pattern of (15.8) and (15.11) extends to cases where logophoric verbs are not involved:

(15.12)   a.   Who did he deny that Mary kissed?
           b.   Who did he forget that Mary kissed?

At the beginning of this chapter, I showed that verbs such as *deny* and *forget* can take non–direct discourse complements. Therefore, if the logophoric rule were the only mechanism for ruling out a coreferential interpretation for (15.8) between *who* and *he*, it should be possible to obtain a coreferential interpretation for (15.12a, b). The fact that these sentences do not allow such an interpretation shows that there is something else going on to block a coreferential interpretation. Application of Condition B' to the higher S-cycle between *he* and *who*, with the latter in the COMP position, is the answer to this question.

Let us now proceed to discuss picture noun reflexives in logophoric complements. The binding conditions given in (15.3) through (15.5) cannot yet distinguish between (15.13a) and (15.13b):

(15.13)   a. $^{\vee}$/?John said to Mary that there was a picture of herself in the
morning paper.
b. *John said about Mary that there was a picture of herself in the
morning paper.

It is clear that the constraint given in (11.5), repeated below for ease of reference, is needed to filter out sentences such as (15.13b):

(15.14)   *Constraint on Picture Noun Reflexives:* The reflexive pronoun in a picture noun construction in a logophoric complement clause is acceptable
if its antecedent is [+logo-1] with respect to the logophoric verb that
takes the complement clause, and acceptable, or marginal, depending upon the speaker, if the antecedent is [+logo-2]. Otherwise, it is
unacceptable.

The only remaining question to be settled is how this constraint is to be applied. Considering the fact that the constraints applying before movement
transformations would disturb the structural relationship between logophoric
verbs and their logophoric NPs and complements, it is best to assume that it
applies cyclically. There is, however, a great deal of overlap between the domain of application of Condition B' and that of the above constraint. I hypothesize that these two conditions apply independently such that a sentence
containing a reflexive is ruled out if either of the two conditions is violated.
This stipulation is consistent with that required for anaphor rules (Conditions
A' and B'); that is, coindexing of two NPs is possible only if neither of the
two rules disallows it. This stipulation, which also applies to the logophoric
rule given in (15.5), sets the cyclical binding conditions apart from the postcyclical nonanaphor rule, which applies only to pairs of NPs whose coindexing or disjoint indexing has not been determined yet by cyclical rules.

3.16 Conclusion

In this chapter, I have shown that NPs in complement clauses of logophoric
verbs require special treatments in determining coreference or disjoint reference and that there are certain syntactic patterns which can appear only in
logophoric complements. It is clear that any theory of grammar would require
some version of the direct discourse perspective described here.

There is a problem with the logophoric rule that is very similar to the one
that we observed with respect to the reflexive rule. Recall that we noted the
following contrast in section 12 of Chapter 2:

(16.1)   a. *Which pictures of John$_i$ did he$_i$ like?
b.   Which of Betty$_i$'s dates did she$_i$ like best?

At the time that Condition B′ applies, we have the following structures:

(16.2)   a.   [$_\bar{s}$ Q [$_s$ he did like which pictures of John]]
          b.   [$_\bar{s}$ Q [$_s$ she did like which of Betty's dates best]]

Condition B′ would apply to *John* and *Betty('s)* and would assign disjoint reference between them and the preceding pronouns. In spite of this, (16.1b) seems to be perfectly acceptable. In order to solve this problem, I had to propose that we need to assign to pairs of NPs that Condition B′ has marked for disjoint reference an index that represents the "strength" of the disjoint indexing. The more deeply embedded the target NP is within larger NPs, the weaker the strength of disjoint indexing. Condition C′, a pronominalization rule, which applies to S-structure after the fronting of *wh*-expressions in these sentences, would then be allowed to ignore weak disjoint indexing and could assign coindices as long as the "precedence and k-command" constraint is not violated.

We need a similar convention for NPs that have been assigned disjoint indices by the logophoric rule. Compare the following sentences:

(16.3)   a.   *Which pictures of John$_i$ did he$_i$ say Mary liked best?
          b.   Which of John$_i$'s pictures did he$_i$ say Mary liked best?

At the time of application of the logophoric rule, we have the following structures:

(16.4)   a.   [Q he [+logo-1] did say [Mary did like which pictures of John best]]
          b.   [Q he [+logo-1] did say [Mary did like which of John's pictures best]]

For both (a) and (b), the logophoric rule would mark *John,* which is in a logophoric complement, for disjoint reference with *he [+logo-1].* In spite of this, (16.3b) seems to be acceptable to most speakers. It seems that this is due to the fact that while *John* in (16.3a) is only once embedded in a larger NP, it is doubly embedded in a larger NP in (16.3b). What this means is that the logophoric rule, like Condition B′, applies with varying strengths, and that a target NP that is multiply embedded within NPs is insulated, to some extent, from the disjoint-indexing power of the rule. The "weak" disjoint indexing can be ignored and condition C′ can be applied. Condition C′ marks as unacceptable sentences such as

(16.5)   a.   *He$_i$ said Mary liked these pictures of John$_i$ best.
          b.   *He$_i$ said Mary liked some of John$_i$'s pictures best.

in which the "precedence" condition remains undisturbed, but it can assign coindexing when the "precedence" condition is removed, as in (16.3b).

The above phenomenon, I suspect, is reducible to the problem of what options the speakers have in choosing expressions to refer to objects. The logophoric rule says that speakers do not have much choice within logophoric complements in referring to the [+logo-1/2] NPs—they have to use the kind of expression that the [+logo-1/2] would have used, that is, a pronominal NP. The acceptability of (16.3b), on the other hand, shows that once the NP that is coreferential with the [+logo-1/2] is moved out of the logophoric complement, speakers are allowed to use their own characterization of the referent of that NP, subject to certain conditions. But reexamination of the coreference and disjoint reference problems from the above perspective must wait for future research.

4 Pronouns and Reflexives (2)

4.1 Introduction

In chapter 2, I showed that reflexives with clause-mate antecedents require that their referents be targets of the actions or mental states represented by the verb phrase. For example, observe the following contrasts:

(1.1)   a.   John$_i$ pulled the blanket over him$_i$.
           b.   John$_i$ pulled the blanket over himself$_i$.
(1.2)   a.   John$_i$ hid the book behind him$_i$.
           b.   John$_i$ hid the book behind himself$_i$.

I noted that for many speakers, (1.1b) necessarily implies that John tried to cover himself up with the blanket to hide under it, while no such implication is necessary for (1.1a). Similarly, I noted that for many speakers (1.2b) necessarily implies that John held the book in his hand and put it behind his back. On the other hand, (1.2a), although it can be used to describe the same situation, need not have this implication of physical contact. Perhaps the book was on the chair, and John stood in front of the chair so that the book could not be seen. What distinguishes (1.1a) and (1.1b), and (1.2a) and (1.2b), is the fact that when the reflexive is used, it is overtly asserted that the referent of the reflexive is the target of the action or mental state represented by the sentence. When the pronoun is used, however, there is no overt or covert assertion to that effect. The same factor also accounts for the following contrast:

(1.3)   a.   John$_i$ has great passion in him$_i$.
           b.   *John$_i$ has great passion in himself$_i$.
(1.4)   a.   *John$_i$ has confidence in him$_i$.
           b.   John$_i$ has confidence in himself$_i$.[1]

In (1.3), the object of *in* is not the target of an action or mental state at all. Hence the impossibility of using a reflexive. In contrast, in (1.4), the object of *in* is the target of the mental state represented by *have confidence in*. Hence the impossibility of using a pronoun.

The above contrast shows that the use of reflexives is a phenomenon sensitive to the semantics of the sentence. In the present chapter, I will further demonstrate the semantic- and discourse-based nature of the constraints on the use of reflexive pronouns.[2]

4.2 The Antecedent of Reflexives

Observe the following sentences:

(2.1)   a.   John$_i$ talked to Mary about himself$_i$.
         b.   *John$_i$ talked to Mary about him$_i$.

As the ungrammaticality of (2.1b) shows, the pattern *x talks to y about w* requires a reflexive pronoun if *w* is coreferential with *x*.[3] This phenomenon is generally dealt with as a case of straightforward, automatic application of a rule of intrasentential reflexivization.

Although reflexivization with a nonsubject trigger in fact occurs, not all speakers find it as acceptable as subject-triggered reflexivization. Observe, for example, the following sentences:

(2.2)   a. $^\lor$/?John talked to Mary$_j$ about herself$_j$.
         b.   *John talked to Mary$_j$ about her$_j$.

There are people who consider (2.2a) perfectly acceptable, but many consider the sentence awkward, and some consider it marginal. Since there are many languages which do not allow reflexivization with a nonsubject trigger, this phenomenon in English is not at all surprising.

Similarly, observe the following sentence:

(2.3)   John talked to Bill about himself.

Most speakers agree that the reflexive pronoun is interpreted primarily as being coreferential with the subject *John,* but many say that the sentence has a secondary meaning in which *himself* is interpreted as coreferential with *Bill.*

There are many sentences, however, that cannot be accounted for by the assumption that subject-triggered reflexivization is automatic and that nonsubject-triggered reflexivization is weaker than subject-triggered reflexivization. Observe the following sentences, some of which were discussed in Kuno and Kaburaki (1975/1977):

(2.4)   a.   I talked to Mary about myself.
         b.   Did you talk to Mary about yourself?
         c.   John$_i$ talked to Mary about himself$_i$.
         d.   (?)One of the students$_i$ talked to Mary about himself$_i$.
         e.   ?A passerby$_i$ talked to Mary about himself$_i$.
         f.   (?)?Someone$_i$ talked to Mary about himself$_i$.

The first three sentences are perfectly acceptable, but from (d) on, acceptability decreases as we go down the list. Example (d) is nearly acceptable if it is assumed that the speaker knew the identity of the person who talked to Mary, but it is marginal otherwise. Example (f) is marginal if it is taken to be an objective description of what happened: someone whom the speaker did not know talked to Mary about his problem/condition/et cetera. On the other hand, the sentence is nearly acceptable if it is assumed that the speaker knew the identity of that *someone* and was simply concealing his identity by using *someone*. The acceptability judgments of (d) and (f) recorded in (2.4) are those that go with the unmarked interpretations of the sentences: namely, the speaker knew the identity in (d), and did not know the identity in (f), of the person who talked to Mary.

Similarly, observe the following sentences:

(2.5)   a.   John$_i$ pulled Mary toward himself$_i$.
        b.   (?)?Someone$_i$ pulled Mary toward himself$_i$.
(2.6)   a.   Someone$_i$, who shall remain nameless, plastered mud all over himself$_i$ and tried to frighten the ladies.
        b.   (?)?Someone$_i$ plastered mud all over himself$_i$ and tried to frighten the ladies.
(2.7)   a.   This good-looking all-American boy$_i$ seated Mary next to himself$_i$.
        b.   (?)?A good-looking all-American boy$_i$ seated Mary next to himself$_i$.

There may be idiolectal variations on the native speakers' judgments on the level of acceptability of the (b) sentences, but most speakers would agree that the (b) sentences are not as good as the corresponding (a) sentences unless the speaker knows the identity of the referent of *someone* or *a good-looking all-American boy* in these sentences but has chosen not to reveal it.

Where does the above contrast come from? Let us first examine (2.4). It seems that what is at issue here is who is responsible for the information represented in the sentences. In (2.4a), the information that the speaker talked to Mary about himself clearly originates from the speaker himself. In (2.4b), the source of information lies in the hearer. Now observe the following sentences:

(2.8)   a.   John talked to Mary about Jane.
        b.   Someone talked to Mary about Jane.

In (2.8a), the source of the privileged information represented by the sentence is either John or Mary.[4] On the other hand, in (2.8b), if the speaker does not know the identity of *someone*, it is most unlikely that he has obtained the information represented by the sentence from the referent of *someone*. Thus, the most unmarked interpretation of the sentence is that the speaker has obtained the information from Mary. In the same way, Mary must have been the source of the information represented by (2.4f). The fact that (2.8b) is acceptable, but that (2.4f) is marginal, suggests that there is something in *himself* in (2.4f) which prevents us from interpreting the sentence as one which represents the information that the speaker has obtained from Mary. We can account for this phenomenon if we can assume that the pattern *x talked to y about x-self* requires that the sentence be interpreted as representing the information that the speaker has obtained from the referent of *x*. Then, the marginality of (2.4f) can be attributed to the fact that while *himself* signals that the information must have been obtained from the referent of *someone,* the pattern *someone talked to Mary about y,* as discussed above, implies that the information must have been obtained, not from the referent of *someone,* but from Mary. It can be hypothesized that the marginality of the sentence derives from this conflict about the source of the privileged information.

Let us now move on to (2.5). If (2.5a) represented simply a physical act of John's dragging Mary in, the speaker could have obtained the information represented by the sentence from John or Mary, or alternatively, the speaker could have been at the scene and observed this event. The fact that (2.5b) is marginal suggests that *x pulled y toward x-self* means more than *x dragged y in.* If the speaker is reporting on what he has heard, the marginality of (2.5b) can be accounted for in the same way as that of (2.4f). That is, the reflexive in this sentence implies that the speaker has obtained the information represented by the sentence from the referent of the reflexive. On the other hand, it is pragmatically most unlikely that the speaker could have obtained this information from a person whose identity he does not know. We can say that (2.5b) is marginal because of this contradiction. Now, how about the situation in which the speaker was at the scene and witnessed someone dragging Mary in? Here we have to assume that the expression *x pulled y toward x-self* implies not only that *x* is the direct target of the action '*x* pulled *y* toward' but also that the whole action is being described by the speaker from *x*'s camera angle (i.e., from *x*'s vantage point). This latter implication is perhaps due to the fact that *toward oneself* represents an internal sensation/realization that the action is being directed toward oneself.

If we assume that *x pulled y toward x-self* requires that the speaker take *x*'s camera angle, then we can account for the marginality of (2.5b) by saying that the reflexive in the sentence forces us to interpret the sentence as having been uttered from the camera angle of the referent of *someone,* while it is difficult for the speaker to take the camera angle of someone whose identity he does not know. The marginality or awkwardness of (2.6b) and (2.7b) seems to be due to the same reason.

This concept of camera angle will be fully developed and systematically described in Chapter 5. For the purpose of the present discussion, let us informally assume that a constraint of the following sort exists for use of reflexives in English:

(2.9)   *Empathy Constraint on Reflexives:* A sentence that contains a reflexive pronoun with a clause-mate antecedent must be interpretable as one produced from the camera angle of the referent of the reflexive.

This constraint automatically accounts for the situation in which the speaker has not witnessed the event represented by the sentence, but in which he has

obtained the information from someone else. In (2.4f), for example, pragmatically speaking, the speaker must have obtained the privileged information from Mary. In other words, it must be that the sentence represents the
event from Mary's camera angle. At the same time, the presence of *himself* in
the sentence, according to the Empathy Constraint on Reflexives, requires
that the sentence represent the point of view of the referent of the reflexive.
These two requirements are incompatible, and hence the marginality of the
sentence.

The above Empathy Constraint on Reflexives requires some modifications.
First, when a reflexive is the direct object of a verb, there does not seem to be
any such requirement. Observe the following sentences:

(2.10)   a.   Someone$_i$ killed himself$_i$.
         b.   Someone$_i$ plastered himself$_i$ with mud and tried to frighten the
              ladies.
         c.   Someone$_i$ seated himself$_i$ next to Mary.

There does not seem to be anything wrong with these sentences. The contrast
between (2.6b) and (2.10b) and between (2.7b) and (2.10c) is particularly interesting. I suspect that this is owing to the fact that the direct object of a verb
is the target of the action or state represented by the verb to a much greater
extent than the object of a preposition is the target of the action or state represented by the predicate, so that it is less affected by discourse factors of the
kind we are discussing here.

Second, the Empathy Constraint on Reflexives does not seem to apply at all
when the antecedent of a reflexive is a generic NP:

(2.11)   a.   Anyone can talk to me about themselves/themself.
         b.   Anyone can talk to me about themselves/themself.
         c.   Anybody can talk to anybody else about themselves/themself.[5]

These sentences are all perfectly acceptable. We will see in Chapter 5 that this
watering down of empathy requirement for reflexives in sentences that involve
generic NPs is not an isolated phenomenon, but that it extends to other
empathy-related areas in English.

Third, the Empathy Constraint is considerably weakened (but not totally
lifted) when the sentence is in the past progressive form. For example, observe the following sentences:

(2.12)   a.   (?)?Someone$_i$ talked to Mary about himself$_i$. (= 2.4f)
         b.   ?Someone$_i$ was talking to Mary about himself$_i$.
(2.13)   a.   (?)?A passerby$_i$ talked to a lady about himself$_i$.
         b.   (?)A passerby$_i$ was talking to a lady about himself$_i$.
(2.14)   a.   (?)?Someone$_i$ plastered mud around himself$_i$.
         b.   ?Someone$_i$ was plastering mud around himself$_i$.

The fact that (2.12b) and (2.13b) are better than the corresponding (a) sentences is undoubtedly owing to the fact that the past progressive in effect removes the privileged access requirement for the information represented in these sentences, so that the speaker need only have overheard a small fraction of the conversation to establish that the referent of the reflexive was talking about himself. The fact that (2.14b) is better than (2.14a) seems to be owing to the fact that sentences in the progressive form in general allow for an interpretation in which the speaker has taken a neutral camera angle.

The above observations necessitate a revision of the Empathy Constraint on Reflexives, as shown below:

(2.15)   *Empathy Constraint on Reflexives* (revised): A sentence that contains a reflexive pronoun that is not a direct object of a verb requires that it be interpreted as one produced from the camera angle of the referent of the reflexive if the sentence is in the tense and aspect that requires an explicit camera angle with respect to the event described in the sentence.

(2.16)   *Empathy and Tense/Aspect*
    (i)   Past tense nonprogressive sentences that are not general truth statements *strongly* require that an explicit camera angle (neutral or nonneutral) be taken.
    (ii)   Past tense progressive sentences *weakly* require that an explicit camera angle be taken.
    (iii) Sentences that represent general truth do *not* require that an explicit camera angle be taken.

Let us now examine reflexives with nonsubject antecedents. Observe, first, the following sentences:

(2.17)   a.   ?Mary talked to John$_i$ about himself$_i$.
          b.   ??Mary talked to a student$_i$ about himself$_i$.
          c.   ??Mary talked to a passerby$_i$ about himself$_i$.
          d.   ?*Mary talked to someone$_i$ about himself$_i$.

As we have already noted, (2.17a) is slightly awkward for many speakers, owing to the fact that nonsubject triggers are weaker than subject triggers. However, the degree of acceptability goes down rather rapidly as we make the dative NP less and less definite.

Similarly, observe the following sentences:

(2.18)   a.   ?Mary talked to John$_i$ about himself$_i$.
          b.   (?)?I talked to John$_i$ about himself$_i$.

As was noted in Kuno and Kaburaki (1975/1977), there are many speakers who consider (2.18b) less acceptable than (2.18a). This must be owing to the fact that it is difficult for the speaker to take John's camera angle while he is describing his own action.

Let us assume that the following constraints are applicable to the use of reflexives in simplex sentences, in addition to the Empathy Constraint on Reflexives stated in (2.15):

(2.19)   *Surface Structure Hierarchy:* Reflexives are better when their antecedents are in subject position than otherwise:

Subject > Nonsubject[6]

(2.20)   *Speech-Act Empathy Hierarchy:* It is difficult for the speaker to describe an action or state involving him while taking someone else's camera angle.

(2.21)   *Anaphoricity Hierarchy:* In sentences that require the speaker to establish an explicit camera angle (cf. (2.15)), the higher their antecedents are in the Anaphoricity Hierarchy, the better reflexives are.

Definite NPs > Indefinite NPs > Indefinite Pronouns

The above hierarchy is a simplified version of Yokoyama's (1979) hierarchy for eligibility of NPs for themehood in sentences.

One way to represent the interaction of the Surface Structure Hierarchy, the Speech-Act Empathy Hierarchy, and the Anaphoricity Hierarchy is to assign to a given trigger (i.e., antecedent) for reflexivization an integral value determined by its relative position on the hierarchies. Let us assign the following weights to items in the hierarchies:

(2.22)   a.   Surface Structure Hierarchy: Subject > Nonsubject
                                                   $(+1)$ (-1)

          b.   Speech-Act Empathy Hierarchy: (-1) if a first-person pronoun
                                                   is elsewhere in the sentence

          c.   Anaphoricity Hierarchy:
                Definite NP > Indefinite NP > Indefinite Pronoun
                                              (*someone, anyone*, etc.)
                $(+1)$ (-1) (-2)

The trigger potential (TP) of a given NP for reflexivization is computed by adding the weights it receives in the above hierarchies. For example, an NP that is in subject position and that is indefinite (e.g., *a student*) receives $(+1)$ $+ (-1) = (0)$ as its trigger potential. The following examples illustrate how this quantitative model works:

(2.23)   a.   John$_i$ talked to Mary about himself$_i$.
                TP of *John:* subject $(+1)$ + definite $(+1)$ = $(+2)$
          b.   ?A student$_i$ talked to Mary about himself$_i$.
                TP of *a student:* subject $(+1)$ + indefinite NP (-1) = (0)
          c.   (?)?Someone$_i$ talked to Mary about himself$_i$.
                TP of *someone:* subject $(+1)$ + indefinite pronoun (-2) = (-1)

      d.   ??Someone$_i$ talked to me about himself$_i$.
            TP of *someone:* subject $(+1)$ + speech-act (-1) + indefinite pronoun $(-2) = (-2)$

The trigger potential values of the subjects in the above sentences decrease from $(+2)$ to (-2), reflecting the corresponding decrease in the level of acceptability of these sentences.

Let us examine some more sentences to see if they show the same correlation between the trigger potential and the observed acceptability status:

(2.24)   a.   ?Mary talked to John$_i$ about himself$_i$.
            TP of *John:* nonsubject (-1) + definite $(+1) = (0)$
       b.   ??Mary talked to a student$_i$ about himself$_i$.
            TP of *a student:* nonsubject (-1) + indefinite NP $(-1) = (-2)$
       c.   ?*Mary talked to someone$_i$ about himself$_i$.
            TP of *someone:* nonsubject (-1) + indefinite pronoun $(-2) = (-3)$
       d.   (?)?I talked to John$_i$ about himself$_i$.
            TP of *John:* nonsubject (-1) + speech-act (-1) + definite $(+1) = (-1)$
       e.   *I talked to someone$_i$ about himself$_i$.
            TP of *someone:* nonsubject (-1) + speech-act (-1) + indefinite pronoun $(-2) = (-4)$
       f. $^\vee$/?Mary talked to me about myself.
            TP of *me:* nonsubject (-1) + definite $(+1) = (0)$
       g.   cf. (?)Mary$_i$ talked to me about herself$_i$.
            TP of *Mary:* subject $(+1)$ + speech-act (-1) + definite $(+1) = (+1)$

In the above examples, also, there is a close correlation between the observed acceptability judgments and the weights that the quantitative model under discussion assigns to the sentences.

When past-tense progressive sentences are involved, empathy control on reflexives gets considerably weakened, as observed in (2.12)–(2.14). We can account for this, as a crude approximation, by assuming that the *negative* weights assigned to entries in the hierarchies given in (2.22) are halved in sentences of this kind. Then we have the trigger potential values as specified below for sentences corresponding to (2.23) and (2.24).

(2.25)   a.   John$_i$ was talking to Mary about himself$_i$.
            TP of *John:* subject $(+1)$ + definite $(+1) = (+2)$
       b.   (?)A student$_i$ was talking to Mary about himself$_i$.
            TP of *a student:* subject $(+1)$ + indefinite NP $(-1/2) = (+0.5)$
       c.   ?Someone$_i$ was talking to Mary about himself$_i$.
            TP of *someone:* subject $(+1)$ + indefinite pronoun $(-2/2) = (0)$

    d.   ?Someone$_i$ was talking to me about himself$_i$.
        TP of *someone:* subject $(+1)$ + speech-act $(-1/2)$ + indefinite
                pronoun $(-2/2)$ = (-0.5)

    e.   Mary was talking to John$_i$ about himself$_i$.
        TP of *John:* nonsubject $(-1/2)$ + definite $(+1)$ = $(+0.5)$

    f.   ?Mary was talking to a student$_i$ about himself$_i$.
        TP of *a student:* nonsubject $(-1/2)$ + indefinite NP $(-1/2)$ =
                (-1)

    g.   (?)?Mary was talking to someone$_i$ about himself$_i$.
        TP of *someone:* nonsubject $(-1/2)$ + indefinite pronoun $(-2/2)$ =
                (-1.5)

    h.   (?)I was talking to John$_i$ about himself$_i$.
        TP of *John:* nonsubject $(-1/2)$ + speech-act $(-1/2)$ + definite
                $(+1)$ = (0)

    i.   ??I was talking to someone$_i$ about himself$_i$.
        TP of *someone:* nonsubject $(-1/2)$ + speech-act $(-1/2)$ + indefi-
                nite pronoun $(-2/2)$ = (-2)

    j.   Mary was talking to me about myself.
        TP of *me:* nonsubject $(-1/2)$ + definite $(+1)$ = $(+0.5)$

    k.   Mary$_i$ was talking to me about herself$_i$.
        TP of *Mary:* subject $(+1)$ + speech-act $(-1/2)$ + definite $(+1)$ =
                $(+1.5)$

Although the above system may be too crude to capture some of the complexities involved in assigning NPs their exact positions on the three hierarchies, which will be discussed in the sections to follow, it in fact accounts for the judgments we have observed in this section remarkably well. The following table shows the correlation between the TP (trigger potential) values of the trigger of reflexivization and the observed acceptability status of the sentences.

(2.26)

TP	Observed Acceptability Status				
+2.0	√	√			
+1.5	√				
+1.0	(?)				
+0.5	√	√	(?)		
0.0	(?)	?	?	?	?
−0.5	?				
−1.0	?	(?)?	(?)?		
−1.5	(?)?				
−2.0	??	??	??		
−2.5					
−3.0	?*				
−3.5					
−4.0	*				

I suspect that idiolectal variations in the acceptability judgments of sentences of the kind that we are discussing here can be attributed to idiolectal variations in the relative weights of the hierarchies involved or to idiolectal variations in thresholds for acceptability status in table (2.26). For example, with respect to the acceptability judgments recorded in (2.26), TP above zero corresponds to "acceptable," TP between zero and -1.0 to "awkward/marginal," and so on. Some speakers might be more tolerant and judge sentences with TP above -1.0 as "acceptable." Alternatively, relative weights assigned to arguments in hierarchies might vary idiolectally. For example, there are speakers who accept almost all sentences with the subject as trigger for reflexivization. These speakers probably have a much higher weight assigned to 'subject' of the Surface Structure Hierarchy of (2.22a): for example, the value of $(+3)$ for 'subject' would put most sentences with the subject as antecedent of a reflexive in the 'above zero' range for the total TP value. As a further example, there are speakers who consider (2.18a) perfectly acceptable. For these speakers, perhaps 'nonsubject' does not have a negative value in the Surface Structure Hierarchy. In any case, with a model of the kind presented here, we can begin to describe idiolectal variations systematically.

4.3 Picture Noun Reflexives

4.3.1 Agenthood of the Trigger

In the previous chapter, we observed that a picture noun reflexive is used in a logophoric complement clause only when it is coreferential with a [+logo-1/2]-marked NP in a higher clause. In this chapter, we will examine picture noun reflexives in simplex sentences, as in

(3.1) a.   John$_i$ showed Mary a picture of himself$_i$.
     b.   *John$_i$ showed Mary a picture of him$_i$.
(3.2) a.   John$_i$ bought from Mary a portrait of himself$_i$.
     b.   *John$_i$ bought from Mary a portrait of him$_i$.
(3.3) a. $^{\vee}$/?John showed Mary$_i$ a picture of herself$_i$.
     b.   *John showed Mary$_i$ a picture of her$_i$.

Because of the unacceptability of sentences such as (3.1b) and (3.2b), it is generally taken for granted that picture noun reflexivization in simplex sentences with the subject as trigger is obligatory. Similarly, it is widely believed that reflexivization into clause-mate picture nouns with the object as trigger is also obligatory because sentences of the pattern of (3.3b) are unacceptable. In this section, I will show that picture noun reflexivization is a phenomenon that is far more complex than has thus far been assumed and that it is controlled by the interaction of many syntactic and semantic conditions.[7]

First, observe the following sentences, which I owe to Jackendoff (1972): the recorded acceptability judgments are Jackendoff's.

(3.4) a.   I hate the story about himself$_i$ that John$_i$ always tells.
       b. *I hate the story about him$_i$ that John$_i$ always tells.
(3.5) a. *I told the story about himself$_i$ that John$_i$ likes to hear.
       b. *I told the story about him$_i$ that John$_i$ likes to hear.
(3.6) a. *John criticized Bill$_i$ in a story about himself$_i$.
       b.   John criticized Bill$_i$ in a story about him$_i$.
(3.7) a. *John learned about Bill$_i$ from a story about himself$_i$.
       b.   John learned about Bill$_i$ from a story about him$_i$.
(3.8) a. *John collaborated with Bill$_i$ on a story about himself$_i$.
       b. *John collaborated with Bill$_i$ on a story about him$_i$.
(3.9) a. *John agreed with Bill$_i$ on an alibi for himself$_i$.
       b. *John agreed with Bill$_i$ on an alibi for him$_i$.

Jackendoff first suggests that the contrast between (3.4) and (3.5) has something to do with the question of whether the subject is marked with the thematic relation "agent" by the verb or not. That is, *tell* has an agent subject,
but *hate* and *like to hear* do not. But Jackendoff does not develop this promis-
ing idea any further.[8] He then notes the impossibility of using reflexives in
(3.6) and (3.7), but does not attempt to account for it. Clearly, he could not
have attributed the unacceptability of (3.6a) and (3.7a) to the fact that *Bill* is
not an agent in these sentences because (3.3a), in which *Mary* is not an agent,
is far better than (3.6a) and (3.7a) and is nearly acceptable for many speakers.
He notes that in (3.8) and (3.9) neither the reflexive nor the pronominal form
would make the sentences acceptable.[9] Jackendoff then conjectures that the
unacceptability of (3.8b) and (3.9b) has something to do with the fact that
Bill is a "co-agent" in these sentences but he leaves the phenomenon unaccounted for.

4.3.2 Awareness Condition

Although there is some truth in Jackendoff's conjecture that the above phenomena have to do with the agenthood or non-agenthood of the trigger of reflexivization, the following examples show that it is not the sole factor in
determining whether reflexives or pronouns should be used in picture nouns.

(3.10) a.   John$_i$ gave that portrait of himself$_i$ to Mary.
        b. ?/??John$_i$ gave that portrait of him$_i$ to Mary.
(3.11) a. *John$_i$ didn't paint that portrait of himself$_i$ on horseback in my
             study. Mary did.[10]
        b. ?John$_i$ didn't paint that portrait of him$_i$ on horseback. Mary did.

John is an agent both in (3.10) and (3.11). In the former, it readily triggers
reflexivization. However, it cannot do so in (3.11). Similarly, observe the following contrast:

(3.12) a.   John$_i$ saw a picture of himself$_i$ in the morning paper.
        b. ??John$_i$ saw a picture of him$_i$ in the morning paper.

(3.13)   a. ??John$_i$ hasn't found out about that horrible book about himself$_i$ yet.[11]

      b. John$_i$ hasn't found out about that horrible book about him$_i$ yet.

John is an experiencer both in (3.12) and (3.13). In the former, it readily triggers reflexivization. However, it cannot do so in (3.13).

The contrast between (3.10, 12) and (3.11, 13) is reminiscent of the contrast involving direct discourse verbs that we observed in the preceding chapter:

(3.14)   a. John$_i$ knows that there is a picture of himself$_i$ in the morning paper.

      b. ?John$_i$ knows that there is a picture of him$_i$ in the morning paper.

(3.15)   a. *John$_i$ still doesn't know that there is a picture of himself$_i$ in the morning paper.

      b. John$_i$ still doesn't know that there is a picture of him$_i$ in the morning paper.

A picture noun reflexive in a subordinate clause requires that the clause represent an utterance or internal feeling of the speaker/perceiver who is the referent of the reflexive. Example (3.14a) is acceptable because the complement clause represents an internal feeling, on the part of John, the referent of *himself,* that "there is a picture of *me* in the morning paper." On the other hand, (3.15a) is unacceptable because the sentence implies that John has never had such an internal feeling.

Returning to our examples involving picture noun reflexives in simple sentences, we can hypothesize the following principle, which originates with Cantrall (1969):

(3.16)   *Awareness Condition for Picture Noun Reflexives* (tentative): Use a picture noun reflexive if, at the point in time that the sentence refers to, the referent of the reflexive perceived/perceives/will perceive the referent of the picture noun as one that involves him. Use a picture noun non-reflexive pronoun otherwise.[12]

Example (3.12) means that John perceived the picture under discussion as one that portrayed him. Hence only the reflexive version is acceptable. On the other hand, (3.13) implies nothing about John's perception about the book under discussion. Hence the impossibility of using a reflexive. Similarly, (3.10) implies that John was aware that the portrait that he gave to Mary was a portrait of himself. Hence a reflexive pronoun is obligatory. On the other hand, (3.11) has nothing to do with John's awareness, or lack thereof, of the portrait under discussion as one involving him. Hence the impossibility of using a reflexive here.

Similarly, observe the following sentences:

(3.17)   a. John$_i$ was asked about all that scandalous gossip about himself$_i$.

      b. ?John$_i$ was asked about all that scandalous gossip about him$_i$.

(3.18)   a.   *John$_i$ was oblivious to all the gossip about himself$_i$.[13]
          b.   John$_i$ was oblivious to all the gossip about him$_i$.

In (3.17), the reflexive version is better because it must have been the case that John perceived the gossip as involving him. On the other hand, in (3.18) the reflexive version is unacceptable. This seems to be owing to the fact that the sentence does not imply at all that John recognized the gossip as involving him. The following (a) sentence is unacceptable for the same reason that (3.18a) is unacceptable; since the dictator died, he could not have been aware concurrently that the statue that crushed him was a statue of himself.

(3.19)   a. ??The dictator$_i$ was crushed to death under a large statue of himself$_i$ on horseback.
          b.   The dictator$_i$ was crushed to death under a large statue of him$_i$ on horseback.

Likewise, compare the following two pairs of sentences:

(3.20)   a. ??The dictator$_i$ was buried under a large statue of himself$_i$ on horseback.
          b.   The dictator$_i$ was buried under a large statue of him$_i$ on horseback.
(3.21)   a.   The dictator$_i$ had himself$_i$ buried under a large statue of himself$_i$ on horseback.
          b. ??The dictator$_i$ had himself$_i$ buried under a large statue of him$_i$ on horseback.

Example (3.20a) is unacceptable because the sentence, for pragmatic reasons, does not imply that the dictator perceived the statue as his own at the time that the sentence refers to. On the other hand, (3.21a) is acceptable because it was his wish before his death that he be buried under a statue of himself. Similarly, compare the following two sentences:

(3.22)   a.   The dictator$_i$ was lying at the foot of that statue of himself$_i$ on horseback.
          b.   The dictator$_i$ was lying at the foot of that statue of him$_i$ on horseback.

For many speakers, (3.22a) implies that the dictator was lying alive and conscious at the foot of the statue, while (3.22b) implies that he was lying dead or unconscious. It must be that this implication, too, derives from the Awareness Condition on picture noun reflexives.

There is a second, marked interpretation for (3.22a), which requires explanation. Namely, the sentence can mean that the dictator was dead but that he had chosen the place where his statue was standing as his place of death. Example (3.20a) is also acceptable in the same kind of marked interpretation: the dictator had asked, while he was alive, that he be buried under a large statue of himself on horseback. The fact that these interpretations exist for (3.22a) and (3.20a) clearly necessitates modification to the Awareness Condition as stated in (3.16), which requires that the Awareness Condition be satisfied at the point in time that the sentence refers to. It seems necessary to allow for the use of a picture noun reflexive exceptionally even when the awareness condition does not hold at the time referred to by the sentence if it has existed sometime prior to that time. For this exceptional use of picture noun reflexives, it is necessary to have fairly explicit discourse contexts that would establish the needed awareness condition. For example, observe the following:

(3.23)   a. *John$_i$ didn't paint that portrait of himself$_i$ on horseback in my study. Mary did. (= 3.13a)

        b. In his study, John had a portrait of himself, and a portrait of his wife. He had painted the portrait of his wife, but he hadn't painted the portrait of himself/*him. It was a work by an artist friend of his.

Example (3.23b) is acceptable, in spite of the fact that John is not the artist who drew the portrait, because the context shows that John had recognized the portrait as a portrait of himself. Similarly, observe the following sentences:

(3.24)   a. ??John phoned Mary$_i$ about a picture of herself$_i$ in the paper.

        b. John phoned Mary$_i$ about that picture of herself$_i$ in the paper.

(3.25)   a. ??John wrote to Mary$_i$ about a picture of herself$_i$ in the paper.

        b. John wrote to Mary$_i$ about that picture of herself$_i$ in the paper.

For many speakers, (3.24a) and (3.25a) are unacceptable because at the time of John's phoning and writing, there was no perception, on Mary's part, of the picture under discussion as one that involved her. In contrast, (3.24b) and (3.25b) are acceptable because the use of the demonstrative *that* makes it easy for us to imagine that Mary knew before John's phone call that there was a picture of herself in the paper. Because of the use of the reflexive *herself*, these two sentences are interpreted as sentences which have been generated from Mary's camera angle, and acquire the meanings which can be paraphrased as 'Mary received a phone call from John about that picture of herself in the paper' and 'Mary received a letter from John about that picture of herself in the paper.' This kind of direct/indirect object-centered interpretation naturally becomes easiest when the first-person pronoun is the object, as in

(3.26)   John wrote to me about that picture of myself in the paper.

The above observations justify the following revision of the Awareness Condition:

(3.27)   *Awareness Condition for Picture Noun Reflexives* (revised): Use of a picture noun reflexive is obligatory if the referent of the reflexive perceived/perceives/will perceive the referent of the picture noun as one that involves him. Use of a picture noun nonreflexive pronoun is obligatory otherwise. The above constraint is the strongest if the awareness is concurrent with the action or state represented by the sentence, and weaker if the awareness is not concurrent with the reference time, but prior to it.

Concurrent awareness > Prior awareness > Nonawareness

The Awareness Condition, as revised above, can also account, at least in part, for the unacceptability of Jackendoff's (3.7a), repeated here for ease of reference:

(3.28)   *John learned about Bill$_i$ from a story about himself$_i$.

It is clear that, with respect to the point in time to which the sentence refers, namely, at the time that John learned about Bill from a story about him, there was no perception, on Bill's part, that the story involved him. Bill might have, prior to John's learning, perceived the same story as one involving him, but the use of an indefinite article makes this kind of situational interpretation very unlikely. Furthermore, even if Bill had perceived the same story as one involving him, this would have little to do with the main thrust of the sentence, which does not imply any active interaction on the part of Bill toward the story about him. It seems that a picture noun reflexivization requires such an interaction. This requirement seems to be related to the constraint discussed briefly in section 3.6 (cf. n. 10) which dictates that the controller for reflexivization be as 'human' as possible. Note that in (3.28), *Bill* means 'what Bill did/was' and is thus semantically inanimate. We will examine this factor later on in this section.

Let us continue to discuss the Awareness Condition, and observe the following sentences:

(3.29)   a.   John promised Mary$_i$ a portrait of herself$_i$.
         b.   ?John promised Mary$_i$ a faithful portrait of herself$_i$.

For some speakers, (a) is acceptable in a 'one of the portraits of Mary that already exist' interpretation, and (b) is not as acceptable as (a).[14] This fact interacts with the Awareness Condition. For the Awareness Condition to permit reflexivization in (a), it is best if portraits of Mary already existed and if she knew about their existence. Hence, we derive the 'one of the portraits of Mary that already exist' interpretation as the primary interpretation of 'a portrait.' On the other hand, the presence of the expression *faithful* makes it difficult to assign the same interpretation to 'a faithful portrait of herself' because the resulting interpretation 'one of the faithful portraits of Mary that already exist' would be pragmatically less plausible.[15]

The Awareness Condition described above originates from an analysis of "irregular" reflexives as "viewpoint" expressions due to Cantrall (1969). For example, he derives (3.30a) from a structure that can be informally represented as (3.30b):

(3.30)   a.   John showed Mary a picture of herself.
         b.   [John showed Mary what she perceived as a picture of herself]

The examples discussed above show that Cantrall's analysis is correct from a semantic, if not from a syntactic, point of view. However, the discussions that follow in this section will show that, although it is a relatively strong condition, the Awareness Condition is just one of many that control picture noun reflexivization, and that it can be violated if other factors make up for the violation.

There are at least five other factors, some of them related to each other, that interact with picture noun reflexivization. They are:

(i)   What is the direct or indirect agent of the picture noun;
(ii)   How active a role the triggering NP plays in the action or state represented by the sentence;
(iii)   What syntactic role the triggering NP plays in the surface structure;
(iv)   How definite the triggering NP is;
(v)   Whether the triggering NP is human or not.

I will discuss the above factors in the order given.

4.3.3 Direct/Indirect Picture Noun Agent

The syntactic type of the direct or indirect agent of the picture noun is as important for conditioning picture noun reflexivization as the Awareness Condition. First of all, observe the following sentences:

(3.31)   a.   *John$_i$ hates Jane's story about himself$_i$.
         b.   John$_i$ hates Jane's story about him$_i$.
(3.32)   a.   *John$_i$ heard Jane's story about himself$_i$.
         b.   John$_i$ heard Jane's story about him$_i$.

As was discussed in Chapter 2, the chain-of-command principle (i.e., if target C has two potential controllers A and B, and if A k-commands B but B does not k-command A, then B controls C) dictates that *Jane* is a stronger controller for reflexivization than *John* is and blocks derivation of (3.31a) and (3.32a). Observe further the following sentences:

(3.33)   a.   John hates Jane$_i$'s story about herself$_i$.
         b.   *John hates Jane$_i$'s story about her$_i$.

The acceptability of (3.33a) and the unacceptability of (3.33b) shows that reflexivization is obligatory with the possessive NP as trigger.

The roles that a possessive NP plays in picture noun reflexivization that have been illustrated in (3.31), (3.32), and (3.33) appear straightforwardly syntactic, and in fact, they seem to be nothing but syntactic in many speakers' idiolects. However, there are speakers who regard the following sentences as acceptable or nearly acceptable:

(3.34)   a.   √/?/??Mary$_i$ isn't interested in anybody's opinion of herself$_i$.
          b.   √/?/??Mary$_i$ doesn't care a bit about anybody's opinion of herself$_i$.
          c.   √/?/??Mary$_i$ wouldn't listen to anybody's opinion of herself$_i$.
          d.   √/?/??Mary$_i$ wouldn't go for anybody's opinion of herself$_i$.

The possessive NP in the above sentences is semantically transparent, and for this reason, serves as a much weaker block than *Jane* in (3.31a) and (3.32a).

By-agentive NPs attached to the right of picture nouns display the same characteristics as the possessive NPs, albeit to a much lesser degree. For example, observe the following sentences:

(3.35)   a.   ?John$_i$ hates stories about himself$_i$ by Jane.[16]
          b.   John$_i$ hates stories about him$_i$ by Jane.
(3.36)   a.   √/?John$_i$ hates stories about himself$_i$ by anybody at all.
          b.   John$_i$ hates stories about him$_i$ by anybody at all.

In (3.35a), the *by*-agentive expression *by Jane* serves as a weak intervening NP in the path between *John* and *himself*.[17] However, the blocking power of *by*-agentive NPs is far weaker than that of possessive NPs. This explains why (3.35a) is considerably better than (3.31a). When the *by*-agentive expression is indefinite and semantically transparent as in (3.36), it serves only as a weak intervening NP in some idiolects, or it loses its blocking power completely in other idiolects.

What is most interesting about agentive NPs on picture nouns is the blocking power of semantically present but syntactically covert agentive NPs. For example, observe the following sentences, which I owe to John Whitman (personal communication):

(3.37)   a.   *Mary criticized Bill$_i$ to his$_i$ face in a long and involved story about himself$_i$.
          b.   Mary criticized Bill$_i$ to his$_i$ face in a long and involved story about him$_i$.
(3.38)   a.   Mary criticized Bill$_i$ behind his$_i$ back for a story about himself$_i$.
          b.   *Mary criticized Bill$_i$ behind his$_i$ back for a story about him$_i$.

In (3.37), Bill was the addressee of Mary's criticism, and therefore he must have recognized the story under discussion as one involving him. In spite of this, reflexivization into the picture noun results in unacceptability. In contrast, in (3.38), Bill was not aware of Mary's criticism either at the point in time that the sentence refers to, or prior to it, but in spite of this, reflexivization into the picture noun is obligatory.

The above contrast is attributable to the fact that in (3.37) *Mary* is the agent of the story, while in (3.38) *Bill* is. In other words, the acceptability status of these sentences can be accounted for if we assume that they have the same structures as the following:

(3.39) a. *$Mary_j$ criticized $Bill_i$ to his_i face in her_j long and involved story about $himself_i$.

   b. $Mary_j$ criticized $Bill_i$ to his_i face in her_j long and involved story about him_i.

(3.40) a. $Mary_j$ criticized $Bill_i$ behind his_i back for his_i story about $himself_i$.

   b. *$Mary_j$ criticized $Bill_i$ behind his_i back for his_i story about him_i.

In (3.39), her_j ($= Mary's$) serves as an intervening NP between the triggering $Bill_i$ and the target $himself_i$ in the picture noun, and hence the unacceptability of (3.39a). On the other hand, in (3.40), there is no intervening NP between the trigger his_i ($= Bill's$) and the target $himself_i$. Hence the acceptability of (3.40a). Since picture noun reflexivization is controlled by a possessive NP in case the picture noun has one, (3.40b) is totally unacceptable. Thus, the acceptability status of the sentences in (3.37) and (3.38) can be accounted for by hypothesizing the presence of her_j ($= Mary's$) as the agent of the picture noun in the former and of his_i ($= Bill's$) as the agent of the picture noun in the latter.

Observe, also, the following sentences offered by John Whitman:

(3.41) a. John gave $Mary_i$ a renewed faith in $herself_i$/*her_i.

   b. $John_i$ gave Mary a renewed faith in *$himself_i$/him_i.

(3.42) a. (With his eyes closed,) John gave $Mary_i$ an accurate description of *$herself_i$/her_i.

   b. $John_i$ gave Mary an accurate description of $himself$/*him_i.

Example (3.41) involves Mary's faith, and hence, the semantic possessive NP *Mary's* triggers reflexivization obligatorily in (a) and blocks reflexivization in (b) as an intervening NP. In contrast, (3.42) involves John's description, and therefore the semantic possessive NP *John's* serves as an intervening NP in (a) and blocks reflexivization, and it triggers reflexivization obligatorily in (b).

It is not the case that all picture nouns must have agentive NPs supplied in the fashion demonstrated in (3.41) and (3.42). For example, observe the following sentences:

(3.43) a. $John_i$ gave Mary a picture of $himself_i$.

   b. *$John_i$ gave Mary a picture of him_i.

Example (3.43a) is noncommittal with respect to who is the agent of the picture under discussion. It could have been John, or it could have been someone else. (But it could not have been Mary.) In the former case, the trigger for reflexivization is not John as the subject of the entire sentence, but the semantic picture noun agent *his* ($= John's$). In the latter case, it is not possible to supply the semantic picture noun agent *someone's* because it would serve as an intervening NP blocking picture noun reflexivization with *John* as trigger for most speaker's idiolects. This implies that the semantic picture noun agent serves as a trigger for reflexivizing a coreferential NP within the picture noun and as an intervening NP if the trigger for reflexivization is somewhere else only when it is coreferential with an overt NP in the sentence.

One might assume that the facts illustrated in (3.39, 40), (3.41, 42), and (3.43) are syntactic facts, and propose that the semantic picture noun agents are physically present as syntactic possessive NPs. Chomsky (1982, pp. 88–100) makes such an assumption. He compares (3.44) and (3.45):

(3.46)   a.   John heard [$_{NP}$ a story about himself] (= 3.44a)
         b.   John$_i$ heard [$_{NP}$ PRO$_{j \neq i}$'s story about him] (= 3.44b)
(3.47)   a.   John$_i$ told [$_{NP}$ PRO$_i$'s story about himself] (= 3.45a)
         b.   John$_i$ told [$_{NP}$ PRO$_i$'s story about him] (= 3.45b)

He notes that in (3.44), "story" is interpreted as someone else's story, while in (3.45) it is interpreted as John's story. He proposes that picture nouns be optionally generated with underlying PRO in the determiner position, and that the controllers of this PRO be assigned by the matrix verb, as in cases of cross-sentential control for complement clause subjects: [John$_i$ wanted [PRO$_i$ to win]] and [John persuaded Bill$_i$ [PRO$_i$ to do it]]. Following this approach, the underlying representations of (3.44) and (3.45) would be as shown below:

(3.46)   a.   John heard [$_{NP}$ a story about himself] (= 3.44a)
         b.   John$_i$ heard [$_{NP}$ PRO$_{j \neq i}$'s story about him] (= 3.44b)
(3.47)   a.   John$_i$ told [$_{NP}$ PRO$_i$'s story about himself] (= 3.45a)
         b.   John$_i$ told [$_{NP}$ PRO$_i$'s story about him] (= 3.45b)

Tell assigns subject control to the PRO in the determiner position of the object picture noun while *hear* does not. In (3.46a), the PRO determiner is optionally not generated, and since the reflexive does not have an accessible SUBJECT within the picture noun, it is bound by *John* of the whole S. In (3.46b), PRO is the accessible SUBJECT within the picture noun, and therefore, *him* is marked for disjoint reference with PRO, but it can be optionally coindexed with *John*. Examples (3.47a) and (3.47b) have PRO as an accessible SUBJECT. Therefore, the picture NP is the governing category for *himself* and *him*. The former is coindexed with PRO, while the latter is marked for disjoint reference with PRO.

The syntactic approach described above seems to work for straightforward cases of "hidden" picture noun agents, but it fails for cases like the following:

(3.48)   a.   John$_i$ wrote for Mary a profile of himself$_i$, which was ten pages long.
         b.   *John$_i$ wrote for Mary a profile of him$_i$, which was ten pages long.
(3.49)   a. $^{\vee}$/?John wrote for Mary$_i$ a profile of herself$_i$ for the application.
         b.   (?)John wrote for Mary$_i$ a profile of her$_i$ for the application.

In order to account for the fact that (3.48b) is unacceptable, Chomsky would have to assume that *write* obligatorily assigns subject control to the PRO in the determiner position of object picture nouns, exactly in the same way that *tell* does in (3.47). But then, (3.49a) should be unacceptable because this PRO (= John) should be the antecedent of *herself*. In spite of this fact, (3.49a) is nearly acceptable for some speakers and acceptable for others. What accounts for the contrast between (3.48a) and (3.49b) is the fact that, while the profile that John wrote in (3.48) is without any question John's profile, the one that John wrote in (3.49) can be regarded either as John's profile of Mary or as Mary's profile of herself. The latter interpretation derives from the fact that it is going to be part of Mary's application, and therefore, in that sense, it is Mary's profile, regardless of who has written it. In other words, the semantic difference between (3.49a) and (3.49b) is that while (3.49b) describes the profile before it has been made part of Mary's application, (3.49a) describes it as it has been integrated into the application. The above discussion points to a basically semantic nature of the phenomenon that we are dealing with here, and to the difficulty in treating it as syntactic, as proposed by Chomsky.[18]

In the preceding section, it was noted that the picture noun reflexive requires that there be an active interaction on the part of its referent toward that of the picture noun. Such an interaction automatically exists when the controller (i.e., the referent of the reflexive) is an overt or covert picture noun agent. When it is neither, it seems necessary that it be interpretable as an indirect agent of the picture noun. Observe, for example, the following sentences:

(3.50)   a.   John talked to Mary$_i$ about the engagement picture of herself$_i$ in the local paper.
         b. $^\checkmark$/?John talked to Mary$_i$ about the picture of herself$_i$ in handcuffs in the local paper.

There are wide idiolectal variations on the acceptability of (3.50b), but many speakers agree that it is not as good as (3.50a). This contrast can be attributed to the fact that while (a) implies that Mary sent in an engagement picture of herself to the local paper to be printed, together with the engagement announcement, (b) pragmatically implies that Mary did not send a picture of herself in handcuffs to the local paper to be printed. In other words, Mary is an indirect agent in (a) but not in (b). This factor seems to reduce the acceptability of (b) to some degree, depending upon the speaker.[19] Those speakers who consider (b) as acceptable as (a) are speakers in whose idiolect either this requirement for indirect agenthood plays only a minor role or the control for reflexivization by the surface object is so strong as to be able to easily override the indirect agenthood requirement.

The following sentences add weight to our argument for the importance of indirect agenthood.

(3.51)   a.   (?)John phoned Mary$_i$ about the picture of herself$_i$ in her$_i$ most recent book.

b.   ??John promised to phone Mary$_i$ about any pictures of herself$_i$ in the paper.

In (a), Mary must have been responsible for the picture of herself in her book, even though she might not have been the person who actually took the picture. Thus, *Mary,* as the indirect agent of the picture noun, makes reflexivization possible. In contrast, in (b), *Mary* is neither a direct nor an indirect agent for the picture noun, and hence the low degree of acceptability of the sentence. The picture noun agent hypothesis predicts that the sentence would be acceptable if it were the case that Mary regularly sends pictures of herself to the paper hoping that they will be printed. The sentence is indeed acceptable if interpreted in this unusual context.

Let us summarize the results that we have obtained thus far:

(3.52)   *Picture Noun Agent as Controller for Reflexivization*
    (a) Possessive NPs as picture noun agents are strong controllers for picture noun reflexivization.
    (b) Semantic picture noun agents which are coreferential with some overt NPs in the sentence are also strong controllers for picture noun reflexivization.
    (c) *By*-agentive NPs of picture nouns are weak controllers for picture noun reflexivization.
    (d) Indirect picture noun agents, namely, overt NPs in the sentence which are not direct agents of picture nouns, but which are responsible for the picture nouns' coming into existence, also serve as relatively strong controllers for picture noun reflexivization.

(3.53)   *Picture Noun Agent as Intervening NP*
    (a) Possessive NPs on picture nouns serve as strong intervening NPs for picture noun reflexivization (except for *anyone's* and *anybody's* in idiolects in which these indefinites serve only as weak intervening NPs).
    (b) Semantic picture noun agents that are coreferential with some overt NPs in the sentence have the same blocking function against picture noun reflexivization.
    (c) *By*-agentive picture noun agents also serve as intervening NPs, but their blocking power is considerably weaker than that of the above two.

4.3.4 Semantic Case of the Triggering NP

As Jackendoff conjectured, there is interaction between the agenthood of the triggering NP and picture noun reflexivization. Reflexivizability is influenced by how agent-like the triggering NP is, as the following pairs illustrate:

(3.54)   a.   John$_i$ repeated to Mary that horrible rumor about himself$_i$.
       b.   John$_i$ tore that horrible picture of himself$_i$ to pieces.

(3.55)   a.   (?)John$_i$ hated that horrible story about himself$_i$. (John not the author)
          b.   (?)John$_i$ knew about that horrible rumor about himself$_i$.

In (3.54), *John* is an agent of the action represented by the rest of the sentence, while in (3.55) it is an experiencer of the state represented by the rest of the sentence. For many speakers, the latter is not as good as the former. I conjecture that this may be owing to the fact that stative sentences involve higher degrees of abstraction, and that unless they are interpreted as sentences that directly represent the experiencer's internal feeling (by an omniscient narrator), they are taken to be sentences that objectively describe the state involved. This objectivity conflicts with the camera angle that is required by the reflexive—namely, the camera angle of the experiencer—and yields awkwardness. This conjecture is supported by the fact that the sentences of (3.55) are even worse in the present tense, which gives them objectivity:

(3.56)   a.   ?John$_i$ hates that horrible story about himself$_i$. (John not the author)
          b.   ?John$_i$ knows about that horrible story about himself$_i$.

The above conjecture is also supported by the contrast found in the following two sentences:

(3.57)   a.   John$_i$ understandably hates that horrible story about himself$_i$.
          b.   ?John$_i$ understandably hates that horrible story about him$_i$.
(3.58)   a.   ?John$_i$ probably hates that horrible story about himself$_i$.
          b.   John$_i$ probably hates that horrible story about him$_i$.

The sentential adverb *understandably* in (3.57) implies that John has expressed his feeling about the story under discussion. Hence the reflexive version, which presumably represents John's own characterization, fits the context better. On the other hand, the use of *probably* in (3.58) makes it impossible to consider the sentence as a statement from John's camera angle, and therefore produces a conflict with the use of the picture noun reflexive in (a).

When a sentence with an experiencer subject represents not a stable state (that is deduced by abstraction) but a temporary state, there does not seem to be any problem with picture noun reflexivization. (This fact may also be accounted for by assuming that picture noun reflexivization conflicts with abstract, objective statements.) For example, observe the following sentences:

(3.59)   a.   John$_i$ heard some strange gossip about himself$_i$ on the radio.
          b.   John$_i$ heard some strange gossip about him$_i$ on the radio.

When a sentence allows both the reflexive and pronominal versions of picture nouns, as in (3.59), there is a subtle difference in meaning between the two. The reflexive version, as predicted, gives the impression that the description is from the point of view of the referent of the reflexive, while the pronominal version gives the impression that it is from the point of view of the speaker.

Thus, in (3.59a), the primary interpretation is that John heard what he felt to be strange gossip about himself on the radio, while that of (3.59b) is that John heard what the speaker thinks is strange gossip about John.

The existence of such pairs where the choice of reflexive or pronominal brings about a subtle meaning difference suggests that the interrelationship between camera angles and semantic cases such as agent and experiencer is extremely complex and cannot be adequately represented by a simple hierarchical relationship between cases. However, I will adopt here a crude approximation, and assume that it is in general easier for the speaker to represent the point of view of an active participant in action than to represent the point of view of an experiencer of a state, and that therefore an agent NP is a stronger trigger for picture noun reflexivization than an experiencer NP.

It is easy for the speaker to represent the point of view of benefactive datives, and indeed, benefactive datives can trigger reflexivization rather readily.[20] For example, observe the following sentences:

(3.60) a. John wrapped up for Mary$_i$ a picture of herself$_i$.
        b. John found for Mary$_i$ a decent picture of herself$_i$.
        c. John painted for Mary$_i$ a portrait of herself$_i$.
        d. John saved for Mary$_i$ all the pieces from an old picture of herself$_i$.
        e. John selected for Mary$_i$ a story about herself$_i$.

The acceptability of the above sentences is conditional on certain contextual interpretations. Example (a) assumes that Mary bought a picture of herself and asked John to wrap it up for her. Example (b) implies that Mary had asked John to look for a decent picture of her or that John had found out that Mary had been looking for one and decided to help. Example (c) implies that Mary had asked John to paint a picture of her. Example (d) implies that Mary had asked John to save the pieces from her favorite picture. Example (e) need not imply that Mary had asked John to select a story for her, but it implies that Mary was there when the selection was made, and she recognized the story as one involving her. It must be that all these implications derive from the Awareness Condition or the (Indirect) Picture Noun Agent Condition, and that when the trigger for picture noun reflexivization is not an active agent for the action represented by the sentence, but is a bystander, it requires that either of the above two conditions (or both) be fulfilled to strengthen the triggerhood of the benefactive NP.

The following examples show that an agent NP in the source expression *from + NP* can trigger picture noun reflexivization, albeit with some difficulty:

(3.61) a. ?John heard from Mary$_i$ about a damaging rumor about herself$_i$ (that was going around).
        b. (?)John heard from Mary$_i$ about a damaging rumor about her$_i$ (that was going around).

(3.62) a. ?John received from Mary$_i$ a graduation portrait of herself$_i$.
      b. ?John received from Mary$_i$ a graduation portrait of her$_i$.

The object of *hear from* and *receive from* represents an agent, and hence the possibility of picture noun reflexivization with it as trigger. On the other hand, the fact that the (a) versions are still awkward or marginal for most speakers shows that an agent NP in the source expression is not as strong a trigger for picture noun reflexivization as an agent NP in subject position.

We saw in (3.3) that a goal can trigger picture noun reflexivization, though it is not as strong a trigger as an agent. The following examples show that an NP which is neither an agent, an experiencer, a benefactive, nor a goal cannot trigger picture noun reflexivization:

(3.63) a. John$_i$ reminded Mary of an old picture of himself$_i$ on horseback.
      b. John$_i$ reminded Mary of an old picture of him$_i$ on horseback.

As is well known, *x reminds y of w* is ambiguous between the agentive interpretation of *x* (i.e., "*x* calls *w* to *y*'s attention") and the nonagentive interpretation of *x* (i.e., "the thought of *x* causes *y* to remember *w*"). Now, (3.63a) has the only the agentive interpretation, and (3.63b) only the nonagentive interpretation. The fact that *John* as subject of the stative verb (where *John* is not an agent) *remind of* cannot trigger reflexivization can be seen clearly in the following examples:

(3.64) a. *John$_i$ reminded Mary of a younger version of himself$_i$.
      b. John$_i$ reminded Mary of a younger version of him$_i$.

For semantic reasons, the sentence allows only the nonagentive interpretation. The fact that (3.64a) is unacceptable shows that the subject *John*, which is neither an agent nor an experiencer, cannot trigger reflexivization. In contrast, the object NP in the nonagentive *x reminds y of w*, which is semantically an experiencer NP, can trigger reflexivization, as shown below:

(3.65) a. John reminded Mary$_i$ of a younger version of herself$_i$.
      b. *John reminded Mary$_i$ of a younger version of her$_i$.

Let us formalize the above observations:

(3.66) *Semantic Case Hierarchy of Picture Noun Reflexives:* An agent NP is the strongest trigger for picture noun reflexives. An experiencer NP and a benefactive NP are the second strongest triggers. A goal NP is a weak but possible trigger. Other NPs cannot trigger picture noun reflexivization.

  Agent > Experiencer/Benefactive > Goal > Other cases

Example (3.64a) is unacceptable partly because it violates the Awareness Condition for Picture Noun Reflexives, but also because the trigger of the reflexive is at the bottom of the Semantic Case Hierarchy.

Similarly, observe the following sentences:

(3.67)   a.   John$_i$ appealed to Mary with a story about himself$_i$.
         b.   *John$_i$ appealed to Mary with a story about him$_i$.
(3.68)   a.   *John$_i$ appealed to Mary in a story about himself$_i$.
         b.   John$_i$ appealed to Mary in a story about him$_i$.

John is an agent in (3.67), but it is not in (3.68).[21]

4.3.5 Syntactic Role of the Triggering NP

Sentences such as (3.65a) show that picture noun reflexivization can be triggered by nonsubjects, but the following examples show that the subject is still a stronger trigger than an object:

(3.69)   a.   John$_i$ showed Mary a picture of himself$_i$.
         b. $^\vee$/?John showed Mary$_i$ a picture of herself$_i$.
(3.70)   a.   ?Mary was shown by John$_i$ a picture of himself$_i$.
         b.   Mary$_i$ was shown by John a picture of herself$_i$.

The fact that (3.69b) is not as good as (3.69a) shows that the nonsubject trigger is weaker than the subject trigger. In contrast, when the sentence is passivized, the new subject, which is semantically a goal, can trigger reflexivization without any difficulty, as can be seen by the acceptability of (3.70a). The fact that (3.70a) is less acceptable than (3.69a) shows that an object NP is a stronger trigger than a *by*-agentive NP for reflexivization. The above facts can be accounted for automatically by revising the Surface Structure Hierarchy for Reflexivization (discussed in the preceding section) as follows:

(3.71)   *Surface Structure Hierarchy for Reflexivization:*
         Surface subject is the strongest trigger for reflexivization. Surface object is the second strongest trigger. Other NPs are weaker triggers than either of the above two.

                    Subject > Object > Others

4.3.6 Anaphoricity of the Triggering NP

At the beginning of this chapter, we saw that reflexivization is subject to the Anaphoricity Hierarchy. It goes without saying that picture noun reflexivization is subject to the same condition. For example, observe the following sentences:

(3.72)   a.   John$_i$ showed Mary a picture of himself$_i$ on horseback.
         b.   ?Someone$_i$ showed Mary a picture of himself$_i$/themself$_i$/ themselves$_i$ on horseback.

The indefinite pronoun *someone* is not as strong a trigger for picture noun reflexivization as the definite NP *John*.

4.3.7 **Humanness Hierarchy**

We now proceed to the last factor for picture noun reflexivization that needs to be discussed in this section. It involves the use of a [+human] NP not to refer to a person in the flesh, but to refer to his/her actions, achievements, personality, and so on. For example, observe the following sentence:

(3.73)   John discussed Mary with Jane.

Mary in this sentence does not refer to Mary in the flesh, but rather to what she was or what she did.

Now, compare the following two sentences:

(3.74)   a.   ?The police interrogated Mary$_i$ about herself$_i$, as well as about her$_i$ close friends.
          b.   ??The police discussed Mary$_i$ with herself$_i$, as well as with her$_i$ close friends.

The awkwardness of (3.74a) seems to derive mainly from the fact that the trigger of reflexivization is not an agent and that it is not in subject position. However, the sentence is considerably better than (3.74b), which is almost unintelligible. This contrast is partly attributable to the fact that the *Mary* which has triggered reflexivization in (3.74b) is not an active participant in the action represented.[22] It seems that the contrast is also partly attributable to the fact that this *Mary* does not represent Mary in the flesh, but 'Mary's matter/problem,' or 'things about Mary.' Similarly, observe the following sentences:

(3.75)   a.   ?The psychiatrist talked to Mary$_i$ about herself$_i$, as well as about her$_i$ close friends.
          b.   *The psychiatrist talked about Mary$_i$ to herself$_i$, as well as to her$_i$ close friends.

The unacceptability of (3.75b) must be de to the same reason that (3.74b) is unacceptable; that is, the *Mary* that has triggered reflexivization is not Mary in the flesh, but it means 'things about Mary.'

Now we are ready to discuss Jackendoff's example (3.7a) again:

(3.76)   *John learned about Bill$_i$ from a story about himself$_i$.

The fact that the sentence is totally unacceptable, and the fact that its acceptability does not improve significantly even if we try to interpret *a story about Bill* as one that has been written by Bill, must be at least partly due to the fact that the triggering NP *Bill* means 'Bill's affairs, things about Bill.'

We can perhaps generalize the above observation and state that an inanimate NP cannot trigger picture noun reflexivization. For example, observe the following sentences:

(3.77)   a.   Ironically, Mary$_i$ owed her$_i$ success partly to that scandalous rumor about herself$_i$ that was going around.

       b.   *Ironically, the book$_i$ owed its$_i$ success partly to that scandalous rumor about itself$_i$ that was going around.

(3.78)   a.   ?They wrapped Mary$_i$ with an enlarged portrait of herself$_i$.

       b.   *They wrapped the diamond$_i$ with an enlarged picture of itself$_i$.

The (b) sentences are considerably worse than the corresponding (a) sentences. The above observations lead to the following generalization:

(3.79)   *Humanness Hierarchy:* The higher the triggering NP is in the humanness hierarchy, the better the result of reflexivization.

Human > Nonhuman animate > Inanimate

The following examples show that nonhuman animate triggers for reflexivization yield sentences with in-between acceptability status:

(3.80)   a.   Fido$_i$ owed his$_i$ enormous popularity in the neighborhood to newspaper articles about himself$_i$.

       b. ??The dog$_i$ owed its$_i$ enormous popularity in the neighborhood to newspaper articles about itself$_i$.

The fact that (3.80a) is acceptable must be due to the fact that the dog has been anthropomorphized in this sentence.

The only circumstance under which we need to make the Humanness Constraint inapplicable is when the reflexive, or a picture noun that contains the reflexive, is the subject of a verb, as in:

(3.81)   a.   The book has overextended itself in its coverage.

       b.   Harvard has published a book about itself.

       c.   The cell has produced a clone of itself.

This is not surprising as we have found in earlier sections that an NP's being a subject is often enough to compensate for its otherwise weak potential to trigger reflexivization.

4.4   More Examples of Picture Noun Reflexives

The following constraints on simplex sentence picture noun reflexivization have so far been discussed:

(4.1)   *Awareness Condition for Picture Noun Reflexives:* Use of a picture noun reflexive is obligatory if the referent of the reflexive perceived/perceives/will perceive the referent of the picture noun as one that involves him. Use of a picture noun nonreflexive pronoun is obligatory otherwise. The above constraint is strongest if the awareness is concurrent with the action or state represented by the sentence and weaker if the awareness is not concurrent with the reference time, but prior to it.

Concurrent awareness > Prior awareness > Nonawareness

(4.2)   *Picture Noun Agent as Controller for Reflexivization:*
    (a)   Possessive NPs as picture noun agents are strong controllers for reflexivization.
    (b)   Semantic picture noun agents which are coreferential with some overt NPs in the sentence are also strong controllers for reflexivization.
    (c)   Indirect picture noun agents also serve as relatively strong controllers for picture noun reflexivization.
    (d)   *By*-agentive NPs of picture nouns are weak controllers for reflexivization.

(4.3)   *Picture Noun Agent as Intervening NP:*
    (a)   Possessive NPs on picture nouns serve as strong intervening NPs for picture noun reflexivization (except in idiolects in which indefinite *anyone's* and *anybody's* serve only as weak intervening NPs).
    (b)   Semantic picture noun agents that are coreferential with some overt NPs in the sentence have the same blocking function against picture noun reflexivization.
    (c)   *By*-agentive picture noun agents also serve as intervening NPs, but their blocking power is considerably weaker than that of the above two.

(4.4)   *Semantic Case Hierarchy of Picture Noun Reflexives:* An agent NP is the strongest trigger for picture noun reflexives. An experiencer NP and a benefactive NP are the second strongest triggers. A goal NP is a weak but possible trigger. Other NPs cannot trigger picture noun reflexivization.

Agent > Experiencer/Benefactive > Goal > Other cases

(4.5)   *Surface Structure Hierarchy for Reflexivization:* Surface subject is the strongest trigger for reflexivization. Surface object is the second strongest trigger. Other NPs are weaker triggers than either of the above two.

Subject > Object > Others

(4.6)   *Anaphoricity Hierarchy:* We assume the following hierarchy regarding the relative degrees of anaphoricity:

First-person pronoun > Other definite NPs > Indefinite NPs > Indefinite pronouns (*someone, anyone,* etc.)

Then, reflexives are better when their antecedents are higher in the Anaphoricity Hierarchy than any other NPs in the same sentence.

(4.7)   *Humanness Hierarchy:* The higher the triggering NP is in the humanness hierarchy, the better the result of reflexivization.

Human > Nonhuman animate > Inanimate

Let us now see how these constraints on picture noun reflexivization interact with each other. First observe the following sentences:

(4.8)   a.   ?John$_i$ hates stories about himself$_i$ by Jane.
        b.   John$_i$ hates stories about him$_i$ by Jane.
(4.9)   a.   John$_i$ gave Mary a portrait of himself$_i$ by his sister.
        b.   John$_i$ got from Mary a portrait of himself$_i$ by his sister.

As noted in the previous section, (4.8a) is awkward because the *by*-agentive picture noun agent *Jane* serves as an intervening NP and blocks reflexivization with *John* as trigger. In contrast, many speakers consider (4.9a) and (4.9b) acceptable. This fact shows that the blocking power of a *by*-agentive NP for picture nouns can be overridden if the triggering NP for reflexivization is strong. Note that while the triggering NP *John* of (4.8a) is not an agent, it is in (4.9). Similarly, compare (4.9) with the following:

(4.10) a.   ?John gave Mary$_i$ a portrait of herself$_i$ by his brother.
        b.   ?John received from Mary$_i$ a portrait of herself$_i$ by her$_i$ brother.

In the above, the triggering NP is not in subject position, and in (a) it is not an agent. The sentences have a lower degree of acceptability than (4.9a, b).
Observe, further, the following sentences:

(4.11) a.   *John gave Mary$_i$ a good evaluation of herself$_i$.
        b.   John gave Mary$_i$ a good evaluation of her$_i$.
(4.12) a.   ??Mary$_i$'s teacher gave her$_i$ a good evaluation of herself$_i$.
        b.   Mary$_i$'s teacher gave her$_i$ a good evaluation of her$_i$.
(4.13) a.   ?Mary$_i$ received from her$_i$ teacher a good evaluation of herself$_i$.
        b.   ??Mary$_i$ received from her$_i$ teacher a good evaluation of her$_i$.
(4.14) a.   Mary$_i$ obtained from her$_i$ teacher a good evaluation of herself$_i$.
        b.   ??Mary$_i$ obtained from her$_i$ teacher a good evaluation of her$_i$.

In (4.11), *John* is the semantic agent of *evaluation*. It serves as an intervening NP for reflexivization into the picture noun with *Mary* as trigger. Hence the unacceptability of (4.11a). In (4.12), too, the semantic agent *Mary's teacher* functions as an intervening NP. The fact that (4.12a) is better than (4.11a) must be owing to the fact that the use of the term *Mary's teacher* in referring to the evaluator under discussion shows that the whole sentence is stated from Mary's point of view. In (4.13), the triggering NP for reflexivization is in subject position and is therefore much stronger than the dative trigger in (4.12a). However, it is still not an agent, and therefore it is not strong enough to completely override the blocking power of the semantic picture noun agent *Mary's teacher*. Hence derives the awkwardness of the sentence. In contrast, *Mary* as subject of *obtained* in (4.14a) is an agent, and it is a very active agent. This fact, and the fact that the use of *Mary's teacher* shows that the sentence is represented from Mary's camera angle, combine to override the blocking

power of the picture noun agent *her teacher's*. Therefore, (4.14a) is acceptable.
Let us now examine Jackendoff's examples with his judgments, repeated here for ease of reference, which involve comitative NPs as antecedents of picture noun reflexives.

(4.15)   a.   *John collaborated with Bill$_i$ on a story about himself$_i$.
       b.   *John collaborated with Bill$_i$ on a story about him$_i$.

Speaker judgments on the acceptability status of (4.15a) vary greatly. Some say the sentence is acceptable, and some say that it is unacceptable. Many say that it is awkward or nearly marginal, but perhaps passable. This seems to be owing to the fact that the sentence involves many conflicting factors regarding reflexivization. Let us first observe that a comitative NP is a weak trigger for picture noun reflexivization:

(4.16)   a. $^\vee$/?John showed Mary$_i$ a picture of herself$_i$.
       b.   ?John talked with Mary$_i$ about a picture of herself$_i$.

Therefore, if *(with) Bill* is the triggering NP for reflexivization in (4.15a), a low degree of acceptability is expected. However, the fact that (4.15a) is considerably worse than (4.16b) still requires explanation.
Let us next investigate what can be the agent of *story* in (4.15). For this purpose, observe the following sentences:

(4.17)   a.   John$_i$ collaborated with Bill$_j$ on his$_j$ story about himself$_j$.
       b.   John$_i$ collaborated with Bill$_j$ on their$_{i,j}$ story about him$_j$ (*himself$_j$).
       c.   *John$_i$ collaborated with Bill$_j$ on his$_i$ story about him$_j$.
          cf. *John$_i$ collaborated with Mary$_j$ on his$_i$ story about her$_j$.

The fact that (4.17c) is unacceptable shows that Bill is the main author and John either an assistant (as is the case with (a)) or a junior co-author (as is the case with (b)). Now, returning to (4.15a), it seems that the speakers who consider the sentence acceptable are those who can interpret it as synonymous with (4.17a), and those who consider the sentence as unacceptable are those who interpret the sentence as synonymous with (4.17b). It seems that for many speakers the agent of *story* is indeterminate and confusing, and I suspect that this gives rise to their judgment that the sentence is somewhere around ?/?? in acceptability. It is interesting to compare (4.15a) with (4.18a):

(4.18)   a.   John assisted Bill$_i$ on a story about himself$_i$.
       b.   ??John assisted Bill$_i$ on a story about him$_i$.

In the above, there is no ambiguity about who is the author of the story: Bill is. Hence, *(Bill's) story about Bill* obligatorily undergoes reflexivization, as shown in (4.18a). The contrast between (4.15a) and (4.18a) makes clear that the low degree of acceptability of (4.15a) is at least partly due to the fact that the sentence is interpreted more in the sense of (4.17b) than in that of (4.18a).[23]

It seems that there is another factor that compounds the complexity of the usage of the expression *x collaborates with y:* it is an expression which, perhaps because it places the main author in the *y* position, requires that the speaker's camera angle be placed closer to *y* than to *x*.[24] For example, observe the following sentences:

(4.19)   a.   John collaborated with me on my book about Einstein.
            b.   ?I collaborated with John on his book about Einstein.

Example (4.19a) is perfectly acceptable because it fulfills both the main author requirement and the camera angle requirement. Example (4.19b) is strange, presumably because it violates the camera angle requirement, although it observes the main author requirement.[25] Now, returning to (4.15), the fact that *Bill*, as an oblique case object of *collaborate with*, is the focus of the speaker's empathy would place it in a stronger position than *John* as the trigger for reflexivization because reflexivization seems to require that the speaker take the camera angle of the referent of the reflexive. The fact that there are wide idiolectal variations in judging the acceptability of (4.15a) seems to be partly owing to the fact that the relative weights of the Surface Structure Hierarchy for Reflexivization and the camera angle requirement for reflexives differ from speaker to speaker. It seems to be owing to exactly this fact that (4.15b) is unacceptable for many speakers also. The expression *x collaborates with y*, because it places *y* in the speaker's empathy focus, points to *Bill* as the trigger for reflexivization. On the other hand, the fact that *Bill* is in an oblique case and that *John* is in subject position points to *John* as the trigger for reflexivization. These two factors are mutually irreconcilable and produce unacceptability judgments for both the reflexive and pronominal versions. In order to represent the semantics of these sentences, the best way is to leave *Bill* unreflexivized and unpronominalized:

(4.20)   John collaborated with Bill$_i$ on a story about Bill$_i$.

4.5 Quantitative Model for Picture Noun Reflexivization

In the preceding sections, I have shown that the picture noun reflexivization is an extremely complex phenomenon and is conditioned by at least seven different factors. Let us extend the simplex quantitative model for reflexivization that was used in section 4.2 to see how different factors interact with each other to produce acceptability judgments. For this purpose, I will assign trigger weights to items in the hierarchies that have been defined by the constraints.

(5.1)   *Awareness Condition:* The trigger NP has
            Concurrent awareness > Prior awareness > Nonawareness
                    (+3)   (+1)   (−5)
            that the picture noun is of/about him/her.

(5.2)   *Picture Noun Agent as Trigger:* The trigger NP is coreferential with

        Overt possessive > Covert picture noun agent > *By*-agentive/
           (+2)   (0)   (−3)

        Indirect agent > Nonagent
           (−3)   (−6)

(5.3)   *Picture Noun Agent as Intervening NP:* There is an intervening NP that is

        Covert picture noun agent > Overt picture noun *by*-agentive >
            (−4)   (−6)

        Overt picture noun possessive agent
               (−8)

(5.4)   *Semantic Case Hierarchy:* The trigger NP is

        Agent > Experiencer/Benefactive > Goal > Other cases
        (+2)   (+1)   (0)   (−5)

(5.5)   *Surface Structure Hierarchy:* The trigger NP is

        Subject > Object > Others
        (+2)   (−1)   (−3)

(5.6)   *Anaphoricity Hierarchy:* The trigger NP is

        Definite NP > Indefinite NP > Indefinite pronoun
        (+2)   (0)   (−2)

(5.7)   *Humanness Hierarchy:* The trigger NP is

        Human > Nonhuman animate > Inanimate
        (+2)   (0)   (−2)

Let us now use a few examples to show how, given a sentence that involves a coreferential NP in a picture noun, the "trigger potential" is assigned to the antecedent of that NP.

(5.8) *John* showed Mary a picture of *himself.* (= 3.1a)

Hierarchies	Weights	Explanation
(1) Awareness:	+3	(John perceived the picture as one involving him.)
(2) Picture noun agent:	−6	(The picture noun does not have a covert or overt agent, or an indirect agent.)
(3) Intervening NP:	0	(The picture noun does not have an intervening NP.)
(4) Semantic case:	+2	(The trigger *John* is an agent of the whole predicate.)
(5) Surface structure:	+2	(The trigger *John* is a subject.)
(6) Anaphoricity:	+2	(The trigger *John* is a definite NP.)
(7) Humanness:	+2	(The trigger *John* is human.)
Trigger potential =	+5	($^{\vee}$himself/*him)

(5.9) $\sqrt{}$/?John showed *Mary* a picture of *herself.* (= 3.3a)

(1) Awareness:	+3	(Mary perceived the picture as one involving her.)
(2) Picture noun agent:	−6	
(3) Intervening NP:	0	
(4) Semantic case:	0	(The trigger *Mary* is a goal.)
(5) Surface structure:	−1	(The trigger is an object.)
(6) Anaphoricity:	+2	(The trigger *Mary* is a definite NP.)
(7) Humanness:	+2	(The trigger is human.)
Trigger potential =	0	($\sqrt{}$/?herself/*her)

(5.10) *Mary liberally quoted from *an American novelist* in a book about *himself.*

(1) Awareness:	−5	(The novelist was not aware of Mary's book about him.)
(2) Picture noun agent:	−6	(The antecedent of the reflexive is not an overt or covert agent, or an indirect agent of the picture noun.)
(3) Intervening NP:	−4	(*Mary* is a covert intervening NP.)
(4) Semantic case:	−3	(The trigger is neither an agent, an experiencer, benefactive, nor a goal.)
(5) Surface structure:	−3	(The trigger is neither a subject nor an object.)
(6) Anaphoricity:	0	(The trigger is an indefinite NP.)
(7) Humanness:	+2	(The trigger is human.)
Trigger potential =	−19	(*himself/$\sqrt{}$him)

The reflexivization potential of *John* of (5.8), which is the total of all the weights derived from the seven hierarchies for picture noun reflexivization, is (+5). Reflexivization results in perfect acceptability; pronominalization in total unacceptability. On the other hand, the reflexivization potential of *Mary* of (5.9) is (0). Reflexivization yields a slightly lower degree of acceptability than (5.8), but pronominalization still yields total unacceptability. In (5.10), five out of seven conditions point against picture noun reflexivization, yielding a reflexivization potential of (−19). The use of *himself* in the sentence results in total unacceptability and the use of *him* in perfect acceptability.

Let us examine some more examples:

(5.11) ??*John* hasn't found out about that horrible book about *himself* yet.

(1) Awareness:	−5	(2) Picture noun agent:	−6
(3) Intervening NP:	0	(4) Semantic case:	+2
(5) Surface structure:	+2	(6) Anaphoricity:	+2
(7) Humanness:	+2		
Trigger potential =	−3 (??himself/$\sqrt{}$him)		

(5.12) *John was destroyed by the scandalous gossip about *himself*.

(1) Awareness:	−5	(2) Picture noun agent:	−6
(3) Intervening NP:	0	(4) Semantic case:	0
(5) Surface structure:	+2	(6) Anaphoricity:	+2
(7) Humanness:	+2		

Trigger potential =   −5 (*himself /$^\vee$him)

(5.13) *John reminded Mary of a younger version of *himself*.

(1) Awareness:	−5	(2) Picture noun agent:	−6
(3) Intervening NP:	0	(4) Semantic case:	−3
(5) Surface structure:	+2	(6) Anaphoricity:	+2
(7) Humanness:	+2		

Trigger potential =   −8 (*himself/$^\vee$him)

(5.14) Mary reminded *John* of a younger version of *himself*.

(1) Awareness:	+3	(2) Picture noun agent:	−6
(3) Intervening NP:	0	(4) Semantic case:	+1
(5) Surface structure:	−1	(6) Anaphoricity:	+2
(7) Humanness:	+2		

Trigger potential =   +1   ($^\vee$himself/*him)

(5.15) ?*John* hates stories about *himself* by Jane. (= 4.8a)

(1) Awareness:	+3	(2) Picture noun agent:	−6
(3) Intervening NP:	−6	(4) Semantic case:	+1
(5) Surface structure:	+2	(6) Anaphoricity:	+2
(7) Humanness:	+2		

Trigger potential =   −2   (?himself/$^\vee$him)

(5.16) *John hates Jane's stories about *himself*.

(1, 2, 4, 5, 6, 7): the same as above	
(3) Intervening NP	−8

Trigger potential =   −4   (*himself/$^\vee$him)

(5.17) John gave *Mary* a renewed faith in *herself*.

(1) Awareness:	+3	(2) Picture noun agent:	0
(3) Intervening NP:	0	(4) Semantic case:	0
(5) Surface structure:	−1	(6) Anaphoricity:	+2
(7) Humanness:	+2		

Trigger potential =   +6   ($^\vee$herself/*her)

(5.18) *John gave Mary a renewed faith in *himself*.

(1) Awareness:	+3	(2) Picture noun agent:	−6
(3) Intervening NP:	−4	(4) Semantic case:	−3

| (5) Surface structure: | +2 | (6) Anaphoricity: | +2 |
| (7) Humanness: | −2 | | |

| Trigger potential = | −8 | (*himself/$^\vee$him) | |

Note in (5.18) that there is nothing agent-like in *John* in this sentence and that it represents, not John in the flesh, but his actions/utterances/personality. Note also that *Mary* is still the covert agent of the picture noun and thus serves as an intervening NP for reflexivization with *John* as trigger.

(5.19) *John gave *Mary* an accurate description of *herself*.

(1) Awareness:	+3	(2) Picture noun agent:	−6
(3) Intervening NP:	−4	(4) Semantic case:	0
(5) Surface structure:	−1	(6) Anaphoricity:	+2
(7) Humanness:	+2		

| Trigger potential = | −4 | (*herself/$^\vee$her) | |

(5.20) *John* gave Mary an accurate description of *himself*.

(1) Awareness:	+3	(2) Picture noun agent:	0
(3) Intervening NP:	0	(4) Semantic case:	+2
(5) Surface structure:	+2	(6) Anaphoricity:	+2
(7) Humanness:	+2		

| Trigger potential = | +11 | ($^\vee$himself/*him) | |

Note above that, contrary to the situation of (5.18), *John* in (5.20) is an agent and it represents John in the flesh. It is also the agent of the picture noun *an accurate description of himself*. Thus, all the factors involved point to reflexivization.

The following table shows the correlation between the trigger potential of the sentences (5.8) through (5.20) and their acceptability status with reflexives and pronouns:

(5.21)

Zone	Trigger Potential Value	Sentence #	Acceptability Status
(A)	+11	(5.20)	$^\vee$himself/*him
	+6	(5.17)	$^\vee$herself/*her
	+5	(5.8)	$^\vee$himself/*him
	+1	(5.14)	$^\vee$himself/*him
	0	(5.9)	$^\vee$/?herself/*her
(B)	−2	(5.15)	?himself/$^\vee$him
	−3	(5.11)	??himself/$^\vee$him
(C)	−4	(5.19)	*herself/$^\vee$her
		(5.16)	*himself/$^\vee$him
	−5	(5.12)	*himself/$^\vee$him
	−8	(5.13)	*himself/$^\vee$him
		(5.18)	*himself/$^\vee$him
	−19	(5.10)	*himself/$^\vee$him

The above correlation table shows that reflexivization results in total acceptability when the trigger potential is in Zone A, in total unacceptability when the trigger potential is in Zone C, and in awkwardness/marginality in Zone B, undoubtedly subject to idiolectal variations. It also shows that pronominalization results in unacceptability when the trigger potential is in Zone A and in acceptability when it is in Zone C. It is expected that the acceptability status of pronominalization is unstable in Zone B and its surrounding borderline areas in Zones A and C.

Let us proceed to examine some sentences that involve violation of the Awareness Condition or the Picture Noun Agent as Intervening NP Constraint but that are nearly or totally acceptable due to the fact that the violation is made up for by the fulfillment of other conditions. First, observe the following example:

(5.22) Under the influence of hypnosis, *John* unconsciously drew a picture of *himself* on a sheet of paper.

(1) Awareness:	−5	(2) Picture noun agent:	0
(3) Intervening NP:	0	(4) Semantic case:	+2
(5) Surface structure:	+2	(6) Anaphoricity:	+2
(7) Humanness:	+2		

Trigger potential =   +3   ($^\vee$himself/*him)

The trigger potential value of ($+3$) puts the sentence in Zone A of the table in (5.21), which predicts that the sentence is acceptable with a reflexive and unacceptable with a pronoun. This prediction is borne out by the observed acceptability status of the sentence.

Observe next the following example:

(5.23) $^\vee$/?John painted for *Mary* a portrait of *herself*.

(1) Awareness:		+3	(Assume that Mary recognized the portrait as one depicting her.)
(2) Picture noun agent:	a.	−3	(if Mary was the instigator or the resulting acquirer of the picture noun)
	b.	−6	(if not)
(3) Intervening NP:		−4	(*John* is an intervening NP.)
(4) Semantic case:		+1	(benefactive)
(5) Surface structure:		−1	(dative object)
(6) Anaphoricity:		+2	
(7) Humanness:		+2	

Trigger potential =	a.	0	($^\vee$/?herself/??her)
	b.	−3	(??herself/$^\vee$her)

If Mary had asked John to paint a portrait of her, or if Mary came to possess the picture, *Mary* is an indirect agent of the picture noun. This nearly overrides the blocking power of *John* as an intervening picture noun agent. The total trigger potential in this interpretation is (0), which puts the sentence at the bottom of Zone A of the table in (5.21). The acceptability status $\checkmark$/? predicted by the table exactly matches the observed acceptability status of the sentence with reflexivization. If, on the other hand, the sentence is followed by a statement that asserts that the picture did not come into Mary's possession, then *Mary* is not an indirect agent. In this interpretation, the trigger potential of *Mary* is (-3), as shown in (b). This puts the sentence on the borderline between Zones B and C of the table, and makes it marginal with a reflexive pronoun and acceptable with a nonreflexive pronoun. This accounts for the intuition that speakers have about the sentence: namely, the sentence with a reflexive implies that Mary told John she wanted to have a portrait of herself, or she commissioned him to paint one for her, while the same sentence with a nonreflexive pronoun implies that John painted a portrait of Mary as a present for her without her prior knowledge.

Next, observe the following sentence:

(5.24) ?/??John collaborated with *Mary* on a story about *herself*. (cf. 4.15)

(1) Awareness:	$+3$	(2) Picture noun agent:	0
(3) Intervening NP:	0	(4) Semantic case:	-3
(5) Surface structure:	-5	(6) Anaphoricity:	$+2$
(7) Humanness:	$+2$		
Trigger potential =	-1	(?/??herself/?/??her)	

I have assumed in the above that *Mary* is the agent of the picture noun. The trigger potential value (-1) puts the sentence in Zone B. The observed acceptability status ?/?? both for the reflexive and nonreflexive versions is as predicted by an extrapolation from the table.

We continue with the following sentence:

(5.25)   John assisted Mary on a book about himself/him.

Both the reflexive and pronominal versions are acceptable, but there is a subtle difference in meaning. The reflexive version implies that John actively helped Mary by taking part in the writing, while the pronominal version implies that John was not actively engaged in the writing. Let us see what our quantitative model says about the two versions:

(5.26) *John* assisted Mary on a book about *himself* by providing her with all the materials she needed and giving comments on her draft manuscript.

(1) Awareness:	$+3$	
(2) Picture noun agent:	-3	(*John* is an indirect agent of the picture noun.)
(3) Intervening NP:	-4	(*Mary* is an intervening picture noun agent.)
(4) Semantic case:	$+2$	
(5) Surface structure:	$+2$	
(6) Anaphoricity:	$+2$	
(7) Humanness:	$+2$	
Trigger potential =	$+4$	($\checkmark$himself/*him)

(5.27) *John* assisted Mary on a book about *himself* by staying abroad and leaving
her alone.

(1) Awareness:	−5	
(2) Picture noun agent:	−6	(*John* is not an indirect agent of the picture noun.)
(3) Intervening NP:	−4	
(4) Semantic case:	+2	
(5) Surface structure:	+2	
(6) Anaphoricity:	+2	
(7) Humanness:	+2	
Trigger potential =	−7	(*himself/$^\vee$him)

In (5.26), it is made clear that John actively contributed to the coming into
existence of Mary's book about him. Therefore, *John* is an indirect agent of
the picture noun. This fact, and the fact that John recognized the book as one
about him, more than make up for the violation of the Picture Noun Agent as
Intervening NP Condition. In this sentence, only the reflexive version is
allowable. In contrast, in (5.27), it is made clear that John did not do anything
active in contributing to the coming into existence of Mary's book about him.
Therefore, *John* is not an indirect agent of the picture noun. Furthermore,
there was neither concurrent nor prior recognition of the book as one about
him. The semantic case of *John* in this sentence, although recorded as agent
(+2) in (5.27), is only slightly agent-like. The trigger potential value of (−7)
puts the sentence in Zone C of the table of (5.21). The sentence is unacceptable with a reflexive and acceptable with a pronoun, as predicted by the table.

Furthermore, observe the following sentence:

(5.28)   John helped Mary with a book about $^\vee$/himself/*him.

The expression *help someone with* implies active participation. Hence, the
kind of interpretation that is represented in (5.27) does not exist for the sentence, and therefore reflexivization is obligatory.

Likewise, observe the following sentence:

(5.29) Mary cost *John*$_i$ a picture of *himself*$_i$ in the paper.

(1) Awareness:	+3/−5	(2) Picture noun agent:	−3
(3) Intervening NP:	0	(4) Semantic case:	+1
(5) Surface structure:	−1	(6) Anaphoricity:	+2
(7) Humanness:	+2		
Trigger potential =	+4/−4		

The primary interpretation of the sentence is that perhaps in order to impress
Mary, John paid for a picture of himself to be printed in the newspaper.[26] In
this interpretation, John was an indirect agent for the picture, and he was
aware of it. The trigger potential value for *John* in this interpretation is (+4),
which, according to the table of (5.21), predicts that the sentence is acceptable

with a reflexive, and unacceptable with a pronoun (i.e., $^{\vee}$/himself/*him). This prediction matches the observed acceptability status of the sentence. The second interpretation of the sentence is that John was publicity-shy and that dating Mary resulted in the appearance of his picture (perhaps with Mary) in the paper. In this interpretation, too, it is possible to interpret John as one who was responsible for the printing of the picture. If he was aware of the picture, the trigger potential is ($+4$) and the same result holds as for the previous case. If John was not aware of the picture, the trigger potential is (-4), which puts the sentence in Zone C, with the predicted acceptability status of *himself/$^{\vee}$him. This prediction agrees with the observed acceptability status of the sentence with the specified interpretation.

Observe, further, the following sentence:

(5.30) *Mary* cost John a picture of *herself* in the paper.

(1) Awareness:	$+3/-5$	(2) Picture noun agent:	-6
(3) Intervening NP:	0	(4) Semantic case:	-5
(5) Surface structure:	$+2$	(6) Anaphoricity:	$+2$
(7) Humanness:	-2		
Trigger potential =	$-6/-14$		

The sentence implies that, in order to please or impress Mary, John paid for her picture to be printed in the newspaper. Just as in (5.29), *John* is the indirect agent for the picture noun, but Mary is not. It is not clear what the semantic case of *Mary* is, but it is clear that it is neither agentive, nor experiencer/benefactive, nor goal. The sentence, by using *Mary* as the subject of *cost,* treats Mary, not as a human being, but as an inanimate object. The trigger potential of *Mary* is $-6/-14$, depending upon whether Mary was aware of the picture. In either case, the value is low enough to predict that the sentence would be unacceptable with a reflexive and acceptable with a pronoun. This prediction is also consistent with the observed acceptability status of the sentence.

We now refine the trigger potential table of (5.21) by incorporating examples (5.23) through (5.30):

(5.31)

Trigger Potential Value	Acceptability Status	
	Reflexive	Pronoun
$+1$ or above	$^{\vee}$	*
0	$^{\vee}$/?	*
-1	?/??	?/??
$-2, -3$	?/??	$^{\vee}$
-4 or below	*	$^{\vee}$

The weights that I have assigned to the items in each hierarchy have been arbitrarily chosen except that they satisfy the condition, "picture noun reflexivization is easier for x than for y." However, the above crude model displays a

strong correlation between the trigger potentials and the observed acceptability status of the reflexive and pronominal versions of the picture nouns
involved. Naturally, different speakers would have different weights assigned
to items in a given hierarchy, and the relative strengths of the hierarchies
would vary from speaker to speaker. However, the model I have described
above seems to approximate the acceptability judgments of the sentences that
I have discussed in this chapter, and, with a full understanding that it is still a
very crude model that requires further refinements, I will use it in the next
section as a model for predicting the acceptability status of picture noun reflexives and pronominals involving relative clauses.

4.6 Picture Nouns and Relative Clauses

As is well known (cf. Cantrall 1969; Jackendoff 1972), picture nouns with
reflexives can appear within the head of a relative clause construction where
the antecedents of the reflexives are downstairs in the relative clause. For
example:

(6.1) a.   This is the picture of himself$_i$ on horseback that John$_i$ told Mary
            about.
       b. $^\vee$/?This is the picture of herself$_i$ on horseback that John told Mary$_i$
            about.

It is clear that the reflexives in these picture nouns are conditioned, in some
way or another, by reflexivization in the relative clauses:

(6.2) a.   John$_i$ told Mary about the picture of himself$_i$ on horseback.
       b. $^\vee$/?John told Mary$_i$ about the picture of herself$_i$ on horseback.

The following (a) sentences are unacceptable because their source relative
clauses, at pre-relativization stage, are unacceptable:

(6.3) a.   ??This is the picture of herself$_i$ that John phoned Mary$_i$ about last
            night.
       b.   ??John phoned Mary$_i$ about a picture of herself$_i$ last night.
(6.4) a.   *This is the evaluation of herself$_i$ that John offered to Mary$_i$.
       b.   *John offered Mary$_i$ an evaluation of herself$_i$.
(6.5) a.   *This is the story about himself$_i$ that Mary criticized John$_i$ in.
       b.   *Mary criticized John$_i$ in a story about himself$_i$.

In order to handle the above phenomenon adequately, it is necessary to have
a mechanism that determines for (6.1a) that the picture noun reflexive has an
appropriate controller, and for (6.3a), (6.4a), and (6.5a) that it does not. In
the interpretive theory of pronouns and reflexives that is adopted here, the
picture noun in (6.1a) has the following underlying structure:

(6.6)   . . . the picture of himself [John told Mary about the picture of himself]

The following interpretive rule is needed to handle the derivation of (6.1a):

(6.7)   *Head Noun Reflexive Rule:* Given a complex NP structure

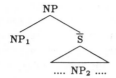

such that NP_1 is the trigger for deleting NP_2, and given that NP_1 and NP_2 are picture nouns each containing a reflexive pronoun, copy the coreference linkage of the reflexive in NP_2 onto that of NP_1.

In the cycle for the relative clause in (6.6), the regular reflexive rule marks *John* and *himself* as coreferential. Next, in the cycle for the S that contains the head noun, the Head Noun Reflexive Rule applies and marks the *himself* of the head noun as coreferential with the *John* of the relative clause.

Rule (6.7) has been formulated in such a way as to be able to handle various other cases. For example, observe the following sentence:

(6.8)   John showed Mary the picture of himself that appeared in the yearbook a few years back.

There are three putative sources for the above sentence:

(6.9)   [John showed Mary the picture of himself [the picture of

$\left\{\begin{array}{ll} \text{a.} & \text{himself} \\ \text{b.} & \text{him} \\ \text{c.} & \text{John} \end{array}\right\}$ appeared in the yearbook a few years back]]

On the lower cycle, neither *himself, him,* nor *John* receives coreference linkage. Thus, the Head Noun Reflexive Rule cannot assign any coreference linkage to *himself* upstairs. However, the regular reflexive rule applies and marks the main clause *John* and *himself* as coreferential.

On the other hand, observe the following sentence:

(6.10)   *This is the story about himself$_i$ that Mary criticized John$_i$ in.

Again, there are three possible underlying structures for the sentence in the interpretive framework.

(6.11)   [This is the story about himself [Mary criticized John in the story about

$\left\{\begin{array}{ll} \text{a.} & \text{himself} \\ \text{b.} & \text{him} \\ \text{c.} & \text{John} \end{array}\right\}$]]

In the cycle for the relative clause, the regular reflexive rule applies. However, *himself* cannot be marked as coreferential with *John* because *John*'s trigger potential is very low (i.e., Awareness: (-5), Picture noun agent: (-6), Intervening NP: (-4), Semantic case: $(+1)$, Surface structure: (0), Anaphoricity: $(+2)$, Humanness: $(+2)$; Total $= (-10)$).[27] Neither can it be marked as coreferential with *Mary* because of lack of gender agreement. In the higher cycle, the Head Noun Reflexive Rule applies, but only vacuously because there is no coreference linkage to be copied onto the higher reflexive. There is no other NP in the main clause that can serve as trigger for reflexivization. Thus, the higher reflexive ends up without being linked to any NP, and the sentence is judged unacceptable for this reason.

Going back to the lower cycle of (6.11), *him* is marked optionally as [+coref] with the object *John*. Since relativization assumes coreferentiality of the head noun and its target, the upstairs *himself* must be coreferential with *him,* and therefore with *John* as well. However, this coreference linkage is established via logical deduction rather than by direct application of a reflexive rule. Thus, the Stranded Reflexive Rule (see (11.80) of sec. 2.11) still applies and marks this derivation of (6.10) as unacceptable.

In the case of (6.11c), the two *John*'s cannot be assigned coreference linkage because they are clause mates. The Head Noun Reflexive Rule does not apply in any case, and therefore the reflexive in the head picture noun is left stranded. Hence, this derivation does not yield a grammatical sentence, either.

The following example involves picture nouns in comparative clauses:

(6.12)   There are more stories about himself$_i$ in newspapers than John$_i$ cares to read.

The underlying structure of the sentence, with unnecessary details omitted, is as shown below.

(6.13)

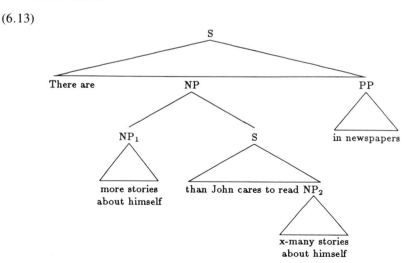

Since the picture noun containing the reflexive (i.e., *more stories about himself*) forms a complex NP together with the *than*-clause, which contains the target of Comparative Deletion, the Head Noun Reflexive Rule applies, and marks *himself* of the main clause as coreferential with the *John* of the embedded clause.[28] Compare the above with the following sentence:

(6.14)   *There are stories about himself in newspapers more often than John cares to read them.

In the above sentence, the *than*-clause forms a sister branch of *more often,* and not of the picture noun, as shown below:

(6.15)

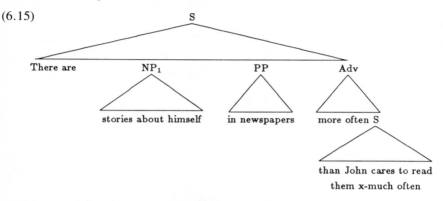

Therefore the Head Noun Reflexive Rule does not apply. Thus, the reflexive in the picture noun upstairs is left stranded without any coreference linkage established; hence the unacceptability of the sentence.

The following example also shows that the Head Noun Reflexive Rule needs to be stated, as in (6.7), as a rule that applies between the head noun and the clause with which it forms a complex NP, and that applies only when the embedded clause involves the same (to-be-deleted) picture noun as the head noun:

(6.16)   *There appear pictures of himself$_i$ in newspapers wherever John$_i$ goes.

All the examples I have used thus far have been of the type in which either the main clause or the embedded clause has a strong trigger for reflexivization, but not both. Interesting interactions take place when both clauses contain potential triggers for reflexivization. First compare the following sentences:

(6.17)   a.   John$_i$ showed Mary the picture of himself$_i$/*him$_i$ that appeared in the yearbook a few years back. (= 6.8)
          b.   Mary threw away a picture of himself$_i$/??him$_i$ that John$_i$ took in Maine a few years back.
          c.   Mary had taken a picture of *himself$_i$/(?)him$_i$ that John$_i$ threw away.

Examples (6.17b) and (6.17c) involve a conflict between the two potential triggers for reflexivization: *Mary* upstairs functioning as a blocking force against reflexivization into *a picture of John,* and *John* downstairs functioning as a trigger for reflexivization (via application of the Head Noun Reflexive Rule). The fact that (6.17b) is acceptable with a reflexive pronoun, but that (6.17c) is not, must be attributable to differences in the trigger potentials between *Mary* and *John* in these sentences.

For the sake of illustration, let us use the quantitative model that was used in the preceding section for simplex sentence reflexives, and attempt to quantify the relative impetus for control of reflexivization in the main and relative clauses. If the trigger potential of NP_1 is A and that of NP_2 is B, I define the relative trigger potential of NP_1 as $(A - B)$ and that of NP_2 as $(B - A)$. Since the upstairs impetus for control of reflexivization is much stronger than the downstairs one, I will hypothesize the following:

(6.18)   *Relative Clause Penalty:* Assign (-3) points to the trigger for picture noun reflexivization in a relative clause.

I will first illustrate how the Relative Clause Penalty applies:

(6.19)   Mary threw away the picture of ??himself$_i$/$^\vee$him$_i$ that John$_i$ hung on the wall.

A.	Upstairs: (*Mary* threw away the picture of himself)			
	(1) Awareness:	+3	(2) Picture noun agent:	−6
	(3) Intervening NP:	0	(4) Semantic case:	+2
	(5) Surface str:	+2	(6) Anaphoricity:	+2
	(7) Humanness:	+2		
	Trigger potential of *Mary:*	+5		

B.	Downstairs: (*John* hung the picture of himself on the wall)			
	(1) Awareness:	+3	(2) Picture noun agent:	−6
	(3) Intervening NP:	0	(4) Semantic case:	+2
	(5) Surface str:	+2	(6) Anaphoricity:	+2
	(7) Humanness:	+2	(8) Relative clause:	−3
	Trigger potential of *John:*	+2		

C.   Relative trigger potential of *John* = B − A = 2 − 5 = −3

Now we are ready to compare (6.17b) and (6.17c).

(6.20)   Mary threw away a picture of himself$_i$/??him$_i$ that John$_i$ took in Maine a few years back. (= 6.17b)

A.	Upstairs: (Mary threw away a picture of himself)	
	Trigger potential of *Mary:*	+5 (cf. (6.19A))

B.   Downstairs: (John took a picture of himself)

(1) Awareness:	+3	(2) Picture noun agent:	0
(3) Intervening NP:	0	(4) Semantic case:	+2
(5) Surface str:	+2	(6) Anaphoricity:	+2
(7) Humanness:	+2	(8) Relative clause:	−3

Trigger potential of *John:*   +8

C.   Relative trigger potential of *John* = B − A = 8 − 5 = +3

(6.21)   Mary had taken a picture of *himself$_i$/(?)him that John$_i$ threw away.
A.   Upstairs: (Mary had taken a picture of himself)
Trigger potential of *Mary:* +11 (same as (6.20B), but without relative clause penalty)
B.   Downstairs: (John threw away a picture of himself)
Trigger potential of *John:* +2 (same as (6.20A), but with relative clause penalty)
C.   Relative trigger potential of *John* = B − A = 2 − 11 = −9

A positive relative trigger potential means that the stronger of the two potential triggers has been used for reflexivization, and a negative one means that the weaker has been used. The positive value of (6.20C) agrees with the acceptability of the sentence with a reflexive, and the negative value of (6.21C) agrees with the unacceptability of the sentence with a reflexive.

Let us further observe the following sentences:

(6.22)   Mary$_i$ threw away a picture of herself$_i$/her$_i$ that John took in Maine a few years back.
A.   Upstairs: (Mary threw away a picture of herself)
Trigger potential: +5 (cf. (6.20A))
B.   Downstairs: (John took a picture of herself . . .)
Trigger potential: +8 (cf. (6.20B))
C.   Relative trigger potential of *Mary* = A − B = −3 ($^\checkmark$herself/$^\checkmark$her)
(6.23)   Mary had taken a picture of herself$_i$/*her$_i$ that John threw away.
A.   Upstairs: (Mary had taken a picture of herself)
Trigger potential: +11 (cf. (6.21A))
B.   Downstairs: (John threw away a picture of herself)
Trigger potential: +2 (cf. (6.21B))
C.   Relative trigger potential of *Mary* = A − B = +9 ($^\checkmark$herself/*her)

The above examples suggest that forward picture noun reflexivization applies without much interference from relative clauses that modify the picture noun, but that picture noun pronominalization is constrained by the relative trigger potential of the upstairs trigger: namely, if the relative trigger potential of the upstairs trigger is too large, pronominalization yields unacceptability.[29]

The above model shows that there is a close correlation between the relative trigger potential of the NP that has actually controlled reflexivization, shown in (C), and the actual degree of acceptability of the surface sentences:

(6.24) *Backward Picture Noun Reflexivization from within Relative Clauses:*

Sentences	Relative Trigger Potential	Acceptability Status
(6.20)	+3	$^\vee$himself/??him
(6.19)	−3	??himself/$^\vee$him
(6.21)	−9	*himself/(?)him

(6.25) *Forward Picture Noun Reflexivization with Relative Clause Interference:*

Sentences	Relative Trigger Potential	Acceptability Status
(6.23)	+9	$^\vee$herself/*her
(6.22)	−3	$^\vee$herself/$^\vee$her

Let us now consider the following sentences, which are patterned after Jackendoff's examples (1972, pp. 166–168):

(6.26) a. Mary hates the story about himself$_i$ that John$_i$ always tells.
  b. *Mary told the story about himself$_i$ that John$_i$ likes to hear.

Jackendoff attempted to account for the above contrast by assuming that there was a rule for duplicating the subject of either the main clause or the relative clause (depending upon the circumstance) in the determiner position of the picture noun, and that this rule was ordered before reflexivization. He assumed that *John's* was inserted in the determiner position of (6.26a) and *Mary's* in the determiner position of (6.26b):

(6.27) a. Mary hates *John's* story about *himself* . . .
  b. *Mary told *her* story about *himself* . . .

If this insertion was carried out before application of the rule for establishing coreference linkage for reflexives, (6.27a) and hence (6.26a) would be marked as acceptable, while (6.27b) and hence (6.26b) would be marked as unacceptable. He conjectured that the conditioning of the duplication rule depended on some semantic property of the verb, and suggested that the property in question might have something to do with the subject's being marked with the thematic relation agent *with respect to the verb*.

The above assumption cannot account for the contrast between (6.17b) and (6.17c) because all the verbs used in these sentences, both upstairs and downstairs, take agent subjects. Note that Jackendoff's thematic relation agent has nothing to do with picture noun agent, but it concerns only agenthood with respect to the verb. Thus the above assumption predicts that (6.17b) and (6.17c) would be both totally unacceptable or perfectly acceptable, depending upon whether the main clause agent NP or the relative clause agent NP gets duplicated in Jackendoff's system.

The contrast between (6.26a) and (6.26b) can be accounted for with the experimental quantitative model under discussion. This model yields the following tabulations:

(6.28)   Mary hates the story about himself$_i$ that John$_i$ always tells. (= 6.26a)

A.	Upstairs: (Mary hates the story about himself)				
	(1) Awareness:	+3	(2) Picture noun agent:	−6
	(3) Intervening NP:	0	(4) Semantic case:	+1
	(5) Surface str:	+2	(6) Anaphoricity:	+2
	(7) Humanness:	+2		
	Trigger potential of *Mary*:	**+4**		

B.	Downstairs: (John always tells the story about himself)				
	(1) Awareness:	+3	(2) Picture noun agent:	0
	(3) Intervening NP:	0	(4) Semantic case:	+2
	(5) Surface str:	+2	(6) Anaphoricity:	+2
	(7) Humanness:	+2	(8) Relative clause:	−3
	Trigger potential of *John*:	**+8**		

C.   Relative trigger potential of *John* = B − A = +4

(6.29)   *Mary told the story about himself$_i$ that John$_i$ likes to hear. (= 6.26b)
    A.   Upstairs: (Mary told the story about himself)
        Trigger potential of *Mary* (same as (6.28B), but without relative clause penalty): +11
    B.   Downstairs: (John likes to hear the story about himself)
        Trigger potential of *John* (same as (6.28A), but with relative clause penalty): +1
    C.   Relative trigger potential of *John* = B − A = −10

The above tabulations, vis-à-vis the table of (6.24), predict that (6.26a) is acceptable with *himself* and marginal with *him*, while (6.26b), with the relative trigger potential of (−10), is unacceptable with *himself* and acceptable, or nearly acceptable, with *him*. These predictions are borne out by the observed acceptability judgments of these sentences by many native speakers.

Next observe the following sentences:

(6.30)   a.   Mary$_i$ liked the portrait of $^\checkmark$herself$_i$/?her$_i$ that John bought.
        b.   John$_i$ bought the portrait of $^\checkmark$himself$_i$/??him$_i$ that Mary liked best.
(6.31)   a.   *Mary liked the portrait of himself that John bought.
        b.   *John bought the portrait of herself that Mary liked best.

Let us examine the predictions our model makes about the acceptability status of these sentences.

(6.32) Mary liked the portrait of herself that John bought. (= 6.30a)

A.	Upstairs: (Mary liked the portrait of herself)			
	(1) Awareness:	+3	(2) Picture noun agent:	−6
	(3) Intervening NP:	0	(4) Semantic case:	+1
	(5) Surface str:	+2	(6) Anaphoricity:	+2
	(7) Humanness:	+2		
	Trigger potential of *Mary:*	+4		
B.	Downstairs: (John bought the portrait of herself)			
	(1) Awareness:	+3	(2) Picture noun agent:	−6
	(3) Intervening NP:	0	(4) Semantic case:	+2
	(5) Surface str:	+2	(6) Anaphoricity:	+2
	(7) Humanness:	+2	(8) Relative clause:	−3
	Trigger potential of *John:*	+2		
C.	Relative trigger potential of *Mary* = A − B = +2			

(6.33)   John bought the portrait of himself that Mary liked best. (= 6.30b)

A.   Upstairs: (John bought the portrait of himself)
Trigger potential of *John* (same as (6.32B), but without relative clause penalty): +5

B.   Downstairs: (Mary liked best the portrait of himself)
Trigger potential of *Mary* (same as (6.32A), but with relative clause penalty): +1

C.   Relative trigger potential of *John* = A − B = +4

The table of (6.25) predicts that reflexivization is unconditionally acceptable for both (6.30a) and (6.30b) and that pronominalization is awkward/marginal for both sentences but (6.30a) is better than (6.30b) with a pronoun. These predictions are also borne out by the observed acceptability status judgments of these sentences.

(6.34)   *Mary liked the portrait of himself that John bought. (= 6.31a)

A.   Upstairs: (Mary liked the portrait of himself)
Trigger potential of *Mary* (same as (6.32A)): +4

B.   Downstairs: (John bought the portrait of himself)
Trigger potential of *John* (same as (6.32B)): +2

C.   Relative trigger potential of *John* = B − A = −2

(6.35)   *John bought the portrait of herself that Mary liked best. (= 6.31b)

A.   Upstairs: (John bought the portrait of herself)
Trigger potential of *John* (same as (6.33A)): +5

B.   Downstairs: (Mary liked best the portrait of herself)
Trigger potential of *Mary* (same as (6.33B)): +1

C.   Relative trigger potential of *Mary* = B − A = −4

The table of (6.24) predicts that both (6.31a) and (6.31b) are within the range of ?? ~ * with reflexivization and $^\vee$ with pronominalization. These predictions reflect the speaker judgments for these sentences fairly closely.

The comparison of (6.28) and (6.34) shows that what is primarily responsible for the acceptability of (6.28) is that the downstairs *John* is also a covert agent of the picture noun in *John told the story about himself.* In contrast, in (6.34), *John* is not an agent of the picture noun in *John bought the portrait of himself.* This does not, however, mean that picture noun reflexivization from the relative clause onto the head noun is allowable only when the postcedent (in the relative clause) of the reflexive is also the picture noun agent. Observe the following example:

(6.36) Nobody was aware of the picture of herself$_i$ that Mary$_i$ hung on the wall of her$_i$ study.

A. Upstairs: (Nobody was aware of the picture of herself)

(1) Awareness:	−3	(2) Picture noun agent:	−6
(3) Intervening NP:	0	(4) Semantic case:	+1
(5) Surface str:	+2	(6) Anaphoricity:	−2
(7) Humanness:	+2		

Trigger potential of *nobody:*   −6

B. Downstairs: (Mary hung the picture of herself on the wall . . .)

(1) Awareness:	+3	(2) Picture noun agent:	−6
(3) Intervening NP:	0	(4) Semantic case:	+2
(5) Surface str:	+2	(6) Anaphoricity:	+2
(7) Humanness:	+2	(8) Relative clause:	−3

Trigger potential of *Mary:*   +2

C. Relative trigger potential of *Mary* = B − A = +8

The fact that *nobody* is an indefinite pronoun, and that the main clause would not satisfy the Awareness Condition, makes *nobody* a very weak potential controller for the picture noun reflexive. On the other hand, the relative clause subject *Mary* is an extremely powerful potential controller for the picture noun reflexive, although it is not the agent of the picture noun. These two factors combine to make (6.36) a perfectly acceptable sentence.

Crude though it is, our model is capable of accounting for most of the contrasts we have observed thus far. Undoubtedly the relative weights are open to empirical verification and many more data need to be analyzed to determine those to be assigned to items for each of the principles, constraints, and hierarchies under consideration. And naturally there are wide idiolectal differences in the values of these weights. Therefore the values that I have used in the above demonstrations should not be taken as anything more than initial approximations. The above results, however, seem to indicate convincingly that the factors that I have identified are all relevant and are needed to account for the picture noun reflexivization phenomenon involving relative clauses.

The question that we have to raise, then, is why so many different factors interact with picture noun reflexivization (as well as with regular simplex sentence reflexivization). In the next chapter, I will attempt to show that many of the conditions are derivable from a higher-order generalization to the effect that picture noun reflexives are "point of view" expressions that are best when they are used with the speaker taking the "camera angle" of the referents of the reflexives.

5 Empathy Perspective

This chapter presents a theory of empathy that was described in Kuno and Kaburaki (1975/1977), introduces revisions that have been made, and adds many more phenomena not discussed in that paper that require an explanation in terms of an empathy perspective. The basic idea of empathy is presented in an intuitive fashion in the first brief introductory section. A formal treatment of the notion of empathy and various principles that involve it are given in subsequent sections.

5.1 Introduction

In describing an event, the speaker can represent his attitude toward its participants in numerous, sometimes subtly different ways. For example, consider the situation in which a man named John hits his brother Bill. The speaker can describe this situation in various ways, which include the following:

(1.1)   a.   Then John hit Bill.
        b.   Then John hit his brother.
        c.   Then Bill's brother hit him.
(1.2)   a.   Then Bill was hit by John.
        b. ??Then John's brother was hit by him.
           ??Then his brother was hit by John.
        c.   Then Bill was hit by his brother.

All the above sentences are identical in their logical content, but they seem to differ from each other with respect to where the speaker has placed himself in relation to John and Bill. Let us use, for illustration, the situation of filming a scene in which John hit Bill. One of the most important decisions that directors must make is where to place the camera while shooting this scene. They can, for example, place the camera equidistant from both John and Bill. The resulting scene will be one in which the event under discussion is presented objectively, with the director taking a detached view. Alternatively, the director can place the camera closer to John than to Bill. In that case, the scene will be presented to the viewer more from John's point of view than from Bill's. As an extreme instance of this situation, the director can give John the camera, so to speak. If this occurs, the scene will be presented to the viewer entirely from John's point of view. John will not appear in the scene because the scene describes what John sees. Alternatively, the director can choose to shoot the scene by placing his camera closer to Bill than to John, or by giving it to Bill. The scenes shot from different camera angles, while capturing the same act of John's hitting Bill, produce different effects on the viewer.

In producing natural sentences, speakers unconsciously make the same kind of decisions that film directors make about where to place themselves with respect to the events and states that their sentences are intended to describe. In describing the event in which John hit his brother Bill, speakers can place themselves in five different positions, (A) through (E), illustrated below:

(1.3)   Partial identification of the speaker ()

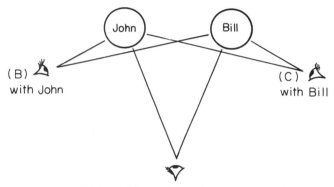

(A) neither with John nor with Bill

(1.4)   Total identification of the speaker

(D) with John

(E) with Bill

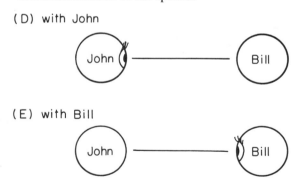

It seems commonsensical that the term *John's brother* (or *his brother*) can be used to refer to Bill only when the speaker has placed himself closer to John than to his brother; the term *John's brother* does not give Bill an independent characterization, but a characterization that is dependent upon John. In the same way, the expression *Bill's brother* (or *his brother*) can be used only when the speaker has placed himself closer to Bill than to John. If the above assumptions are correct, we can say that (1.1b) is a sentence that the speaker has produced by placing himself closer to John than to Bill, and that (1.1c) and (1.2c) are sentences that the speaker has produced by placing himself closer to Bill than to John.

Let us also assume that passive sentences in general signify speaker placement closer to the new subject than to the old. Again, if this assumption is correct, we can say that (1.2a) and (1.2c) are both sentences in which the speaker is placed closer to Bill than to John. Incidentally, sentences such as (1.1a) do not use either of the two devices that are under discussion, and therefore there is no way for us to tell what camera angle the speaker has taken in producing them.

I am claiming that both expressions such as *John's brother* and passive sentence patterns are used by speakers to show their closer placement to one participant in a sentence than to another. When a possessive NP is used, the speaker is closer to the referent of the possessive than to that of the entire NP. And when a passive sentence pattern is used, the speaker is closer to the referent of the new subject than to that of the old one. Although both claims seem intuitively correct, the real tests of their validity depend upon what predictions they can make to account for data involving possessive NPs and the passive sentence pattern.

We can summarize the above observations by showing which of the sentences of (1.1) and (1.2) are appropriate or inappropriate for the five camera positions shown in (1.3) and (1.4). In the following, # signifies that the sentence is inappropriate as a sentence used in the specified camera angle.

(1.5)

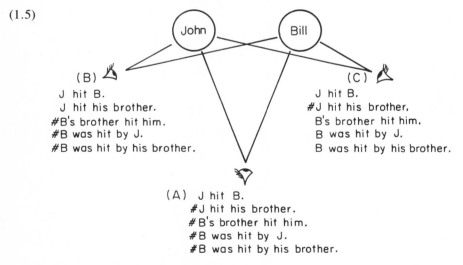

The total identification of the speaker with John or Bill, as illustrated in (1.4D) and (1.4E), seldom occurs in conversations, but it occurs very often in narratives. The appropriateness or inappropriateness of the sentences under discussion for these two situations is identical with the situations shown in (1.5B) and (1.5C), respectively.

What is most interesting here is that the sentences of (1.2b), repreated below, are marginal:

(1.6)   a.   ??Then John's brother was hit by him.
        b.   ??Then his brother was hit by John.
        c.   cf. ??Then his brother was hit by him.

The fact that (1.6c) is also marginal shows that the marginality of (1.6a, b) has little to do with the problem of forward or backward pronominalization.

The above phenomenon is predictable on the basis of the two assumptions that we have made about camera angles. The term *John's brother* (or *his brother*), according to our first assumption, indicates that the speaker has placed himself closer to John than to Bill. On the other hand, the use of the passive sentence pattern, according to our second assumption, signifies that the speaker has placed himself closer to the referent of the new subject, Bill, than to the referent of the old subject, John. These two positions are mutually irreconcilable, and clearly cannot be occupied by a single speaker/camera. The fact that the sentences of (1.6) are marginal suggests that in producing a single sentence the speaker can use only one "camera." Just as a film director must choose a single camera position for a given scene, the speaker must predetermine his camera position and maintain that position through the production of a single sentence.

Thus, the consideration of camera angles or points of view in sentence production makes it possible to account for the marginality of (1.6), which would be unexplainable otherwise. In the rest of this chapter, I will formalize the above observations and develop a theory of "empathy," demonstrating its usefulness in accounting for various phenomena in language.

5.2 Empathy

Let us use the term empathy for the notion of the camera angle that we discussed in the preceding section:

(2.1)   *Empathy:* Empathy is the speaker's identification, which may vary in degree, with a person/thing that participates in the event or state that he describes in a sentence.

(2.2)   *Degree of Empathy:* The degree of the speaker's empathy with x, $E(x)$, ranges from 0 to 1, with $E(x) = 1$ signifying his total identification with x, and $E(x) = 0$ signifying a total lack of identification.

The concept "a camera angle on x rather than y" can be represented as $E(x) > E(y)$ (namely, the degree of the speaker's identification with x is greater than with y). I will refer to relationships such as $E(x) \gtreqless E(y)$ as empathy relationships.

The two assumptions that we discussed in the preceding section are formalized below:

(2.3)   *Descriptor Empathy Hierarchy:* Given descriptor x (e.g., *John*) and another descriptor $f(x)$ that is dependent upon x (e.g., *John's brother*), the speaker's empathy with x is greater than with $f(x)$.

$$E(x) > E(f(x))$$

E.g. E(John) > E(John's brother)

(2.4)   *Surface Structure Empathy Hierarchy* (tentative): In a passive sentence, it is easier for the speaker to empathize with the referent of the subject than with that of the *by*-agentive.

$$E(\text{subject}) > E(by\text{-agentive})$$

The explanation of the marginality of (1.2b) discussed in the previous section can be formalized in the following manner:

(2.5)   ??Then John's brother was hit by him.
   a.   Descriptor Empathy Hierarchy:
        E(John) > E(John's brother)
   b.   Surface Structure Empathy Hierarchy:
        E(subject = John's brother) > E(*by*-agentive = John)

If we assume that empathy relationships are transitive, we obtain the following result from (2.5a) and (2.5b):

(2.6)   *E(John) > E(John's brother) > E(John)[1]

The constraint informally stated in the preceding section—that only one camera can be used in the production of a single sentence—can now be formulated in the following manner:

(2.7)   *Transitivity of Empathy Relationships:* Empathy relationships are transitive.

(2.8)   *Ban on Conflicting Empathy Foci:* A single sentence cannot contain logical conflicts in empathy relationships.

A single sentence may contain more than one empathy relationship as long as they are not logically contradictory. For example, observe the following sentence:

(2.9)   John and his brother talked to Mary about her sister.
   a.   E(John) > E(John's brother)
   b.   E(Mary) > E(Mary's sister)

The above sentence does not give us any means of determining the empathy relationship between John and Mary/her sister or between John's brother and

Mary/her sister. Therefore, the two relationships (2.9a) and (2.9b) cannot be collapsed into one. This situation does not yield marginality or unacceptability because there is no logical conflict between the two relationships.

Similarly, there is no logical conflict in the relationships in the following sentence:

(2.10)   John talked to his wife about her sister.
      a.   E(John) > E(his wife)
      b.   E(his wife) > E(her sister)

The expressions *John* and *his wife,* according to the Descriptor Empathy Hierarchy, determine the empathy relationship shown in (2.10a). Likewise, the expressions *his wife* and *her sister* (= his wife's sister) determine the empathy relationship shown in (2.10b). These two relationships can be collapsed into one according to the transitivity principle:

(2.11)   E(John) > E(his wife) > E(her sister)

Example (2.10) is acceptable because there is no logical conflict in (2.11).

Returning to cases that involve conflicts in empathy relationships, observe the following sentences:

(2.12)   a.   *Then Bill$_j$'s sister$_i$ hit her$_i$ brother$_j$.
      b.   *Then Bill$_j$'s friend$_i$ came to see his$_i$ friend$_j$.

The unacceptability of these sentences can be accounted for also as a conflict between two empathy relationships. For example, (2.12a) involves the following two relationships:

(2.13)   a.   *Bill's sister:* E(Bill) > E(his sister)
      b.   *her brother:* E(her = Bill's sister) > E(her brother = Bill)
      c.   according to the transitivity principle:
          *E(Bill) > E(his sister) > E(her brother = Bill)

We can say that (2.12a) is unacceptable because (2.13a) and (2.13b) are logically contradictory, as shown by (2.13c).

Now compare the above sentences with the following:

(2.14)   a.   *The alcoholic$_j$'s wife$_i$ killed her$_i$ husband.
      b.   ??An alcoholic$_j$'s wife$_i$ killed her$_i$ husband.
      c.   An alcoholic's wife should not criticize her husband.

Example (2.14a), like (2.12), is clearly unacceptable. In contrast, (2.14c) is perfectly acceptable. The acceptability status of (2.14b) lies somewhere in between. It can be conjectured that this difference in acceptability judgments has something to do with the fact that in (2.14b) the noun phrase in question, *an alcoholic,* is specific but not anaphoric, and that in (2.14c) it is generic and does not have any specific referent. The following examples show that the phenomenon under discussion has something to do with whether the NP involved is referential or not:

(2.15)   a.   *Mary's husband talked to his wife about this problem.
         b.   Mary's husband needs his wife only when he is hungry.
         c.   cf. Mary's husband needs her only when he is hungry.

Example (2.15b) is acceptable for many speakers. Even those speakers who consider it less than perfect feel that it is considerably better than (2.15a). Furthermore, there is a slight difference in meaning between (2.15b) and (2.15c). The latter is a sentence describing when Mary's husband needs Mary. Mary is treated here as a person. On the other hand, (2.15b) is a statement with respect to when Mary's husband needs a wife. In other words, *his wife* in this sentence does not really refer to Mary, but it rather represents the function of a wife as he sees it. Naturally, there is only one person who plays the role of his wife, namely, Mary. Therefore, *his wife* refers to Mary, but this reference is only by implication and does not seem to be a stipulated reference.

Similarly, observe the following exchange:

(2.16)   Speaker A: Is there anyone who loves his wife?
         Speaker B: Yes, Mary's husband loves his wife.

Here again, it seems that *his wife* in (2.16B) is nonreferential. This sentence means that Mary's husband is wife-loving. It happens that the goal of this wife-loving is Mary, but this reference is not stipulated, only implied.

The above observations establish that empathy constraints apply only when noun phrases are used referentially.[2]

5.3   Reciprocal Verbs as Empathy Verbs

Assume that a person named Mary, whom the speaker knows well, went to a party with Bill, whom the speaker also knows well, and that the following three events took place there: (i) Mary was harassed by an eight-foot-tall rowdy; (ii) she slapped an eight-foot-tall boxer in the face; and (iii) she met an eight-foot-tall basketball player. The speaker, having heard about these events from Bill, reports them individually to others:

(3.1)   Mary had quite an experience at the party she went to last night.
        a.   An eight-foot-tall rowdy harassed her.
        b.   She was harassed by an eight-foot-tall rowdy.
        (So, she complained about it to the host . . .)
(3.2)   Mary had quite an experience at the party she went to last night.
        a.   She slapped an eight-foot-tall boxer in the face.
        b.   *An eight-foot-tall boxer was slapped in the face by her.
        (The hostess was upset and asked her to leave . . .)

(3.3)   Mary had quite an experience at the party she went to last night.
    a.   She met an eight-foot-tall basketball player.
    b.   *An eight-foot-tall basketball player met her.
    (They started talking about . . .)

Why is it that the passive sentence pattern is possible in (3.1) but impossible in (3.2)? Why is it that (3.3b) is unacceptable in spite of the fact that if person A met person B, it is also true that B met A? The framework of the empathy perspective provides answers to these questions.

Let us first compare (3.1b) and (3.2b). It is clear that the difference in acceptability between these two sentences is owing to the fact that the surface subject is coreferential with the discourse topic in (3.1b) but that it is not in (3.2b).[3] Then the acceptability of (3.1b) and the unacceptability of (3.2b) can be explained by assuming that the following hierarchy holds:

(3.4)   *Topic Empathy Hierarchy:* Given an event or state that involves A and B such that A is coreferential with the topic of the present discourse and B is not, it is easier for the speaker to empathize with A than with B:
    E(discourse-topic) $\geq$ E(nontopic)

The equality sign is included in the formula because it is possible for the speaker to describe the event or state objectively, with no empathy with either A or B.[4]

Now let us examine the empathy relationships that (3.1b) and (3.2b) involve:

(3.5)   Empathy relationships of (3.1b):
    a.   Topic Empathy Hierarchy: E(she) $\geq$ E(an eight-foot-tall rowdy)
    b.   Surface Structure Empathy Hierarchy:
        E(subject = she) $>$ E(*by*-agentive = an eight-foot-tall rowdy)
(3.6)   Empathy relationships of (3.2b):
    a.   Topic Empathy Hierarchy: E(she) $\geq$ E(an eight-foot-tall boxer)
    b.   Surface Structure Empathy Hierarchy:
        E(subject = an eight-foot-tall boxer) $>$ E(*by*-agentive = her)

As is shown in (3.5), there is no logical conflict in (3.1b) between the two empathy relationships defined by the Topic Empathy Hierarchy and the Surface Structure Empathy Hierarchy. Hence the acceptability of the sentence. In contrast, the two empathy relationships that (3.2b) involves are irreconcilably contradictory, as is shown in (3.6). The sentence thus violates the Ban on Conflicting Empathy Foci, and hence comes its unacceptability.

The following examples show that the Topic Empathy Hierarchy should be defined on the basis of topic versus nontopic, as it has been in (3.4), and not on the basis of anaphoric versus nonanaphoric:

(3.7)   Mary had quite an experience at the party she went to last night.
    a.   John, who had had too much to drink, harassed her.
    b.   She was harassed by John, who had had too much to drink.

(3.8)   Mary had quite an experience at the party she went to last night.
   a.   She slapped John, who had had too much to drink, in the face.
   b.   ??John, who had had too much to drink, was slapped in the face by her.

Example (3.8b) is unacceptable in spite of the fact that *John*, the subject of the passive sentence, is as anaphoric as the *by*-agentive *Mary*. Clearly the unacceptability of this passive sentence derives from the fact that *John*, which is not coreferential with the discourse topic, has been placed in the subject position, and *Mary*, which is coreferential with the discourse topic, has been placed in the *by*-agentive position.

Now let us move to (3.3). The explanation for the unacceptability of (3.3b) lies in the fact that sentences involving *meet* in the sense of an accidental encounter share one characteristic with passive sentences: the subject of these sentences has been chosen as subject by the speaker's design. In the case of passivization, an optional transformation that need not be applied has been used.[5] In (3.1b) and (3.2b), the speaker has chosen to apply passivization, and in that sense, chosen *she* and *an eight-foot-tall basketball player* as the subjects of the respective sentences. Sentences with reciprocal verbs such as *meet* are not derived via optional transformation, but the same choice on the part of the speaker is present. Since (3.9a), for example, is true when (3.9b) is true, and conversely,

(3.9)   a.   John met Mary.
         b.   Mary met John.

in describing an event in which John and Mary met each other, the speaker can choose between John and Mary as subjects. Thus, both (3.9a) and (3.9b) are like passive sentences in that their respective subjects have been placed in subject position by the speaker's design.

Let us revise our Surface Structure Empathy Hierarchy (from 2.4) in the following way:

(3.10)   *Surface Structure Empathy Hierarchy (revised):* It is easier for the speaker to empathize with the referent of the subject than with the referents of other NPs in the sentence.[6]
         E(subject) > E(other NPs)

The unacceptability of (3.3b) can now be accounted for as deriving from the conflict in empathy relationships that the sentence involves:

(3.11)   Empathy relationships of (3.3b):
         a.   Topic Empathy Hierarchy:
               E(her) ≥ E(an eight-foot-tall basketball player)
         b.   Surface Structure Empathy Hierarchy:
               E(an eight-foot-tall basketball player) > E(her)
         (a) and (b) are contradictory.

The moment we invoke (3.10) for explanation of the unacceptability of (3.3b), we are required to explain why (3.1a) is acceptable in spite of the fact that it, too, involves the same conflict in empathy relationships that (3.3b) involves. That is, the Topic Empathy Hierarchy dictates that E(her) ≥ E(an eight-foot-tall rowdy) be the case, while the Surface Structure Empathy Hierarchy dictates that E(an eight-foot-tall rowdy) > E(her) be the case. We can solve this apparent contradiction by hypothesizing that the following meta-rule generally holds in application of discourse principles:

(3.12)   *Markedness Principle for Discourse-Rule Violations:* Sentences that involve marked (or intentional) violations of discourse principles are unacceptable. On the other hand, sentences that involve unmarked (or unintentional) violation of discourse principles go unpenalized and are acceptable.[7]

As I have already mentioned, (3.3b) is unacceptable because it violates the Ban on Conflicting Empathy Foci, as shown in (3.11), *and* because this violation has been caused by the speaker's intentional choice of *an eight-foot-tall basketball player* as the subject of the sentence. On the other hand, (3.1a) is acceptable, in spite of the fact that it violates the Ban on Conflicting Empathy Foci, because the violation is not by the speaker's design—that is, *harass* is a verb that places an agent in subject position and a victim in object position, and therefore the positioning of *an eight-foot-tall rowdy* in subject position in this sentence has been determined by this requirement as to the use of *harass*, and not by the speaker's design. The speaker could have chosen to apply passivization and placed *she* in subject position—then there would have been no violation of the ban.[8] However, this nonapplication of passivization arises from benign neglect and is not an intentional choice.

Observe next the following sentences, in which the verb *meet* is intended to mean 'meet for the first time' and not 'meet as arranged':[9]

(3.13)   a.   I met John at the party last night.
          b.   ??John met me at the party last night.
(3.14)   a.   I met you at the party last night.
          b.   ??You met me at the party last night.
(3.15)   a.   You met my brother at the party last night. (Right?)
          b.   My brother met you at the party last night.

The above phenomenon can be accounted for by assuming that the following principle holds:

(3.16)   *Speech Act Empathy Hierarchy:* The speaker cannot empathize with someone else more than with himself.[10]

$$E(\text{speaker}) > E(\text{others})$$

Note that the acceptability of (3.15b) shows that empathy hierarchy between the hearer and a third party cannot be predetermined. Whether the third party is higher than the hearer in empathy hierarchy or not depends upon the speaker's psychological relationship, at the time of utterance, with the third party and with the hearer.

There are occasions when sentences of the pattern of (3.13b) and (3.14b) are acceptable. For example, observe the following discourses:

(3.17)   Speaker A: I met you at the Smiths' before.
         Speaker B: a.   You met me where?
                      b.   *I met you where?
(3.18)   Speaker A: Have I met you somewhere before?
         Speaker B: a.   Yes, you met me at the party last night.
                      b.   ??Yes, I met you at the party last night.
(3.19)   Speaker A: John was telling me yesterday that he hadn't met you before.
         Speaker B: a.   He met me at the party last night.
                      b.   ??I met him at the party last night.

Example (3.17B) is a parrot question. Parrot questions, in general, are formed by duplicating the sentence pattern of the preceding statement, with changes only in the first- and second-person pronouns, and with the portion that the speaker has not understood replaced by a *wh*-expression.[11] Thus, (3.17Ba) is a sentence that automatically obtains if speaker B wants to query speaker A's statement with respect to the locative adverb. The violation of the Ban on Conflicting Empathy Foci resulting from the fact that *you* is the subject of *met* instead of *I* (as in (b)) is thus unintentional, and therefore there is no penalty arising from this violation. Hence the acceptability of the sentence. Moreover, the rule for forming parrot questions is an obligatory syntactic one that does not allow (3.17Bb), although this sentence is correct in terms of empathy relationships.

Similarly, the fact that *you met me* is used in (3.18Ba), rather than *I met you*, as in (3.18Bb), is attributable to the general principle that dictates that the same sentence pattern be used in answers as in questions. Therefore, the violation that this answer involves of the Ban on Conflicting Empathy Foci is unintentional, and therefore there is no penalty for this violation.

In (3.19), speaker B is correcting what John said (as reported by speaker A). Corrective sentences, just like parrot questions, follow the same sentence pattern as the sentence which is being corrected, and therefore the illegitimate empathy relationship E(he) > E(me) in (3.19Ba) goes unpenalized on account of its unintentionality.[12] Again, the strength of the rule is such that it makes (3.19Bb) almost unacceptable.

In (3.17)–(3.19), I have shown that sentences of the pattern of (3.13b) and (3.14b), which are otherwise questionable, can be used legitimately in the parrot question context and the corrective context. They are used in (3.17)–(3.19) in response to overt questions or statements which satisfy the empathy requirements. There are situations in which sentences of the pattern of (3.13b) and (3.14b) can be used without overt statements such as (3.17A, 18A, 19A). (I am indebted to Vicky Bergvall for this observation.) Imagine that John Smith, a student, wallks into Professor Margaret Doyle's office the day after meeting her at a party:

(3.20)   (John Smith says to Prof. Doyle's secretary)
          Professor Doyle should remember me.
          a.   She met me at the party last night.
          b.   ?I met her at the party last night.

Example (3.20a) is a kind of precorrective statement, giving Professor Doyle the information before she has a chance to react negatively.

Finally, in situations like (3.17)–(3.20), there is always a way to get out of the problems of empathy conflict that sidesteps the problem of hierarchy overrides. (I am indebted to Vicky Bergvall for this observation also.) It is the use of the 'A and B met' pattern instead of the 'A met B' pattern. For example, observe the following:

(3.21)   Speaker A: I met you at the Smiths' before.
          Speaker B: We met where?
(3.22)   Speaker A: Have I met you somewhere before?
          Speaker B: Yes, we met at the party last night.

Let us return to the normal context, in which sentences such as (3.13b) and (3.14b) are marginal or unacceptable. This, as I have already argued, is due to the fact that given ??*John/you met me,* the Surface Structure Empathy Hierarchy dictates that E(John/you) > E(me) in violation of what the Speech Act Empathy Hierarchy dictates, *and* that this conflict has been created "intentionally" by the speaker's choice of *John/you* as subject of the reciprocal verb *meet.* This characteristic of *meet* is shared by other reciprocal verbs. For example, observe the following discourses:

(3.23)   Mary had quite an experience at the party she went to last night.
          a.   She ran into a private detective who was wearing a Sherlock Holmes cap.
          b.   *A private detective who was wearing a Sherlock Holmes cap ran into her.
(3.24)   Guess what happened to Mary on her way to the protest meeting.
          a.   She encountered a large, armed riot policeman.
          b.   *A large, armed riot policeman encountered her.
(3.25)   Did you hear the latest about Mary?
          a.   She married a ninety-year-old millionaire.
          b.   ??A ninety-year-old millionaire married her.

Run into, encounter, and *marry* are reciprocal verbs, and as such allow the speaker to choose the subject from either of the two NPs involved in the action expressed by the verb. Therefore, the violation of the Ban on Conflicting

Empathy Foci in the (b) sentences is by the speaker's design; hence the unacceptability of the sentences.

The above observations do not mean that sentences of the pattern of (b) are always unacceptable. If the context forces the use of an indefinite NP as subject, the Markedness Principle for Discourse-Rule Violations comes in and makes the sentences acceptable. For example, observe the following discourse:

(3.26)   Speaker A: No one wants to marry Mary.
          Speaker B: a.   A ninety-year-old millionaire has just married her.
                        b.   She has just married a ninety-year-old millionaire.

Example (3.26A) is acceptable, in spite of the fact that the underlying subject of *marry* is coreferential with indefinite NP *no one* because the main-clause verb *wants* forces the use of *no one* in subject position, and *Mary* in object position. Example (3.26Ba) is acceptable, in spite of the fact that it places an indefinite NP *a ninety-year-old millionaire* in subject position and discourse-topic NP *her* in object position, because this arrangement has been dictated by speaker A's statement. This statement, which violates the Ban on Conflicting Empathy Foci, has the overtone of being a "corrective" sentence. In (3.26Bb) the empathy relationship deriving from the Topic Empathy Hierarchy (i.e., E(she) ≥ E(a ninety-year-old millionaire)) and the relationship deriving from the Surface Structure Empathy Hierarchy (i.e., E(she) > E(a ninety-year-old millionaire)) are mutually consistent. This sentence is a possible response to speaker A's statement, but it does not have a "corrective" overtone. Speaker B is simply revealing a new piece of information to speaker A.

Similarly, observe the following sentence:

(3.27)   A nineteen-year-old high school dropout married Mary for her money and then tried to kill her.

It seems that there are two reasons for having an indefinite NP as subject and an anaphoric NP (i.e., *Mary,* which can very easily be interpreted as referring to the discourse topic) as object of *married* in this sentence. First, *for money* is a purpose expression which designates the purpose of the surface subject. Therefore, if it is the case that the person who was after money was the nineteen-year-old high school dropout under discussion, and not Mary, then the choice of the former as subject of *married* is automatically dictated. Another way of expressing what has been said above is to say that *marry for money* is no longer a middle verb, and therefore it behaves like verbs such as *harass,* which, as we have seen in (3.1) and (3.7), can readily take a nontopic NP as subject and a topic NP as object.

The second reason for the speaker to use *a nineteen-year-old high school dropout* as the subject of *married* in (3.27) is the fact that it is the subject of the second predicate as well. Since *tried to kill* is clearly not a reciprocal verb, the speaker did not have the option of using *Mary* as the subject of this expression. The pressure on conjoined elements to have parallel structure thus motivates the use of *a nineteen-year-old high school dropout* as the subject of *married* as well as of *tried to kill*.

In order to see how strong this pressure is for maintaining the same subject for conjoined structures, let us observe the following discourses:

(3.28)   Speaker A: What's happening with Mary?
        Speaker B: a. ??A nineteen-year-old high school dropout married her.
                  b.   A nineteen-year-old high school dropout proposed to her.
                  c.   ?A nineteen-year-old high school dropout married her for her money.
                  d.   ?A nineteen-year-old high school dropout married her and tried to kill her.
                  e.   A nineteen-year-old high school dropout married her for her money and tried to kill her.
                  f.   She married a nineteen-year-old high school dropout, and he tried to kill her.

The contrast between speaker B's responses (a) and (b) is as predicted: *married* is a reciprocal verb but *proposed* is not. The contrast between (c), (d), and (e) shows that the presence of *for her money* alone is not enough to justify the choice of nontopic NP *a nineteen-year-old high school dropout* as the subject of *married* over discourse topic *Mary,* and that the parallel structure pressure alone is not enough, either. As shown in (e), which is perfectly acceptable, we need both of the redeeming factors to justify the choice of the indefinite NP as subject. Example (f) is an acceptable answer to speaker A's question, but it has a nuance that is different from that of (e). That is, while (e) describes the high school dropout's having married Mary for her money and his having tried to kill her as a single event, (f) presents these two as two more or less independent events, with no cause-effect implication.[13]

In this section, I have shown that reciprocal verbs, because they give the speaker an alternative of selecting either one of the two NPs involved as subject, do not allow violations of empathy-related principles unless the violations can be justified on some other limited and well-defined grounds. In the next section, we will look into verbs which represent actions from the point of view of those who are acted on rather than from the point of view of agents.

5.4 *Hear From* and *Receive From* as Empathy Verbs

Observe the following sentences:

(4.1)   a.   I told Mary yesterday that John was sick.
       b.   Mary told me yesterday that John was sick.

(4.2)   a.   I heard from Mary yesterday that John was sick.
      b.   ??Mary heard from me yesterday that John was sick.

Let us examine the empathy relationships that each of the above sentences involves:

(4.3)   Empathy relationships of (4.1a)
      a.   Surface Structure Empathy Hierarchy: E(I) > E(Mary)
      b.   Speech Act Empathy Hierarchy: E(I) > E(Mary)
(4.4)   Empathy relationships of (4.1b)
      a.   Surface Structure Empathy Hierarchy: E(Mary) > E(me)
      b.   Speech Act Empathy Hierarchy: E(me) > E(Mary)
(4.5)   Empathy relationships of (4.2a)
      a.   Surface Structure Empathy Hierarchy: E(I) > E(Mary)
      b.   Speech Act Empathy Hierarchy: E(I) > E(Mary)
(4.6)   Empathy relationships of (4.2b)
      a.   Surface Structure Empathy Hierarchy: E(Mary) > E(me)
      b.   Speech Act Empathy Hierarchy: E(me) > E(Mary)

As shown above, the two empathy relationships that each of (4.1a) and (4.2a) contains are mutually consistent, and therefore these sentences do not violate the Ban on Conflicting Empathy Foci. In contrast, the empathy relationships in each of (4.1b) and (4.2b) are logically contradictory, and therefore these sentences violate the ban. In spite of this, (4.1b) is perfectly acceptable, and it is only (4.2b) that is marginal or unacceptable.

The acceptability of (4.1b) can be easily explained. Since *tell* is a verb that places an agent in subject position and a hearer in dative position, the positioning of *Mary* as subject and *me* as dative object is unintentional. The Markedness Principle for Discourse-Rule Violations, which was discussed in section 5.3 (see (3.12)), dictates that there be no penalty for the violation of the Ban on Conflicting Empathy Foci here since the violation is unintentional. The unacceptability of (4.2b), on the other hand, can be accounted for by the same empathy perspective if we can assume that the speaker's choice of *Mary* as subject of (4.2b) was intentional. We observe that *hear from* is an exceptional verb in that it places the agent of the action in an oblique case (i.e., as object of *from*) and places a nonagent perceiver in subject position. In that sense, *hear from* is very much like the passive *be told by,* which places a goal NP in subject position and an agentive NP in an oblique case as object of *by.* We can extend the above observation and claim that, as a general principle, the choice of a given NP as subject is intentional if the verb involved is one which places an agent NP in an oblique case and a nonagent NP in subject position.

On the basis of the above observation, we can say that (4.2b) involves an intentional violation of the Ban on Conflicting Empathy Foci in that the speaker, while he could have used an unmarked verb *tell* and uttered (4.1a), has *intentionally* chosen to use the marked verb *hear from,* and produced a violation of the ban as shown in (4.6). As the Markedness Principle for Discourse-Rule Violations dictates, the penalty for this intentional violation is unacceptability.

The expression *receive from* behaves very much like *hear from.* Observe the following contrast:

(4.7) a. I sent Mary a package containing Japanese noodles.
       b. Mary sent me a package containing Japanese noodles.
(4.8) a. I received from Mary a package containing Japanese noodles.
       b. ??Mary received from me a package containing Japanese noodles.

The explanation for the marginality, out of context, of (4.8b) is exactly the same as for (4.2b). *Receive from* is a marked verb in that it places an agent NP in an oblique case and a nonagent NP in subject position. In describing the semantics of (4.8b), the speaker could have used *send,* as in (4.7a), which would have placed *I* in subject position, and *Mary* in object position, with no violation of the Ban on Conflicting Empathy Foci. Instead, he has chosen the marked verb *received from,* and intentionally placed *Mary* in subject position and *me* in an oblique case, and thus produced a conflict between the Surface Structure Empathy Hierarchy and the Speech Act Empathy Hierarchy. Hence the unacceptability of the sentence.[14]

The above observation does not mean that sentences of the pattern of (4.8b) are always unacceptable. If other factors force the use of this pattern, there is no penalty. For example:

(4.9) Speaker A: Who did Mary receive the package from?
       Speaker B: She received the package from ME.

In the above, speaker B follows the sentence pattern of the question and puts *me* in the place of the *wh*-expression. Just as has been shown with reciprocal verbs, the parallel pattern requirement between the question and the answer justifies the violation of the Ban on Conflicting Empathy Foci, and therefore the sentence goes unpenalized. In fact, there is a further reason why (4.9B) is acceptable. That is, in this sentence, *she* is the discourse topic and *me* a focus. Thus, according to the Topic Empathy Hierarchy, E(she) $\geq$ E(me) holds. This clearly enhances the acceptability of the sentence.

Observe, also, the following sentence:

(4.10) It was two days after Tom received the package from me that he took it to Mary and opened it with her.

If the point in time of the receipt of the package is under discussion, *x received something from me* becomes a perfectly acceptable sentence pattern.[15] In other words, addition of a time adverb makes *x received something from y* logically nonsynonymous with *y sent something to x.* Given modern postal systems, the following two sentences clearly are not synonymous.

(4.11)   a.   John sent Mary a package yesterday.
          b.   Mary received a package from John yesterday.

The embedded clause *Tom received the package from me* of (4.10) involves an understood time adverb (i.e., Two days after THE DAY THAT Tom received . . .), and therefore it is no longer a marked version of the corresponding unmarked sentence with *I sent the package to Tom.* Therefore, the choice of the sentence pattern of (4.10) was not by the speaker's design, but it has been forced by the actual situation that the speaker wanted to describe. Hence the Markedness Principle for Discourse-Rule Violations dictates that the sentence go unpenalized.

We can perhaps further generalize the above observation and state that *x receives something from y* constitutes a marked verb when used to refer to the totality of event "*y* sends something to *x* and *x* receives it," but it is not a marked verb when used to point to only the receiving part of the event. The presence of a time adverb, as in (4.10) and (4.11b), makes clear that only the receiving part of the event is under discussion. The following sentences (for which I am indebted to Shelley Waksler) are acceptable, in spite of the fact that they do not contain time adverbs, because it is clear that the events represented by *received from* do not contain the sending part.

(4.12)   a.   The fact that Tom received a package from me didn't prove that I was the drug dealer.
          b.   Mary found out that Tom received a package from me because she saw my return address on the box.

5.5   Complex Sentences

Let us now see how empathy principles apply to complex sentences. First observe the following:

(5.1)   a.   Jane told John what he had told her two days before.
         b.   Jane told John what she had heard from him two days before.
         c.   John heard from Jane what he had told her two days before.
         d. ??John heard from Jane what she had heard from him two days before.

The above four sentences represent logically identical content. For many speakers, the first three are acceptable but the fourth is marginal or unacceptable. Let us see whether these judgments are in agreement with the predictions the empathy perspective makes about the acceptability status of these sentences. According to the Surface Structure Empathy Hierarchy, the expressions *x told y something* and *x heard something from y* both define the empathy relationships $E(x) > E(y)$. However, there is a difference. In the former case this relationship has derived automatically, since the verb *tell* places an agent in subject position and a hearer in dative object position; in the latter case, the $E(x) > E(y)$ relationship has been obtained intentionally by using the marked verb *hear,* which places an agent in an oblique case and a nonagent in subject position. In the following, I will designate empathy relationships derived from such uses of marked verbs with a prefixed *m.*

(5.2) a. *Jane told John* what *he had told her* two days before.
       $E(Jane) > E(John)$ $E(John) > E(Jane)$

       *$E(Jane) > E(John) > E(Jane)$: unintentional violation

       b. *Jane told John* what *she had heard from him* two days before.
       $E(Jane) > E(John)$ $mE(Jane) > E(John)$

       $E(Jane) > E(John)$: no contradiction

       c. *John heard from Jane* what *he had told her* two days before.
       $mE(John) > E(Jane)$ $E(John) > E(Jane)$

       $E(John) > E(Jane)$: no contradiction

       d. ??*John heard from Jane* what *she had heard from him* two days before.
       $mE(John) > E(Jane)$ $mE(Jane) > E(John)$

       *$E(John) > E(Jane) > E(John)$: intentional violation

The Markedness Principle for Discourse-Rule Violations given in (3.12) enables us to explain why speakers judge (5.1d) as far less acceptable than (5.1a)–(5.1c). Examples (5.2a) and (5.2d) (= (5.1a) and (5.1d)) both involve violations of the Ban on Conflicting Empathy Foci. However, in the former case, the violation has derived from the use of unmarked verb *tell.* Therefore, it is an unintentional violation, and the Markedness Principle for Discourse-Rule Violations marks the sentence acceptable. In contrast, (5.2d) involves an intentional violation of the ban in that it has been created by using the marked verb *hear.* Therefore, the Markedness Principle cannot let the violation go unpenalized and marks the sentence unacceptable.

The following four sentences show the same contrast as in (5.1):

(5.3) a. *Jane sent back to John* the package that *he had sent her.*
       $E(Jane) > E(John)$ $E(John) > E(Jane)$

       *$E(Jane) > E(John) > E(Jane)$: unintentional violation

       b. *Jane sent back to John* the package that *she had received from him.*
       $E(Jane) > E(John)$ $mE(Jane) > E(John)$

       $E(Jane) > E(John)$: no contradiction

       c. *John received from Jane* the package *he had sent her.*
       $mE(John) > E(Jane)$ $E(John) > E(Jane)$

       $E(John) > E(Jane)$: no contradiction

d.   ??*John received from Jane* the package that *she had received from him.*

   $\underbrace{\text{mE(John)} > \text{E(Jane)} \hspace{4cm} \text{mE(Jane)} > \text{E(John)}}$

   $*\text{E(John)} > \text{E(Jane)} > \text{E(John)}$: intentional violation

Here again, only (d) involves a marked (intentional) violation of the Ban on Conflicting Empathy Foci, and this accounts for the great degree of unacceptability of the sentence.

Observe, further, the following sentences:

(5.4)   a.   The woman who met (= encountered) the reporter heard from him that her sister was a suspect in a murder case.

   b.   *The woman who the reporter met (= encountered) heard from him that her sister was a suspect in a murder case.

As discussed in section 5.3, violation of the Ban on Conflicting Empathy Foci involving a use of the reciprocal verb *meet* is deemed to be intentional, and the resulting sentence is therefore marked as unacceptable. The contrast between (5.4a) and (5.4b) is accounted for in the empathy perspective in the following way:

(5.5)   Empathy relationships of (5.4a)
   a.   Main clause: The woman heard from the reporter . . .
                          mE(the woman) > E(the reporter)
   b.   Relative clause: The woman met the reporter.
                          mE(the woman) > E(the reporter)
   c.   Combined: E(the woman) > E(the reporter)

(5.6)   Empathy relationships of (5.4b)
   a.   Main clause: The woman heard from the reporter . . .
                          mE(the woman) > E(the reporter)
   b.   Relative clause: The reporter met the woman.
                          mE(the reporter) > E(the woman)
   c.   Combined: *E(the woman) > E(the reporter) > E(the woman)
                          (intentional violation)

The empathy relationships in (5.4a) are mutually consistent; hence the acceptability of the sentence. In contrast, those that (5.4b) contains are mutually contradictory, as shown in (5.6); hence the unacceptability of the sentence.

Thus far, all the cases of inconsistency between the main-clause and embedded-clause empathy relationships have been either those in which both relationships are unmarked, as in (5.2a) and (5.3a), or those in which both relationships are marked, as in (5.2d), (5.3d), and (5.6). We now examine cases in which one of the two relationships is marked, while the other is unmarked. Observe the following sentences:

(5.7)   a.   Two days after Mary met John at a party, she was invited by him
                        mE(Mary) > E(John)   mE(Mary) > E(John)
              to dinner.

        b.   Two days after Mary met John at a party, he invited her to dinner
                        mE(Mary) > E(John)   E(John) > E(Mary)

(5.8)   a.   Two days after Mary humiliated John at a party,
                        E(Mary) > E(John)
              she met him at a bus stop.
              mE(Mary) > E(John)

        b.   ᵛ/?Two days after Mary humiliated John at a party,
                        E(Mary) > E(John)
              he met her at a bus stop.
              mE(John) > E(Mary)

It seems that all the above four sentences are acceptable, given the assumption
the last sentence requires that John has been the discourse topic. These sentences show that inconsistency in the main-clause and embedded-clause empathy relationships does not result in marginality/unacceptability unless both
relationships are marked. This conclusion is again consistent with the Markedness Principle for Discourse-Rule Violations.

The fact that (5.8b) requires a richer context to be acceptable than does
(5.7b) is also the result of interaction with the Markedness Principle. I hypothesize that a test for consistency in empathy relationships applies from left
to right and that the first empathy relationship established in a given sentence
sets a tone for the rest of the sentence. In (5.7b), it is not possible to assume
that John, rather than Mary, has been the topic of the preceding discourse because the ensuing empathy relationship E(topic = John) ≥ E(Mary) would be
inconsistent with the empathy relationship mE(Mary) > E(John) dictated by
Mary met John. Thus, mE(Mary) > E(John) gets firmly established first in
the sentence. The right-hand empathy relationship E(John) > E(Mary) is inconsistent with this relationship, but it is an unmarked one, and therefore
there arises no penalty for the sentence. In contrast, in (5.8b), it is possible to
assume that John, rather than Mary, has been the topic of the preceding discourse because the inconsistency between the ensuing relationship E(topic =
John) ≥ E(Mary) and the E(Mary) > E(John) defined by *Mary humiliated
John* goes unpenalized due to the fact that the latter relationship is an unmarked one. This makes it possible, in proper context, to firmly establish
E(John) ≥ E(Mary) as the first empathy relationship. The sentence is acceptable because this relationship is not contradicted by the right-hand empathy
relationship mE(John) > E(Mary), defined by *he met her*.

There is one additional fact to be considered with regard to (5.8b). This is
that its complete acceptance requires the assumption that a nonsubject in the
first clause—John—is the topic of the discourse. Ordinarily, subjects are most
likely to be regarded as discourse topics, and thus, ordinarily (especially

out of context) Mary is regarded as the discourse topic, firmly establishing $E(Mary) \geq E(John)$. This relationship is then contradicted by the marked relationship $mE(John) > E(Mary)$ defined by *he met her,* yielding the marginality of the sentence. This explains why some speakers feel that there is something wrong with (5.8b) the first time they see the sentence in isolation, but they conclude, after some deliberation, that the sentence is acceptable in the right context.

The assumption that, out of context, the subject is the most likely discourse topic is not the only factor that tends to fix the subject NP as empathy focus in sentences where the first subject-verb-object clause is an unmarked one, as in (5.8). Observe the following:

(5.9) a. John drove Mary, who he met at the party, to her apartment.
       b. ??John drove Mary, who met him at the party, to her apartment.

Many speakers consider (5.9b) marginal, and considerably worse than (5.8b). It seems that the marginality comes from its being difficult to consider a participant NP that is modified by a nonrestrictive relative clause as a previously established discourse topic. Not only is it more likely (though not necessary) that *John* is the discourse topic as a result of its being the sentence subject; it is highly unlikely that *Mary* is the topic, since it is modified by a nonrestrictive relative clause. Such clauses, by definition, are not required, and speakers therefore intentionally choose to use them. Their function is to give additional information about the NP they modify, information that would normally not be necessary for a previously established topic, which would already have been characterized in the preceding discourse. For example, consider the following contrast:

(5.10) a. Mary, who was at the party, saw John.
        b. Mary saw John, who was at the party.

If we have mentioned the party (which is likely from the use of *the*), then it is to be expected that our discourse topic (assuming it not to be the party) will have been located there in the preceding context. Therefore, the NP that is modified by *who was at the party* is not likely to be the topic, and in fact, many speakers take Mary to be the topic in (b), but not in (a), in spite of the fact that *Mary* is the subject of both sentences.

I have hypothesized that a test for consistency in empathy relationships applies from left to right, and that the first empathy relationship established in a given sentence sets a tone for the rest of the sentence. The following sentence gives further support to this hypothesis:

(5.11) John, who Mary had met at the party, drove her to her apartment.

This sentence, unlike (5.9b), is perfectly acceptable. I hypothesize that, since *drove her (= Mary)* does not occur until after the nonrestrictive relative, the main-clause empathy relationship between *John* and *Mary* cannot be established before the embedded-clause empathy relationship. Thus, the embedded-clause empathy relationship mE(Mary) > E(John) dictated by *Mary had met who (= John)* sets a tone for the rest of the sentence. The sentence is acceptable because this relationship is not contradicted by the empathy relationship of the main clause *John drove her to her apartment,* which, considering the fact that *John* is not the discourse topic, is most likely to be E(Mary) > E(John).

Parallelism must also be considered in predicting speakers' judgments. Observe the following contrast:

(5.12) a.   John repeated to Mary the same story that he had told her a few days before.
        b.   ✓/?John repeated to Mary the same story that she had been told by him a few days before.
(5.13) a.   John told Mary the same story that he had told her a few days before.
        b.   ??John told Mary the same story that she had been told by him a few days before.

For many speakers, (5.13b) is considerably worse than (5.12b). The awkwardness of (5.12b) derives from the fact that it is not easy to assume that Mary, rather than John, has been the discourse topic. The fact that (5.13b) is much less acceptable than (5.12b) suggests that we look for other factors involved in the sentence. I hypothesize that the badness of (5.13b) is partly due to the fact that the same verb with the same agent and the same goal appears in two different voices, active and passive, in the same sentence. That is, it is attributable to the fact that the sentence lacks parallelism. Observe that (5.12b) uses different verbs and that *repeated to* cannot be passivized to make Mary its subject. We can perhaps invoke the Markedness Principle for Discourse-Rule Violations here: the lack of parallelism in (5.12b) is unintentional, and therefore the sentence goes unpenalized, but it is intentional in (5.13b), and hence the marginality of the sentence.

5.6 *Come Up To* and *Go Up To* as Empathy Expressions

Observe the following sentences:

(6.1)   a.   He shouldn't have come up to me and told me that he was tired of studying with me.
        b.   You shouldn't have come up to me and told me that you were tired of studying with me.
(6.2)   a.   *I shouldn't have come up to him and told him that I was tired of studying with him.
        b.   *I shouldn't have come up to you and told you that I was tired of studying with you.[16]

(6.3) a. *He shouldn't have gone up to me and told me that he was tired of studying with me.

  b. *You shouldn't have gone up to me and told me that you were tired of studying with me.

(6.4) a. I shouldn't have gone up to him and told him that I was tired of studying with him.

  b. I shouldn't have gone up to you and told you that I was tired of studying with you.

X comes up to Y is one of the few expressions in English that are exceptions to the Surface Structure Empathy Hierarchy (i.e., E(subject) > E(other NPs)), and it requires that the speaker describe the action from the camera angle of Y rather than X. In contrast, *X goes up to Y* requires that the speaker describe the action from the camera angle of X rather than Y. Example (6.1a) is acceptable because the empathy relationship E(goal = me) > E(subject = he) dictated by *come up to* agrees with the empathy relationship dictated by the Speech Act Empathy Hierarchy given in (3.16). On the other hand, (6.2a) is unacceptable because the empathy relationship E(goal = him) > E(subject = I) that is dictated by *come up to* contradicts the empathy relationship E(I) > E(him) that is dictated by the Speech Act Empathy Hierarchy. All the other sentences in (6.1) through (6.4) can be accounted for in a similar manner in the empathy perspective under discussion.

The above constraints on the use of *come up to* and *go up to* partly interact with the constraints on the use of *come* and *go*.[17] That is, (i) *X goes to Y* if the speaker is closer to X than to Y such that X moves away from the speaker, or if he describes X's movement to Y from a distance objectively; and (ii) *X comes to Y* if the speaker is closer to Y than to X such that X moves toward the speaker (as well as toward Y), or if Y is the hearer. Thus, observe the following sentences:

(6.5) John's student $\begin{Bmatrix} \text{a. came up to} \\ \text{b. went up to} \end{Bmatrix}$ him and complained about the lecture.

(6.6) John $\begin{Bmatrix} \text{a. *came up to} \\ \text{b. \ went up to} \end{Bmatrix}$ his teacher and complained about the lecture.

Since E(John) > E(John's student) holds, the situation described in (6.5) should call for *come up to,* which requires empathy on the object, and not *go up to,* which requires empathy on the subject. In spite of this, (6.5b) is perfectly acceptable. Between (6.5a) and (6.5b), the former is the unmarked form, and it does not require any special context to justify its use. In contrast, in order to use (6.5b), the speaker either must position himself closer to John's student than to John or must take a very detached view of the whole event. For example, if the speaker positions himself at the opposite end of the classroom from the teacher (i.e., John), and observes his student walking up to him, then he must describe this situation using *go* as in (6.5b) because the student's movement toward John was a movement away from the speaker. In other words, the deictic constraint on the use of *come* and *go* supersedes the empathy constraint of *come up to* and *go up to*.

Now let us examine (6.6a) and (6.6b). Most speakers consider (6.6a) considerably worse than (6.5b). If the speaker observed the class by positioning himself closer to the teacher at the podium, and noticed John *coming* to the podium to complain to his teacher, the deictic constraint on the use of *come* and *go* should supersede the empathy requirement of *come up to* and *go up to* and should make (6.6a) acceptable. The fact that most speakers consider this sentence unacceptable seems to be owing to the fact that it is unlikely for a class observer who has positioned himself close to the teacher to know one of the students well but not to know the teacher's name. In case the observer in the same physical setup does not know the student's name, the sentence becomes acceptable:

(6.7)   (uttered by a class observer who was at the podium side of the classroom)
         After class, a student came up to his teacher and complained about the lecture.

The deictic requirement of *come* has superseded the empathy requirement of *come up to* in the above sentence. The situation described above, contrary to that of (6.6a), is not an unlikely one, because the observer does not know the Similarly, observe the following examples:

(6.8)   A student $\left\{ \begin{array}{l} \text{a. came up to} \\ \text{b. went up to} \end{array} \right\}$ John and complained about the lectures.

(6.9)   John $\left\{ \begin{array}{l} \text{a. *came up to} \\ \text{b. \ went up to} \end{array} \right\}$ a psychology professor and complained about the lecture

Since E(John) $\geq$ E(a student) holds, the situation described in (6.8) should call for *come up to*, which requires empathy on the goal, and not *go up to*, which requires empathy on the subject. In spite of this, (6.8b) is acceptable. In this instance, also, the version with *come up to* is the unmarked form, and it does not require any special context to justify its use. In contrast, in order to use (6.8b), the speaker must either position himself, for example, at the back of a classroom, in such a way that the student's movement toward John is a movement away from him (= the speaker), or distance himself far away from both John and the student so that the use of the objective *went* can be justified. In (6.9), on the other hand, since E(John) $\geq$ E(a psychology professor) holds, the acceptability of (6.9b) and the unacceptability of (6.9a) is as predicted by the requirement of *come up to* and *go up to*. The fact that (6.9a) is not regarded as acceptable must be due to the fact that it would be strange for the speaker to position himself close to a psychology professor unknown to him, observe John coming toward the professor as well as toward himself, and describe the situation as he saw it. If the speaker had observed the event from the psychology professor's camera angle, it must have been that he knew his name.

Finally, let us examine the use of *come up to* and *go up to* when the first- and second-person NPs are involved. Observe, first, the following sentences:

(6.10)   (a student speaking to the teacher right after class at the podium)

If I get lost during class, can I $\begin{Bmatrix} \text{a. come up to} \\ \text{b.*go up to} \end{Bmatrix}$ you after the lecture and ask questions?

The unacceptability of (6.10b) is undoubtedly owing to the fact that when the goal of the speaker's movement is the hearer at the place of utterance, it is not possible to use *go*. Example (6.10), as well as the preceding ones, might appear to show that there is no basic difference between *come up to, go up to and go to, come to*. However, the following examples show that there is:

(6.11)   (a student speaking to the teacher in his office)

If I get lost during class, can I $\begin{Bmatrix} \text{a. come up to} \\ \text{b. go up to} \end{Bmatrix}$ you after the lecture and ask questions?

(6.12)   (a student speaking to the teacher in his office)

If I get lost during class, can I $\begin{Bmatrix} \text{a. come to} \\ \text{b. ??go to} \end{Bmatrix}$ you after the lecture and ask questions?

In the above example, the place of utterance (the teacher's office) and the location of the target of the speaker's movement (the teacher at the podium) are not identical. As shown in (6.12b), *go to* cannot be used in this context because the movement involved is not a movement away from the place of utterance.[18] The fact that (6.11b) is acceptable shows that *go up to* is an expression which is partly controlled by the physical locations of the speaker, the hearer, and the third parties involved but which has an independent status from *go to* in that its use is partly controlled by the empathy perspective of the speaker vis-à-vis the hearer and the third parties.

5.7 *Envy*

The verb *envy* can occur in surface structures followed by two NPs as in the following:

(7.1)   I envy John his good looks.

The second NP after *envy* can be a simple NP, as in (7.1), or any type of complex NP, either a relative clause construction or a *rumor*-type clause:

(7.2) a. I envy John the girls who flock around him all the time.
       b. I envy John the way his mother treats him.
       c. I envy John the fact that he is able to go to Europe every year.

Joseph (1976) has examined the *envy* NP_1 NP_2 pattern in which there is an overt NP in NP_2 that is coreferential with NP_1. Joseph first notes that it appears that there is little or no syntactic restriction on where in NP_2 this coreferent NP may occur, both as to position and as to grammatical relation: for example, observe the following sentences, which are patterned after Joseph's:

(7.3) a. I envy John the way *he* can talk with Sue like that.
       b. I envy John the fact that *he* always catches the most fish.
(7.4) a. I envy John the way Sue smiles at *him*.
       b. I envy John the gift which Sally gave (to) *him* for his birthday.
(7.5) I envy John the fact that there are lots of people who are willing to volunteer to take care of *him*.

In (7.3), the coreferential NP appears as the subject of the relative clause in NP_2. In (7.4), it appears as a constituent of the predicate in the relative clause. In (7.5), it appears in a relative clause that is embedded in the *fact*-clause.

In spite of the above apparent freedom of this coreferential NP to appear in any position or grammatical relation, there are sentence pairs that differ only in the position and grammatical relation of this coreferential NP but in which this difference affects the acceptability of the sentences. For example, observe the following sentences, which are again due to Joseph. The acceptability judgment assigned to each sentence is his:

(7.6) a. I envy John the girl *he* married.
       b. ?*I envy John the girl who married *him*.
(7.7) a. I envy John the fact that Betty could come up to *him* like that.
       b. ?*I envy John the fact that *he* could come up to Betty like that.
(7.8) a. I envy John the fact that *he* could go up to Betty like that.
       b. ?*I envy John the fact that Betty could go up to *him* like that.
(7.9) a. I envy John the fact that *he* discovered helium.
       b. ?*I envy John the fact that helium was discovered by *him*.

There are speakers for whom sentences of the pattern of *envy* NP_1 NP_2 are less than perfect, but even for these speakers, the (a) sentences above are considerably better than the corresponding (b) sentences.

Joseph has proposed the following constraint on the use of *envy*:

(7.10) *Constraint on Envy* NP_1 NP_2: In the structure *envy* NP_1 NP_2, the NP in NP_2 that is coreferent to NP_1 must be in a position to receive the speaker's empathy.[19]

The relative clause of (7.6a) involves *marry*, which, as we have seen in section 5.3, requires that E(subject) > E(object) hold. Thus, we obtain E(he =

John) $>$ E(the girl), which fulfills Joseph's constraint on the use of *envy*. Hence the acceptability of the sentence. On the other hand, the underlying structure of the relative clause of (7.6b), due to the same constraint on the use of *marry*, dictates that E(the girl) $>$ E(John) hold. This violates the constraint on the use of *envy* and hence results the unacceptability of the sentence. Similarly, *come up to* of (7.7a) dictates the E(John) $>$ E(Betty) hold. This satisfies the constraint on *envy*, and therefore the sentence is acceptable. In contrast, *come up to* of (7.7b) dictates that E(Betty) $>$ E(John) be the case. This violates the constraint under discussion, and hence comes the unacceptability of the sentence. The expression *go up to* of (7.8), on the other hand, requires that the speaker's empathy be with the subject. Thus, (7.8a) satisfies Joseph's constraint; hence the acceptability of the sentence. On the other hand, (7.8b) dictates that E(Betty) $>$ E(John) hold, violating the constraint on *envy*. The sentence is unacceptable for this reason. Example (7.9b) is unacceptable because *John* has been downgraded in the Surface Structure Empathy Hierarchy by passivization, and he cannot receive the speaker's empathy.

The above explanation of the acceptability of the (a) sentences and the unacceptability of the (b) sentences in (7.6) through (7.9) is consistent with the acceptability of the sentences of (7.3) through (7.5). In (7.4a), for example, the constraint on the use of *envy* dictates that E(John) $>$ E(Sue) hold. On the other hand, since *him* ($=$ John) is the object and *Sue* the subject of the verb *smiles at*, the Surface Structure Empathy Hierarchy dictates that E(Sue) $>$ E(John) hold. Therefore, there is an apparent logical conflict between these two empathy relationships. However, the sentence is deemed acceptable because the latter relationship has arisen nonintentionally, due to the fact that *smile at* takes an agent as subject and a goal as object. In other words, the violation of the Ban on Conflicting Empathy Foci that (7.4a) contains is nonintentional, and therefore the Markedness Principle for Discourse-Rule Violations dictates that there be no penalty for the violation. The acceptability of (7.4b) and (7.5) can be accounted for in the same fashion.

It is important to note that *envy* NP_1 NP_2 does not require that NP_1 be in the highest position in the empathy relationships that are expressed in the sentence. For example, all the acceptable sentences that have been discussed in this section have the first-person pronoun as subject. The Speech Act Empathy Hierarchy dictates that E(I) $>$ E(John) be the case. Thus, the empathy relationship that (7.6a), for example, contains is E(I) $>$ E(John) $>$ E(the girl). The sentence is acceptable because there is no intentional downgrading of *John* in empathy hierarchies. Similarly, observe the following sentence:

(7.11)   I envy John the fact that he is far brighter than I am.

In this sentence, also, there is no intentional downgrading of *John* in NP_2. Hence, the sentence is acceptable in spite of the fact that E(I) $>$ E(John) holds in NP_2. Likewise, compare the following three sentences:

(7.12) a. I envy John the fact that he always outdoes me at chess.
        b. I envy John the fact that even I can't beat him at chess.
        b. *I envy John the fact that I am always outdone by him at chess.

Even those speakers who consider (7.12a, b) as less than perfect agree that they are considerably better than (7.12c). The difference must be attributable to the fact that although the *fact*-clauses of these sentences have E(I) > E(John), only (7.12c) involves an intentional downgrading of *John* by passivization.

5.8 Syntactic Prominence

In section 5.2, I accounted for the marginality or unacceptability of (8.1b) as arising from a conflict between the Descriptor Empathy Hierarchy and the Surface Structure Empathy Hierarchy:

(8.1) a. Then John hit his brother.
      b. ??Then John's brother was hit by him.

The term *John's brother* shows that the speaker is describing the event from John's camera angle rather than John's brother's (i.e., E(John) > E(John's brother)). On the other hand, the use of the passive construction shows that the speaker is describing the event from the point of view of the new subject rather than the old subject (i.e., E(John's brother) > E(John)). These two camera angles are irreconcilably contradictory, and hence comes the unacceptability of (8.1b).

The Surface Structure Empathy Hierarchy interacts not only with the Descriptor Empathy Hierarchy, but also with other empathy hierarchies that are relevant. For example,

(8.2) a. Then John hit a boy on the head.
      b. ??Then a boy was hit on the head by John.

There is nothing wrong with (8.2a), but one would need a rich context to justify (8.2b). The marginality or unacceptability of (8.2b) can be attributed to a conflict between the Surface Structure Empathy Hierarchy, which dictates that E(a boy) > E(John) hold, and the Topic Empathy Hierarchy, which dictates that E(John) ≥ E(a boy) be the case. Since this conflict has been produced intentionally by applying passivization, the Markedness Principle for Discourse-Rule Violations dictates that the sentence be marked as unacceptable.

Similarly, observe the following sentences:

(8.3) a. Then I hit John on the head.
      b. *Then John was hit on the head by me.

The unacceptability of (8.3b) derives from the fact that while the Surface Structure Empathy Hierarchy dictates that E(John) > E(me) hold, the Speech

Act Empathy Hierarchy dictates that E(me) > E(John) be the case. Again, the two empathy relationships are logically contradictory, and hence arises the unacceptability of the sentence.

As has been shown with other examples, the above observations do not mean that sentences of the pattern of (8.2b) and (8.3b) are always unacceptable. Given rich contexts which would justify the use of the passive construction, their acceptability status increases accordingly. For example, observe the following discourse:

(8.4) Speaker A: Then Mary was hit on the head by John.
        Speaker B: No, no. I know that a BOY was hit on the head by John, so it couldn't have been Mary.

Speaker B corrects speaker A's statement by using the same sentence pattern. This redeems the violation of the Ban on Conflicting Empathy Foci in (8.4B) and makes the sentence acceptable. Similarly, observe the following sentences:

(8.5) a. (?)A boy sneaked into the room and was immediately hit on the head by John.
      b. ??A boy sneaked into the room and was immediately hit on the head by me.

The pressure for using a parallel structure with the same subject has lifted the acceptability status of (8.5a) and made it far more acceptable than (8.2b). The fact that (8.5b) is still marginal can be attributed to the fact that, while (8.5a) violates only the Topic Empathy Hierarchy on account of the parallel structure pressure, (8.5b) violates both the Topic Empathy Hierarchy and the Speech Act Empathy Hierarchy. Note that since the speaker is talking about an event in which he is involved, *me* both refers to the speaker and is coreferential with the discourse topic.

In (8.5a), I showed that the pressure for using a parallel structure with the same subject has redeemed the violation of the Ban on Conflicting Empathy Foci. The following discourse shows the operation of the pressure for parallel structures between sentences:

(8.6) Several children were injured in the melee that ensued. A girl had her finger bitten off by Mary. *A boy was hit on the head by John.*

The fact that *several children* is the subject of the first sentence supplies pressure for the use of *a girl* and *a boy* as subjects of the succeeding sentences.

Next observe the following sentences:

(8.7) a. John and his sister went to Paris.
      b. *John's sister and he went to Paris.
      c. *His sister and John went to Paris.
      d. *His sister and he went to Paris.

According to the Descriptor Empathy Hierarchy, given a descriptor x and another descriptor $f(x)$ that is dependent upon x, $E(x) > E(f(x))$ holds. The fact that (8.7b, c, d) are marginal or unacceptable suggests that when x and $f(x)$ appear in a coordinate structure, they must be arranged in that order. This constraint can be stated in the following manner:

(8.8)   *Word Order Empathy Hierarchy:* It is easier for the speaker to empathize with the referent of a left-hand NP in a coordinate structure than with that of a right-hand NP.

   E(Left-hand NP) > E(Right-hand NP)

Considering the fact that the left-hand position in a coordinate structure is more prominent than the right-hand position, and considering the fact that, given the subject and nonsubject NPs, the first is the most prominent position, the Surface Structure Empathy Hierarchy and the Word Order Empathy Hierarchy can be considered to be two different manifestations of the same principle:

(8.9)   *Syntactic Prominence Principle:* Give syntactic prominence to a person/object that you are empathizing with.

The Surface Structure Empathy Hierarchy deals with the manifestation of syntactic prominence in terms of structural configuration, and the Word Order Empathy Hierarchy deals with the manifestation of syntactic prominence in terms of linear order.

Let us examine some more examples relevant to the Word Order Empathy Hierarchy:

(8.10)   a.   I saw John and a student walking together yesterday.
         b.   ??I saw a student and John walking together yesterday.
(8.11)   a.   I saw you and a blonde girl walking together yesterday.
         b.   ??I saw a blonde girl and you walking together yesterday.
(8.12)   a.   I thought you and John were good friends.
         b.   I thought John and you were good friends.
(8.13)   a.   I thought you and my brother were good friends.
         b.   I thought my brother and you were good friends.

The marginality or unacceptability of (8.10b) and (8.11b) arises from a conflict between the Word Order Empathy Hierarchy and the Topic Empathy Hierarchy. Examples (8.12b) and (8.13b) are acceptable because the Speech Act Empathy Hierarchy does not predetermine the hierarchical relationship between the hearer and a third party. For example, (8.12b) is acceptable if *John* has been the discourse topic or if the speaker considers himself closer to John than to the hearer.

The Word Order Empathy Hierarchy interacts in an interesting way with a "modesty" principle derived from normative grammar. For example, observe the following sentences:

(8.14)   a.   ??I and John are good friends.
       b.   John and I are good friends.

According to the Speech Act Empathy Hierarchy, $E(I) > E(John)$ holds. Therefore, (8.14a) rather than (8.14b) is the expected form. However, as shown in (8.14), the actual acceptability judgments are reversed. This seems to be due to a principle that says that the speaker should be modest and give himself the lowest priority.

(8.15)   *The Modesty Principle:* In the coordinate NP structure, give the least prominence to yourself.[20]

The Modesty Principle is an artificial one that is taught repeatedly at the grade school level. There are adult speakers, as well as child speakers, who have not acquired this principle. What is interesting is that these speakers seem not to have acquired some of the rules of case marking, either, and say:

(8.16)   Me and John are good friends.

Observe, further, the following examples:

(8.17)   a.   Me and John went to Boston last night.
       b.   John and me went to Boston last night.

The fact that (8.14a) is heard much less often than (8.17b) shows that the case selection rule is more difficult than the Modesty Principle to master, and that those speakers who have acquired the former have also acquired the latter, but not vice versa.

There is another apparent counterexample to the Word Order Empathy Hierarchy. Observe the following sentence:

(8.18)   Standing in line there were Bill, John's sister, and John, in that order.

There is nothing wrong with this sentence in spite of the fact that *John's sister, and John* establishes the empathy hierarchy $E(\text{right-hand NP}) > E(\text{left-hand NP})$ in contradiction with the Word Order Empathy Hierarchy. This apparent contradiction, too, can be explained by the Markedness Principle. Examples (8.7b)–(8.7e) are unacceptable because they involve marked violations of the Word Order Empathy Hierarchy—the speaker has had an option of placing either *John/he* or *John's/his sister* in the left-hand position and has intentionally chosen the latter. Hence arises the unacceptability of these sentences. On the other hand, in (8.18), the placement of *John's sister* to the left of *John* has been forced by a physical situation that the sentence is meant to describe. Since the sentence involves only an unmarked (or unintentional) violation of the Word Order Empathy Hierarchy, the Markedness Principle dictates that there be no penalty for the violation. Hence the acceptability of (8.18).[21]

5.9 Empathy Adjectives

Observe the following sentence:

(9.1)   John talked to Bill about his wife.

The sentence has a three-way ambiguity with respect to the referent of *his:* (i) someone other than John and Bill who has been talked about in the preceding discourse; (ii) John; and (iii) Bill. Between the latter two interpretations, there does not seem to be any preference. Only context can tell which interpretation is intended.

In contrast, the following sentence is not as ambiguous:

(9.2)   John talked to Bill about his beloved wife.

As Kaburaki (1973) observed about the corresponding sentence in Japanese, the primary interpretation that one gets for the sentence is that of 'about John's wife.' It might be possible for some speakers to obtain the interpretation 'about Bill's wife,' but this interpretation is only secondary and is rather weak. Similarly, observe the following sentence:

(9.3)   John talked to Bill about his dear old friend.

Again, the primary interpretation of the sentence is 'about John's dear old friend.'

The above phenomenon can be accounted for by assuming that *beloved* and *dear old* are expressions that can be used only when the speaker places himself close to the experiencer of these feelings. As the Surface Structure Empathy Hierarchy states, it is easier for the speaker to empathize with the referent of the subject than with the referent of the object. Hence, the experiencer of *beloved* and *dear old* is identified as the referent of the subject of these sentences.

It is clear why *beloved* and *dear old* behave the way they do. As adjectives that describe internal feelings that do not usually have an external manifestation, they are best suited for describing the speaker's own feeling, as in *my beloved wife* and *my dear old friend.* If the speaker is expressing, not his own internal feeling, but someone else's, then that person must be close enough to the speaker for him to be able to tell what is going on in his mind. These expressions come out sounding like sarcasm or quotations when a nonanaphoric noun phrase is used as experiencer.

(9.4)   a.   ??Someone talked to Mary about his beloved wife.
         b.   ??A visitor talked to Mary about his beloved wife for two hours.
         c.   ??A stranger talked to Mary about his dear old friend.

Returning to (9.2) and (9.3), the fact that the primary interpretation of *his* is *John's* and not *Bill's* naturally derives from the fact that the subject and object NPs are of the same kind (*John* vs. *Bill*). These two NPs contain no overt indication of where the speaker has placed himself vis-à-vis John and Bill. In such a situation, the Surface Structure Empathy Hierarchy is the only factor that gives a clue about the speaker's camera angle, and hence, *John* is understood to be the experiencer of *beloved* and *dear old*. In contrast, observe the following sentences:

(9.5)   a.   John talked to me about my beloved wife.
        b.   John has written to me about my dear old friend Mary.

These sentences are acceptable because E(me) > E(John) makes clear that the speaker himself is the focus of his empathy. Similarly, observe the following sentences:

(9.6)   a.   ?John started talking to Mary about her dear old friend Jane.
        b.   ∨/(?)Someone started talking to Mary about her dear old friend Jane.

Many speakers consider (b) to be slightly better than (a). This must be due to the fact that *someone* in (b), although it is the subject of the sentence, cannot be considered to be a strong candidate as the experiencer of the feeling 'dear old,' and hence *Mary* has a better chance in this sentence for being interpreted as the experiencer than in (a).

The expression *embarrassing* displays behavior similar to that of *beloved* and *dear old*. First, observe the following sentences: ·

(9.7)   a.   John told Mary something embarrassing.
        b.   John had to tell Mary something embarrassing.

At issue here is the person to whom that something was embarrassing. There are four possible interpretations: (i) embarrassing to John; (ii) embarrassing to Mary; (iii) embarrassing to John and Mary; and (iv) embarrassing to the speaker. For many speakers, the first and strongest interpretation of (9.7) is that of (iii) or (iv) because if the deliverer of the news is embarrassed, the hearer gets also embarrassed, and vice versa, and a third party who is present, who is the speaker of the sentence, also gets embarrassed. In other words, embarrassment, for most people, is a reciprocal event. I will exclude the interpretations (iii) and (iv) from consideration because they are not relevant to the problem under discussion, that is, whether the subject or object controls the expression *embarrassing*. For many speakers, interpretation (i) is stronger than interpretation (ii) both in (9.7a) and (9.7b). This intuition can be confirmed by the fact that *to her* can be added after *embarrassing*, but not *to him:*

(9.8)   a.   John told Mary something embarrassing to her.
        b.   John had to tell Mary something embarrassing to her.
(9.9)   a.   (?)/?John told Mary something embarrassing to him.
        b.   (?)/?John had to tell Mary something embarrassing to him.

The fact that *to him* cannot be added after *embarrassing* must be related to the fact that (9.7a) and (9.7b) already mean 'embarrassing to John,' and therefore there is no need for specifying the experiencer as John overtly. On the other hand, the fact that *to her* can be added after *embarrassing*, as shown in (9.8), or rather, the fact that for some speakers *to her* must be added if the intended meaning is 'embarrassing to Mary,' shows that (9.7a) and (9.7b) ordinarily do not have the 'embarrassing to Mary' interpretation. That the subject tends to be interpreted more readily as representing the experiencer of *embarrassing* is also attributable to the working of the Surface Structure Empathy Hierarchy.

The choice of experiencer for emotive adjectives interacts with the Descriptor Empathy Hierarchy also. For example, observe the following sentences:

(9.10)   a.   John told Mary something embarrassing.
         b.   John told his sister something embarrassing.
         c.   Her brother told Mary something embarrassing.

As already stated, the primary interpretation of (a) is that of 'embarrassing to John.' However, it is possible to obtain a secondary 'embarrassing to Mary' interpretation. In contrast, it is much more difficult to obtain an 'embarrassing to his sister' interpretation for (b). Furthermore, in (c), the primary interpretation is that of 'embarrassing to Mary' rather than of 'embarrassing to her brother.' This fact can be explained by assuming that the focus of the speaker's empathy is chosen as the experiencer of *embarrassing*. In (a), only the Surface Structure Empathy Hierarchy is relevant. Thus, *John* is ordinarily considered to be the focus of the speaker's empathy, but it is also possible to consider *Mary* as the empathy focus. On the other hand, in (b), both the Surface Structure Empathy Hierarchy and the Descriptor Empathy Hierarchy point to *John* as the focus of the speaker's empathy. Therefore, it is next to impossible to obtain an 'embarrassing to his sister' interpretation. In contrast, in (c), the Descriptor Empathy Hierarchy shows that *Mary* is the focus of the speaker's empathy. Therefore, the 'embarrassing to Mary' interpretation becomes the primary interpretation of the sentence.

Similarly, observe the following sentence:

(9.11)   No one told Mary anything embarrassing.

The sentence unambiguously means 'embarrassing to Mary.' This must be due to the fact that the Topic Empathy Hierarchy favors *Mary* over *no one* as the focus of the speaker's empathy.

In the above, I have shown that the nature of the subject and the nature of the object interact with each other to determine the preference for the experiencer choice of *embarrassing*. Whether the subject controls the expression *embarrassing* or the object does is also highly influenced by the semantics of verbs. For example, compare the following sentences:

(9.12)   a.   John told Mary something embarrassing. (= 9.7a)
         b.   John asked Mary something embarrassing.

It is much easier to get the 'embarrassing to Mary' interpretation for (b) than for (a). The above contrast reminds us of the contrast we observed in the previous two chapters with reflexives:

(9.13)   a. $^\vee$/?John talked to Mary about herself.
         b.   John asked Mary about herself.
(9.14)   a. $^\vee$/?John told Mary about the picture of herself in the post office.
         b.   John asked Mary about the picture of herself in the post office.

For many speakers, the (b) sentences are better than the corresponding (a) sentences. As I mentioned in Chapters 3 and 4, this seems to be attributable to the fact that *ask* involves the object in the action represented by the sentence much more than *talk to* and *tell* do. If this comparison between *embarrassing* and the reflexive is relevant, we can say that reflexives in English, even in simple sentences, are empathy-loaded expressions which show that the speaker has identified himself with their referents to a certain degree.

5.10 **Reflexives as Empathy Expressions**

In the preceding chapters, I presented, among others, the following conditions on the use of reflexive pronouns in English:

(10.1)   a.   *Surface Structure Hierarchy:* Surface subject is the strongest trigger for reflexivization. Surface object is the second strongest trigger. Other NPs are weaker triggers than either of the above two. (cf. sec. 4.3)

Subject > Object > Others

         b.   *Anaphoricity Hierarchy:* Reflexives are better when their antecedents are higher in the Anaphoricity Hierarchy than any other NPs in the same sentence. (cf. sec. 4.2)

First-person pronoun > Other definite NPs > Indefinite NPs >
Indefinite pronouns (*someone, anyone*, etc.)

         c.   *Awareness Condition:* Use of a picture noun reflexive is obligatory if the referent of the reflexive perceived/perceives/will perceive the referent of the picture noun as one that involves him. Use of a picture noun nonreflexive pronoun is obligatory otherwise. This constraint is the strongest if the awareness is concurrent with the action or state represented by the sentence, and weaker if the awareness is prior to the reference time. (cf. sec. 4.3)

Concurrent awareness > Prior awareness > Nonawareness

         d.   *Semantic Case Hierarchy of Picture Noun Reflexives:* An agent NP is the strongest trigger for picture noun reflexives. An experiencer NP and a benefactive NP are the second strongest triggers. A goal NP is a weak, but possible trigger. Other NPs cannot trigger picture noun reflexivization (cf. sec. 4.3).

Agent > Experiencer/Benefactive > Goal > Other cases

e. *Humanness Hierarchy:* The higher the triggering NP is in the Humanness Hierarchy, the better the result of reflexivization (cf. sec. 4.3).

Human > Nonhuman animate > Inanimate

Now we can reexamine these conditions in the framework of the empathy perspective. The Surface Structure Hierarchy has already been revised and renamed as the Surface Structure Empathy Hierarchy. I will show later on in this section how the three-way formulation of (10.1a) and the two-way formulation E(subject) > E(other NPs) hypothesized in section 3 of this chapter can be reconciled. The Anaphoricity Hierarchy can be obtained by combining, with additional refinements, the Speech Act Empathy Hierarchy and the Topic Empathy Hierarchy. The Awareness Condition on Picture Noun Reflexives is very much like the constraint on the use of *beloved, dear old,* and *embarrassing* that was discussed in the previous section. In particular, observe the following sentences:

(10.2) a. John talked to Mary about his beloved wife.
        b. John talked to Mary about a picture of himself.

Example (10.2a) can be used only when John regards his wife to be *beloved* to him. In the same way, (10.2b) can be used only when John recognizes that the picture is one of himself. In other words, picture noun reflexives are expressions which require the speaker to enter into their referents' internal feeling.

The fact that the above three nonsyntactic constraints—namely, the Speech Act Empathy Hierarchy, the Topic Empathy Hierarchy, and the Awareness Condition—control the use of reflexives in English firmly establishes that reflexives in English are empathy expressions. The Semantic Case Hierarchy of Picture Noun Reflexives is also relatable to empathy factors as well—specifically, it seems to be the case that, other things being equal, the more agentive or experiencer-like a role an NP plays vis-à-vis the action/state represented in the sentence, the easier it is for the speaker to empathize with its referent. The Humanness Hierarchy clearly derives from empathy considerations—that is, it is easier to empathize with a human than with an animal or inanimate thing.[22]

In the above, I have likened English reflexives to expressions such as *beloved, dear old,* and *embarrassing.* I hasten to add that English reflexives are nevertheless less empathy-loaded expressions than these adjectives. For example, observe the following sentences:

(10.3) a. (?)?Mary was talking to someone about himself.
　　　　b.　　　Someone was talking to Mary about himself.
(10.4) a.　　　*Mary was talking to someone about his beloved wife.
　　　　b.　　　??Someone was talking to Mary about his beloved wife.

As mentioned in section 4.2, (10.3a) is marginal because surface object is a weaker controller for reflexivization than surface subject and an indefinite pronoun is the weakest controller for reflexivization. In contrast, (10.3b), in which the antecedent of the reflexive is also an indefinite pronoun, is perfectly acceptable in the situation when the speaker overheard someone talking to Mary. This fact shows a marked contrast with the fact that (10.4b) is not acceptable even in the same kind of situation. The subject-triggered reflexivization, as in (10.3b), does not require the speaker to enter into the internal feeling of the referent of the reflexive, but empathy adjectives such as *beloved* do require the speaker to enter into the experiencer's internal feelings. This contrast is clearly due to the fact that while the topic of conversation can be identified objectively by a bystander, whether or not someone holds his wife *beloved* to him cannot be determined objectively by a casual bystander.

Observe, further, the following sentences (in which John and Mary are assumed to be siblings):

(10.5) a. Mary talked to John about herself.
　　　　b. Mary talked to her brother about herself.
　　　　c. John's sister talked to him about herself.

It seems that these sentences have more or less the same degree of acceptability. This shows that the Descriptor Empathy Hierarchy does not affect the subject-triggered reflexivization. Now compare the above with the following sentences:

(10.6) a. √/?Mary talked to John about himself.
　　　　b.　　??Mary talked to her brother about himself.
　　　　c. √/?His sister talked to John about himself.

Example (10.6b) is considerably worse than (10.6a) or (10.6c). This shows that non-subject-triggered reflexivization is an empathy-conditioned phenomenon: (b) is awkward or marginal because, in addition to the fact that its trigger is in nonsubject position, the choice of descriptors in referring to Mary and John (i.e., the use of *Mary* and *her brother*) makes clear that the trigger for reflexivization is not the focus of the speaker's empathy.

I will show now how the three-argument hierarchy of subject > object > others for reflexivization shown in (10.1a) can be reduced to the two-argument hierarchy of E(subject) > E(others) for empathy. Recall that the former hierarchy was motivated by examples such as the following:

(10.7)   a.   John$_i$ showed Mary a picture of himself$_i$.
         b. $^\vee$/?John showed Mary$_i$ a picture of herself$_i$.
(10.8)   a.   ?Mary was shown by John$_i$ a picture of himself$_i$.
         b.   Mary$_i$ was shown by John a picture of herself$_i$.

The three-argument hierarchy for reflexivization is designed to account for the difference between (10.7b) and (10.8a). More specifically, it was necessary to be able to say that (10.7b) is better than (10.8a) because the trigger for reflexivization for the former is an object, while that for the latter is an "other" NP. However, we can now make use of the same kind of consideration that we have tried to capture by the Markedness Principle for Discourse-Rule Violations introduced in Section 3 of this chapter. In (10.7b), *John* is a stronger control for reflexivization than *Mary*. However, this relationship has automatically obtained because *John* is the agent and *Mary* the goal of the action represented by *showed*, which places the former in subject position and the latter in dative object position. In contrast, in (10.8a), the relative strength for control of reflexivization has been intentionally switched by application of passivization, an optional rule. Thus, *Mary* is a much stronger control for reflexivization vis-à-vis *John* in (10.8a) than *John* is vis-à-vis *Mary* in (10.7b). Conversely, *John* is a much weaker control for reflexivization vis-à-vis *Mary* in (10.8a) than *Mary* is vis-à-vis *John* in (10.7b). Hence, (10.8a) is less acceptable than (10.7b).

5.11 The Empathy and Direct Discourse Perspectives

Various empathy phenomena that have been discussed in this chapter interact in interesting ways with the direct discourse perspective. First, observe the following sentences:

(11.1)   a.   John told Mary that everything was all right.
         b.   Mary was told by John that everything was all right.

In (11.1a), *John* is [+logo-1a] (i.e., a speaker NP) and *Mary* [+logo-2] (i.e., a hearer NP). The fact that (11.1b) is perfectly acceptable establishes that there is nothing wrong with downgrading a [+logo-1] NP and upgrading some other NP. Next observe the following sentences:

(11.2)   a.   John$_i$ assured Mary$_j$ that he$_i$ would not harm her$_j$ in any way.
         b.   Mary$_j$ was assured by John$_i$ that he$_i$ would not harm her$_j$ in any way.

In these sentences, too, *John* is a [+logo-1a] NP, and *Mary* a [+logo-2] NP. Observe that in (11.2b), the main clause establishes the empathy relationship E(Mary) > E(John), while the complement clause establishes that E(he = [+logo-1a]) > E(her = [+logo-2]) via the Speech Act Empathy Hierarchy. The fact that (11.2b) is perfectly acceptable suggests that, unlike in the case of relative clauses, the tests for empathy relationship consistency are applied independently to main clauses and to indirect discourse complements, and not to the entire sentences. Indirect discourse complements have the status of independent clauses as far as empathy tests go. This makes sense because indirect discourse complements, after all, represent the words and thoughts of the main clause speaker/experiencer NPs.

Observe, further, the following sentences:

(11.3)   a.   John$_i$ assured Mary$_j$ that he$_i$ would not harm her$_j$ in any way.
         b.   ??John$_i$ assured Mary$_j$ that she$_j$ would not be harmed by him$_i$ in any way.

The marginality of sentences such as (11.3a) led Ross (1970) to hypothesize the following:

(11.4)   *Ross's constraint:* If a deep structure subject NP and some other NP in the same deep structure are coreferential, then the former NP may not become a passive agent.

It is clear that if the above constraint were used to account for the marginality of (11.3b), it would erroneously predict that (11.2b) would be as marginal as (11.3b).

The marginality of (11.3b) can be attributed to the fact that its indirect discourse complement clause violates the Speech Act Empathy Hierarchy. Note that *she* is coreferential with a [+logo-2] NP, and *him* with a [+logo-1a] NP, and that both are in the indirect discourse complement of the verb (i.e., *assured*) that takes the logophoric NPs *John* and *Mary* as its arguments. Thus, the empathy relationship dictated by the complement clause is E(she = [+logo-2]) > E(him = [+logo-1a]), which violates the Speech Act Empathy Hierarchy E(speaker) > E(others).

The above observations establish the following two points:

(11.5)   a.   The Ban on Conflicting Empathy does not apply between the main clause and the embedded clause if the latter is a logophoric complement.
         b.   An NP within a logophoric complement that is coreferential with the [+logo-1] NP of the logophoric verb is considered to have a "speaker" status vis-à-vis application of the Speech Act Empathy Hierarchy. However, the [+logo-1] NP of the logophoric verb does not have a "speaker" status.

Example (11.5b) is owing to the fact that in logophoric complements an NP that is coreferential with the main clause [+logo-1] NP corresponds to the first-person pronoun "I," but the [+logo-1] NP in the main clause does not have such a correspondence.

Let us examine several more examples to contrast the above analysis with Ross's. First observe the following sentence:

(11.6)   The boy who had been refused by the girl$_i$ resented her$_i$ and started spreading malicious rumors about her$_i$.

The sentence is acceptable in spite of the fact that it violates Ross's constraint. The acceptability of the sentence is readily explainable in the empathy and direct discourse perspectives. Example (11.6) does not involve a logophoric complement, and therefore the direct discourse perspective does not play any role here. The relative clause *the boy had been refused by the girl*, due to the Surface Structure Empathy Hierarchy, establishes E(the boy) > E(the girl). This relationship is a marked one because passivization, an optional rule, has been used. The main clause *the boy resented her (= the girl)* also establishes E(the boy) > E(the girl). This relationship is an unmarked one because it is simply owing to the fact that the verb *resent* places its experiencer (i.e., *the boy*) in subject position and the goal NP (i.e., *her*) in object position. In any case, since these two relationships are perfectly consistent with each other, there is nothing wrong with the sentence with respect to the empathy perspective.

Similarly, observe the following sentence:

(11.7)   Mary met John$_i$ at the home of a woman who had been started off in business by him$_i$.

The sentence also violates Ross's constraint, but again there does not seem to be anything wrong with it. This fact, too, is readily explainable in the empathy perspective. As we saw in section 5.3, the expression *x meets y* is one that requires that E(x) > E(y) because of the marked nature of the reciprocal verb *meet*, which, like the passive construction, gives the speaker an option of placing either x or y in subject position. Thus, the main clause of (11.7) dictates that the relationship E(Mary) > E(John) hold. The passive construction in the relative clause establishes the E(a woman) > E(John) relationship. *John* is downgraded in both relationships, and therefore there is no empathy conflict in the sentence. Example (11.7) is acceptable for this reason.

Let us return to the problem of how empathy expressions behave in logophoric complements. Observe the following sentences:

(11.8)   a.   ??He met me at a party a few years ago.
          b.   This man told me that he had met me at a party a few years ago.

As was discussed in section 5.3, (11.8a) is marginal or unacceptable out of context. However, (11.8b), whose complement clause is identical with (11.8a), is perfectly acceptable. This phenomenon is automatically explainable in the direct discourse perspective because the sentence, after application of interpretive rules for pronominal coreference, has the following structure, in which [+logo-1a] marks the speaker NP, and [+logo-2], the hearer NP:

(11.9)   [This man [+logo−1a] told me [+logo−2] that [he had met me at . . .]]

        [+coref]

                                [+coref]

Since a logophoric complement is involved, the empathy consistency tests apply independently to the main clause and to the embedded clause. The sentence is acceptable because the E(he = [+logo-1a]) > E(me = [+logo-2]) relationship dictated by the verb *met* in the complement clause is consistent with the Speech Act Empathy Hierarchy E(speaker) > E(others).

Parallel to (11.8b), we have the following sentence:

(11.10)   This man told me that I had met him at a party a few years ago.

These two sentences are not exactly synonymous. Example (11.10) implies that the speaker did not originally think that they had met before or that he still does not believe that they had met before. On the other hand, (11.8b), although it can be used in such a context, does not require it, and is primarily used for simply reporting what the man said. The above contrast is attributable to the fact that while the underlying structure of (11.8b) is as shown in (11.9), that of (11.10) is as shown below:

(11.11)   [This man [+logo−1a] told me [+logo−2] that [I had met him . . .]]

                          [+coref]

                        [+coref]

Since the subject *I* of the embedded clause is coreferential with the [+logo-2] NP (i.e., the hearer NP) of the sentence, and the object *him* with the [+logo-1a] NP (i.e., the speaker NP), the empathy relationship of the embedded clause parallels that of

(11.12)   "You met me . . ."

As was mentioned in section 5.3, this expression can be used only in special contexts such as the "corrective" one. The implication in (11.10) that the speaker did not originally think, or still does not think, that he and the man under discussion met before, is derived from the implication that (11.12) carries with it.

I suspect that there is a weak reading of (11.10) that does not involve "corrective" contexts. This interpretation arises, if it ever does, owing to the fact that a [+logo-1b] marking (i.e., an experiencer-NP marking) can be associated, with some difficulty, with a [+logo-2] marking (i.e., a hearer-NP marking). This means that an indirect discourse complement can, with some difficulty, be interpreted as representing not what a [+logo-1a] NP (i.e., the speaker NP) said, but what the hearer NP has felt internally as the result of hearing what the speaker NP has said.[23] When this [+logo-1b] marking is attached, the [+logo-1a] marking originally associated with the speaker NP is erased:

(11.13)

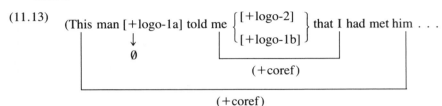

Thus the empathy relationship that derives from the complement clause of (11.13) is E(I [+logo-1b]) > E(him), which is consistent with the E(speaker) > E(other NPs) dictated by the Speech Act Empathy Hierarchy.

The assignment of a [+logo-1b] marking to a [+logo-2] NP that is not in subject position seems to be highly constrained, and limited to those cases where there is a strong overt indication that the nonsubject NP is the focus of the speaker's empathy, and where for some reason or another the interpretation of the complement clause as representing what the [+logo-1a] NP has uttered is blocked. It is difficult to obtain this [logo-1b] interpretation of the complement clause for (11.10) because it is readily interpretable as representing what the man has uttered. However, observe the following sentence:

(11.14)   This man didn't tell me that I had met him before, and I recalled it only after he left.

Since the main clause is negated, it is easy to interpret the complement clause as representing, not what the man might have said, but rather the speaker's restatement of what the man might have said. Hence it is easy to interpret the complement clause without imagining a "corrective" context.

In section 3.12, I proposed the following rule:

(11.15)   *Logophoric Feature Assignment Rule:* If an NP is in the subject position and if it is marked as [+logo-1a] or [+logo-2], optionally mark it as [+logo-1b].

What this rule means is that an indirect discourse complement of a passive saying verb can be interpreted, *without any difficulty,* as representing the internal feeling of the hearer NP (which is the subject of the passive saying verb) rather than the utterance of the speaker NP (which is in *by*-agentive position). It is for this reason that the complement clause of the following sentence does not have a "corrective" force:

(11.16)   I was told by this man that I had met him at a party a few years ago.

In this sentence, the speaker is restating what the man told him in his (= the speaker's) words. The main clause subject *I* is [+logo-1b], namely, an experiencer NP, and therefore, *I had met him* of the complement clause simply defines the empathy relationship E(I = [+logo-1b]) > E(him), which is consistent with the Speech Act Empathy Hierarchy. Hence there is no need to imagine a corrective context to justify the complement clause.

Let us now observe the passive version of (11.8b):

(11.17)   I was told by this man that he had met me at a party a few years ago.

That this sentence is perfectly acceptable requires explanation. The main clause dictates that the empathy relationship E(I) > E(this man) hold. Since the passive sentence pattern is used in the sentence, this relationship is supposed to be inviolable. In contrast, the logophoric complement dictates that the empathy relationship E(he = this man [+logo-1a]) > E(me = [+logo-2]) hold. These two relationships appear to be contradictory. However, the condition (11.5a), which dictates that the Ban on Conflicting Empathy Foci not apply between the main clause and its logophoric complement, accepts the sentence because both relationships are consistent with the Speech Act Empathy Hierarchy.

5.12 Empathy Phenomena in Japanese—Giving Verbs

So far in this chapter, I have presented a set of principles, all pertaining to camera angles, or the position of the speaker vis-à-vis the event/state that he describes in the sentence, which must be observed in sentence production. I have discussed a number of phenomena in English which give justification to these principles. In this section, I will show that there is a language which has a built-in mechanism for overtly specifying what the speaker's camera angle is. I am referring here to Japanese and its use of giving verbs as supporting verbs to represent the speaker's empathy with the referent of the subject or nonsubject NPs in nonstative sentences.

Japanese has two series of giving verbs, as shown below:

(12.1)			*A-series*	*B-series*
	a.	*Informal:*	yar-u	kure-ru
	b.	*Semi-Honorific:*	age-ru (receiver-honorific)	—
	c.	*Honorific:*	sasiage-ru (receiver-honorific)	kudasar-u (giver-honorific)

I will use the informal forms *yar-u* and *kure-ru* as illustrative members of the two series. For example, observe the following sentences:

(12.2) a. Taroo ga Hanako ni okane o *yar*-u.
                    to money give
          b. Taroo ga Hanako ni okane o *kure*-ru.
                    to money give

Both (a) and (b) mean 'Taroo gives money to Hanako.' They both imply that the act described is beneficial to the recipient. Beyond these two common features, the two sentences are very different with respect to whose point of view the speaker is representing. It is felt that (a) is, more or less, a statement from Taroo's point of view (or a statement with the speaker's empathy with Taroo), while (b) is a statement from Hanako's point of view. Let us make a tentative formulation of this intuitive feeling:

(12.3) *Giving Verbs in Japanese (tentative): yar-u* and *kure-ru* are subject to the following empathy constraint:
          a. *Yar-u* requires that E(subject) > E(dative)
          b. *Kure-ru* requires that E(subject) < E(dative)

Kure-ru thus constitutes an exception to the Surface Structure Empathy Hierarchy, which dictates that the relationship E(subject) > E(other NPs) hold. Let us observe some sentences to see how well the above formulation can account for their acceptability status.

(12.4) a. Boku ga Hanako ni okane o *yar*-u.
                I   to money give
                'I give money to Hanako.'
          b. *Boku ga Hanako ni okane o *kure*-ru.
(12.5) a. *Taroo ga boku ni okane o *yar*-u.
                        me to money give
          b. Taroo ga boku ni okane o *kure*-ru.

The acceptability status of each of the four sentences can be predicted in the following way:

(12.6)   *Subject*   *Dative*
     (12.4a)
       yar-u: E(I) > E(Hanako) ⎫
       Speech Act Empathy Hierarchy   E(I) > E(Hanako) ⎭ no contradiction
     (12.4b)
       kure-ru: E(I) < E(Hanako) ⎫ contradiction
       Speech Act Empathy Hierarchy   E(I) > E(Hanako) ⎭
     (12.5a)
       yar-u: E(Taroo) > E(I) ⎫ contradiction
       Speech Act Empathy Hierarchy   E(Taroo) < E(I) ⎭
     (12.5b)
       kure-ru: E(Taroo) < E(I) ⎫ no contradiction
       Speech Act Empathy Hierarchy   E(Taroo) < E(I) ⎭

In (12.4a), the use of *yar-u* 'give' shows that the speaker is empathizing with the subject rather than with the dative object. This empathy relationship is consistent with the Speech Act Empathy Hierarchy, which places the speaker higher than others in the speaker's empathy hierarchy. Hence the acceptability of the sentence. In contrast, in (12.4b), the use of *kure-ru,* according to the hypothesis presented in (12.3), shows that the speaker is empathizing with the dative rather than with the subject. This places *Hanako* higher than the speaker himself in his empathy hierarchy, which is a violation of the Speech Act Empathy Hierarchy. Hence the unacceptability of the sentence. The unacceptability of (12.5a) and the acceptability of (12.5b) can be explained in the same way.

Now observe the following sentences:

(12.7)   a.   Boku ga kimi ni okane o *yar*-u.
             I   you to money give
             'I give money to you.'
         b. *Boku ga kimi ni okane o *kure*-ru.
(12.8)   a. *Kimi ga boku ni okane o *yar*-u.
             you   me   to money give
             'You give money to me.'
         b.   Kimi ga boku ni okane o *kure*-ru.

The acceptability judgments of these sentences are exactly the same as those for (12.4) and (12.5). This is consistent with the claim of the Speech Act Empathy Hierarchy, which places the hearer below the speaker by dictating that $E(speaker) > E(others)$ be fulfilled.

Observe further the following sentences:

(12.9)   a.   Kimi ga Hanako ni okane o *yar*-u.
              you   to money
              'You give money to Hanako.'
          b.   Kimi ga Hanako ni okane o *kure*-ru.
(12.10)   a.   Taroo ga kimi ni okane o *yar*-u.
                    you to money
              'Taroo gives money to you.'
          b.   Taroo ga kimi ni okane o *kure*-ru.

The fact that all the above sentences are acceptable supports the claim (implicit in the Speech Act Empathy Hierarchy) that the empathy relationship between the hearer and the third person cannot be predetermined. Comparing (12.9a) and (12.9b), one gets the impression that while the speaker is closer to the hearer than to Hanako in (a), he is closer to Hanako than to the hearer in (b).

Having established the fact that the empathy constraint of *yar-u* and *kure-ru* is consistent with the Speech Act Empathy Hierarchy, let us proceed to the Descriptor Empathy Hierarchy, which dictates that given descriptor x (e.g.,

John) and another descriptor that is dependent upon x, that is, f(x) (e.g., *John's brother*), the relationship $E(x) > E(f(x))$ hold.

Observe the following sentences.

(12.11) a.   Taroo ga (Taroo no) imooto   ni okane o *yar*-u.
                          little sister to money give
                'Taroo gives money to his little sister.'
         b.   *Taroo ga (Taroo no) imooto ni okane o *kure*-ru.
(12.12) a.   (?)Hanako no niisan ga Hanako ni okane o *yar*-u.
                's big brother   to money give
                'Hanako's big brother gives money to Hanako.'
         b.   Hanako no niisan ga Hanako ni okane o *kure*-ru.

The unacceptability of (12.11b) is attributable to the conflict between the E(Taroo's little sister) > E(Taroo) relationship that the use of *kure-ru* requires, and the E(Taroo) > E(Taroo's little sister) relationship that the Descriptor Empathy Hierarchy dictates. On the same ground, (12.12a) should be unacceptable because there is conflict between the E(Hanako's big brother) > E(Hanako) relationship that the use of *yar-u* dictates and the E(Hanako) > E(Hanako's big brother) relationship that the Descriptor Empathy Hierarchy dictates. The fact that the sentence is nearly acceptable suggests that the empathy requirement of *yar-u* is not as strong as that of *kure-ru*.

On the basis of the above observation, let us revise the empathy condition of *yar-u* and *kure-ru* given in (12.3) in the following way:

(12.13) *Empathy Condition on Giving Verbs in Japanese:*
         a. *yar-u* $E(\text{subject}) \geq E(\text{dative})$
         b. *kure-ru* $E(\text{subject}) < E(\text{dative})$

We can say that (12.11b) is totally unacceptable because the two empathy relationships—one dictated by (12.13b) and the other dictated by the Descriptor Empathy Hierarchy—are completely opposite. On the other hand, (12.12b) is nearly acceptable because the difference between the two empathy relationships is just that between "=" and "<."

Observe, further, the following sentences:

(12.14) a.   Taroo ga toorigakari-no hito   ni okano o *yatta*.[24]
                          passing-by   person to money give-Past
                'Taroo gave money to a passerby.'
         b.   *Taroo ga toorigakari-no hito ni okane o *kureta*.
(12.15) a.   Toorigakari-no hito ga Taroo ni okane o *yatta*.
                passing-by   person   to money gave
                'A passerby gave money to Taroo.'
         b.   Toorigakari-no hito ga Taroo ni okane o *kureta*.

The Topic Empathy Hierarchy, which dictates that the relationship E(discourse-topic) ≥ E(nontopic) hold, establishes for (12.14) the relationship E(Taroo) ≥ E(a passerby). This exactly matches the requirement that is dictated by *yatta* in (12.14a). Hence the acceptability of the sentence. In contrast, in (12.14b), *kureta* 'gave' requires that E(Taroo) < E(a passerby). Since this requirement, which is a very strong one, contradicts the Topic Empathy Hierarchy requirement, unacceptability results, as shown in (12.14b). In (12.15a), the use of *yatta* requires that E(a passerby) ≥ E(Taroo). This is not contradictory with the Topic Empathy Hierarchy because of the shared equality relationship. Hence the acceptability of the sentence. In (12.15b), the use of *kureta* requires that E(a passerby) < E(Taroo), which is consistent with the requirement of the Topic Empathy Hierarchy. Therefore, this sentence, too, is acceptable.[25]

I have shown above that empathy factors condition the use of the two series of giving verbs in Japanese. However, the scope of empathy effect in Japanese is much wider than the above discussion might have suggested. This is because giving verbs are used in Japanese as supporting verbs to specify the camera angle of the speaker. For example, observe the following sentences:

(12.16) a.   Taroo ga Hanako ni hanataba o okutta.
                          to bouquet   sent
             'Taroo sent Hanako a bouquet of flowers.'
         b.   Taroo ga Hanako ni hanataba o okutte   *yatta*.
                          to bouquet   sending gave
         c.   Taroo ga Hanako ni hanabata o okutte   *kureta*.
                                  sending gave

The above three sentences represent the same event, that is, that of Taroo's sending a bouquet of flowers to Hanako. However, they are different with respect to where the speaker has placed himself in describing the event. Example (a) is a neutral sentence, in which the speaker has placed himself at a distance from both Taroo and Hanako. In contrast, (b) is a sentence in which the speaker has placed himself closer to Taroo than to Hanako, while (c) is a sentence in which the speaker has placed himself closer to Hanako than to Taroo. Both (b) and (c) also have an additional implication that the act was beneficial to Hanako, but this implication is not our primary concern here.

The empathy conditions for the use of *yar-u* and *kure-ru* as supporting verbs are exactly the same as those of *yar-u* and *kure-ru* as independent verbs, except that *yar-u* cannot be used for neutral description. For example, observe the following sentences:

(12.17) a.   Toorigakari-no hito ga Taroo ni okane o kasita.
              passing-by   person   to money lent
             'A passerby lent Taroo some money.'
         b.   ?Toorigakari-no hito ga Taroo ni okane o kasite *yatta*.
                                            lending gave

We can account for the marginality of (12.17b) by assuming that *yar-u* as a supporting verb requires that the relationship E(subject) > E(dative) hold. This is different from the empathy requirement of *yar-u* as an independent verb in that it lacks an equality sign. Then, the marginality of the sentence can be attributed to the conflict between the E(a passerby) > E(Taroo) relationship dictated by the use of *V-te yar-u,* on one hand, and the E(Taroo) ≤ E(a passerby) relationship dictated by the Topic Empathy Hierarchy. Intuitively, the fact that *yar-u* as a supporting verb does not allow neutral description can be attributed to the fact that if this supporting verb, whose use is optional, is used, it must be for some good reason, that is, for overtly specifying that the sentence is from the point of view of the subject. Appearance of the supporting verb *yar-u* in a neutral description would not accomplish any useful purpose.

Since *yar-u* and *kure-ru* can be combined with almost any action verbs, the scope of empathy effect in Japanese is indeed extensive. Furthermore, when a nonsubject NP refers to the speaker or to someone close to him (i.e., to someone whose point of view he can readily represent), Japanese forces the speaker to make explicit that he is representing the point of view of the referent of that NP. For example, compare the following sentences:

(12.18)   a.   Taroo ga *Hanako* ni hanataba o *okutta.* (= 12.16a)
                           to bouquet   sent
                    'Taroo sent Hanako a bouquet of flowers.'
           b.   *Taroo ga *boku* ni hanataba o *okutta.*
                           me to bouquet   sent
                    'Taroo sent me a bouquet of flowers.'
           c.   Taroo ga boku ni hanataba o *okutte   kureta.*
                           me to bouquet   sending gave
           d.   Taroo ga boku ni hanataba o *okutte   kita.*
                           me to bouquet   sending came

As we have already seen, (12.18a) is a neutral sentence describing the designated event from a distance. However, when the recipient is the speaker himself, it is not possible to describe the event neutrally, as shown by the unacceptability of (b). It is necessary to add *kure-ta* 'gave' to overtly show that the E(recipient) > E(agent) relationship holds, or to use *kita* 'came' to show that the act of sending a bouquet of flowers was directed toward the speaker.[26]

Similarly, observe the following sentences:

(12.19)   a.   ??Yamada-kun ga boku no kanai ni hanataba o *okutta.*
                                my   wife to bouquet   sent
                    'Mr. Yamada sent my wife a bouquet of flowers.'
           b.   Yamada-kun ga boku no kanai ni hanataba o   *okutte kureta.*

c.   Yamada-kun ga boku no kanai ni hanataba o *okutte kita.*

The marginality or unacceptability of (12.19a) in ordinary context shows that when the recipient is someone close to the speaker, such as his wife, he cannot describe the designated event neutrally.[27] He has to overtly show that the statement is from that person's camera angle (and therefore from his), by using *kure-ta* or *kita.*

The above facts are not the peculiarities of the verb used (i.e., *okur-u* 'send'). Many other verbs show the same behavior. Observe that the following (b) sentences are all marginal or unacceptable and that *kure-ru* 'give' or *ku-ru* 'come' must be used as a supporting verb:

(12.20)   a.   Taroo ga Hanako ni denwa o kaketa.
                        to phone   placed
                'Taroo called up Hanako.'
          b.   *Taroo ga boku ni denwa o kaketa.
                'Taroo called me up.'
(12.21)   a.   Taroo ga Hanako o tazuneta.
                        visited
                'Taroo called on Hanako.'
          b.   *Taroo ga boku o tazuneta.[28]
                'Taroo called on me.'
(12.22)   a.   Taroo ga Hanako o yuusyoku ni yonda.
                        dinner   to invited
                'Taroo invited Hanako to dinner.'
          b.??Taroo ga boku o yuusyoku ni yonda.[29]
                'Taroo invited me to dinner.'
(12.23)   a.   Taroo ga Hanako ni okane o kasita.
                        to money   lend
                'Taroo lent money to Hanako.'
          b.??Taroo ga boku ni okane o kasita.[30]
                'Taroo lent me money.'

In addition to these giving verbs, which are used extensively in Japanese to specify overtly where the speaker's camera is placed in describing events and actions, Japanese has a series of receiving verbs that perform the same function: *moraw-u* 'receive (informal),' and *itadak-u* 'receive (giver-honorific).' For example,[31]

(12.24)   a.   Taroo ga Hanako ni okane o *moratta.*
                        to money   received
                'Taroo received money from Hanako.'[32]
          b.   Boku wa Hanako ni okane o *moratta.*
                'I received money from Hanako.'

c.   ??Hanako ga *boku* ni okane o *moratta.*
'Hanako received money from me.'

These examples show that the following constraint holds on the use of *moraw-u* 'receive':

(12.25)   *Empathy Condition on Receiving Verbs in Japanese*
moraw-u 'receive':   E(subject) > E(*Ni*-marked NP)

Now receiving verbs, like giving verbs, can be used as supporting verbs, coupled with main verbs, to show that the speaker's camera angle is that of the subject of the sentence.

(12.26)   a.   Yamada-kun ga uta o utatta.
                                  song sang
'Yamada sang a song.'
b.   Yamada-kun ga uta o utatte   *kureta.*
                          song singing gave
'Yamada gave me (the favor of) singing a song.'
c.   Boku wa Yamada-kun ni uta o utatte   *moratta.*
                                  to song singing received
'I received from Yamada (the favor of his) singing a song.'

Example (a) is a neutral sentence. Example (b) is a sentence from the speaker's camera angle, with the additional implication that Yamada's singing was beneficial to the speaker. Example (c) is also a sentence from the speaker's (i.e., the subject's) point of view, and it also implies that Yamada's act was beneficial to the speaker. The difference between (b) and (c) is that, while the former describes the event involved strictly as one initiated by its agent (i.e., Yamada-kun), the latter describes it as one originally initiated by the subject of *moraw-u* 'receive' (i.e., *boku* 'I'). Thus, (c) is in fact paraphrasable as 'I asked of, and received from, Yamada (a favor of) singing a song.'

I have given in this section a point-of-view analysis of giving and receiving verbs in Japanese. The following is a summary of the observations:

(12.27)
a. *yar-u* 'give'   (i)   independently: E(subject) ≥ E(dative)
                                (ii) supporting verb: E(subject) > E(dative)
b. *kure-ru* 'give'   for (i) and (ii):   E(subject) < E(dative)
c. *moraw-u* 'receive' for (i) and (ii):   E(subject) > E(*Ni*-marked NP)

The above conditions on the use of giving and receiving verbs naturally interact with the direct discourse perspective. For example, observe the following sentences:

(12.28)   a.   *John ga *boku* ni okane o *yatta.*
                          me   to money gave
'John gave me money.'

  b. cf. John ga boku ni okane o *kureta.*
          me   to money gave   .
  c. John wa [*boku* ni okane o *yatta*] to huityoosite iru. (cf. (a))
          me   to money gave   that bragging is
      'John is bragging that he gave me money.'
  d. ??John wa [*boku* ni okane o *kureta*] to   huityoosite iru. (cf. (b))
          me   to money gave   that bragging is

What is interesting is the fact that (c), which contains the ill-formed clause
(a), is acceptable and that (d), which contains the well-formed clause (b), is
marginal for many speakers. This is clearly due to the fact that the subject of
yatta in (c) is coreferential with the [+logo-1] NP (i.e., *John*) in the main
clause, while the dative object of *yatta* is coreferential neither with [+logo-1]
nor [+logo-2] NP in the main clause. To put it in more informal terms, (c) is
acceptable because the direct discourse representation of what John is bragging about would be

(12.29)   "Boku wa *x* ni okane o *yatta.*"
            I   to money gave
           'I gave money to *x*.'

where *x* stands for whatever descriptor John chose to use to refer to the
speaker of (c). We can say that (12.28c) is acceptable because the direct discourse representation of what John said, (12.29), is acceptable. Similarly, we
can say that (12.28d) is marginal or unacceptable for many speakers because
the direct discourse representation of John's bragging is unacceptable, as
shown in (12.30).

(12.30)   "*Boku wa *x* ni okane o *kureta.*"
            I   to money gave
           'I gave money to *x*.'

There are many speakers who consider both (12.28c) and (12.28d) acceptable. These are the speakers for whom sentences involving indirect speech are
acceptable if the empathy conditions for use of giving and receiving verbs are
fulfilled either at the level of the direct discourse representation of the indirect
speech or at the level of surface sentence.

    The facts that I have described in this section would be extremely difficult
to account for in a non–ad hoc fashion without resource to the empathy perspective and the direct discourse perspective.[33]

5.13 Some Other Empathy Expressions in Japanese

In the preceding section, I showed that giving and receiving verbs in Japanese
are empathy expressions that force the speaker to take specific camera angles.
I also showed that these giving and receiving verbs combine with main verbs

and overtly specify the speaker's camera angles in his description of events represented in the sentences. These devices make Japanese a language that is extremely rich in empathy expressions.

I briefly showed in section 3.14 that one of the functions of Japanese reflexive *zibun* 'self' is as a logophoric (more specifically, [+logo-1]) pronoun. As is the case with the English reflexives, we can characterize *zibun* as an empathy expression. Compare the following two sentences:

(13.1) a. Yamada$_i$ wa, *kare$_i$* o nikunde iru onna to kekkonsite simatta.
              him   hating   is woman with marrying ended up
            'Yamada$_i$ ended up marrying a woman who hated him$_i$.'
        b. Yamada$_i$ wa, *zibun$_i$* o nikunde iru onna to kekkonsite simatta.

Examples (a) and (b) are different only with respect to whether the pronominal *kare* 'he' or the reflexive *zibun* 'self' is used to refer to the main clause subject *Yamada*. Semantically, these two sentences are different in that while (a) is a sentence in which the speaker gives an objective description of what happened by placing himself at a distance from Yamada, (b) gives the impression that the speaker is omniscient and has identified himself with Yamada. The latter sentence ordinarily implies that Yamada knew at the time of the marriage that the woman he married hated him, or that he later came to know it. In other words, the sentence ordinarily represents Yamada's internal feeling. Thus, the sentence (b) can be characterized as one in which the speaker has overtly expressed his high degree of empathy with Yamada.

Observe, further, the following sentences:

(13.2) a. Taroo$_i$ wa, Hanako ga *zibun$_i$* ni kasite *kureta* hon o nakusite
                                      self   to lending gave   book losing
            simatta.
            ended up
            'Taroo has lost a book that Hanako lent him(self).'
        b. *Taroo$_i$ wa, Hanako ga *zibun$_i$* ni kasite *yatta* hon o nakusite simatta.

In the preceding section, I showed that *yar-u* 'give' and *kure-ru* 'give' as supporting verbs have the following empathy requirements:

(13.3) a. V-te *yar-u:*   E(subject) > E(dative)
        b. V-te *kure-ru:* E(subject) < E(dative)

Let us assume that the above hierarchies not only represent the relative degrees of the speaker's empathy with the subject and dative object but that they indicate that the dative for *yar-u* and the subject for *kure-ru* have been *downgraded* in the speaker's empathy.[34] The reflexive *zibun*, on the other hand, dictates that the speaker empathize with its referent.[35] More particularly, the speaker is not allowed to use *zibun* to refer to an NP that has been downgraded. The above requirements for the use of *yar-u/kure-ru* and *zibun*, put together, can account for the contrast between (13.2a) and (13.2b):

(13.4) (13.2a):	the use of *kureta*	dictates	E(Hanako) < E(Taroo) with E(Hanako) downgraded
	the use of *zibun* = Taroo	"	E(Taroo) be high and not downgraded

no contradiction

(13.2b):	the use of *yatta*	dictates	E(Hanako) > E(Taroo) with E(Taroo) downgraded
	the use of *zibun* = Taroo	"	E(Taroo) be high and not downgraded

contradiction

Example (13.2b) is unacceptable because the camera angle required for the use of *zibun* and that required for the use of *yatta* are incompatible. Similarly, observe the following sentences:

(13.5)   a.   Taroo$_i$ wa *zibun*$_i$ ni ai ni *kita* hito ni wa, dare-demo, syokuzi o dasu.
              self   to see to came people whoever   meal   offer
              'Taroo offers a meal to anybody who has *come* to see him(self).'
        b.   *Taroo$_i$ wa *zibun*$_i$ ni ai ni *itta* hito ni wa, dare-demo syokuzi o dasu.
              self   to see to went people whoever   meal   offer
              'Taroo offers a meal to anybody who has *gone* to see him(self).'

The use of *kita* 'came' in the relative clause of (a) makes clear that the whole sentence is a statement from Taroo's camera angle. It upgrades Taroo and downgrades the subject (i.e., visitors) in empathy. Note that *zibun* 'self' can be used in the relative clause in reference to Taroo. In contrast, the use of *itta* 'went' in (b) shows that Taroo has been downgraded in the speaker's empathy. Note that *zibun* cannot be used here. Examples such as (13.5a) and (13.5b), as well as (13.2a) and (13.2b), firmly establish *zibun* as an empathy expression.
Observe, further, the following examples:

(13.6)   a.   Kawada-kyoozyu$_i$ wa, *zibun*$_i$ no byoozyoo o kizukau hitotati
                          prof.   self   's condition   worry   people
              ni yotte, atatakaku kanbyoosareta.
              by   warmly   was-looked-after
              'Professor Kawada was warmly looked after by those who were worried about his health condition.'
        b.   *Kawada-kyoozyu$_i$ wa, *zibun*$_i$ no si o kanasimu hitotati ni yotte,
                          prof.   self   's death mourn   people by
              teityoo ni hoomurareta.
              reverently was-buried

'Professor Kawada was reverently buried by those who mourned his death.'

The above two sentences have an identical structure, but (a) is acceptable and (b) is unacceptable. This must be due to the fact that there is a discourse principle such as (13.7) that is applicable at least to Japanese, and perhaps to many other languages:

(13.7)   *Aliveness Requirement for Empathy:* It is possible to describe an action or state with the camera angle only of a living person. (In other words, it is not possible to empathize with a dead person.)

We observe the same principle in operation in the following:

(13.8)   a.   Yamada$_i$ wa, Tanaka ga *zibun*$_i$ o *korosoo* to sita toki,
                                    self   try-to-kill did when
             hitokoto mo   koe o tatenakatta.
             even one word voice uttered-not
             'Yamada, when Tanaka tried to kill him, didn't utter a word.'

         b.   *Yamada$_i$ wa, Tanaka ga *zibun*$_i$ o *korosita* toki,
                                    self   killed   when
             itiokuen no   syakkin o kakaete ita.
             100-million-yen debt   had
             'Yamada, when Tanaka killed him, had 100 million yen in the hole.'

In (a), Yamada, as the result of Tanaka's trying to kill him, might have died a moment later. However, at the time that the sentence refers to, Yamada was still alive. Therefore, the speaker can legitimately empathize with him and use *zibun* in referring to him. On the other hand, at the time that (b) refers to, Yamada was dead. Therefore, the speaker is not allowed to empathize with him, and hence it is not possible to use *zibun* here.

The above discussion does not mean that *zibun* can never be used in reference to a dead person. Its use is legitimate as long as the smallest clause or noun phrase that contains *zibun* describes an action, state, or relationship that existed before the death of the referent. For example, observe the following sentences:

(13.9)   a.   Kawada-gahaku$_i$ wa, desitati ga *zibun* no tame ni tatete   kureta
                   painter   disciples self 's sake for building gave
             atelier de, saigo no iki o hikitotta.
                   in last   breath breathed
             'Painter Kawada breathed his last in the atelier which his disciples had built for him(self).'

         b.   *Kawada-gahaku$_i$ wa, desitati ga *zibun*$_i$ no tame ni setti sita
                   painter   disciples self 's sake for prepared
             soogizyoo   ni hakobareta.
             funeral place to carried

'Painter Kawada was taken to the funeral place that his disciples arranged for him.'

Example (13.9) is acceptable because painter Kawada knew that his disciples had built an atelier for him. In contrast, (13.9b) is unacceptable because he did not recognize the funeral place, while he was still alive, as one that his disciples arranged for him. Similarly, observe the following contrast:

(13.10)   a.   Kawada-kyoozyu$_i$ wa sigo   suguni,   *zibun*$_i$ no ie kara,
                      prof.   after-death immediately self's house from
          soogizyoo   ni utusareta.
          funeral home to transferred-was
          'Prof. Kawada was transferred from his (self's) house to a funeral home immediately after his death.'
          b.   *Kawada-kyoozyu$_i$ wa, sigo suguni, *zibun*$_i$ no soogizyoo
                                                         funeral home
          ni utusareta.
          to was-transferred
          'Prof. Kawada was transferred to his (self's) funeral home immediately after his death.'

In (a), the relationship 'self's house' existed while Kawada was alive. Hence the acceptability of the sentence with *zibun*. On the other hand, the relationship 'self's funeral home' did not exist while Kawada was still alive. In other words, there was no recognition of the funeral home, on the part of Kawada, as "my own funeral home." Hence the impossibility of using *zibun* in (b).

In the above, I have shown that the Japanese reflexive pronoun *zibun* functions as an empathy expression. In Chapter 3, I showed that it functions as a logophoric (more specifically, as a [+logo-1]) pronoun. What is the common feature between these two uses? Since the clause that contains a logophoric pronoun represents a statement or feeling on the part of the referent of the logophoric NP in the main clause, and since this representation is from the camera angle of the logophoric NP, we can say that the use of *zibun* as a logophoric pronoun is a special case of its use as an empathy expression. However, the following examples show that it is necessary to keep these two functions of *zibun* separate:

(13.11)   a.   Taroo$_i$ wa Hanako o *zibun*$_i$ no syuzyutu o tantoosita isya ni
                               self   's surgery   was-in-charge doctor to
          syookaisita.
          introduced
          'Taroo$_i$ introduced Hanako to the doctor who was in charge of his$_i$ surgery.'

    b. *Hanako wa Taroo$_i$ ni *zibun*$_i$ no syuzyutu o tantoosita
                 by self   's surgery   was-in-charge
      isya ni syookaisareta.
      doctor to was-introduced
      'Hanako was introduced by Taroo$_i$ to the doctor who was in charge
      of his$_i$ surgery.'

The Japanese reflexive normally requires a sentence subject as trigger. It cannot be coreferential with the *by*-agentive of a simple passive sentence. Thus, in (a), *zibun* is coreferential only with *Taroo*, and not with *Hanako*, while in (b), it is coreferential with *Hanako*, and not with *Taroo*.

Now compare the above phenomenon with the following:

(13.12)   a.   Taroo$_i$ wa Hanako ni *zibun*$_i$ no tokoro ni sugu   kite
                              to self   's place to immediately coming
          kure to   tanonda.[36]
          give that asked
          'Taroo$_i$ asked Hanako to come to self$_i$'s place immediately.'
       b.   Hanako wa Taroo$_i$ ni *zibun*$_i$ no tokoro ni sugu   kite
                           by self   's place   to immediately coming
          kure to   tanomareta.
          give that was-asked
          'Hanako was asked by Taroo$_i$ to immediately come to self$_i$'s place.'

The reflexive pronoun *zibun* can be coreferential with the *by*-agentive *Taroo (ni)* in the passive sentence (b). This must be due to the fact that *zibun* in (13.12a, b) is a [+logo-1] pronoun and is not subject to the requirement for surface subject control.

Japanese has emotive adjectives which behave like *dear old, beloved*, and *embarrassing*. For example, observe the following sentences:

(13.13)   a.   Taroo was Hanako ni tegami o kaita.
                      to letter   wrote
       b.   Taroo wa *itosii*   Hanako ni tegami o kaita.
                   longed-for   to letter   wrote
          'Taroo wrote a letter to his dear old Hanako.'
(13.14)   a.   Taroo wa Hanako no tegami o yonda.
                       's letter   read
          'Taroo read Hanako's letter.'
       b.   Taroo wa *natukasii*   Hanako no tegami o yonda.
                   fondly-memorable   's letter   read
          'Taroo read a letter from Hanako, of whom he has sweet memories.'

Examples (13.13a) and (13.14a) do not make the speaker's camera angle clear. They can be neutral, objective sentences, or ones with the speaker's empathy with Taroo, or they can even be interpreted as having the speaker's empathy with Hanako. On the other hand, (13.13b) and (13.14b) make explicit where the speaker stands vis-à-vis Taroo and Hanako. They are both sentences which have been produced with the speaker empathizing with Taroo. This is because of the emotive nature of *itosii* 'longed for' and *natukasii* 'fondly memorable.' The speaker, in order to be able to use these expressions representing Taroo's feeling toward Hanako, must have a high degree of empathy with Taroo.

Now compare the following two sentences:

(13.15)   a.   Taroo wa Ziroo ni *itosii*   Hanako kara   no tegami o miseta.
                                to longed-for   from   's letter   showed
              'Taroo showed Ziroo a letter from (his) dear old Hanako.'

         b.   Taroo wa Ziroo ni *itosii* Hanako kara no tegami o misete *kureta*.
                                                                          gave

         c.   Taroo wa Ziroo ni *itosii* Hanako kara no tegami o misete *yatta*.
                                                                          gave

These three sentences have the following interpretations with respect to who the experiencer is of the feeling *itosii* 'dear to':

(13.16)   (13.15a)   Taroo > Ziroo
          (13.15b)   Ziroo
          (13.15c)   Taroo

The primary interpretation of (13.15a) is that of 'dear to Taroo,' but it is possible to get a 'dear to Ziroo' interpretation as a secondary interpretation. On the other hand, (13.15b) seems to allow only a 'dear to Ziroo' interpretation. This must be due to the fact that the use of *kureta* 'gave,' which requires the speaker's empathy focus on the dative object, makes clear that Ziroo is the focus of empathy. Similarly, (13.15c) seems to allow only for a 'dear to Taroo' interpretation. This interpretation seems to be imposed on the sentence because the use of the supporting verb *yatta* 'gave,' which requires the speaker's empathy on the subject, makes clear that Taroo is the focus of empathy in the sentence.

Observe also the following sentences:

(13.17)   a.   Taroo wa Hanako o *natukasii* Nara   no ryokan ni sasotta.
                                   fondly-memorable 's inn   to invited
              'Taroo invited Hanako to the fondly-memorable inn in Nara.'

         b.   Hanako wa Taroo ni *natukasii* Nara   no ryokan ni sasowareta.
                                   fondly-memorable 's inn   to was-invited
              'Hanako was invited by Taroo to the fondly-memorable inn in Nara.'

Here again, the experiencer of *natukasii* 'fondly-memorable' in (a) is primarily *Taroo* and secondarily *Hanako*. In contrast, in (b), it has to be *Hanako*.[37] This must be due to the fact that the former subject *Taroo* has been downgraded to *by*-agentive position with the use of the passive construction, and therefore it cannot win over *Hanako* in its control of *natukasii*. Similarly, compare the following two sentences:

(13.18) a. Taroo ga neesan   ni *natukasii*   tomodati no hanasi o sita.
                       big-sister to fondly-memorable friend   talked-about
             'Taroo talked to his big sister about (lit.) the fondly-memorable friend.'

         b. Taroo no neesan   ga, Taroo ni *natukasii*   tomadati no
               's big-sister   to fondly-memorable friend
             hanasi o sita.
             talked-about
             'Taroo's big sister talked to Taroo about (lit.) the fondly-memorable friend.'

In (a), the experiencer of the feeling *natukasii* is the subject of the sentence, while in (b) it is predominantly the dative object and secondarily the subject. This contrast clearly results from the interaction of the Surface Structure Empathy Hierarchy with the Descriptor Empathy Hierarchy.

Further examples can be found in Kaburaki (1973), in which are considered expressions such as *Tanaka-kun* 'friend Tanaka/student Tanaka, etc.' and *otoosan* 'Dad':

(13.19) a. Yooko wa, *Tanaka-kun* ga issyoni kite   kureru node,
                                   together coming give   since
             ooyorokobi datta.
             great-joy   was
             'Yoko was very happy that friend Tanaka was coming with her.'

         b. Yooko wa, *Tanaka-kun* ga nyuuinsita   toki,   mada Amerika
                                       hospitalized-was when yet
             kara kaette   inakatta.
             from returning was-not
             'Yoko hadn't returned from America when friend Tanaka was hospitalized.'

The question here is, who is the person who has such a relationship with Tanaka as to be able to call him *Tanaka-kun* 'friend Tanaka' (instead of, say, *Tanaka-san* 'Mr. Tanaka' or *Tanaka-sensei* 'Teacher Tanaka')? There is no problem with interpreting *Tanaka-kun* of (a) and (b) as meaning 'my friend Tanaka.' In addition, (a) can mean 'her (= Yoko's) friend Tanaka,' while (b) does not have such a meaning. This must be owing to the fact that Yoko, since she was in America, did not have an internal feeling to the effect that her friend Tanaka was hospitalized. This behavior of . . .-*kun* parallels that of emotive adjectives such as *itosii* 'longed-for' and *natukasii* 'fondly memorable,' and establishes it as an empathy expression.

5.14 Reflexives in Other Languages

In section 3.14, I showed that reflexive pronouns in Turkish perform the function of logophoric pronouns. They can also be characterized as empathy expressions. For example, compare the following two noun phrase expressions:

(14.1)   a.   siyaset adamının *kendisini* görmeğe *geldiği* söylentisi kimsenin
politics man's   self   to-see   coming rumor   nobody's
dilinden   düşmeyen şebeke başkanı
tongue-from not-falling gang   leader
'the gang leader who the fact that the politician *came* to see *him(self)*
is widespread'

   b. √/?/??siyaset adamının *kendisini* görmeğe *gittiği* söylentisi
politics man's   self   to-see   going rumor
kimsenin dilinden   düşmeyen şebeke başkanı
nobody's tongue-from not-falling gang   leader
'the gang leader who the fact that the politician *went* to see *him(self)*
is widespread'

The use of *geldiği* 'coming' in the relative clause of (a) makes clear that the description given here is from a camera angle of the gang leader. Note that the reflexive pronoun *kendisini* is acceptable for all speakers. On the other hand, in (b), the use of *gittiği* 'going' in the relative clause makes clear that the description is not from the viewpoint of the gang leader. The acceptability of (b) varies greatly among speakers, but they are in agreement that (a) is better than (b) and that (b) can be used only in a special style of writing such as newspaper reporting. We can say that the reflexive pronouns in Turkish are empathy expressions, at least in colloquial speech, though to a lesser degree than their Japanese counterpart *zibun* 'self.'

Similarly, observe the following noun phrases:

(14.2)   a.   profesörün *kendisini* okuttuğu gerçeği herkesçe   bilinen çocuk
professor's self-to   teaching truth   by-everyone being-known boy
'the boy who the fact that the professor taught him(self) is well
known'

   b. ?/??şebeke başkanın *kendisini* öldürdüğü söylentisi kimsenin
gang   leader's self   killing   rumor   nobody's
dilinden   düşmeyen profesör
tongue-from not-falling professor
'the professor who the rumor that the gang leader killed him(self)
is widespread'

All speakers accept (14.2a), but they consider (b) a little strange, awkward, or marginal. This must be due to the fact that in (b) the reflexive pronoun refers to a dead person. It must be that it is difficult to take a camera angle of a dead person in Turkish, as well as in Japanese, although the force of this constraint seems to be considerably weaker in Turkish than in Japanese.[38]

In section 3.14, I showed that the Korean reflexive *caki* performs the function of a logophoric pronoun (more specifically, a [+logo-1] pronoun). There are wide idiolectal variations in the acceptability judgments of Korean speakers on the use of *caki*, but it is safe to say that most speakers consider the (b) sentences below less acceptable than the corresponding (a) sentences, and many regard them as unacceptable:

(14.3) a. John$_i$-un   *caki*$_i$ (-uy) cip-ey   *o*-nun   salam
            topic self('s)   house-to come-ing people
            nwukwu-eykeytunci swul-ul   ceykongha-n-ta.
            whoever-to   drinks-acc. offers
            'John offers drinks to whoever *comes* to his (self's) house.'
        b. ??/*John$_i$-un,   *caki*$_i$ (-uy) cip-ey   *ka*-nun   salam
            topic self('s)   house-to come-ing people
            nwukwu-eykeytunci swul-ul   ceykongha-n-ta.
            whoever-to   drinks-acc. offers
            'John offers drinks to whoever *goes* to his (self's) house.'

(14.4) a. John$_i$-un, Mary-ka macimakulo *caki*$_i$-lul po-la w-ass-ul-ttay,
                topic   nom. last   self-acc. see-to come-Past-when
            aph-ass-ta.
            sick-was
            'John was sick when Mary *came* to see him(self) last.'
        b. ??/*John$_i$-un, Mary-ka macimakulo *caki*$_i$-lul po-la *ka*-ss-ul-ttay,
                topic   nom. last   self-acc. see-to go-Past-when
            aph-ass-ta.
            sick-was
            'John was sick when Mary *went* to see him(*self*) last.'

Assuming that the verb *o-ta* 'come' requires the speaker's empathy with the goal and the verb *ka-ta* 'go' requires empathy with the agent, the above fact can be accounted for only if we assume that the Korean reflexive *caki* can be used only when its referent is the focus of the speaker's empathy.[39]

The empathy-based nature of reflexive pronouns in Russian is well documented. According to Yokoyama (1979, 1980), possessive NPs that are coreferential with the clause mate subject in Russian are realized in pronominal or reflexive form:

(14.5) a. Ja podal *moj* stakan.
             I gave my cup
             'I offered my cup.'
          b. Ja podal *svoj* stakan.
             I gave self's cup
             'I offered my cup.'

(14.6) a. On podal *ego* stakan.
             he gave his cup
             'He offered his cup.'
          b. On podal *svoj* stakan.
             he gave self's cup
             'He offered his cup.'

Because of the ambiguity of *ego* 'his' in (14.6a) with respect to whether it refers to the subject or to some other third-person masculine NP that has appeared in the preceding discourse, grammars usually do not recommend the usage of third-person possessive pronouns which refer to the subject. As for first- (and second-) person possessives, the choice between the reflexive and nonreflexive pronouns is considered to be optional.

For the first person, the use of the reflexives is marked, and it signals that the speaker is referring to his split ego, or to an identity that is apart from himself. For example, observe the following sentence, which Yokoyama attributes to Peškovskij (1974):

(14.7) Kto ni umret, ja vsex ubijca tajnyj:
       who ever dies I all's killer secret
       Ja uskoril   Fedora končinu,
       I hastened F's   death
       Ja ostravil *svoju* sestru caricu,
       I poisoned self's sister queen
       Monaxinju smirennuju . . . vse ja! (Puškin 7.26)
       nun   meek   all I
       'No matter who dies, I am the secret murderer of everyone: I hastened Feodor's demise, I poisoned my sister the czarina, the meek nun . . . I do it all!'

According to Peškovskij, the use of the reflexive *svoju* in (14.7) is motivated by the fact that here the speaker is referring not to the real facts but to rumors which he considers false. Substituting *moju* 'my' for *svoju* 'self's' in this sentence would imply that the speaker admits that he actually poisoned his sister.

Yokoyama hypothesizes the choice between reflexive and personal possessive pronouns is determined by the degree to which the speaker of an utterance identifies with his inner self in the process of speech performance. She assumes that reflexivization takes place when the speaker's dissociation with his inner self takes place. In (14.7), the person that the speaker is talking about is not his inner self, but what other people consider him to be. This necessitates the use of a reflexive pronoun.[40]

Yokoyama also hypothesizes that it is natural for the speaker to efface himself when he is concerned with a third-person subject. Hence, the speaker's dissociation with his inner self is nearly obligatory, and therefore the use of the reflexive possessive becomes necessary.

The above characterization of the use of the reflexive and nonreflexive possessive pronouns in Russian is an elegant way to account for the apparently inconsistent use of reflexives. For the first- and second-person subjects, reflexives are used when the speaker does not have empathy with their referents, and for the third-person subjects, the reflexives are used when (or rather because) the speaker shows his empathy with their referents. However, it seems there is some problem in claiming that the speaker ordinarily effaces himself when he is concerned with a third-person subject. In many languages, the speaker can describe a third party's action or state objectively, without effacing himself, at least as easily as he can describe it by identifying himself with the third party. It is difficult to believe that Russian regularly forces the speaker to take the third party's point of view. There might be some mechanically syntactic aspects to the use of reflexive possessives with a clause mate subject as its antecedent.

In looking into clause mate reflexivization phenomena in Russian, one is struck with the fact that reflexivization takes place much more pervasively in the language than in English. However, it is still possible to find some evidence that it is in part controlled by the kind of constraints that we observed for English reflexivization. For example, observe the following sentences:

(14.8)   Ivan$_i$ videl etot *svoj*$_i$/**ego*$_i$ portret v gazete.
         saw   this self's   his   picture in newspaper
         'Ivan saw that picture of himself in the newspaper.'

(14.9)   Ivan$_i$ ne videl etot *svoj*$_i$/*?ego*$_i$ portret v gazete.
         not saw   that self's   his   picture in newspaper
         'Ivan did not see that picture of himself/him in the newspaper.'

The fact that *ego* 'his' is much better in (14.9) than in (14.8) suggests that something like the Awareness Condition is in operation. When the condition is not met, it has the effect of upgrading the status of the nonreflexive pronouns in Russian, instead of downgrading the acceptability of the reflexive.

Observe, further, the following sentences:

(14.10)   Ivan$_i$ byl razočarovan sluxami   o   *sebe*$_i$/**nem*$_i$.
          was disappointed rumors-with about self/him
          'Ivan was disappointed with the rumors about himself.'

(14.11)   Ivan$_i$ rešil   ujti s raboty iz-za   sluxov o   ?*sebe$_i$/*nem$_i$*.
           decided leave work   because-of rumors about self/him
           'Ivan decided to resign because of rumors about himself.'
(14.12)   Ivan$_i$ byl uvolen iz-za   sluxov o   **sebe*$_i$/*nem*$_i$.
           was fired   because-of rumors about self/him
           'Ivan was fired because of rumors about him.'

The nonreflexive pronoun is unacceptable for (14.10) and (14.11), but it is acceptable in (14.12), in which a reflexive pronoun cannot be used. This must be due to the fact that while *Ivan* is an agent or experiencer in the first two sentences, it is neither in the third. Furthermore, undoubtedly related to this fact, there is an active interaction on the part of *Ivan* toward the picture noun expression in (14.10, 11) but not in (14.12). In addition, (14.12) does not assert or imply that Ivan was aware of the rumors. These examples also show an empathy-related nature for the reflexive in Russian.

Last, observe the following sentences:

(14.13)   Ivan$_i$ napominaet ej   **svoego*$_i$/?*ego*$_i$ brata.
           reminds   her self's   his   brother
           'Ivan reminds her of his brother.'

Here is another instance in which the subject-triggered reflexivization yields an unacceptable sentence. This must be due to the fact that *Ivan* is neither agent, nor experiencer, nor benefactive. Ivan does not interact with his brother in any way. Furthermore, at the time that the sentence refers to, Ivan need have no awareness that Mary is thinking of his brother. All these factors must be responsible for the unacceptability of (14.13) with the reflexive *svoego*. The fact that (14.13) is awkward even with *ego* 'his' is perhaps related to the fact that in the following sentence, it is difficult to interpret *ego* as referring to *Ivan:*

(14.14)   Ivan napominaet Sashe   **svoego*/*ego* brata.
           reminds   to-Sasha self's   his brother
           'Ivan reminds Sasha of his brother.'

The predominant interpretation of (14.14) is that Ivan reminds Sasha (male) of 'Sasha's brother.' It is difficult to obtain the 'Ivan's brother' interpretation. Returning to (14.13), since *ej* 'to her' is feminine and *ego* 'his' masculine, there is no possibility of interpreting *ego* as coreferential with *ej*. Nevertheless, it seems that the factors that force the 'Sasha's brother' interpretation in (14.14) are also making it difficult in (14.13) to establish a coreference linkage between *ego* and *Ivan.*

Yokoyama's work, and the data presented in (14.8)–(14.14), make clear that the distribution of reflexive and nonreflexive pronouns in Russian is a phenomenon that is controlled by various empathy factors. However, there are still wide unexplored areas concerning this phenomenon in Russian, and further research is needed to formulate the conditions on more definite terms.

5.15 **Conclusion**

The concept of "point of view" is one which other scholars have used. It has, for example, been taken into account in analyzing narratives, of which there are said to be two styles: reportive and nonreportive. Reportive-style narratives are those in which a single narrator maintains his identity and describes a series of events and states as he has observed them. For example, (15.1), as a part of a reportive-style narrative, represents the narrator's judgment of the situation:

(15.1)   John was hungry.

In other words, (15.1), in this interpretation, really means (as Ross would like to indicate syntactically):

(15.2)   I tell you that John was hungry.

On the other hand, (15.1), as a part of a nonreportive-style narrative, represents not the narrator's point of view, but John's. In nonreportive style, there is no narrator present as an interpreter or observer of the situation. Example (15.1) is the direct way of representing John's internal feeling:

(15.3)   John: "I am hungry."

In this style of storytelling, the narrator in effect has the ability to become John, or any other central character in the story.

The concept of point of view, as it has been commonly utilized for analysis of literary texts, has been considered to be an all-or-nothing concept (total identification or total lack of identification) and has not been looked at as a continuum. It has been considered useful for literary analysis but irrelevant to the syntax of colloquial speech or with the theory of grammar.

As far as I know, Cantrall (1969) was the first attempt to introduce the concept of point of view in analysis of a syntactic phenomenon in colloquial speech. As I mentioned in section 4.3, Cantrall observed that "irregular reflexives" appear in clauses that represent the "viewpoint" of the speaker, his addressee, or referents mentioned in the discourse. He hypothesized that these clauses are dominated in the deep structure by a higher verb of thinking, knowing, or perceiving. For example, he assumed that the (a) sentences below are derived from the underlying structure of the corresponding (b) sentences:

(15.4)   a.   Mary represents to John some hope for himself.
          b.   Mary represents to John [what he sees as] some hope for himself.
(15.5)   a.   The fact that there is a picture of himself hanging in the post office frightens John.

b. The fact that there is a picture of [one that he would perceive/has perceived to be] himself hanging in the post office frightens John.

There is a great deal of truth in the above observation, which has been incorporated into the analysis of reflexive pronouns discussed in Chapter 4.3 as the Awareness Condition. However, Cantrall's viewpoint was of a limited nature because it was still an all-or-nothing concept. Furthermore, he did not make any attempt to generalize the concept and apply it to other areas of English syntax.

The observation that some peculiar syntactic phenomena occur in non-reportive-style narratives was first explicitly made by Kuroda (1971).[41] Kuroda observed that there are expressions in Japanese which normally require first-person subjects, such as

(15.6) a. Watasi wa   kanasii.
            I   thematic-particle sad
            'I am sad.'
        b. *Anata wa kanasii.
            you   sad-are
            'You are sad.'
        c. *Mary wa kanasii.
            'Mary is sad.'

Such expressions represent the sensations or emotions of the referent of the subject. The fact that (15.6b, c) are not acceptable in Japanese must be owing to the fact that the speaker is not expected to know what is going on in someone else's mind.

Kuroda noted that these expressions, which normally require the first-person subject, are sometimes allowable with a third-person subject, as in

(15.7) Yamadera no kane o kiite, Mary wa kanasikatta.
        mountain-temple bell hearing   was-sad
        'Hearing the bell of the mountain temple, Mary was sad.'

He observed that sentences such as (15.7) are acceptable as nonreportive-style sentences in which the narrator has adopted the point of view of the third-person subject. In the framework of the empathy perspective, (15.7) is allowable only as a sentence in which E(Mary) = 1, in which the speaker has totally identified himself with the referent of *Mary*.

Enlightening as it was, Kuroda's point-of-view analysis still did not go beyond the special narrative style—one that is heavily used in literature but not in daily conversations. Moreover, owing to the narrative style analyzed, it was similar to Cantrall's work in maintaining an all-or-nothing approach.

Still in the analysis of literature, we find a departure from the all-or-nothing concept in Uspensky's study of points of view in verbal work ("Point of View on the Phraseological Plane"), which is part of his comprehensive study of points of view in works of art (Uspensky 1973). This study is well regarded in the field of literary criticism, but its significance to linguistics is rather limited. However, it is important to us here because it recognizes that more than one point of view can be represented in the same sentence. Uspensky addresses himself to two major topics: the speaker/narrator's choice of names in referring to persons in sentences, and different modes of quotations—direct discourse, indirect discourse, quasi-direct discourse, and mixtures of the three. As an illustration of the first problem, Uspensky quotes the following example from Tolstoy's *War and Peace:*

(15.8)   "In spite of Count Bezuhov's enormous wealth, Pierre ever since he had inherited it, and had been, as people said, in receipt of an annual income of five hundred thousand, had felt much less rich than when he had been receiving an allowance of ten thousand from his father."

The same character is being called *Count Bezuhov* and *Pierre* in the same sentence. The former, which is a formal name for the character together with his title, is used in the phrase which deals with his wealth, representing the author's objective attitude toward the character; but *Pierre* is used when the point of view shifts to that of the man himself. It is important to note that Uspensky is dealing here with shifts in the narrator's point of view vis-à-vis a single person described in a sentence. This phenomenon is totally different in nature from the shifts that the Ban on Conflicting Empathy Foci, which I have hypothesized in this chapter, is intended to disallow. The latter deals with illegitimate switches in camera angles from one person to another in a single sentence.

Regarding the different modes of quotations the author can use in representing different points of view, Uspensky observes, for example, that Tolstoy, in *War and Peace,* often made deliberate use of someone else's speech by marking it in the text regularly by italics:

(15.9)   Anna Pavlovna had been coughing for the last few days: she had an attack of *la grippe,* as she said—*grippe* was then a new word only used by a few people."

Observe that (15.9) represents a mixture of Tolstoy's own speech and that of his character Anna Pavlovna.

Although Uspensky's work on points of view centering around choice of names and modes of quotation is extremely interesting and important for understanding the narrator's changing perspectives in literary pieces, it does not seem to have much to do with the *syntax* of language. It does not offer generalizations that would explain what makes some sentences unacceptable.

Finally, I want to mention a recent work on a hypothesis that is closely related to the empathy perspective but has its own independent domain of research and application; I refer to the work of Kamio (1979) on "the speaker's territory of information." In this paper, Kamio observes that Japanese is a language which requires the speaker to overtly mark a sentence with respect to whether the information that is represented in it belongs to his territory or not. For the present purpose, it is enough to say that only those events, actions, and states that the speaker has direct knowledge of (for example, via direct observation) belong to his territory of information. Kamio observes that Japanese requires the speaker to represent information that does not belong to his territory by using nondirect forms such as *rasii* 'it appears that,' *soo da* 'I hear that,' *daroo* 'I suppose,' and so on, at sentence-final position. Thus, observe the following sentences:

(15.10)   a. *Anata wa kanasii. (= 15.6b)
                'You are sad.'
            b. *Mary wa kanasii. (= 15.6c)
                'Mary is sad.'

Kamio hypothesizes that these sentences are unacceptable because none of these nondirect forms appear, even though the speaker expresses information that he cannot have direct knowledge of.

Kamio's concept of "territory of information" extends far beyond the emotive expressions, exemplified in (15.10), that Kuroda has focused on. As Kamio observes, even expressions such as

(15.11)   Taroo wa byooki da.
                     sick   is
            'Taroo is sick.'

require that the speaker have direct knowledge of Taroo's sickness. Even if Taroo's mother has told the speaker that Taroo is sick, or even if Taroo himself has called him up and told him that he is sick, the speaker still is not justified in treating the information as belonging to his territory and therefore is not allowed to convey the information to others using (15.11). In order to be able to use (15.11), he must have had a direct observation of Taroo's sickness, such as having seen him in bed, or having seen him vomit, and so on. Kamio's work promises to have wide ramifications not only in syntactic and semantic analysis of Japanese, but also in sociolinguistic analysis of the language because what kind of information belongs to whose territory involves interpersonal and intercommunity relationships.

There is clearly some commonality between the territory of information perspective and the empathy perspective. Given a piece of information that belongs to the territory of a person with whom the speaker is empathizing and a piece of information that belongs to the territory of a person with whom the speaker is not empathizing, it is safe to assume that the former would be easier for the speaker to treat as if it belonged to his own territory than the latter would be. However, sentences such as the following firmly establish that the empathy perspective and the territory of information perspective belong to two separate planes:

(15.12)   a.   Yuube, Hanako ga kanozyo no kateikyoosi to   eiga o mi ni itta.
last-night   her   tutor   with movie see to went
'Last night, Hanako went to see a movie with her tutor.'

   b.   Yuube, Hanako ga kanozyo no kateikyoosi to   eiga o mi ni itta
last-night   her   tutor   with movie see to went
soo da.
I-hear
'I hear that last night, Hanako went to see a movie with her tutor.'

Example (15.12a) is possible if the speaker witnessed Hanako's going out to see a movie with her tutor or was informed of it by Hanako at its inception. It is impossible otherwise. If Hanako told the speaker about it after (but not before) she had seen the movie, the speaker would not be able to use (15.12a) to describe the event. He would have to use (15.12b) and explicitly mark the proposition as not belonging to his territory. This is in spite of the fact that the speaker, by referring to Hanako as Hanako and to the tutor as Hanako's tutor, overtly signifies that he is describing the event from Hanako's camera angle rather than from her tutor's. In other words, the empathy relationship E(Hanako) > E(her tutor) in (15.12a) and (15.12b) is independent of the problem of whether the information about Hanako's viewing a movie with her tutor belongs to the speaker's territory, as in (15.12a), or not, as in (15.12b).

As I have shown above, other scholars have made use of point of view and related concepts for linguistic analysis. However, as far as I know, Kuno and Kaburaki (1975, 1977), on which this chapter has been partly based, was the first attempt to build a theory of point of view as part and parcel of a theory of grammar, and to apply it to wide varieties of *syntactic* phenomena in daily speech. Although it represents considerable development from this previous work, the analysis presented in this chapter is of a preliminary nature; undoubtedly, many phenomena will be uncovered in the future which would constitute counterexamples to the specific empathy-based principles as they have been stated in this chapter. At least some revision and introduction of new principles can be expected. However, there does not seem to be any doubt that the empathy perspective as a whole will stay intact, and will continue to play a crucial role in providing natural explanations for a wide range of otherwise mysterious linguistic phenomena.

6 Conclusions

In this book, I have examined the behavior of pronouns, reflexives, reciprocals, and many other syntactic phenomena, and have shown that the conditions for their use cannot be stated without recourse to two nonsyntactic perspectives, the direct discourse perspective and the empathy perspective. I have often called to the reader's attention the kind of mistaken syntactic generalizations that have been made by scholars who have not had access to these perspectives or who have chosen to underestimate them. To the extent that my analyses of these phenomena are correct, I have demonstrated the usefulness of these perspectives for analyzing "syntactic" phenomena. I am not, naturally, claiming that every syntactic phenomenon should be described in the framework of these perspectives. Given a syntactic phenomenon, there is no telling a priori whether either the direct discourse or the empathy perspective is involved. What I am claiming here is that having these two perspectives at our disposal, and being familiar with the kind of discourse factors that interact with syntax, results in an important advantage; it guards us against making single-minded syntactic generalizations. It has been the aim of this book to show that syntactic and nonsyntactic factors interact, and that both bear on the acceptability of certain structures.

As I discussed at the end of the Introduction, the direct discourse and empathy perspectives are only two of many functional perspectives that have been identified and studied thus far. For example, the functional sentence perspective, which examines sentences in discourse from the points of view of "a flow of information," "presupposition," "topic and comment," and so on, is well known to be an indispensable perspective for analysis of numerous syntactic patterns in many languages. In this book, I have demonstrated the need for this perspective only in my discussion of extraction from picture nouns in Chapter 1 (cf. secs. 1.2 and 1.3). I do not wish to imply that this issue is less important than the direct discourse and empathy perspectives, and in fact, I originally planned to include this perspective and many other topics relating to my research in this book. However, I have had to give up this plan owing to time and space limitations. I leave it for a future book.

Many syntacticians persist in the belief that, given a "syntactic" phenomenon, they can isolate the syntactic factors that are involved in it without knowing what nonsyntactic factors are involved. I hope that this book has added to the ever-mounting proofs that they are wrong. As I have amply demonstrated, what constitutes the acceptability status of sentences involving a given syntactic pattern is very often the result of the interaction of numerous factors, both syntactic and nonsyntactic. Those who are not familiar with what kind of nonsyntactic factors exist in what kind of phenomena are apt to attempt to capture nonsyntactic facts by mistaken syntactic generalizations, and to ignore true syntactic facts by mistakenly considering them as performance/discourse facts. Should this book succeed in making some of these syntacticians more cautious and less liable to make blind syntactic generalizations, it will have achieved its goal.

Notes

Chapter 1

1. See Moravscik and Wirth (1980) and Newmeyer (1980) for outlines of some of these theories.

2. Facts described in this section and the analysis which is proposed (including analogies to Necker cube interpretations) are from Kuno (1972a, 1974a).

3. What I have called "contextual meaning" here is somewhat different from, although clearly related to, what is often referred to as "context-dependent meaning." The latter concept is used in discussion, for example, of the referents of pronouns in sentences such as

(i)   John hates his mother, and Bill hates his father.

and in discussion of the intentionality or unintentionality of actions in sentences such as

(ii)   John hit the wall.

See Lakoff (1970) and Bosch (1983) for interesting discussion of this latter concept.

4. The observation that it is not possible to obtain mixed interpretations for sentences such as (1.9) was first made by Lakoff (1970).

5. Right-Node Raising is a process in which the common rightmost constituent in conjoined clauses is extracted from the clauses and attached to the right of the topmost sentence structure. Thus, Right-Node Raising applied to

(i)   [[John loved Mary]$_S$ but [Tom hated Mary]$_S$]$_S$

yields

(ii)   [[[John loved]$_S$ but [Tom hated]$_S$]$_S$ Mary]$_S$

6. Examples (1.15b) and (1.16b) involve a process, sometimes called *Respectively-*Transformation (cf. Kuno 1970) which extracts from conjoined clauses structurally identical but lexically different rightmost constituents and attaches them to the right of the topmost sentence structure by conjoining them with *and*. This process applied to:

(i)   [John [loved Mary]$_{VP}$] and [Tom [hated Jane]$_{VP}$]

yields

(ii)   [John and Tom] [[loved Mary]$_{VP}$ and [hated Jane]$_{VP}$], respectively.

The same process applied to (1.15a) conjoins the two rightmost NPs (*a policeman* and *a fireman*), attaches them to the topmost sentence structure, and yields (1.15b). Observe that this process applies to *a policeman* and *a fireman* in spite of the fact that the former is [object], and the latter [agent].

The same process applied to (1.16a) yields:

(iii)   The children and the parents respectively liked the teachers [object] and were liked by the teachers [experiencer].

Right-Node Raising then applies to the rightmost common constituent *the teachers* of the conjoined VPs and attaches it to the topmost sentence structure, yielding (1.16b). Note that this extraction process (i.e., Right-Node Raising) has ignored the difference in semantic cases between the first and second tokens of *the teachers*.

7. For most people, the first interpretation is one with the surface ABCD facing them. It seems that this preference is due to the fact that we are more accustomed to looking at a boxlike object from above than from below. (I am indebted to Charles K. Bergman for this observation.)

8. I am indebted to Terry Langendoen for this observation (personal communication, 1972).

9. The fact that the interpretation of a linguistically ambiguous element is more stable than that of a visually ambiguous figure, and that it is not subject to a constant oscillation that characterizes the latter, is perhaps due to the fact that the linguistic element, once parsed and understood (in one way), is stored in memory in an unambiguous formal (semantic) representation. Since there is no ambiguity concerning that element in this representation, there is no switching to the second interpretation as time passes. I am indebted to Akio Kamio for this observation.

10. This section is based on section 1 of my earlier paper (Kuno 1980).

11. In Chomsky's government and binding theory (see Chomsky 1981), the Specified Subject Condition is allowed to apply only to reflexives and reciprocals, and therefore it does not apply to (2.2b). There does not seem to be any explanation for the unacceptability of (2.2b) in Chomsky (1981). Fiengo and Higginbotham (1981) and Gueron (1981) assume that there is a Specificity Condition, i.e., that extraction from specific NPs is prohibited. They claim that NPs with possessive NPs in determiner position are specific and block extraction. My discussion in this section will show that the Specificity Condition is also difficult to maintain.

In this section, I will use Chomsky (1973) because the unacceptability of sentences such as (2.2b) has been discussed most extensively in that framework.

12. In fact, the fronting of *who* both in (2.4a) and (2.4b) violates Chomsky's Subjacency constraint. I will discuss this constraint fully in sec. 1.3. Until then, we will assume that (2.1b) does not involve violation of any constraint and that (2.2b) involves violation of only the Specified Subject Condition.

13. I am indebted to a participant in my course on functional syntax at the 1977 Linguistic Institute, University of Hawaii at Manoa, where I discussed similar but less natural counterexamples to the Specified Subject Constraint.

14. I am indebted to Yukio Otsu for this sentence.

15. The information that a given element in a sentence in discourse represents is old and predictable if the information is recoverable, with a high degree of reliability, from the preceding discourse context even when that part of the sentence is garbled with noise, and it is new and unpredictable if otherwise. For example, observe the following discourse:

(i)   Speaker A: What does John like?
       Speaker B: He likes fish.

In (iB), *He likes* represents old, predictable information because even if that part of the sentence is garbled with noise, it is recoverable from the preceding context (iA). This is exactly why it does not have to show up in Speaker B's response. On the other hand, *fish* in (iB) represents new, unpredictable information. If this part of the sentence is garbled, there is no way for Speaker A to determine what it is.

Predictability/unpredictability is a matter of degree. In this book, I will use the expression "the focus of expression x" to refer to the element in x that represents highly unpredictable information. See Prince (1981) for different definitions of the concepts related to 'old' and 'new' information that have been used in discourse analysis.

16. Japanese, unlike English, allows relativization of constituents in adverbial clauses, as well as those in doubly embedded relative clauses. For example, observe the following sentences:

(i)   a.   [Sono kodomo ga kawaigatte ita] neko ga sinde simatta.
              the   child   loved   cat   died
              'The cat that the child loved died.'
       b.   Kore wa [[Ø kawaigatte ita] neko ga sinde simatta] kawaisoo na
              this   loved   cat   died   poor
              kodomo desu.
              child   is
              'This is a poor child who (lit.) the cat that (he) loved died.'

See Kuno (1973, 1978a) for discussion of relativization out of these types of constructions.

17. The suggestion that what is relativized in English is the topic of the relative clause was first made by Gundell (1974). Erteschik-Shir (1973) proposed the concept of 'bridge,' which is similar to that of 'topic,' to account for extraction facts in Danish, English, and Japanese.

18. Grosu gives contexts which would make sentences such as (2.22) acceptable but does not explain why such contexts make them acceptable. The hyper-topic explanation given here is mine.

19. The acceptability judgment assigned to this sentence is Bach and Horn's (1976). There are situations which would make this sentence readily acceptable, which will be discussed below.

20. Thus, according to Chomsky, the unacceptability of sentences such as

(i)   *Who did you buy Mary's portrait of?

is due to violations of two conditions: Specified Subject Condition, which we discussed in the preceding section, and Subjacency, which is given in (3.6).

21. For many speakers, (3.7b) is less than perfect, but I am here representing Bach and Horn's acceptability judgment. It is clear that all speakers find (3.7b) considerably better than (3.8b).

22. The *it*-cleft pattern behaves in the same way as *Wh*-Q Movement. For example, observe the following sentences:

(i)   a.   John wrote a book about physics.
       b.   It was physics that John wrote a book about.
       c.   It was about physics that John wrote a book.
(ii)   a.   They destroyed a book about physics.
       b.   *It was physics that they destroyed a book about.
       c.   *It was about physics that they destroyed a book.

Bach and Horn would claim that (ib) and (ic) are both acceptable because *about physics* can be extraposed out of the picture noun in (ia), while (iib) and (iic) are both unacceptable because *about physics* in (iia) cannot be extraposed out of the picture noun. This parallelism also dissolves when we examine further data:

(iii) a. I borrowed a book about physics.
       b. ?It was physics that I borrowed a book about.
       c. *It was about physics that I borrowed a book.
(iv)   a. I bought a book about physics.
       b. It was physics that I bought a book about.
       c. *It was about physics that I bought a book.

In the above, the (b) sentences are only slightly awkward, if ever, while the (c) sentences are totally unacceptable.

23. For many speakers, it is difficult to prepose *about*-phrases:

(i)   ?/??About whom was the teacher asking you for so long?

However, for the same speakers, (3.9b), (3.10b), and (3.11b) are considerably worse than (3.7b).

24. Incidentally, Koster (1978) correctly rejects Bach and Horn's and Chomsky's restructuring analysis, but for the wrong reason. He observes that "the very restructuring rules that Chomsky invokes to allow extraction have in general just the opposite effect in that they make extraction impossible" and attributes this observation to Huybregts (1976):

(i)   a. He saw a book about farming, yesterday.
       b. He saw a book, yesterday, about farming.
       c. *What did he see a book, yesterday, about Ø?

This is a misdirected criticism on the restructuring analysis because the unacceptability of (ic) is independent of restructuring. There is a rule in English which says that a preposition cannot be left dangling after a major break. Thus, the following (c) sentence is also unacceptable.

(ii)   a. He talked to Mary and many others yesterday.
       b. He talked, yesterday, to Mary and many others.
       c. *Who did he talk, yesterday, to Ø?

Thus, (ic) is unacceptable for the same reason that (iic) is unacceptable. Since the restructuring analysis assumes that extraposition can take place vacuously without requiring an intervening element after extraposition between the original head NP and the PP, Koster's counter-argument against the restructuring analysis is ineffective in those cases. The proponents of the restructuring analysis can easily claim that

(iii)   What did he buy a book about?

is acceptable because there is no major break between *a book* and *about*.

25. See Sperber and Wilson (1982) for a definition of relevance on the basis of contextual implications, and for a characterization of "degrees of relevance" in terms of number of contextual implications and amount of processing involved in deriving them.

26. As far as I know, Bierman (1972) was the first to note that this fact is related to the extractability or unextractability of the object of picture nouns.

27. Example (3.25) could follow (3.24b), but it would be as a side remark to let the hearer know who John Irving is, and a real continuation of (3.24b), which can be about the book (but not about the author) or about what happened as a consequence, for example, is still to come.

Chapter 2

1. Or, alternatively, Ross's formulation would be consistent with the assumption that there is no rule of adverb preposing or postposing but that there is a base-generated position for adverbs both at the end and beginning of the sentence: $S \rightarrow$ (Adv) NP VP (Adv.).

2. There are speakers who find (2.1a) to be less than perfect, and (2.1d) even less acceptable. I will attempt to account for this fact later on in this chapter. However, even those speakers consider (2.1a, d) more acceptable than (2.1b, c).

3. For reasons that I do not have space here to reproduce, Ross hypothesized that pronominalization must apply both cyclically and obligatorily.

4. See (1.17) for the definition of the concept of "k-command."

5. Jackendoff's system works equally well if the *wh*-expression is fronted to clause-initial position in the S_2 cycle via successive cyclic movement.

6. Alternatively, if it is assumed that Lasnik's formulation applies not to the surface structure, but to the structure that has not undergone stylistic rules such as adverb fronting, it would apply to (5.2a) and (5.2b), and it would correctly predict the acceptability status of (5.9a) and (5.9b) because (5.9a) would derive from a structure (i.e., (5.2b)) that has been marked unacceptable, and (5.9b) from a structure (i.e., (5.2a)) that has been marked acceptable. However, this approach would fail to account for the acceptability of (ia):

(i)   a.   Near the girl John$_i$ was talking with, he$_i$ found a snake.
        b.   Near the girl he$_i$ was talking with, John$_i$ found a snake.

7. For example, S and $\overline{S}$ belong to the same category type. Quite strangely, as I will point out later, Reinhart's analysis requires that $\overline{\overline{S}}$ not be regarded as belonging to the same category types as S and $\overline{S}$.

8. In Lasnik's framework, the distinction between S and $\overline{S}$ does not exist. Therefore, for the purpose of applying his condition to structures which distinguish between S and $\overline{S}$, his cyclical nodes must be expanded to include $\overline{S}$.

9. In Reinhart's formulation, in order for NP_1 and NP_2 to be regarded as coreferential, it must be that both left-to-right and right-to-left applications of her rule are free from violation of coreference interpretation. In (6.6b), NP_1 does not c-command NP_2 and therefore, her rule does not apply in the left-to-right application. But this does not allow coindexing of the two NPs because the right-to-left application blocks a coreferential interpretation.

10. See sec. 2.12 for discussion of the idiolects in which (6.7a) is nearly acceptable.

11. The following is Postal's formulation of the constraint: "Given a transformation T which moves NP and a phrase marker P to which T is otherwise applicable, T cannot apply to P if the operation of T on P will result in one NP in P crossing another with which it is coreferential, where these NPs are clause mates" (1971, p. 68).

12. Note that Reinhart's c-command formulation can correctly predict the impossibility of a coreferential interpretation between *whose* and *he* for (7.11a) but not for (7.11b). This is because *he* c-commands *whose* via a projection of S to $\overline{S}$ in the surface structure of (7.11a) but not in that of (7.11b).

13. We will discuss this problem further in the next section.

14. In fact, as will be discussed in sec. 2.11, Chomsky revises the definition of "governing category" for other purposes, but this revision causes a problem with the coindexing of *John* and *his* in (8.4b).

15. In Chomsky (1981) and Chomsky (1982), there is a considerable degree of vacillation as to where the binding conditions apply. For example, observe the following quotations:

> We have so far been assuming that the binding theory applies at the LF-level. Another possibility is that it applies at S-structure (N.B. the S-structure is a structure that obtains after application of *Wh*-Q and *Wh*-Relative Movements, which are one and the same rule in GB theory, but before application of "stylistic" rules such as Subject-Aux Inversion). . . . There are a number of considerations that suggest that in fact the binding theory does apply at S-structure. . . . Therefore these examples provide *prima facie* evidence that the binding theory applies at S-structure, a conclusion that I will now adopt. (Chomsky 1981, pp. 196–97)

> While certain questions remain open, I think the weight of evidence currently suggests that the binding theory applies at the S-structure level. (Chomsky 1982, p. 7)

> In forthcoming work, Youssef Aoun presents evidence that the binding theory also applies at the LF level. . . . (Chomsky 1982, p. 91)

> Therefore, the binding theory holds at LF' (N.B. LF' is a representation that obtains after the rule of Predication, applying to the LF-representation, identifies the index of the head noun and that of the relative pronoun). (Chomsky 1982, p. 94)

> There is good reason to suppose that the binding theory applies at S-structure. . . . If the binding theory applies at S-structure and at LF', then it is plausible to suppose that it also applies at LF, hence, at all syntactic levels apart from D-structure (N.B. i.e., deep structure). (Chomsky 1982, p. 94)

In the present section, I will first examine some crucial sentences in the framework in which the binding conditions apply to LF-representation, simply because Chomsky (1981) discusses those or similar sentences in that framework, and not in the framework in which the binding conditions would apply to S-structure. Later on in this section, I will discuss the same sentences in the latter framework.

16. Another problem with the binding conditions is that they predict that pronouns and reflexives show complementary distributions. But there are many instances in which they can co-occur. For example, observe the following sentences:

(i)   a.   John$_i$ hid the book behind him$_i$.
      b.   John$_i$ hid the book behind himself$_i$.
(ii) a.   John$_i$ put the blanket under him$_i$.
      b.   John$_i$ put the blanket under himself$_i$.

I will discuss how to deal with the above problem in secs. 2.9–2.11.

17. The rule which is responsible for the fronting of *near John* in (8.21) must be a syntactic rule and not a "stylistic rule" in GB theory because it changes coreference possibilities of NPs:

(i)   a.   *He$_i$ found a snake near the girl John$_i$ was talking with.
      b.   Near the girl John$_i$ was talking with, he$_i$ found a snake.

If the assumption that a rule cannot be a "stylistic" one if it changes quantifier interpretations and NP reference possibilities is to be taken seriously, which it must be, not many rules can remain in this category. For example, observe the following:

(ii)   Subject-Predicate Inversion
    a.   The news that Mary$_i$ had been exonerated was not revealed to her$_i$.
    b.   ??Not revealed to her was the news that Mary$_i$ had been exonerated.
cf.   c.   Not revealed to Mary$_i$ was the news that she$_i$ had been exonerated.
(iii)   Relative Clause Extraposition
    a.   The news that Mary$_i$ had been exonerated finally reached her$_i$.
    b.   ??The news finally reached her$_i$ that Mary$_i$ had been exonerated.
cf.   c.   The news finally reached Mary$_i$ that she$_i$ had been exonerated.
(iv)   VP Fronting
    a.   *She$_i$ wasn't fond of everyone Mary$_i$ came in touch with.
    b.   Fond of everyone Mary$_i$ came in touch with she$_i$ wasn't.
(v)   NP Fronting
    a.   John$_i$'s mother loves him$_i$ dearly.
    b.   *Him$_i$, John$_i$'s mother loves dearly.

18. There are sentences of the pattern of (9.15) and (9.16) that allow both the reflexive and pronominal versions, with totally different semantics. For example, observe the following sentences:

(i)   a.   John$_i$ has confidence in himself$_i$.
    b.   John$_i$ has confidence in him$_i$.

Example (ia) means that John trusts himself, while (ib) means that John is a person who is confident. Similarly, observe the following pairs of discourses, which I owe to Elanah Kutik (personal communication, 1981):

(ii)   a.   Sidney$_i$ is self-deprecating. He$_i$ has a great deal of hatred in/of himself$_i$. (the emotion is directed towards Sidney.)
    b.   Sidney$_i$ is a bitter person. He$_i$ has a great deal of hatred in him$_i$. (i.e., Sidney hates other people.)
(iii)   a.   My cousin Mabel$_i$ is absolutely eccentric. She$_i$ has the craziest beliefs in herself$_i$. (about her own self, her abilities and so forth.)
    b.   My cousin Mabel$_i$ is absolutely eccentric. She$_i$ has the wildest beliefs in her$_i$. (i.e., about the world, other people, etc.)

In all the above examples, when a reflexive pronoun is used, its referent is the target of the state represented by the expression "have X in," while when a pronoun is used, its referent is not a target of the state involved.

The (a) and (b) sentences above have different constituent structures (I am indebted to J. McCawley for this observation):

(iv)   a.   Confidence in himself$_i$/*him$_i$ is the one thing that John$_i$ has.
    b.   The confidence in himself$_i$/*him$_i$ that John$_i$ has pleases me.

These examples show that in the (a) sentences in (i)–(iii), *NP in himself* is a constituent, while in the (b) sentences, *NP in him* does not form a constituent. However, this distinction in constituent structures is not directly responsible for the distribution of reflexive and non-reflexive pronouns. In (9.10), for example, *the letter* and the prepositional phrase that follows it do not form a constituent, but a reflexive rather than a pronominal is required.

19. The fact that (9.24a) implies an intentional action while (9.24b) implies a nonintentional action can be seen clearly when we insert *accidentally:*

    (i)   a.   ??John$_i$ accidentally spilled the gasoline all over himself$_i$.

           b.   John$_i$ accidentally spilled the gasoline all over him$_i$.

20. See Kuno (1983) for comparison of this constraint in English with a similar, but crucially different constraint for French nonclitic reflexive pronouns (*lui-même, elle-même,* etc.) proposed by Zribi-Hertz (1980).

21. It goes without saying that the above semantic filter applies to reflexives that have satisfied certain syntactic conditions, which will be discussed in detail in sec. 2.11.

22. The hypothesis that surface nonnominative pronouns are ambiguous between [−reflexive] and [+reflexive], which, as far as I know, first appeared in Kuno (1972c), has since been independently proposed by at least two others. Chomsky (1981) hypothesizes that in sentences such as

    (i)   John lost his way.

in which possessive pronouns must be coreferential with the subject, the possessive pronouns are anaphors (i.e., [+reflexive] in my framework). But he assumes that in

    (ii)   John lost his book.

his is a regular pronoun regardless of whether it is coreferential with *John* or not. Thus, in Chomsky's framework, anaphoric pronouns have extremely limited usage (limited to possessive pronouns as they appear in idiomatic expressions such as (i)).

Bouchard (1982) assumes that reflexive forms, rather than pronouns, are ambiguous between core reflexives and "fake" reflexives, or pronouns in disguise. He assumes that reflexives in sentences such as

    (i)   a.   John shaved himself.

           b.   John is proud of himself.

are core reflexives, but those in

    (ii)   a.   John turned the argument against himself.

           b.   John hid the book behind himself.

are in fact pronouns. The difference between (ib) and (ii), according to him, lies in the assumption that while the preposition has been reanalyzed with preceding elements in the former, it is not the case with the latter. Underlying this assumption is the claim that core reflexives appear only in direct object position. Thus, he does not attempt to account for the sometimes possible and sometimes impossible alternations between the surface reflexive and surface pronominal forms in sentences such as (10.1) and (10.2) other than noting that *himself* in these sentences is not a core reflexive.

In a somewhat different vein, McCawley (1976) proposes that $[\Delta]_{NP}$, an "empty NP" in Jackendoff's interpretive framework (cf. sec. 2.4), is ambiguous between [−reflexive] and [+reflexive]. This is in order to correctly interpret (ib), which represents the structure corresponding to (ia):

(i)   a.   Larry kicked himself, but Jake didn't.
     b.   [[Lary [kick]$_V$ [himself]$_{NP}$ but [Jake not [Δ]$_V$ [Δ]$_{NP}$]

Unless Δ is marked as [+reflexive], Jackendoff's interpretive rule that assigns disjoint indices between *Jake* and *him* in *Jake kicked him* would assign disjoint indices to *Jake* and Δ and would make it impossible to obtain the most obvious interpretation of (ia), in which the second clause means "Jake kicked himself."

23. Example (10.10b) is perfectly acceptable for Lakoff and many other speakers, but there are some speakers who consider the sentence awkward or marginal. This seems to be due to a conflict between the discourse function of fronting, which implies contrast, and stressibility of pronouns. The reason for fronting *near him* from an inside-VP position to sentence-initial position must be to give a contrastive implication to the phrase. On the other hand, the pronoun *him* is not easily stressible: a stress on *him* would force a noncoreferential interpretation between *him* and *John*. Note that this is true even for (10.10a) when *him* is stressed:

(i)   John found a snake near HIM.

In (i), *John* and *HIM* can receive only a disjoint reference interpretation. Thus, the awkwardness or marginality of (10.10b) for these speakers can be accounted for as resulting from the above conflict. In order to represent a contrast that is intended, an emphatic reflexive must be used:

(ii)   a.   John found a snake near HIMSELF.
      b.   Near HIMSELF, John found a snake.

24. There are speakers for whom (10.21b) becomes nearly acceptable with heavy contrastive stress on *sister*. I will return to this problem later in sec. 2.12.

25. It is generally assumed that *each other* is conditioned more or less purely by syntax, and is free from the kind of discourse factors that influence the use of reflexives. However, there are speakers who consider the sentences in (ii) marginal:

(i)   a.   John and Mary watched over each other's children.
     b.   John and Mary carried each other's trunks.
     c.   John and Mary patted each other's heads.
     d.   John and Mary cried on each other's shoulders.
(ii)   a.   ??John and Mary saw each other's children on the street.
     b.   ??John and Mary dislike each other's spouses.
     c.   ??John and Mary took a nap in each other's rooms.
     d.   ??John and Mary died on each other's birthdays.

It is clear that (i) and (ii) cannot be distinguished on the basis of phrase structure configuration. A semantic comparison of (i) and (ii) shows that *each other* sentences of the pattern under discussion are acceptable to the extent that the actions or states represented by the sentences *directly* involve the referent of *each other* as their "target." For example, compare (ia) and (iia). Example (ia) is acceptable, not as a sentence which objectively describes what happened, but as a sentence which describes the situation in which there was an agreement between John and Mary to the effect "I will watch over your child, so you watch over mine." In this sense, (ia) involves "active reciprocity" between John and Mary. On the other hand, in (iia), John's seeing Mary's child and her seeing John's child was accidental, and there is no "active reciprocity." Hence the marginality of (iia). Example (iib) is acceptable to those speakers who can visualize the situation in which John is constantly telling Mary that he doesn't like her spouse, and vice versa, but marginal otherwise. Example (iic) is acceptable to those speakers who can read into this sentence an agreement between John and Mary for swapping rooms for the purpose of taking a nap but is marginal otherwise. Finally, (iid) is acceptable if it is intended to mean planned timing for John and Mary's deaths but marginal otherwise. There are many speakers who consider (ii) as acceptable as (i). These speakers simply do not have the semantic constraint mentioned above for the use of *each other* in the possessive case.

26. The reason that the concept of c-command is inappropriate for the above chain-of-command principle is that it would block *John* in the following sentence from serving as a controller for the reflexive:

(i)   John showed Bill a picture of himself.

Note that *John* c-commands *Bill*, but *Bill* does not c-command *John* in the structure corresponding to (i). Therefore, the principle (11.7) will apply to (i) and determine that only *Bill* could be the controller for the reflexive. On the other hand, if k-command is used as the command concept for (11.7), the principle does not apply to (i) because *John* and *Bill* are in a symmetric command relationship. Similarly, the concept of S-command is inappropriate because it cannot deal with the picture-noun context under discussion:

(ii)   *John looked at Mary's picture of himself.

Note that in (ii), *Mary* S-commands *John*, and therefore, the chain-of-command principle cannot block derivation of the sentence.

27. *John* would c-command *himself* only if, at the time of application of Condition A, it were in subject position (i.e., *John's criticism of himself*), or only if an extremely ad hoc restructuring analysis that would incorporate the preposition into N (i.e., *criticism-from/by*) were introduced. The former solution would contradict the assumption made for (11.11b) that *(from/by) John* does not constitute an accessible SUBJECT in this sentence.

28. Another factor that might be involved in the contrast between (11.11b) and (11.12b) is the relative order of the two prepositional phrases *of NP* and *from/by NP* in the basic word order:

(i)   Mary had never been willing to listen to criticism of herself from/by John.
(ii)   ??Mary had never been willing to listen to criticism of himself from/by John.

In (i), which corresponds to (11.11b), the reflexive follows its antecedent *Mary*, while in (ii), the reflexive precedes its antecedent *John*. I am indebted to Akio Kamio for this observation.

29. Such a restructuring analysis has been proposed by Williams (1980) and Hornstein and Weinberg (1981).

30. It might be argued that sentences of the pattern of (11.16a, b) can be handled by assuming that there is a small clause in the sense of Stowell (1981) in underlying structure:

(i)   a.   [John found a snake [, PRO near him]]
       b.   [John put a blanket [, PRO under him]]

Let us assume, for a moment, that "?" is an S in these structures, with PRO as SUBJECT. Then Condition B would simply require that *him* be free within this small clause, thus allowing for the possibility of coindexing *him* with *John*.

The above approach would have difficulty in accounting for the following sentences, in which full sentences corresponding to the putative small clauses are unacceptable.

(ii)   a.   John$_i$ pulled the rope toward him$_i$.
        b.   [John pulled the rope [PRO toward him]]
        c.   *The rope was toward him.

Whatever semantic filter that would mark (c) as anomalous would mark the small clause in (b) as anomalous.

Furthermore, observe the following sentences:

(iii)   a.   John$_i$ found a snake near him$_i$.
        b.   ??John$_i$ found a snake near himself$_i$.
(iv)   a.   John found a snake in the basket.
        b.   This is the basket which John found a snake in.

For many speakers, (iiib) is marginal. In the framework of the small clause analysis, this must mean that *find* cannot take a plain locative expression, but must take a small clause that contains a locative expression. Now, observe (ivb). This sentence, which is acceptable, violates Chomsky's Subjacency Condition because *which* has been fronted crossing over two S boundaries, one of which is for the small clause by assumption. Therefore, the small clause analysis based on the assumption that "?" is an S cannot be taken seriously unless the condition for Subjacency is more satisfactorily stated.

What makes the above small clause analysis even less tenable is the fact, pointed out by Bouchard (1982, pp. 84–85), that indicates that the small clause analysis leads to internal contradictions. Observe the following sentences (the acceptability judgments are Bouchard's):

(v)   a.   *They saw snakes near themselves.
        b.   They saw snakes near them.
        c.   They saw snakes near each other.

The fact that (a) is unacceptable and (b) acceptable, as was the case with (iiia, b), would necessitate an obligatory "small clause" analysis for the pattern "*see* + NP + PP." But the fact that (c) is acceptable indicates that the underlying structure does not have [PRO *near each other*], but simply a prepositional phrase. But then, there is no explanation as to why this option of not inserting a PRO in the structure is not available for a reflexive in (va).

In the above, I have assumed that "?" for a small clause is an S. Alternatively, let us assume, as Stowell (1981) in fact did, that small clauses are of the same category as their heads. Then, "?" in (ia) and (ib) is a PP, which is not a governing category. Since the governing category for *him* would thus be the S for the entire sentences, Condition B would apply and would erroneously block the coindexing of *him* with *John*. It does not seem that the small clause analysis can be invoked to solve the dilemma that GB theory finds itself in.

31. Thus, in Chomsky's framework, given

(i)   a.   John lost his way.
        b.   John lost his book.

Condition A would establish coreference between *John* and *his* (an anaphor) for (ia), according to the assumption that *his* (an anaphor) does not have an accessible SUBJECT within the NP for *his way,* while the coreferential interpretation between *John* and *his* for (ib) is established by default, i.e., by virtue of the fact that there are no conditions that would block the coindexing of the two NPs (note that Condition B, combined with Huang's hypothesis that the SUBJECT accessibility requirement does not apply to pronouns, says that *his* in (ib) must be free within the NP for *his book,* thus allowing for the possibility for coindexing it with *John*). This approach requires unnecessary complications—it requires (i) specifications of the distribution of possessive pronouns as anaphors and (ii) the assumption that the SUBJECT accessibility requirement does not apply to regular possessive pronouns. Note that once it is recognized that surface possessive pronouns are sometimes anaphors, it is best to let such anaphoric pronouns appear freely in deep structure. Thus, both (ia) and (ib) would have two different underlying structures, one with *his* as pronominal and the other with *him* as anaphor. Condition B would then establish disjoint reference between *John* and the pronominal *his,* while Condition A would establish obligatory coreference between *John* and *his* as anaphor. (Note that in this framework, NP is not a governing category.) Then, pragmatics would filter out (ia) with *his* as a pronominal because one does not lose somebody else's way. In this latter approach, which is being proposed in this section, there are no ad hoc conditions necessary, and the same rule (i.e., Condition A) is responsible for the coreferential interpretation of (ia) and (ib).

32. In GB theory, sentences that involve fronting of NPs are derived not from the structure with the NPs in the original position but from the structure that contains relative clauses. Thus, (ia), in this theory, is derived from the structure informally represented in (ib):

(i)   a.   Mary, John likes.
        b. $[_{\bar{s}}$ Mary $[_{\bar{s}}$ COMP $[_{S}$ John likes who]]]
        c. $[_{\bar{s}}$ Mary $[_{\bar{s}}$ who(m)$_i$ $[_{S}$ John likes $[e]_i]]$

It is claimed that the *wh*-expression gets fronted into the COMP position by a general rule for fronting *wh*-words, and it then gets deleted by a general rule for deleting relative pronouns in the accusative case.

33. Reinhart (1981) naturally considers sentences such as (11.32b) and (11.33b) acceptable. Solan (1983), on the other hand, rejects such sentences and proposes the following constraint:

(i)   *Backward Anaphora Restriction* (Solan): Pro$_i$ . . . NP$_i$ is impossible if
        (i)   Pro c-commands NP; or
        (ii)   Pro and NP are within the same minimal S, and Pro d-commands (= k-command) NP.

34. The claim that there are two rules that apply to R-expressions, one applying in reflexive contexts and the other applying in nonreflexive contexts, is found in Jackendoff (1972), Reinhart (1981), and Solan (1983). Jackendoff assumes that both rules operate under the S-command condition, while Reinhart assumes that both apply under the c-command condition. Solan, as mentioned in n. 33, assumes that the rule applying in reflexive contexts uses k-command and the one applying in nonreflexive contexts uses c-command. Solan's reflexive context rule applies only for backward anaphora, but it should be generalized to apply to all cases in which the right-hand NP is an R-expression. For example,

(i)   a.   *John received a letter from Mary$_i$ about Mary$_i$.
        b.   *In the mail, there was a letter from Mary$_i$ about Mary$_i$.
        c.   *John heard from Mary$_i$ about Mary$_i$.

should be marked unacceptable by the same reflexive context rule.

35. As pointed out in sec. 2.6, Reinhart's disjoint reference rule, which applies at surface structure, cannot account for either the unacceptability of (11.36b) or the acceptability of

(11.37b). Recall that Reinhart attributes the unacceptability of (11.36b) to the fact that *he* c-commands *John* via an S to $\bar{S}$ projection of the c-command domain. As Carden (1980) has shown, this analysis fails to explain why (i), in which *he* does not c-command *John*, is also unacceptable.

(i)   *Near John$_i$, I believe he$_i$ found a snake.

Similarly, whatever principle that would mark (11.36b) unacceptable would also mark (11.37b) unacceptable because the same command relationship holds in the surface structure between *he* and *John* in these sentences.

Solan (1983) observes that Reinhart's analysis cannot account for the unacceptability of

(ii)   *In John$_i$'s bed, Sam put him$_i$. (Solan)

because *him* does not c-command *John('s)*. He assumes that his constraints (i.e., in clause-mate contexts PRO$_i$ cannot both precede and k-command NP$_i$, and in non-clause-mate contexts PRO$_i$ cannot both precede and c-command NP$_i$) apply at the levels of S-structure and LF-representation. He assumes that at these levels, *he/him* both precedes and k-commands *John* in (11.36) and (ii).

It is clear that Solan's constraints make the wrong prediction on the acceptability status of (11.37b). Since his non-clause-mate rule applies to the prefronting structure represented by (11.37a), it marks it unacceptable, thereby predicting that (11.37b), which he assumes is derived by applying a "stylistic" rule of fronting, is also unacceptable.

Furthermore, Solan's assumption that the fronting of prepositional phrases *near John* and in *John's bed* of these sentences has not yet taken place at S-structure seems to be difficult to maintain. As shown in (11.37), the fronting rule under discussion changes coreference possibilities of NPs. Therefore, the rule cannot be a "stylistic" one and must have applied before the S-structures of (11.36b), (11.37b), and (ii) are obtained.

Finally, as will be shown below, some of the sentences of the pattern of (ii) are acceptable, suggesting that the unacceptability of (ii) should not be attributed to a violation of the binding conditions.

36. I will use the term "postcyclical" here as synonymous with "applying to the S-structure."

37. The claim represented here that the reflexive rules are cyclical, while the pronominal rule is postcyclical, was first presented in Kuno (1972c, pp. 313–314). The claim that Condition C' applies to the S-structure and not to the LF-representation will be justified below.

The k-command formulation of a reflexive rule allows for coindexing of *himself* and *him/John* in the following sentences because the latter k-commands the former:

(i)   a.   *Himself talked to Mary about him.
        b.   *Himself talked to Mary about John.

However, Condition B' blocks the coindexing because the nonreflexive *him/John* is k-commanded by the clause-mate *himself*.

38. There are at least two independent arguments for assuming that sentential adverbs originate in sentence-initial position. First, the sentence-initial position is the most unmarked position for sentential adverbs:

(i)   a.   To my great surprise, he showed up on time.
        b.   ??He showed up on time to my great surprise.

(ii)   a.   Luckily, he didn't fall off the cliff.
        b.   ??He didn't fall off the cliff luckily.

The (b) sentences are acceptable only if there is a big pause before the sentential adverbs such that they can be interpreted as an afterthought addition to the main sentences.

Second, there are sentential adverbs which *cannot* appear in any other places than sentence-initial position:

(iii)   a.   Once upon a time, there lived an old fisherman . . .
        b.   *There lived an old fisherman . . . once upon a time.
(iv)   a.   As for her, she won't be invited.
        b.   *She won't be invited, as for her.
(v)   a.   Between John and Mary, Mary is the brighter.
        b.   *Mary is the brighter between John and Mary.

There does not seem to be any good reason why these sentential adverbs would have to originate at sentence-final position and undergo obligatory fronting.

39. See Kuno (1975a) for a transformational version of the above explanation of the contrast between (11.42a) and (11.42b). See Kuno (1975b) for various tests that distinguish between sentential adverbs and VP adverbs and Reinhart (1976, 1983) for additional tests. Jackendoff (1975) attempted to account for the contrast between (11.42a) and (11.42b) on a purely semantic ground. He hypothesized that the contrast between the two could be attributable to the fact that the subject of *found a scratch* in (11.42a) represents a Real-Mary, while that of *looks terribly sick* in (11.42b) represents an Image-Mary. However, the following examples show that this line of approach does not work:

(i)   a.   From a recent portrait of Mary, people believe that she removed stains.
        b.   From a recent portrait of Mary, people believe that she is sick.

As in (11.42), a coreferential interpretation is impossible for (a) and possible for (b). However, the subjects of *removed stains* and *is sick* are both Real-Mary. Therefore, the contrast between Real-Mary and Image-Mary cannot be the explanation for the contrast between the (a) and (b) sentences. Naturally, the explanation lies in the fact that while the *from*-NP expression in (a) has been placed in sentence-initial position by fronting, it is a sentential adverb representing a basis of judgment in (b) and has been in that position from the beginning.

Reinhart (1976, 1981) attempted to account for the contrast by using the same distinction that I had used: sentential adverbs vs. VP adverbs. She assumed, however, that sentential adverbs, too, originate from sentence-final position and are placed in sentence-initial position by some kind of a fronting process. She then hypothesized that while a fronted VP adverb is attached to the COMP node of the $\bar{\text{S}}$, a fronted sentential adverb is attached to $\bar{\bar{\text{S}}}$:

(ii)   a.

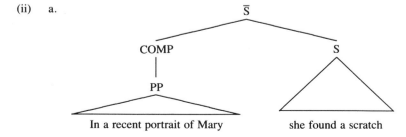

b.

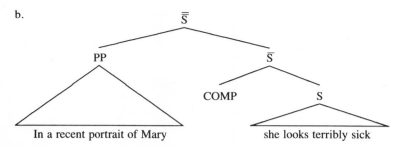

$\overline{\overline{S}}$

PP

$\overline{S}$

COMP   S

In a recent portrait of Mary   she looks terribly sick

She defined c-command in such a way as to allow an S to $\overline{S}$ projection but not an $\overline{S}$ to $\overline{\overline{S}}$ projection. Note that, according to this definition of c-command, *she* c-commands *Mary* in (iia) (and hence there is no coreferential interpretation between the two NPs) but not in (iib) (hence allowing for a coreferential interpretation). It is clear that this line of approach cannot explain the phenomenon under discussion because in (i) *she* does not c-command *Mary* either in (a) or (b).

40. A comprehension test for pronominal reference was conducted by Carden (personal communication, 1982) utilizing the following four sentences:

(i)   a.   Above her, Mary noticed a crack developing in the snow.
       b.   Above Mary, she noticed a crack developing in the snow.
(ii)   a.   Above her skis, Mary noticed a crack developing in the snow.
       b.   Above Mary's skis, she noticed a crack developing in the snow.

Example (ib) patterns after (11.43b) and (iib) after (11.49b). According to Carden, coreferential interpretation between *Mary* and *she/her* is significantly inhibited for (ib)—as opposed to (ia), for which almost all subjects can get coreferential interpretation—but it is significantly less inhibited for (iib) than for (ib), for which few subjects can get coreferential interpretation.

41. Example (11.57a) is awkward for some speakers, but its awkwardness does not seem to be any different from that of, for example,

(i)   John took her to the mirror and showed her himself.

Therefore, the awkwardness of the sentence does not seem to be due to the fact that the dative NP has been used as antecedent for a reflexive. It seems to be due to the fact that two proforms are juxtaposed next to each other without prepositions. (cf. ??They showed him her in the mirror.)

42. Compare the following two sentences:

(i)   a.   *Mary talked to himself$_i$ about himself$_i$.
       b.   John$_i$ talked to himself$_i$ about himself$_i$.

Example (a) is unacceptable because the coindexed reflexives do not have an independent NP that binds them. In contrast, (b) is acceptable because they do. In (b), it is not the case that each of the two reflexives has the other reflexive as its antecedent. Each has *John* as its antecedent. A similar observation is found in Lakoff (1968).

43. It is not the case that all sentences of the pattern of (11.58a, b) are acceptable. For example, observe the following sentences:

(i)   a.   *Articles about himself$_i$ frequently attack the President$_i$.
       b.   *The latest book about himself$_i$ described the Senator$_i$ as an alcoholic.

(I am indebted to Kyle Johnson for (a).) As I will show in Chap. 4, picture noun reflexives are subject to various semantic and discourse-based constraints, one of which states that picture noun reflexives are acceptable to the extent that the sentences make clear that the referents of the reflexives are "aware" that the referents of the picture nouns involve them. Examples (11.58a) and (11.58b) are acceptable because the sentences make clear that John recognized the picture and the rumor as involving him, while (ia) and (ib) are unacceptable because there is nothing in the sentences that indicates that such a recognition existed.

44. See pp. 77–78 for the difficulties that a restructuring analysis would have and p. 78 for the problem with excluding PP nodes from the set of domain-limiting nodes for c-command.

45. In fact, there is another reason for lack of coreferential interpretation in (11.60). There is a rule in English, as well as in many other languages, which bans use of a full NP in complement clauses of saying, knowing, and feeling verbs when it is coreferential with the main clause NP that represents the agent/experiencer of the saying, knowing, and feeling action/state. I will develop this hypothesis fully in Chap. 3.

46. Sentences of the pattern of (11.63b), as well as those of the pattern of (11.65b), which follows, were used by Jacobson and Neubauer (1976) to show that reflexivization must apply cyclically (in the transformational framework). McCawley (1976) and Hasegawa (1983) used sentences of the pattern of (11.56b) to show that an interpretive rule for reflexives is both cyclical and optional.

47. Hasegawa acknowledges Joan Bresnan (personal communication) for (11.70a) and (11.70b).

48. I am indebted to John Whitman (personal communication) for (c), which shows that sentences of the pattern under discussion can be acceptable not only when the "accessible SUBJECT" is a dummy *it* as in (a) or an indefinite unspecific NP as in (b), but also when it is an anaphoric demonstrative pronoun.

49. The *i*-within-*i* condition against coindexing seems to be a valid condition and should be invoked to disqualify *it* in (11.76b) from serving as an accessible SUBJECT for *each other.*

50. The following example shows that *each other* can readily enter into a relative clause:

(i)   They were pleased with the reputations that each other's latest papers generated.

Here again, I suspect that the acceptability of the sentence is due to the fact that it is easy to visualize the situation in which the persons that *they* and *each other* refer to were congratulating each other for the success of their papers. Compare (i) with

(ii)   ??John and Mary lost newspapers in which each other's pictures appeared.
(iii)   ??They were buried in the cemeteries where each other's parents had been buried.

It is difficult or impossible to assume that the persons that *they* refers to were aware of the reciprocity of the actions represented in (ii) and (iii). I assume that these sentences are marginal for this reason.

The following example shows that reflexives, too, can enter into a relative clause:

(iv)   John was pleased with the reputations that stories about himself in the national papers had generated.

As will be shown in Chap. 4, the acceptability of sentences of the pattern ⟨
dependent upon the condition that the referent of the reflexive is "aware" t'
noun involves him. So, compare (iv) with the following:

(v)   *John$_i$ was killed by a lunatic who stories about himself$_i$ in the newspapers had
        infuriated.

51. Once it is realized that the primary factor involved here is that of "awareness" or
"mutual interaction," it becomes difficult to produce sentences which are unacceptable with
the object reference interpretation. Examples (11.84a, b) become perfectly acceptable if one
can visualize the kind of context that is described in (11.87). Similarly, observe the following
sentences:

(i)   a.   They asked the two about each other.
        b.   They asked the couple in succession if each other's success in business af-
              fected the way they treated each other.

It seems that it is easier to get the object-control interpretation than the subject-control one
for these sentences.

52. Asymmetry between the domains of anaphors and pronominals is also recognized
in Huang's hypothesis that the requirement for an accessible SUBJECT applies to anaphors
but not to pronominals.

Chapter 3

1. What is responsible for the awkwardness of (1.8b) has little to do with pronominalization because the following sentence is equally awkward:

(i)   ?That John was the best boxer in the world was claimed by Ali repeatedly.

The awkwardness is due to the presence of a heavy sentential subject which has not been
extraposed to sentence-final position:

(ii)   a.   It was claimed by Ali repeatedly that he was the best boxer in the world.
        b.   It was claimed by Ali repeatedly that John was the best boxer in the world.

The marginality of (1.8b) must be attributed in part to the above factor, also.

2. There is not much semantic difference between (3.3b) and (3.3c). This is because
Ali would not have said, "I am not the greatest boxer in the world" unless there was someone
else's statement "Ali is the best boxer . . . ," and because if Ali denied someone else's statement to the effect that he was the best boxer, it is most likely that he said, "I am not the
greatest boxer in the world."

3. There are speakers who accept (3.4a). This can be attributed to the fact that in
spreading the rumor, John need not have actually allowed it to be known that he was speaking
about himself. He could have had others act for him or even gone so far as to contact anony-
mously newspapers to give them a story about "John" without anyone knowing it was him. It
seems that speakers who can readily imagine such a situation consider (3.4a) acceptable. I
am indebted to Eileen Nam (personal communication, 1985) for this observation.

4. There are speakers who consider (3.2b), (3.4b), and (3.5b) to be as unacceptable as
(3.1b), (3.4a), and (3.5a), respectively. It seems that for these speakers, passive sentences
with pronominal by-agentives which have heavy clausal subjects are already marginal: for

this reason, they would reject the following sentences as well when *her* is unstressed and nondeictic.

(i)   a.   That Ali$_i$ was the greatest boxer was claimed by her$_j$.
       b.   That Ali$_i$ was the greatest boxer was denied by her$_j$.

For these speakers, the level of unacceptability that derives from this sentence pattern, irrespective of the coreferentiality problem, is so great that it is indistinguishable from the level of unacceptability that derives from the illegitimate coreferentiality intended in (3.1b), (3.4a), and (3.5a). What is important is that there are many speakers who regard (3.2b), (3.4b), and (3.5b) as much less unacceptable than (3.1a), (3.4a), and (3.5a) but that, as far as I know, there are no speakers who make the reverse judgment.

5. It might be possible to use (4.2b) in contexts in which it is made clear that John later realized that he had a medical appointment that afternoon. However, the sentence in itself does not imply that he realized it later.

6. For many speakers, (5.11c) is acceptable if it is interpreted as representing a habitual situation. For these speakers, the following sentence is perfectly acceptable:

(i)   That Mary never said hello to John$_i$ worried him$_i$.

On the other hand, if it is clear that the sentence represents a one-time-only event in the past, it becomes marginal or unacceptable.

(ii)   ??That Mary forgot to say hello to John$_i$ worried him$_i$.

This phenomenon can be accounted for if we hypothesize that habitual or customary action has a better chance, all other things being equal, of becoming common knowledge.

7. I owe (5.12), (5.13), and the observations that follow them to John Whitman (personal communication).

8. I am indebted to James McCawley (personal communication, 1985) for these sentences.

9. Sentence (6.2b) is marginal to speakers for whom an R-expression cannot be both preceded and k-commanded by a coindexed NP. See sec. 2.11 for discussion of this constraint. For those speakers who accept (6.2b), it seems that there is a subtle difference in connotation between this sentence and (6.2a). That is, the complement clause of (6.2b) can be read as if it were in quotation marks. For example, compare the following two sentences:

(i)   a.   People often said about their new mayor$_i$ that he$_i$ was a lunatic.
       b.   ?/??People often said about him$_i$ that their new mayor$_i$ was a lunatic.

If (ib) is any good, it strongly implies that people did indeed say, "Our mayor is a lunatic," while (ia) does not have that implication: people might have said, "Mr. Thompson is a lunatic," "That man is a lunatic," or any other expressions that could have been used to refer to the mayor.

10. It might be argued that (6.1b) is unacceptable because restructuring has taken place in such a way as to make *say to* act as a single verb, and that the same kind of restructuring has taken place in (6.4b) also, originally starting with *make the statement* as V and ending up with *make the statement to* as V. The restructuring analysis, however, fails to account for the contrast such as the following:

(i)   a.   *People often made the uncalled-for statement to her$_i$ that Mary$_i$ was a lunatic.

  b. (?)People often made the uncalled-for statement about her$_i$ that Mary$_i$ was a lunatic.

Since *statement* can be modified by attributives, it is difficult to maintain that *make the statement* is a V.

The restructuring analysis is also used for accounting for the contrast of the following type:

  (ii) a. I spoke to the men about each other.
  b. *I spoke about the men to each other.

Chomsky (1981, pp. 225–226) hypothesizes that (iib) is unacceptable because *the men* does not c-command *each other*, but he conjectures that (iia) might be the result of a "reanalysis" applying to *speak to*, thus permitting c-command in this case.

The contrast of the sort that we see between (iia) and (iib) was first observed by Lakoff (1968) using reflexive pronouns:

  (iii) a. Mary talked to John$_i$ about himself$_i$.
  b. *Mary talked about John$_i$ to himself$_i$.

Lakoff attempted to block the derivation of (iiib) by a crossover constraint. It was shown in Kuno and Kaburaki (1975, p. 38) that it is not possible to account for the unacceptability of (iiib) on a syntactic basis. Observe the following sentence:

  (iv) *Mary discussed John$_i$ with himself$_i$.

This sentence does not involve any word order shift. Therefore, Lakoff's crossover account would be helpless. Also, in this sentence, *John* c-commands *himself*. Therefore, Chomsky's c-command analysis is also helpless. I assumed that there is a humanness hierarchy for reflexivization, and that it is not possible to use a nonhuman *John* (note that the left-hand *John* in (iiib) and (iv) does not refer to a human being, but to what John did/was) as controller for reflexivizing a human *John*. This condition, if extended to anaphors in general, can account for the unacceptability of (iib), thus making the "reanalysis" explanation unnecessary. See Chaps. 4 and 5 for details of the above nonsyntactic account.

  11. Incidentally, those speakers who do not like (9.1a), (9.3a), and (9.4a) do not accept (9.5a), either. Since (9.5b) is also unacceptable to them, there is no way for these speakers to state the content of (9.5) using a reflexive pronoun.

  12. If we can assume, as Ross has, that there is a performative clause in the underlying structure of an ordinary sentence, then this condition can account for the acceptability of (ia, b) and the unacceptability of (ic) automatically:

  (i) a. This paper was written by Ann and myself.
  b. This paper was written by Ann and yourself.
  c. *This paper was written by Ann and himself.

This is because these sentences would then be derived from the underlying structures shown below:

  (ii) a. [I$_i$ [+logo-1] SAY TO YOU$_j$ [+logo-2] THAT [this paper . . . by Ann and myself$_i$]]
  b. [I [+logo-1] SAY TO YOU$_j$ [+logo-2] THAT [this paper . . . by Ann and yourself$_j$]]

$$*[I_i [+\text{logo-1}] \text{ SAY TO YOU}_j [+\text{logo-2}] \text{ THAT [this paper} \dots \text{ by Ann and}$$
$$\text{himself}_k]]$$

‍‑‍‑e that it is impossible to coindex *himself* in (c) with either the [+logo-1] or the [+logo-2] NP in the main clause.

13. There are speakers who consider (9.9b) to be perfectly acceptable. These must be the speakers who can interpret *know from* as more or less synonymous as *hear from*. There are also speakers who do not have the "x knows y from w" pattern in their idiolect.

14. For some speakers, the acceptability of (9.15b) increases if *it* is inserted between *hear* and *from John*.

    (i)   MARY didn't hear it from John$_i$ that the paper had been written by Ann and himself$_i$. JANE heard it from him$_i$.

The use of *it* in (i) seems to have the function of making the complement clause factive and thus strongly suggesting that John did say that the paper had been written by Ann and himself. I am indebted to John Whitman (personal communication) for this observation.

15. I am indebted to James McCawley (personal communication, 1985) for (9.16b).

16. I am claiming here that the instability of judgments on the acceptability status of (10.5b) and that of (10.5c) are due to two different reasons. That is, I assume that the fluctuation of the speaker judgments on the acceptability status of (10.5b) is due to an idiolectal bifurcation concerning whether a [+logo-2] NP is a legitimate antecedent for the reflexive in the *NP like x-self* pattern. On the other hand, I assume that the fluctuation of judgments on the acceptability status of (10.5c) is due to an idiolectal bifurcation concerning how easy or difficult it is for the speaker to deduce that "w said y" from "x hears from w." In fact, the speakers who find (10.5b) less than perfect are not coextensive with those who find (10.5c) less than perfect, which seems to support my claim that two independent factors are involved here.

17. Example (11.7c) is better than (11.6d). I suspect that this is owing to the fact that it is easier to assume that John nevertheless knew (i.e., held the internal feeling) that his picture appeared in the morning paper for (11.7c) than for (11.6d).

18. It has been pointed out by John Whitman (personal communication) that (11.11e) is possible only in a context where, for example, a giant newspaper photo is plastered on the wall directly behind where John is sitting. It seems that the implication that John should know makes it possible to use a reflexive in such a situation.

19. Here again, if it is clear that at some time in the future John might come to be aware of the picture, the use of reflexive becomes acceptable:

    (i)   John$_i$ still doesn't know that there is a picture of himself$_i$ in the morning paper, but he$_i$ will soon.

20. This fact parallels the following phenomenon:

    (i)   a.   John heard that as for Jane, she wouldn't have to move.
            b.   John heard from Mary that as for Jane, she wouldn't have to move.
    (ii)   a.   John was told that as for Jane, she wouldn't have to move.
            b.   John was told by Mary that as for Jane, she wouldn't have to move.

What is at issue here is who is comparing Jane with other members of the group under discussion; namely, who is engaged in a chain of thought involving Jane and others. The person doing the comparison is John in the (a) sentences, but it is Mary in the (b) sentences. From this point of view, the constraint on the use of the *as for x-self* pattern that we have seen in the above is simply a special case of the behavior of the *as for y* pattern in sentences that have a [+logo-2] NP in subject position that is not also [+logo-1b].

21. See Grinder (1970) and Jackendoff (1972).

22. Sentences of the patterns of (13.7c) are acceptable as nonreportive narrative-style sentences in which the speaker, or rather the narrator, has completely identified himself with the person whose inner thought he is describing:

(i)   The exam period was approaching, but Mary was not in the mood for studying. There were more important things in life than studying. Anyway, she had only one course with a final exam. *It would be easy ∅ to prepare herself for the exam.*

In the same nonreportive narrative-style writing, *as for himself, as for herself,* etc., which cannot be used in the main clause, as we observed in sec. 3.12, are also acceptable. Observe the following sentences, which are taken from Fraser (1970):

(ii)   John was worried about what Sheila should do. As for himself, he knew the best plan of attack.

(iii) Mary tried to convince both Tom and me to go. As for herself, she wasn't sure what she would do.

23. Indirect reflexivization is allowable for adverbial clauses and even for relative clauses in subjunctive complement clauses:

(i)   Jón$_i$ sagði að hann$_i$ væri   glaður ef María kyssti *sig$_i$*.
       said that he   would be-glad if   would-kiss(subj.)
       'John$_i$ said that he$_i$ would be glad if Mary kissed him(self)$_i$.'

(ii)   Jón$_i$ segir að hann$_i$ komi ekki nema María kyssi *sig$_i$*.
       says that he   won't come unless   kiss (subj.)
       'John$_i$ says that he$_i$ won't come unless Mary kisses him(self)$_i$.'

(iii) Jón$_i$ segir að þetta sé   stúlkan sem elski *sig$_i$*.
       says that this is (subj.) girl   that loves (subj.)
       'John$_i$ says that this is the girl that loves him(self)$_i$.'

24. Thráinsson entertains the possibility that indirect reflexivization in Icelandic is conditioned by my direct discourse perspective but rejects it for the reason that I will mention below. The direct discourse analysis of the phenomenon was first presented during my course on functional syntax at the 1975 LSA Institute, University of New York at Oswego. It was also briefly described in Kuno (1978c).

25. Example (14.17a) can also mean that John says that Harold$_j$ knows that Mary loves him$_j$.

26. *Sig* in (14.17b) cannot be coreferential with *Haraldur*, either, because it appears in a complement clause in the indicative.

27. The reflexive pronoun is also acceptable in infinitival clauses which have the corresponding subjunctive clause counterparts:

(i)   La signora$_i$ mi dice di giacere presso di sè$_i$.
       the woman me orders to lie (inf.) near self
       'The woman orders me to lie near (lit.) herself.'

28. In fact, the (understood) subject and the genitive NP of the complement clause in (a) are fourth-person pronouns, which refer not to immediately mentioned NPs but to "aforementioned" NPs.

29. I am indebted to Pat Tiller (personal communication, 1985) for this example.

30. These examples are from Clements (1979).

31. In (15.7b), *John* is k-commanded, but not preceded, by *him*. Therefore, Condition C′ cannot apply to *John* to mark it for disjoint reference with *him*. Removing the "precede" condition from Condition C′ would make it possible to mark (15.7b) unacceptable with a coreferential interpretation, but the same revision would mark (15.7a) also as unacceptable on a coreferential reading between *John* and *him*.

Chapter 4

1. Example (1.4a) is acceptable if it is intended to mean that confidence is what John has. In this marked interpretation, the sentence has the same syntactic and semantic structures as (1.3a). (I am indebted to Elanah Kutik for this observation.) See sec. 2.9 for more examples of minimal pairs such as (1.4).

2. In sec. 2.9 I proposed that nonnominative personal pronouns (e.g., *him, his, her*) are ambiguous between [−reflexive] and [+reflexive]. Since the subject matter of the present chapter is the distribution of surface reflexive forms with *-self/selves* spelling and surface pronominal forms, I will use the term "reflexives" exclusively for forms ending with *-self/selves* and the term "personal pronouns" for forms without *-self/selves* (including [+reflexive] *him, her*, etc.), in the rest of the chapter.

3. The following sentences might appear to be counterexamples to this generalization.

(i) a. ??John$_i$ talked to Mary about himself$_i$ not getting enough moral support from her.

     b. (?)John$_i$ talked to Mary about him$_i$ not getting enough moral support from her.

However, the fact that the use of a pronoun in (b) does not result in unacceptability is due to the fact that there is a clause boundary after the preposition *about:*

(ii) [John$_i$ talked to Mary about [him$_i$ not getting enough moral support from Mary]]

Therefore, these sentences do not exemplify the pattern *x talks to y about w* (where *x* and *w* are coreferential) under discussion. Many speakers prefer (iii) to (ia) or (ib).

(iii) John$_i$ talked to Mary about his$_i$ not getting enough moral support from her.

4. It might have been Jane, but in that case, Jane must have obtained the information directly or indirectly from either John or Mary.

5. For some speakers, the unmarked reflexive for *anyone* is plural *themselves*, and for others, it is singular uni-gender *themself*.

6. Note that while (2.15) is a condition that is sensitive to the grammatical function of a reflexive pronoun, (2.19) is one that is sensitive to the grammatical function of the antecedent of a reflexive.

7. There are speakers who consider the (b) sentences above nearly acceptable if the pronouns are lightly stressed and noncontracted and if they do not carry contrastive inter-

pretation. It seems that, even for these speakers, the relative degrees of acceptability that are discussed in the following still hold.

8. In discussing the contrast between (3.4) and (3.5), Jackendoff states the following: "I suggest that the property in question may have something to do with the subject's being marked with the thematic relation agent *by the verb*" (the italics mine). He would have been closer to the mark if he had used the same concept, not with respect to the verb, but with respect to the picture noun. That is, in (3.4), *John,* and not *I,* is the agent of *the story* (i.e., John's story) while in (3.5), *I,* not *John,* is the agent of *the story*. I will show later that agenthood in this sense, although it is relevant for picture noun reflexivization, is only one of many factors that control the phenomenon.

9. This point is disputable because (3.8a) and (3.9a) are nearly acceptable for some speakers. Also, the following sentence is acceptable for many speakers:

(i)   John collaborated with Mary$_i$ on a story about herself$_i$.

We will examine these sentences shortly in this section.

10. There are contexts which make sentences of the pattern of (3.11a) acceptable, one of which will be discussed shortly.

11. There are speakers who consider (3.13a) acceptable. I will discuss this problem later on in this section.

12. There is a productive class of exceptions to this constraint, which will be described below.

13. For many speakers, (3.18a) is unacceptable if it means "John was unaware of all the gossip . . .' but acceptable if it means 'John knew about the gossip, but was not bothered by it.'

14. I am indebted to John Whitman (personal communication) for this observation.

15. Another factor that might be involved here is the difference in the meaning of *promise* between (3.29a) and (3.29b). These two sentences can be paraphrased as follows:

(i)   a.   John promised Mary$_i$ to give her$_i$ a portrait of herself$_i$.
      b.   *John promised Mary$_i$ to draw a faithful portrait of herself$_i$.

The *promise* in (3.29a) means 'promise to give,' while it means 'promise to draw' in (3.29b). Note that (ib) is unacceptable because *herself* is not coreferential with the underlying subject of *draw*, which is *John*. The fact that *John* is the implicit Agent of *a faithful portrait of Mary,* as well as the awareness condition, seems to weakly block reflexivization in (3.29b). I am indebted to Akio Kamio (personal communication) for this observation.

16. In sec. 2.11, I stated that the following sentence is acceptable or nearly acceptable:

(i)   Mary had never been willing to listen to criticism from/by John of herself.

Many speakers consider (3.35a) less acceptable than (i). I will discuss this problem later on in this section.

17. Recall that in sec. 3.16, the concept of "intervening NP" was defined in an order-free way on the basis of Langacker's chain-of-command principle. The principle states that if (i) two identical nodes A_1 and A_2 both k-command some other node B; (ii) A_1 k-commands A_2; and (iii) A_2 does not k-command A_1, then any transformational operation involving A and B can apply only with respect to A_2 and B, and not A_1 and B. Thus, A_2 blocks, with varying strength, application of the transformational operation as an "intervening NP." In (3.36a), *John* and *anybody* both k-command *himself, John* k-commands *anybody,* but not

vice versa. Therefore, *anybody* is an intervening NP in the path for reflexivization between *John* and *himself*.

18. I am indebted to John Whitman for (3.48) and (3.49).

19. I am indebted to John Whitman for this observation about indirect agent.

20. I am indebted to Shelley Waksler for this observation and the following data.

21. Sentence (3.68a) is acceptable on the reading that John as he was described in his (= John's) book about himself appealed to the speaker. In this interpretation, John is the picture noun agent, and he was naturally aware that the book was about him.

22. The underlying *Mary* that is the object of *(discussed . . .) with* is an active participant, but the *Mary* that is the object of *discussed* is not.

23. The following sentence is not too bad in spite of the fact that the trigger is not the agent of the picture noun:

(i)   (?)Mary$_i$ assisted Bill on a story about herself$_i$.

We will examine this sentence in the following section.

24. I am indebted to John Whitman for this observation.

25. However, (4.19b) would be perfectly acceptable if "what I have been doing" or "what I have published" is the topic of the conversation. In such a context, it is expected that sentences with the first-person subject appear one after another. (I am indebted to Vicky Bergvall for this observation.) What the above phenomenon shows is that the camera angle violation of (4.19b) requires a contextual justification, and in the absence of any such justification, as when the sentence is given in isolation in (4.19b), it is felt that there is something odd about the sentence.

26. It is also possible to interpret (5.29) as "John could have had his picture in the paper if it hadn't been for Mary." The trigger potential value of *John* in this interpretation of the sentence is the same as the one for the interpretation being discussed here.

27. Recall that the reflexive rule (Condition A′) as discussed in sec. 2.11, must be cyclical and optional. Therefore, even when a reflexive in the lower S has a strong potential control, it can be left uncoindexed.

28. See Bresnan (1973), for example, for the claim that expressions such as *more caviar than he can eat* form complex NPs.

29. Since the reflexive rule (Condition A′) applies cyclically but optionally, it is possible to leave a reflexive in the lower S uncoindexed even if its potential controller downstairs has a strong trigger potential. Note that in (6.22B) *John* is an extremely powerful controller, but it is still possible not to apply the reflexive rule to *herself* in the lower S cycle.

Chapter 5

1. In this chapter, I use the symbol * to mark empathy relationships that are logically contradictory. But whether a sentence that involves such a contradictory empathy relationship is judged as totally unacceptable (*), marginal (??), or awkward (?) depends upon the strength that the empathy principles that have been violated have in each person's idiolect, and upon whether mitigating circumstances can be readily found that would make up for the violation. This explains why I have marked (2.6) with *, but the sentence (2.5) that involves this contradictory relationship only with ??.

2. Observe the following discourse, which is due to John Goldsmith (personal communication, 1985):

(i)   Mary$_i$'s mother$_j$ talked to the school doctor about her$_j$ daughter$_i$'s ever-worsening depression. He gave her$_j$ some excellent advice; that Mary$_i$ might consider a different major was perhaps his most important suggestion. He then noted that it was not uncommon for students like her$_i$ to try several fields before making a decision.

The first sentence in (i) involves a violation of the Ban on Conflicting Empathy Foci, and therefore, it should be unacceptable, but it is only slightly odd to some speakers and perfectly acceptable to others. This contrasts interestingly with the fact that the first sentence in the following discourse is awkward at best and marginal to most speakers:

(ii)   ?/??Mary$_i$'s mother$_j$ talked to the school doctor about her$_j$ daughter$_i$. She$_j$ told him that she$_i$ was suffering from ever-worsening depression. He gave her$_j$ some excellent advice; . . .

The contrast is clearly attributable to the fact that in the first discourse *her daughter* is in genitive position, while in the second discourse it is not. However, it is not the case that violations of the Ban on Conflicting Empathy Foci involving the Descriptor Empathy Hierarchy are always mitigated if the second of the two descriptors is in genitive position:

(iii)   ??Mary$_i$'s mother$_j$ talked to her$_j$ daughter$_i$'s boyfriend.

Sentences of this type are acceptable only when a switch in descriptors (e.g., from *Mary$_i$* to *her$_j$ daughter$_i$*) carries with it some significant implication. For example, compare (iii) with the following:

(iv)   Mary$_i$'s mother$_j$ married her$_j$ daughter$_i$'s boyfriend.

The above sentence, which is perfectly acceptable, expresses the speaker's value judgment about marrying one's daughter's boyfriend. This value judgment is totally absent in

(v)   Mary$_i$'s mother$_j$ married her$_i$ boyfriend.

Returning to (i), we can say that it is acceptable because it describes Mary's mother's act as one that parents of schoolchildren are often engaged in, that is, speaking to the school doctor about their children's problems. In other words, it depicts a common scene in which a parent would tell a school doctor, "I want to speak to you about *my daughter's* problem." This vividness of depiction would be totally absent if *her daughter's* in (i) were replaced with *her* or *Mary's*.

The above observation shows that the Ban on Conflicting Empathy Foci can be violated without resulting in unacceptability if there is a good reason for the violation. This phenomenon can be dealt with in a principled way by the Markedness Principle for Discourse-Rule Violations, which will be introduced in the next section.

3. There are apparent counterexamples to this generalization. For example, observe the following discourse:

(i)   Guess what happened at the party that my eight-foot boa constrictor terrorized last night.
a.   It bit an eight-foot-tall basketball player on the thumb.
b.   An eight-foot-tall basketball player was bit on the thumb by it.

The leading sentence of (i) establishes the speaker's eight-foot boa constrictor as the topic of the discourse. In spite of this fact, (ib) seems to be acceptable. As I will show later, this is because of a principle which states that it is generally easier for the speaker to take the point of view of a human being than that of a nonhuman animal. Examples in this section will involve only human dramatis personae to isolate them from interference from other factors such as this.

4. The justification for the equality sign for the Topic Empathy Hierarchy will be made in sec. 4.12.

5. Alternatively, in theoretical frameworks in which passive sentences are derived not by applying passivization to the corresponding active sentences, but from underlying structures that already have agent NPs in *by*-agentive position, these "passive" underlying structures must be regarded as "marked" constructions that have corresponding more "basic" constructions, so that the choice of subject NPs in these sentences could be regarded as being due to the speaker's design.

6. In Kuno and Kaburaki (1975/1977), the following hierarchy was hypothesized:

(i)   E(subject) $\geq$ E(object) $\geq$ . . . $\geq$ E(*by*-agentive)

However, the following examples show that the relative position of the object and the *by*-agentive in the hierarchy is not predeterminable:

(ii)   a.   Mary was introduced by *John* to three of *his students*.
        b.   Mary was introduced to *John* by *his teacher*.

Sentence (iia) shows that E(*by*-agentive) > E(dative object) holds. On the other hand, (iib) shows that E(dative object) > E(*by*-agentive) holds. Hence, the impossibility of specifying the relative position of the dative object and *by*-agentive in the Surface Structure Empathy Hierarchy.

Similarly, observe the following:

(iii)   a.   John was led away from *Mary* by *her bodyguard*.
        b.   John was rescued by *Mary* from *her inquisitive parents*.

These examples show that the relative position of the *by*-agentive and *from*-expression in the empathy hierarchy is not predeterminable, either.

Likewise, observe the following examples:

(iv)   a.   John was locked up with *Mary* by *her mean old stepmother*.
        b.   Mary was locked up by *the King* yesterday with *his fierce-looking bulldog*.

These examples show that the relative position of the comitative expression and *by*-agentive cannot be specified in the hierarchy, either.

All the above show that the only relative position in the empathy hierarchy that is predeterminable is that between the subject and nonsubject.

7. This hypothesis was first discussed informally in Kuno and Kaburaki (1975/1977), but was formulated as shown in (3.12) in Kuno (1978d) and Kuno (1979).

8. In fact, for many speakers (3.1b) is better than (3.1a) in the given context.

9. *Meet* for 'meet as arranged' is not a middle verb. For example, observe the following sentences:

(i)   a.   Mary met John at the airport as arranged, and he looked really surprised to see her there.
        b.   *John met Mary at the airport as arranged, and he looked really surprised to see her there.

The subject of *meet* for 'meet as arranged' must be involved in the arrangement, but the object need not be.

Now observe the following contrast:

(ii)   a.   I met John at the party last night for the first time.
      b.   ??John met me at the party last night for the first time.
(iii) a.   I met John at the party last night as arranged.
      b.   John met me at the party last night as arranged.

The acceptability of (iiib) shows that *meet* for 'meet as arranged' is not an empathy verb.

10. In Kuno and Kaburaki (1975/1977), the following hierarchy was proposed:

(i)   E(speaker) > E(hearer) > E(third person)

Example (3.16), for the reason given below, places the hearer and the third person in the same category.

11. This requirement for a switch between the first- and second-person pronouns makes (3.17Bb) unacceptable.

12. As is the case with parrot questions, corrective sentences also require a switch between the first- and second-person pronouns:

(i)   Speaker A: You took me to this restaurant last month.
      Speaker B: No, I took you to this one two months ago.

This is why (3.19Bb) is marginal/unacceptable.

13. In colloquial American, the expression "x married y" is not used much outside of idioms such as "marry y for (the) money." Instead, "x got married to y" is used. This latter expression seems to be even more empathy-loaded than "marry." For example, observe the following exchange:

(i)   Speaker A: What's happening with Mary?
      Speaker B: *A nineteen-year-old high school dropout got married to her.

Example (iB) is worse than (3.28Ba).

14. The general principle proposed above that verbs with agents in an oblique case and nonagents in subject position are *marked* does not apply to verbs with agents in an oblique case whose "nonagent" subjects acquire a high degree of agenthood. For example, observe the following sentences:

(i)   Mary learned how to talk like that from me.

The subject of *learn from* has a considerably higher degree of agenthood than the subject of *be taught by* or *receive from*. This can be witnessed by the fact that it can be used in the imperative sentences:

(ii) a.   Learn how to write papers from your teachers.
      b.   ??Be taught how to write papers by your teachers.
      c.   ??Receive homework assignments from your teachers.

The fact that (i) is a completely acceptable sentence in spite of its violation of the E(subject) > E(other NPs) principle must be attributable to the fact that *learn from* has an agent NP as its subject, and thus does not constitute a marked verb. Another expression which shows the same characteristic (perhaps to a much greater degree) is *buy from* (as opposed to *sell*).

Observe, further, the following examples, which were suggested by John Whitman:

(iii) a. I gave Mary a bad impression of linguists in general.
       b. ?Mary received from me a bad impression of linguists in general.

It seems that (iiib) is considerably better than (4.8b). This can be explained in the following way. First, note that (iiia) is ambiguous between the following two interpretations:

(iv) Interpretation I: I told Mary all kinds of negative things about the behavior of linguists, and thereby caused her to believe what I believe: that linguists in general are no good.
      Interpretation II: My performance as a linguist—and as a person, in her view—warranted the tarnishing of all other linguists' reputations as well (in Mary's mind).

Interpretation I has *I* as an agent, while interpretation II does not. Note that (iiib), to the extent that it is acceptable, is acceptable only on interpretation II. That is, *me* of (iiib) is not an agent. Thus, the principle that "verbs with agents in an oblique case and nonagents in subject position are marked" does not apply to (iiib).

15. I am indebted to Michael Szamosi for this observation.

16. I will discuss the kind of context that would make (6.2b) acceptable later on in this section.

17. I am indebted to Vicky Bergvall (personal communication, 1981) for this important observation.

18. The use of *go to* in (6.12) would be acceptable if, for example, the hearer were moving to another office or building, or going on a trip right after class and the student were saying that he would go to see the teacher at the place of his destination to complain about the lecture.

19. The pattern "one envies NP_1 NP_2" implies that one thinks that NP_2 is beneficial to NP_1. Sentences of this pattern are acceptable when the logic for this implication is immediately clear to the hearer, but is marginal when it is not. For example, compare the following two sentences:

(i) a. I envy John the woman he chose.
     b. ??I envy John the woman who chose him.

In (ia), there can be numerous obvious reasons why the speaker thinks that the woman John chose is beneficial to John. Since John presumably controlled selection of the girl, he must have used a set of qualifications that appealed to him and that would also appeal commonsensically to others. Example (ia) says that the speaker is envious of John on account of the woman who he chose because her qualifications are beneficial to him. In contrast, in (ib), the woman who chose John chose him because of his qualifications and not hers. Therefore, there are no explicitly stated or implied qualifications that the woman might possess which the speaker considers to be beneficial to John. Hence, the marginality of the sentence. Now, compare (ib) with the following sentences:

(ii) a. ?I envy John the woman who chose him as her life-long companion.
      b. (?)I envy John the friendly audience which chose him as the best orator in the competition.
      c. I envy Billy Graham the friendly audiences which year after year have chosen him the best preacher in America.

Example (iia) is better than (ib) because it hints at the qualifications that the woman possesses which the speaker considers as beneficial to John—that is, the woman possesses good qualifications for a wife. Example (iib) and (iic) are acceptable because the second NP in each sentence states explicitly why the speaker considers NP_2 to be beneficial to NP_1.

20. The fact that this rule is not a mechanical rule that is applied blindly can be seen by observing the following sentences:

(i)   a.   ??I and my teacher went to Paris.
        b.   ?I and my wife went to Paris.
        c.   (?)I and three of my students went to Paris.
        d.   cf. ?I and three students went to Paris.
(ii)   a.   I and someone else went to Paris.
        b.   *Someone else and I went to Paris.
(iii)   a.   I and three others went to Paris.
        b.   *Three others and I went to Paris.

Example (i) involves the Descriptor Empathy Hierarchy because the term *I* and a term that is dependent on *I* (e.g., *my teacher*) are involved in each of the first three sentences. The Descriptor Empathy Hierarchy dictates that *I* be given syntactic prominence, while the Modesty Principle dictates that *I* be placed second. The fact that (ia) is marginal shows that the Modesty Principle is stronger than the Descriptor Empathy Hierarchy. At the same time, the fact that (ib) is better than (ia), and that (ic) is nearly acceptable shows that the Modesty Principle weakens *a little* when social convention does not require the speaker to be modest vis-à-vis the referent of the other NP. On the other hand, the awkwardness of (id) shows that (ic)'s near acceptability is due to the fact that the Descriptor Empathy Hierarchy has won over the weakened Modesty Principle in this sentence. Examples (ii) and (iii) show that when the other NP contains expressions such as *else* and *others,* the logic of the expressions requires that the NP which represents the set with which the other NP is disjoint, be stated first. Thus, the violation of the Modesty Principle that (iia) and (iiia) involve is "unintentional," and the Markedness Principle for Discourse-Rule Violations dictates that there be no penalty for this violation. Hence the acceptability of these sentences.

In this connection, observe that (iib) and (iiib) are totally unacceptable in the intended reading "one person besides myself" and "three people besides myself," but that they are acceptable if they are intended to mean "one person/three people besides those mentioned, and in addition, I."

Observe, further, the following sentences:

(iv)   a.   (?)/?I and my student went to Paris.
        b.   (?)I and three of my students went to Paris.
        c.   I and three of my students from MIT went to Paris.
        d.   ?Three of my students from MIT and I went to Paris.

The fact that (ivc) is perfectly acceptable while (iva) is marginal shows that the length of the other NP also is involved. That is, the longer the other NP is, the easier to place the first person pronoun at the head of the list.

The Modesty Principle applies less stringently in nonsubject position. For example, observe the following:

(v)   a.   The teacher praised Mary and me during the class.
        b.   The teacher praised me and Mary during the class.

Example (vb) still gives the impression that the speaker is placing himself in the forefront and is more marked than (va), but it is considerably better than (8.14a). This fact can be attributable to several factors. First, it is possible to consider "and Mary" as an added-on afterthought. Alternatively, the order might represent the chronology of the teacher's praising—he might have first praised the speaker, and then Mary. In this connection, note that the following sentence, which does not involve a chronological sequence of events, is worse than (vb):

> (iv)   ?The teacher likes me and Mary best of all.

The sentence seems to have a "substandard English" flavor, which (vb) lacks.

Finally, the Modesty Principle does not apply when listing by recollection is involved. For example, observe the following exchange:

> (vii) Speaker A: Who was at the party?
> Speaker B: a.   Well, me, John, Bill, and your brother.
> b.   Well, John, Bill, me and your brother.

Speaker B gives a list of people at the party as he recalls their names, and therefore, the order of names in the list is conditioned by the speaker's memory, and not by any empathy-related principles. Note, also, that in this kind of context, the sequence *John's brother and he/John* that is otherwise banned shows up:

> (viii) Speaker A: Who made the honors list?
> Speaker B: Well, Bill, Mary, Tom, John's brother, and, I believe, John, also.

21. It would not be amiss to introduce here another piece of evidence for the existence of the Markedness Principle for Discourse-Rule Violations. Observe, first, the following sentences:

> (i)   a.   John gave the book to her.
> b.   John gave her the book.

Many double object verbs in English alternate between a periphrastic *to*-dative, as shown in (ia), and an incorporated dative, as shown in (ib). I will assume here that the periphrastic dative pattern represents the underlying order of the direct and indirect object of double object verbs, and that (ib) is derived from (ia) by application of an optional syntactic rule called Dative Incorporation.

Now observe the following sentences:

> (ii)   a.   John gave the book to a boy.
> b.   ??John gave a boy the book.

Example (iia) is a perfectly natural sentence, and it does not require any special context for the speaker to accept it as such. On the other hand, (iib), which should be derivable by application of Dative Incorporation to (iia), is marginal and would be uttered only in a peculiar context. This fact can be accounted for if we assume that English is also subject to the well-known "From-Old-To-New Principle," which states that in languages in which word order in sentences is relatively free, the unmarked word order of constituents is "old, predictable information first, and new, unpredictable information last." According to this principle, (iia) is acceptable because the old information *the book* appears before the new information *a boy*. On the other hand, (iib) is marginal because the new information *a boy* appears before the old information *the book*. (As far as I know, Tsuneko Yokoyama (personal communication, 1975) was the first to note the marginality of (iib), and to attempt to account for it on the basis of the From-Old-To-New Principle.)

But the moment we invoke the From-Old-To-New Word Order Principle for the explanation of the marginality of (iib), we are faced with the problem of explaining why (iiia) is perfectly acceptable:

(iii)   a.   John gave a book to the boy.
          b.   John gave the boy a book.

The direct object *a book* of (iiia), which is most likely to represent new, discourse-unpredictable information, precedes the dative object *the boy,* which is most likely to represent old, discourse-predictable information. Therefore, (iiia) is as much a violation of the From-Old-To-New Word Order Principle as (iib) is, and yet (iiia) is perfectly acceptable and (iib) is marginal.

The above dilemma can be solved by assuming, as we did, that (iiia) represents an underlying word order, and (iiib) a word order derived by application of Dative Incorporation, which is an optional rule. That is to say, (iiia) represents a word order that automatically obtains given *a book* as object, and *the boy* as recipient of the act of giving. The sentence involves a violation of the From-Old-To-New Word Order Principle, but this violation is unmarked or unintentional. Hence, there is no penalty for the violation, and the sentence is acceptable. On the other hand, (iib) has been produced by "intentionally" applying Dative Incorporation, which did not have to be applied. Thus, the violation of the From-Old-To-New Word Order Principle that this sentence involves is a marked and intentional one. Hence, as the Markedness Principle for Discourse-Rule Violations dictates, there is a penalty for the violation in the form of marginality of the sentence.

For further justification of the Markedness Principle under discussion, see Kuno (1978b, 1979).

22. The Semantic Constraint on Reflexives discussed in sec. 2.5, which states that reflexive pronouns ending with *-self* or *-selves* are used in English if and only if their referents are the direct recipients or targets of the actions or mental states represented by the sentences, is perhaps an idiosyncratic condition that is not relatable to the empathy perspective, although one is tempted to treat it also as deriving from the empathy perspective. Soga (1980) claims that this condition is also empathy-related. She bases this claim on Cantrall's claim that (i) and (ii) below, for example, are different in that the use of a reflexive pronoun implies that the speaker has taken the point of view of the referent of the reflexive:

(i)   John seated Mary behind him.
(ii)   John seated Mary behind himself.

However, as I showed in sec. 2.9, the primary difference between the two seems to be whether the referent of the object of preposition is the target of the action involved or not. To see this point, observe the following two sentences:

(iii)   I hid the book behind me.
(iv)   I hid the book behind myself.

Both sentences clearly represent the speaker's own point of view, but they are different in that the latter sentence implies, obligatorily, that the speaker hid the book by holding it behind his back, while there is no such implication for (iii). Perhaps the book was on a chair, and the speaker stood in front of the chair. Extending the concept of empathy to cases such as (ii) and (iv) seems to be stretching it a little too much.

23. In this interpretation, the sentence would be paraphrasable as "I was told, and therefore, I know, that . . ."

24. *yar* + *ta* → *yatta*

25. The Topic Empathy Hierarchy includes an equality sign in order to account for the acceptability of sentences such as (12.15a). Intuitively, what this means is that the speaker can describe an event/state that involves a person who he has been talking about and a person who he has just introduced into discourse without empathizing with the former. In other words, the speaker can place himself at a far distance from both, and describe the event/state objectively.

26. Note that *kita* 'came' in this sentence does not imply at all that Taroo came. It does imply, though, that the bouquet of flowers 'came' to the speaker.

27. Example (12.19a) is acceptable in contexts which make clear that the speaker is making an objective statement. For example, if the speaker is describing a sequence of events that took place at his wedding, he can use (12.19a).

28. The reason that *okur-u* 'send,' *denwa o kake-ru* '(lit.) place call, call up,' and *tazune-ru* '(lit.) ask around, visit' behave the way described in (12.18b), (12.20b), and (12.21b) seems to be that the actions that these expressions represent do not include the end-result portion that directly involves the goal. For example, *okur-u* refers only to the agent-initiated act of sending, and its semantics does not include the "arriving of the object at the goal" portion. Similarly, *denwa o kake-ru* refers to the agent-initiated act of dialing a number, and its semantics does not include the portion that refers to the goal's answering the phone. Likewise, *tazune-ru* represents the process of travelling towards the goal, and does not include the "arrival at the goal" part.

Kamio (1979) has shown that in Japanese the concept of "territory of information" is vital, and that the speaker can represent only those pieces of information that fall under his own "territory of information" in direct affirmative forms. According to this extremely insightful observation, the fact that a third person arranged for a bouquet of flowers to be delivered to the speaker belongs to the sphere of that third person, and not to the speaker's territory because the latter could not have had a direct observation of the action. Hence the unacceptability of (12.18b). The explanation for the unacceptability of (12.20b) and (12.21b) follows the same line.

The following sentences show that in case that the speaker overtly states that the information represented does not belong to his territory, *okur-u* 'send' and *denwa o kake-ru* 'call up' can be used with the first-person object:

(i)   a.   Kimi boku ni denwa o kaketa?
             you me to phone placed
             'Did you call me up?'
       b.   Yamada-kun, boku ni denwa o kaketa rasii.
                      me to phone placed seems
             'Yamada seems to have tried to phone me.'
(ii)   a.   Kimi boku ni nani-ka okutta?
             you me to something sent
             'Did you send anything to me?'

b.   Yamada-kun, boku ni nani-ka okutta rasii.
            me   to something sent seems
      'It seems that Yamada sent me something.'

In (ia) and (iia), the speaker is inquiring about the information that falls under the hearer's territory. In (ib) and (iib), the speaker, by using *rasii* 'it seems,' overtly signals that the information represented does not belong to his territory.

29. Since nothing moves towards the speaker, *yonde kita* '(lit.) inviting came' is unacceptable. (*Yonde kureta* '(lit.) inviting gave' is the correct form.) This fact shows an interesting contrast with the fact that *sasotte kita* 'inducing came' is acceptable:

(i)   a.   *Taroo ga boku o yuusyoku ni *yonde   kita.*
                                       inviting came
       b.   Taroo ga boku o yuusyoku ni *sasotte   kita.*
                                       inducing came

This contrast seems to be due to the fact that while *yob-* '(lit.) call, invite' does not have a corresponding nominal form, *sasow-* 'ask, induce' does:

(ii)   a.   *Yobi* ga kita.
             invitation came
       b.   *Sasoi* ga kita.
             inducement came

The form *o-yobi* 'invitation' with an honorific prefix exists, but the verb that goes with it is not *ku-ru* 'come,' but *kakar-u* '(lit.) hang, hover.'

30. Since the act of lending money necessarily involves the act of borrowing the money on the part of the dative object, the event represented by (12.23b) must belong to the dative object's (i.e., the speaker's) territory of information. Therefore, the unacceptability of (12.23b) requires an empathy perspective for explanation.

31. *moraw + ta → moratta*

32. The dative particle *ni* 'to' after *Hanako* designates a secondary agent. See Kuno (1978a).

33. I presented the above analysis of giving and receiving verbs in Japanese first in Kuno (1976b) and Kuno and Kaburaki (1975/1977). Kyoko Inoue (1979) rejects my empathy analysis of giving verbs primarily on the basis of the fact that sentences such as the following exist (I use Inoue's orthographic conventions for her examples):

(i)   (a man talking about his inheritance)
       chichi-wa watashi-ni zaisan-o *yar-i* tai- to   it-te   i-ru
       father   I   property give want Quot. saying be-Nonpast
       'My father is saying that he wants to give me the property.'
(ii)   (a man trying to talk his friend out of saying that he was the one who gave his
       friend the gift in question)
       watashi-ga *kure-ta* -to   anmari hito -ni iw-anai de kudasai.
       I   give   Quot. much   people to say not   please
       'Please don't say to too many people that I gave (it) to you.'

What is at issue is the use of *yar-i* in (i) with a first-person dative object, and the use of *kure-ta* 'gave' in (ii) with a first-person subject. Inoue states that "Kuno's first principle, namely the Speech-Act Empathy Hierarchy, which simply says that the primary empathy of the speaker rests with himself, obviously cannot explain sentences such as (i) and (ii)." But what these sentences show is no different from what (12.28c) shows—that is, an interaction of the direct discourse perspective with the empathy conditions on the use of giving and receiving verbs. It seems that Inoue was not aware that this interaction was discussed, with (12.28c, d), (12.29), and (12.30) as illustrative examples, in the latter half of Kuno and Kaburaki (1975/1977), which are two of the three papers that Inoue uses as basis for her criticism of the empathy analysis of *yaru* and *kureru*.

34. The fact that the empathy relationships dictated by *V-te yar-u* and *V-te kure-ru* are not only inequality relationships of the degrees of empathy, but also involve absolute downgrading of the lesser argument, is due to the working of the Markedness Principle for Discourse-Rule Violations discussed in sec. 5.3. That is, in (13.2), the speaker had an option of using either the stem verb without a supporting verb (i.e., *kasita* 'lent'), or using the other supporting verb (*yatta* instead of *kureta* and vice versa). Thus, the fact that he has used *kureta* in (13.2a), and *yatta* in (13.2b) is due to his own design. He has "intentionally" upgraded *Hanako* and downgraded *Taroo* in (13.2a) by using *kureta*, and he has "intentionally" upgraded *Taroo* and downgraded Hanako in (13.2b) by using *yatta*. Thus, the downgraded NPs cannot serve as the focus of the speaker's empathy.

35. Note that this condition on the use of *zibun* does not dictate that its referent be higher than the referents of any other NPs in the sentence with respect to the speaker's empathy. This is due to the fact that sentences of the following pattern are in general acceptable:

(i)   a.   Taroo$_i$ wa, boku o *zibun*$_i$ no ie   ni yobitagatte   iru.
              me   self   's house to invite-wanting is
       'Taroo is anxious to invite me to his house.'
       b.   Taroo$_i$ wa, *zibun*$_i$ ga boku ni syookaisita hito o   waruku   itte   iru.
              self   me   to introduced person slanderously saying is
       'Taroo is speaking ill of the person who he has introduced to me.'

If *zibun* required that the degree of the speaker's empathy with its referent be the highest in the sentence, the above sentences should be unacceptable because they dictate that E(Taroo) > E(speaker) hold, while the Speech Act Empathy Hierarchy dictates that E(speaker) > E(Taroo) be true. The fact that these sentences are acceptable shows that the empathy relationship that they define is simply that of E(speaker) > E(Taroo) = high.

36. In this sentence, we have an extremely interesting mixture of direct and indirect discourse. The main verb of the quoted clause ending with the quotative particle *to* is in the imperative. Therefore, this in English would have been a direct quote in quotation marks. On the other hand, the genitive pronoun of "Please come to *my* house immediately" has been changed to *zibun* 'self' via application of Indirect Discourse Formation. Japanese allows this kind of mixed speech types rather freely. For example, observe the following sentence:

(i)   Tanaka$_i$ ga imakara sugu *yatu*$_i$ no uti ni *koi* to iu kara,
                   now-from immediately him's house to come (Imp.) that say since
       itte kuru.
       going come
       'Since Tanaka says that "Come to" his house right now, I am going.'

The main verb of the quoted speech *koi* 'come' is in the imperative. At the same time, the goal of this imperative verb is represented in an indirect quotation mode as *yatu no uti ni* 'to that guy's house.' Similarly, observe the following:

(ii)   Tanaka$_i$ ni, *yatu*$_i$ no ie de   rusubansite *kure*   to   tanomareta.
          by him   's house in house-sitting give (Imp.) that was-asked
        'I was asked by Tanaka to (lit.) "Please house-sit" at his house.'

The main verb of the quoted speech *rusubansite kure* is in the imperative, but *yatu* 'that guy' is in the third person.

37. Both (a) and (b) also have an interpretation in which Nara is "fondly-memorable" to both Taroo and Hanako. This interpretation, although a legitimate one, is not relevant to the present discussion, which concerns the relative ease with which *Taroo* and *Hanako* in different syntactic functions can be the focus of the speaker's empathy.

38. Turkish has two reflexive pronouns *kendi* and *kendisi*. Sezer (1979/1980) hypothesizes that while *kendi* is an empathy-loaded reflexive, *kendisi* is a neutral, empathy-free reflexive. However, the contrasts observed in (14.1) and (14.2) show that *kendisi,* too, is controlled by empathy factors.

39. I am indebted to Young-Se Kang for (14.3) and (14.4).

40. It is interesting to note that the first person reflexives in English sometimes have the same "dissociation with inner self" effect. For example, compare the following sentences:

(i)   a.   The experiments reported on in this paper have been carried out by John
             Smith, Mary Turner, and *me.*
       b.   The experiments reported on in this paper have been carried out by John
             Smith, Mary Turner, and *myself.*

Both (a) and (b) are acceptable, but (a) has a flavor of a personal statement, while (b) has a flavor of an impersonal statement. This must be due to the fact that *myself* in (b) signals that the speaker/writer has dissociated himself with his inner self. This dissociation results in various different effects. In appropriate contexts, (ib) is interpreted as a "modest" statement, while in some different contexts, sentences of this pattern are considered to be "cocky." Note that the use of "editorial we" is also sometimes interpreted as a sign of modesty and sometimes as a sign of "cockiness."

41. Fraser (1970) noted, without explanation, that (ib) and (ic) are acceptable in spite of the fact that (ia) is unacceptable:

(i)   a.   *As for himself,* he won't be invited.
       b.   John was worried about what Sheila should do. *As for himself,* he knew the
             best plan of attack.
       c.   Mary tried to convince both Tom and me to go. *As for herself,* she wasn't
             sure what she would do.

As observed by Ross (1970) and discussed in sec. 3.12, the pattern *as for x-self* normally requires a first-person reflexive pronoun. It is clear that *as for himself* is allowable in (ib) and (ic) only in the interpretation in which the narrator has totally identified himself with the referent of the reflexive. That is, these sentences are acceptable only as nonreportive style narrative sentences. From this point of view, it is interesting to observe that for many speakers, (ic) is at best awkward, and that it improves considerably if *me* is replaced by, say, *Jane:*

(ii)   Mary tried to convince both Tom and Jane to go. *As for herself,* she wasn't sure what she would do.

This is due to the fact that the whole discourse of (ii) can be interpreted as a nonreportive style narrative. This point requires explanation. In nonreportive style narrative sentences, the first person pronoun referring to the narrator never shows up because then, the narrator would be maintaining his own identity and describing the event from his point of view (thus yielding reportive style sentences). Therefore, the first sentence of (ic), because of the presence of *me,* cannot be a nonreportive style narrative sentence, and must be taken as a reportive style sentence. On the other hand, the second sentence, due to the presence of *as for herself,* has to be interpreted as a nonreportive style sentence. This switch from reportive to nonreportive style is too abrupt, and makes the second sentence awkward or marginal for some speakers.

Bibliography

Akmajian, A., and S. Anderson. 1970. "On the Use of Fourth Persons in Navajo, or Navajo Made Harder." *International Journal of American Linguistics* 36(1):1–8.

Allen, J. B., and J. B. Greenough. 1883, 1903. *New Latin Grammar.* New York: Ginn & Co.

Bach, E., and G. M. Horn. 1976. "Remarks on 'Conditions on Transformations.'" *Linguistic Inquiry* 7(2):265–299.

Bierman, M. H. 1972. "Aspects of Pied Piping." Unpublished honors thesis, Department of Linguistics, Harvard University.

Bosch, P. 1983. *Agreement and Anaphora: A Study of the Role of Pronouns in Syntax.* New York: Academic Press.

Bouchard, D. 1982. "On the Content of Empty Categories." Doctoral dissertation, MIT.

Bresnan, J. W. 1973. "Syntax of the Comparative Clause Construction in English." *Linguistic Inquiry* 4(3):275–343.

Cantrall, W. L. 1969. "On the Nature of the Reflexive in English." Doctoral dissertation, University of Illinois. Published as *Viewpoint, Reflexives, and the Nature of Noun Phrases.* Paris: Mouton, 1974.

Carden, G. 1980. "Blocked Forward Anaphora: C-Command the Surface-Interpretation Hypothesis." Presented at the Fifty-fifth Annual Meeting of the Linguistic Society of America, San Antonio, December 28–30.

————. 1981. "Blocked Forward Coreference." Presented at the Fifty-sixth Annual Meeting of the Linguistic Society of America, New York, December 27–30.

Cattell, R. 1979. "On Extractability from Quasi-NPs." *Linguistic Inquiry* 10(1):168–172.

Chomsky, N. 1965. *Aspects of the Theory of Syntax.* Cambridge, Mass.: MIT Press.

————. 1973. "Conditions on Transformations." In S. R. Anderson and P. Kiparsky, eds., *A Festschrift for Morris Halle.* New York: Holt, Rinehart & Winston.

————. 1975. *Reflections on Language.* New York: Pantheon Books.

————. 1977. "On Wh-Movement." In P. W. Culicover, T. Wasow, and A. Akmajian, eds., *Formal Syntax.* New York: Academic Press.

————. 1981. *Lectures on Government and Binding.* Dordrecht: Foris Publications.

————. 1982. *Some Concepts and Consequences of the Theory of Government and Binding.* Linguistic Inquiry Monograph 6. Cambridge, Mass.: MIT Press.

Clements, G. N. 1979. "The Logophoric Pronoun in Ewe: Its Role in Discourse." *Journal of West-African Linguistics* 10(2):141–177.

Erteschik-Shir, N. 1973. "On the Nature of Island Constraints." Doctoral dissertation, MIT. Reproduced by the Indiana University Linguistics Club, 1977.

————. 1981. "More on the Extractability from Quasi-NPs." *Linguistic Inquiry* 12(4):665–670.

Fiengo, R., and J. Higginbotham. 1981. "Opacity in NP." *Linguistic Analysis* 7:395–421.

Fillmore, C. 1968. "The Case for Case." In E. Bach and R. Harms, eds., *Universals in Linguistic Theory.* New York: Holt, Rinehart & Winston.

Fraser, B. 1970. "A Reply to 'On Declarative Sentences.'" *Mathematical Linguistics and Automatic Translation.* Report no. NSF-24, Computation Laboratory, Harvard University.

Grinder, J. T. 1970. "Super Equi-NP Deletion." *Papers from the Sixth Regional Meeting of Chicago Linguistic Society,* pp. 297–317.

Grosu, A. 1978. "On Unbounded Extraction Phenomena and the So-called Specified Subject Condition." *CUNY Forum* (Queens College, New York) 4:58–115.

Gueron, J. 1981. "Logical Operators, Complete Constituents, and Extraction Transformations." In R. May and J. Koster, eds., *Levels of Syntactic Representation.* Dordrecht: Foris Publications.

Gundell, J. M. 1974. "The Role of Topic and Comment in Linguistic Theory." Doctoral dissertation, Department of Linguistics, University of Texas at Austin.

Haig, J. 1978. "Topics in Japanese Grammar." Doctoral dissertation, Harvard University.

Hasegawa, K. 1983. "Bunpoo no Waku-gumi (Grammatical Framework), Part 2." *Gengo* (Taishukan Publishing Co.), 12(6):100–108.

Hornstein, N., and A. Weinberg. 1981. "Case Theory and Preposition Stranding." *Linguistic Inquiry* 12(1):55–91.

Huang, J. 1983. "A Note on the Binding Theory." *Linguistic Inquiry* 14(3):554–561.

Huybregts, M. A. C. 1976. "Vragende(r)wijs: Progressieve Taalkunde." In G. Koefoed and A. Evers, eds., *Lijnen van Taalkundig Onderzoek.* Groningen: Tjeenk Willink.

Inoue, Kyoko. 1979. "'Empathy and Syntax Re-examined: A Case Study from the Verbs of Giving in Japanese." *Papers from the Fifteenth Regional Meeting of Chicago Linguistic Society,* pp. 149–159.

Jackendoff, R. 1972. *Semantic Interpretation in Generative Grammar.* Cambridge, Mass.: MIT Press.

————. 1975. "On Belief-Contexts." *Linguistic Inquiry* 6(1):53–93.

Jacobson, P., and P. Neubauer. 1976. "Rule Cyclicity: Evidence from the Intervention Constraint." *Linguistic Inquiry* 7(3):429–462.

Joseph, B. 1976. "ENVY: A Functional Analysis." *Linguistic Inquiry* 7(3):503–508.

Kaburaki, E. 1973. "Nihongo Saiki-Daimeisi *Zibun* ni tuite no Teigen (Some Proposals concerning the Japanese Reflexive Pronoun *Zibun*)." *Nebulus* (Meiji-Gakuin Daigaku-in Eibungaku-Senkooka, Tokyo) 2:19–52.

Kamio, A. 1979. "On the Notion *Speaker's Territory of Information:* A Functional Analysis of Certain Sentence-Final Forms in Japanese." In G. Bedell, E. Kobayashi, and M. Muraki, eds., *Explorations in Linguistics: Papers in Honor of Kazuko Inoue.* Tokyo: Kenkyusha.

Keenan, E. 1974. "The Functional Principles: Generalizing the Notion of 'Subject of.'" *Papers from the Tenth Regional Meeting of the Chicago Linguistic Society,* pp. 298–309.

Koster, J. 1978. "Conditions, Empty Nodes, and Markedness." *Linguistic Inquiry* 9(4):551–594.

Kuno, S. 1970. "Some Properties of Non-referential Noun Phrases." In R. Jacobson and S. Kawamoto, eds., *Studies in General and Oriental Linguistics.* Tokyo: TEC Co.

————. 1972a. "Natural Explanation for Some Syntactic Universals." *Mathematical Linguistics and Automatic Translation.* Report no. NSF-28. Cambridge, Mass.: Computation Laboratory, Harvard University.

————. 1972b. "Pronominalization, Reflexivization, and Direct Discourse." *Linguistic Inquiry* 3(2):161–195.

————. 1972c. "Functional Sentence Perspective: A Case Study from Japanese and English." *Linguistic Inquiry* 3(3):269–320.

————. 1973. *The Structure of the Japanese Language.* Cambridge, Mass.: MIT Press.

————. 1974a. "Lexical and Contextual Meaning." *Linguistic Inquiry* 5(3):469–477.

————. 1974b. "Super Equi-NP Deletion is a Pseudo-Transformation." In E. Kaisse and J. Hankamer, eds., *Papers from the Fifth Annual Meeting of the North Eastern Linguistic Society,* Department of Linguistics, Harvard University.

————. 1974c. "A Note on Subject Raising." *Linguistic Inquiry* 5(1):137–144.

————. 1975a. "Three Perspectives in the Functional Approach to Syntax." *Papers from the Parasession on Functionalism.* Chicago Linguistic Society, pp. 276–336. Also in L. Matejka, ed., *Sound, Sign and Meaning: Quinquagenary of the Prague School Linguistic Circle.* Michigan Slavic Contribution 6. Ann Arbor: University of Michigan, 1976.

————. 1975b. "Condition for Verb Phrase Deletion." *Foundations of Language* 13: 161–175.

————. 1976a. "Subject, Theme and the Speaker's Empathy—A Reexamination of Relativization Phenomena." In C. Li, ed., *Subject and Topic.* New York: Academic Press.

————. 1976b. "The Speaker's Empathy and Its Effect on Syntax: A Reexamination of *yaru* and *kureru* on Japanese." *Journal of the Association of Teachers of Japanese* (2/3): 249–271.

————. 1976c. "Super Equi-NP Deletion is a Pseudo-Transformation." (A revised version of Kuno [1974b]). *Studies in English Linguistics.* Vol. 4. Tokyo: Asahi Press.

————. 1978a. "Japanese: A Characteristic OV Language." In W. Lehmann, ed., *Syntactic Typology.* Austin: University of Texas Press.

————. 1978b. "Generative Discourse Analysis in America." In W. Dressler, ed., *Current Trends in Textlinguistics.* New York: Walter de Gruyter.

————. 1978c. *Danwa no Bunpoo* (Discourse Grammar). Tokyo: Taishukan Publishing Co.

————. 1978d. "Two Topics on Discourse Principles." In *Descriptive and Applied Linguistics* 11. Tokyo: International Christian University.

————. 1979. "On the Interaction between Syntactic Rules and Discourse Principles." In G. Bedell, E. Kobyashi, and M. Muraki, eds., *Explorations in Linguistics: Papers in Honor of Kazuko Inoue.* Tokyo: Kenkyusha.

————. 1980. "Functional Syntax." In E. Moravscik, ed., *Syntax and Semantics.* Vol. 11. *Current Approaches to Syntax.* New York: Academic Press.

————. 1983. "Reflexivization in English." *Communication and Cognition* 16(1/2):65–80.

Kuno, S., and E. Kaburaki. 1975. "Empathy and Syntax." In S. Kuno, ed., *Harvard Studies in Syntax and Semantics.* Vol. 1. Department of Linguistics, Harvard University, Cambridge, Mass., pp. 1–73. Also in *Linguistic Inquiry* 8:4, 1977, pp. 627–672.

Kuroda, S.-Y. 1971. "Where Epistemology, Style and Grammar Meet—A Case Study from Japanese." In S. R. Anderson and P. Kiparsky, eds., *A Festschrift for Morris Halle.* New York: Holt, Rinehart & Winston.

Lakoff, G. 1968. "Pronouns and Reference." Unpublished paper, distributed by the Indiana University Linguistic Club, Bloomington.

————. 1970. "A Note on Vagueness and Ambiguity." *Linguistic Inquiry* 1:357–359.

Langacker, R. 1969. "On Pronominalization and the Chain of Command." In D. A. Reibel and S. A. Schane, eds., *Modern Studies in English*. Englewood Cliffs, N.J.: Prentice-Hall.

Lasnik, H. 1976. "Remarks on Coreference." *Linguistic Analysis* 2(1):1–22.

McCawley, J. D. 1976. "Notes on Jackendoff's Theory of Anaphora." *Linguistic Inquiry* 7(2):319–341.

Moravscik, E. A., and J. R. Wirth. 1980. *Syntax and Semantics*. Vol. 13. *Current Approaches to Syntax*. New York: Academic Press.

Napoli, D. J. 1979. "Reflexivization across Clause Boundaries in Italian." *Journal of Linguistics* 15:1–28.

Newmeyer, F. J. 1980. *Linguistic Theory in America: The First Quarter-Century of Transformational Generative Grammar*. New York: Academic Press.

Peškovskij, A. M. 1974. *Russkij Sintaksis v Naučnom Osveščenii*. Moscow.

Postal, P. 1970. "On Coreferential Complement Subject Deletion." *Linguistic Inquiry* 1(4):439–500.

———. 1971. *Cross-Over Phenomena*. New York: Holt, Rinehart & Winston.

———. 1974. *On Raising*. Cambridge, Mass.: MIT Press.

Prince, E. 1981. "Toward a Taxonomy of Given-New Information." In P. Cole, ed., *Radical Pragmatics*. New York: Academic Press.

Random House. 1964. *The American College Dictionary*. New York: Random House.

Reinhart, T. 1975. "Whose Main Clause? (Point of View in Sentences with Parentheticals)." In S. Kuno, ed., *Harvard Studies in Syntax and Semantics*. Vol. 1. Department of Linguistics, Harvard University, Cambridge, Mass.

———. 1976. "The Syntactic Domain of Anaphora." Doctoral dissertation, MIT, Cambridge, Mass.

———. 1981. "Definite NP Anaphora and C-Command Domains." *Linguistic Inquiry* 12(4):605–635.

———. 1983. *Anaphora and Semantic Interpretation*. London: Croom Helm.

Ross, J. R. 1967a. "On the Cyclic Nature of English Pronominalization." In *To Honor Roman Jacobson*. The Hague: Mouton. Reprinted in D. Reibel and S. Schane, eds., *Modern Studies in English*. Englewood Cliffs, N.J.: Prentice-Hall, 1969.

———. 1967b. "Constraints on Variables in Syntax." Doctoral dissertation, MIT, Cambridge, Mass.

———. 1970. "On Declarative Sentences." In R. A. Jacobs and P. S. Rossenbaum, eds., *Readings in English Transformational Grammar*. Waltham, Mass.: Ginn & Co.

Sezer, E. 1979–1980. "On Reflexivization in Turkish." *Harvard Ukrainian Studies* 3/4:748–759.

Smyth, H. W. 1920/1956/1973. *Greek Grammar*. Cambridge, Mass.: Harvard University Press.

Soga, Machiko. 1980. "Empathy Constraints on Reflexives in English." In K. Araki, ed., *Linguistics and Philosophy*. No. 1. Tokyo: Aratake Shuppan.

Solan, L. 1983. *Pronominal Reference—Child Language and the Theory of Grammar*. Dordrecht: D. Reidel Publishing Co.

Sperber, D., and D. Wilson. 1982. "Mutual Knowledge and Relevance in Theories of Comprehension." In N. V. Smith, ed., *Mutual Knowledge*. New York: Academic Press.

Stowell, T. A. 1981. "Origins of Phrase Structure." Doctoral dissertation, MIT, Cambridge, Mass.

Thráinsson, H. 1975. "Reflexives and Subjunctive in Icelandic." *Papers from the Sixth Meeting of the North Eastern Linguistic Society* 6:225–239.

Uspensky, B. 1970. *A Poetics of Composition: The Structure of the Artistic Text and Typology of a Compositional Form*, trans. V. Zavarin and S. Wittig. Berkeley: University of California Press.

Wasow, T. 1972. "Anaphoric Relations in English." Doctoral dissertation, MIT, Cambridge, Mass.

———. 1979. *Anaphora in Generative Grammar.* Ghent: E. Story-Scientia.

Williams, E. 1980. "Predication." *Linguistic Inquiry* 11(1):203–238.

Yokoyama, O. T. 1979. "Studies in Russian Functional Syntax." Doctoral dissertation, Department of Slavic Languages and Literatures, Harvard University. Also in *Harvard Studies in Syntax and Semantics* 3(1980):451–774.

Zribi-Hertz, A. 1980. "Coreferences et Prénoms Reflechis: Notes sur le Contraste Lui/Lui-même en Français." *Linguisticae Investigationes* 4(1):131–179.

Index